Working with Families

An Integrative Model by Level of Need

FOURTH EDITION

Allie C. Kilpatrick

Professor Emerita, The University of Georgia

Thomas P. Holland

The University of Georgia

Boston   New York   San Francisco
Mexico City   Montreal   Toronto   London   Madrid   Munich   Paris
Hong Kong   Singapore   Tokyo   Cape Town   Sydney

Series Editor: Patricia Quinlin
Series Editorial Assistant: Sara Holliday
Marketing Manager: Laura Lee Manley
Production Editor: Patrick Cash-Peterson
Editorial-Production Service: Omegatype Typography, Inc.
Composition Buyer: Andrew Turso
Manufacturing Buyer: JoAnne Sweeney
Electronic Composition: Omegatype Typography, Inc.
Cover Administrator: Rebecca Krzyzaniak

For related titles and support materials, visit our online catalog at www.ablongman.com.

Between the time website information is gathered and then published, it is not unusual for some sites to have closed. Also, the transcription of URLs can result in typographical errors. The publisher would appreciate notification where these errors occur so that they may be corrected in subsequent editions.

Library of Congress Cataloging-in-Publication Data

Kilpatrick, Allie C.
   Working with families : an integrative model by level of need / Allie C. Kilpatrick, Thomas P. Holland. — 4th ed.
      p.   cm.
   Includes bibliographical references and index.
   ISBN 0-205-44619-1 (paperbound)
      1. Family psychotherapy.   2. Family social work.   I. Holland, Thomas P.   II. Title.
   RC488.5.K55   2006
   616.89'156—dc22

                                                                        2005051217

Printed in the United States of America

10   9   8   7   6   5   4   3   2   1   RRD-VA   09   08   07   06   05

This book is lovingly dedicated to our families:

Past: our families of origin
Parents and grandparents who gave us a wonderful heritage
Hammond & Lena Callaway (Allie's parents)
Webster & Maria Callaway (Allie's grandparents
Thomas W. & Dorothy Holland (Tom's parents)

Present: our families of procreation
Spouses and children who give us so much pleasure and joy
Rev. Ebb G. Kilpatrick, Jr. (Allie's deceased husband)
Charles E. Hill (Allie's present husband)
Gray & April Kilpatrick and Galen & Doug Smith (Allie's children)
Daphne & Todd Hyatt and Stevens & Louise Hill (Allie's stepchildren)
Myra Blackmon (Tom's wife)
Kimberly Bolton (Tom's daughter)

Future: our descendants
Grandchildren and great-grandchildren who will carry on our heritage
Nick & Jessie Smith (Allie's grandchildren)
Courtland & Allie Hyatt and Griffin & Graham Hill (Allie's step-grandchildren)
Trevor & Zachary Bolton (Tom's grandchildren)

Contents

PART TWO • *First Level of Family Need: Basic Survival* 75

5 *Interventions with Level I, Neglectful Families:
A New Model of Family Preservation* 76

Jackie Ellis and R. Kevin Grigsby

6 *A Family Case Management Approach
for Level I Needs* 94

Roberta R. Greene and Nancy P. Kropf

**PART THREE • *Second Level of Family Need:
Structure, Limits, and Safety*   *115***

7   *Structural Family Interventions*   *116*

Harry J. Aponte

8   *Social Learning Family Interventions*   *128*

Arthur M. Horne and Thomas V. Sayger

PART FOUR • *Third Level of Family Need: Boundaries and Control   145*

9 *Solution-Focused Family Interventions   146*

Jeffrey J. Koob

Foreword

As both a family practitioner and an educator for almost 40 years, I have been aware of the need to formulate a theoretical base for family practice that explains family dynamics and provides clear guidelines for effective interventions. In this book, the goal of bringing together family levels of need and practice models is accomplished in a manner that is both comprehensive and easy to grasp.

For me, the most valuable material in this book relates to the use of the practitioner's self in the helping process. Clearly, as in all helping endeavors, the person of the practitioner is the vital factor for facilitating change. Murray Bowen, in my opinion, accurately addresses the essence of family practice in his insistence that practitioners can progress with a family only as far as they have progressed in their own family relationships. Linking the maturity level of the practitioner to the overall conditions of the problem context captures a powerful dynamic in the helping process.

In this fourth edition of *Working with Families,* Kilpatrick and Holland outline ways to approach the diversity of family dynamics, family need levels and lifestyles, and the many commonalities shared by all human aggregates throughout the life cycle. Major additions to this work include an Instructor's Manual, which includes PowerPoint presentations; relevant Internet resources; and an "Ethical Challenges" section. In this text, the emphasis on diversity and difference has not obscured the common human needs, capacities, and coping styles of people. Chapters dealing with various strategies to meet different levels of need are written by national and international experts in the field.

Some of the most cogent and thought-provoking parts of *Working with Families* are to be found in the constant emphasis on family strengths and coping capacities. While the authors assert that no single theory is adequate to deal with all family needs or styles, the theories presented here all contain a basic strategy that focuses on levels of need rather than on levels of pathology.

The expanded attention to the domains of family spirituality and professional ethics is especially relevant for the present period of rapid cultural change. The importance of the spiritual dimension cuts across all levels of family need. For many families, the spiritual dimension is crucial for their moral and behavioral guidelines. How can family practitioners understand family needs if they are unaware of the specific moral underpinnings for a particular family?

Family spiritual considerations and professional ethics form a critical part of the ecology of the treatment process for each family with whom we work, and all chapters have been revised and edited to reflect current thinking and practice. The attention *Working with Families* gives to spiritual and ethical considerations deserves careful reading.

Finally, this book directs attention to the specific needs of each specific family and to the specific interventions needed to address the uniqueness of the family. The content of this book provides the basis for reflective consideration of the meaning of the spiritual and ethical dimensions of family work.

> D. Ray Bardill
> Professor Emeritus, School of Social Work
> Florida State University
> Past President, American Association for Marriage
>   and Family Therapy

Preface

Working with Families: An Integrative Model by Level of Need was written especially for use as a text for students in social work, marriage and family therapy, counseling, psychology, and human service courses. Faculties in over 100 colleges and universities nationally and internationally are using this text in both undergraduate and graduate courses. This book is especially geared toward applications with families that are usually seen in social service and family agencies, ones that students would typically be working with in their internships and practicum experiences. However, it also addresses family needs at higher levels. Practitioners in the various disciplines have also found it to be useful in their practices.

The purpose of *Working with Families* is to fill the need in social work and family therapy literature for an appropriately relevant textbook on family interventions, addressing the needs of families that students and practitioners typically see. Previous texts have focused on overviews of different models of family therapy, emphasizing primarily one model, a special population, or a problem group. Some have been geared toward middle-class, private-practice clients. Most have presented the therapist as the expert within a family systems context. What is needed is an integrative model for practice, one based on an assessment of the level of need in the family and the particular problems clients are facing within a wider ecological context. Once this assessment is done, then different interventions can be selected that are appropriate for that family's particular level of need at that point in time, around their specific problem area. Our goal was to meet the need for such a selective approach.

When students are given a broad overview of all the different models of working with families, they often come away from the course not knowing which specific approach to use in which particular situation. On the other hand, when only one model is taught, students are tempted to use that model with every family, even when it may not be suitable. When the focus is on a special population or problem group, students have difficulty generalizing appropriately to other populations or problem groups. Many family therapy texts are geared toward middle-class, walking-wounded, private-practice clients. These are *not* the families that students or practitioners typically see in agency settings.

This book presents an integrative model to help students and practitioners make the fit between therapeutic style and family need. An overall ecosystems–social constructionism metatheory serves as the philosophical and theoretical base for working with families on four levels of family need. Examples are given of specific approaches to intervention that would be relevant to use on each level of family need.

Revisions to the Fourth Edition

This fourth edition of *Working with Families* has been revised and updated to reflect current content and methods. The revisions include:

- An Instructors' Manual. This is a major addition to this edition. The Instructor's Manual will be an aid to instructors and to the learning experiences of students. This manual includes PowerPoint presentations for each chapter.
- Relevant Internet Resources. These are given for each chapter and provide more resources for study.
- An Ethical Challenges section. This new section is included for each method-of-practice chapter so that instructors and students will give special thought to this important area of practice.
- New chapters and a new author. Chapter 5, on meeting basic needs in families, has been rewritten, building on the work of the previous author. Chapter 11, on meeting fourth-level family needs, has also been rewritten.
- All chapters have been revised and edited to reflect current thinking and practice.

An increased student and client interest in spirituality has led us to emphasize this area of sensitive practice in a specific chapter as well as in various chapters devoted to practice. This added emphasis reflects the current state of knowledge, interest, and attention surrounding this subject area. A framework for spiritual assessment is given. The concepts of resilience and family strengths are emphasized as the base on which to build. Ethically informed practice is a current issue. For this reason, we have added Internet resources that contain the NASW, AAMFT, and Counselors' Codes of Ethics. The seven ethics cases with commentaries from experts in the field, along with references to specific standards of the code of ethics relevant to that particular case remain in the text. The glossary has been expanded to include terms used in the new chapters.

Organization of the Text

Part One of *Working with Families* covers the theory base and contextual and practice concerns that are useful with families at any level of need. Chapter 1, by Kilpatrick, presents a framework of the four levels of needs of families. This framework serves as a priority-setting guide that enables students and practitioners to determine which methods approach one would use with a specific family. As such, the chapter is a beginning assessment tool grounded in the therapeutic assumption that interventions must start addressing the level of the most basic need before moving on to higher levels of needs and interventions. In Chapter 2, the theory that undergirds this integrative approach is discussed by Holland and Kilpatrick. The metatheories of ecosystems and social constructionism form the philosophical and theoretical foundations for the needs of families and for the methods used to meet these needs as presented in this book.

In Chapter 3, Hopps and Kilpatrick discuss the importance of the helping relationship/therapeutic alliance and the contexts of client diversities that must be addressed on any level of need. The focus on ethnic-sensitive practice, multiculturalism, and cultural democracy gives a global perspective to students and practitioners and requires the practitioner to think in terms of a multisystem, interactive, international approach. Whether practiced in the United States or elsewhere, this perspective on diversity is crucial as our world becomes one community. A cultural assessment grid is presented, and client diversity in terms of gender, power, poverty, and family structures is discussed. Although the focus is on diversity issues, the emphasis is on commonalities that unite us rather than on differences that divide us.

In the last chapter in Part One, Chapter 4, Kilpatrick, Becvar, and Holland provide suggestions for creating a practice that is well informed relative to ethical decision making and sensitive to the role of spirituality in the lives of both practitioners and clients. Guides for ethical decision making are presented, relevant codes of ethics discussed, and Internet resources given. The discussion on spirituality has been greatly enlarged and emphasized. A Framework for Spiritual Assessment that students and practitioners should find very helpful is included. Specific examples of spiritually oriented helping activities that students and practitioners could utilize with their clients are also presented.

Parts Two through Five focus on interventions that are appropriate for families on each of the four levels of family need. Each chapter includes examples of interventions that would be relevant, but they are not the only ones that could be used on that level. With a shift in emphasis, some of the approaches could be used on more than one level of family need. Each chapter discusses how a specific approach could be applied to families that have needs on levels other than the one that we focus on in that chapter.

Each chapter in Parts Two through Five follows a similar format, addressing and containing the following subjects and features:

- Needs presented by the family
- Assessment, especially determining the level of need of the family
- Goals of the intervention
- Intervention approach used, including the basic tenets of the approach, application to a family, specific interventions, and how the interventions are evaluated for effectiveness
- Application to families on other levels of need
- Ethical challenges
- Summary
- Discussion questions
- Suggested readings
- References
- Internet resources

Page numbers indicating where each of these subjects can be found in each chapter are given in the Outline of Approaches on p. xxvi.

In Part Two, the first level of family need is addressed. This first level deals with basic survival issues. The chapters in this part present two approaches to family practice that are appropriate for families on the first level of need. Chapter 5, by Ellis and Grigsby, presents the family-preservation approach with neglectful families, which is designed to address basic needs in high-risk families with children. Greene and Kropf, in Chapter 6, present the case management approach, which is a process for assisting families who have multiple service needs.

The second level of family need is presented in Part Three. This level is concerned with structure, limits, and safety. In Chapter 7, Aponte, internationally known as one of the founders and developers of structural family therapy, presents this systems-based model that places a special focus on the internal organization of relationships within families. In Chapter 8, Horne and Sayger present the social learning family interventions approach to families. This approach deals with both internal and external, or environmental, factors that affect family needs and focuses on learning more effective social skills.

Part Four deals with the third level of family need, which is concerned with boundaries and control. Both chapters in this part present approaches to intervention. In Chapter 9, Koob discusses solution-focused interventions, one of the brief intervention approaches that are appropriate for families at this level of need. The emphasis on health and strengths makes it an especially useful model for families at this level of need. In Chapter 10, Walsh presents family systems theory, a widely utilized approach to family assessment and intervention. It provides a comprehensive conceptual framework for understanding how *emotional ties* within families of origin influence the lives of individuals and pays attention to multigenerational family processes and interventions.

Part Five addresses interventions at the fourth level of family need: family and personal growth. This higher level of need is represented by a focus on inner richness and quality of life. In Chapter 11, a revised chapter, Williams discusses narrative family interventions. This approach emphasizes the *meaning* that families make of their experiences instead of the cause of the problem. It makes use of a collaborative, co-learning therapeutic relationship. The second approach, presented in Chapter 12 by Kilpatrick and Trawick, is object relations family interventions (ORFI). ORFI is a bridge between working with individuals and working with families and is essentially interactional in its intervention processes. It gives primacy to the need for a human relationship, even at birth.

In Part Six, the final chapter looks at the larger issues of the family in the community context. Chapter 13, by Kilpatrick, Turner, and MacNair, discusses the ecosystem implications of working with families at the macrosystem level, thus integrating the previous intervention approaches with the theoretical and philosophical foundations presented earlier.

Acknowledgments

Our great appreciation goes to all the contributors to this fourth edition. They are experts in their fields, and we are grateful for the time and energy they have given.

The reviewers of the first, second, and third editions made some very valuable suggestions that made the book more relevant, readable, and user friendly. These suggestions and ideas were helpful and have been incorporated into later editions.

Dr. Ray Bardill kindly agreed to write the foreword for this fourth edition. Many thanks go to him for taking time out of his busy schedule, and also for his many contributions and insights as well as the inspiration he has provided the senior author of this book, Allie Kilpatrick, in working with families. He has been a role model in having the courage to write and speak about spirituality when it was not popular to do so.

Thanks are due to the reviewers of this fourth edition: Charles Barke, Southwest Missouri State University; Steven Harris, Texas Tech University; Thomas Smith, Florida State University; and Barbara Thomlison, Florida International University. We are very grateful to Patricia Quinlin and the editorial staff of Allyn and Bacon. They have been most supportive and cooperative even while gently pushing to get this new edition into production. Their contributions have been helpful, timely, and professional. Thank you!

Allie would like to pay special tribute to her extended familiy. The four living generations of my sisters, brother, and countless cousins inspire my study and appreciation of families. My parents and grandparents, and those ancestors who came before, left our generation with a vital spiritual heritage that has sustained, nurtured, and challenged us. For this I will be eternally grateful.

Tom would like to pay special tribute to his extended family also: my parents and parents-in-law have been important models; my daughter and grandsons are sources of hope for the future.

Our families have been very patient and loving during this process, and they contributed in unique ways to our ideas about families. To them we send a heartfelt note of appreciation.

Authors

Allie C. Kilpatrick, M.S.W., M.C.E., Ph.D., is Professor Emerita of the University of Georgia School of Social Work, where she taught for almost 25 years. She has published extensively in areas of family and social work practice and was instrumental in the development of the interdisciplinary certificate program in Marriage and Family Therapy (MFT) at the University of Georgia, where she served as its coordinator. She is a Diplomate in Clinical Social Work, member of the Academy of Certified Social Workers, and Clinical Member and Approved Supervisor for AAMFT and is licensed in Georgia as a Clinical Social Worker and as a Marriage and Family Therapist.

Thomas P. Holland, Ph.D., is Professor and Director of the Institute for Nonprofit Organizations, University of Georgia. He also has been Associate Dean and Chairman of the doctoral program at the Mandel School of Applied Social Sciences, Case Western Reserve University, Cleveland, Ohio. Dr. Holland has published extensively on management and governance of nonprofit organizations. He was recently recognized by the University of Georgia as Outstanding Teacher of the Year and by his school as Outstanding Scholar of the Year.

Contributors

Harry J. Aponte, L.C.S.W., L.M.F.T., has conducted workshops, lectured, and trained therapists in a variety of locations within and outside of the United States. He has an appointment as Clinical Associate Professor in the Couple's and Family Therapy Program of Drexel University. He is advisory editor on a variety of professional journals in this country and abroad, including *Family Process*. Dr. Aponte was a teacher of family therapy at the Menninger Clinic, and director of the Philadelphia Child Guidance Clinic. He has published *Bread & Spirit* (Norton, 1994), a book that addresses therapy with today's poor in the context of ethnicity, culture, and spirituality.

Dorothy S. Becvar, Ph.D., M.S.W., is an Associate Professor in the School of Social Service at Saint Louis University. A Licensed Clinical Social Worker and a Licensed Marital and Family Therapist with over 25 years of experience in both academia and private practice, Dorothy has published extensively. She is the author of many journal articles and book chapters and of the books *In the Presence of Grief: Helping Family Members Resolve Death, Dying, and Bereavement Issues* (Guilford Press, 2001) and *Soul Healing: A Spiritual Orientation in Counseling and Therapy* (Basic Books, 1997), as well as the editor of *The Family, Spirituality, and Social Work* (Haworth, 1997). With her husband, Raphael J. Becvar, she has coauthored four books: *Family Therapy: A Systemic Integration*, fifth edition (Allyn and Bacon, 2003), *Pragmatics of Human Relationships* (Geist and Russell, 1998), *Hot Chocolate for a Cold Winter's Night: Essays for Relationship Development* (Love Publishing, 1994), and *Systems Theory and Family Therapy: A Primer*, second edition (University Press of America, 1999). She is coeditor, with William Nichols, Mary Anne Pace-Nichols, and Augustus Napier, of the *Handbook of Family Development and Intervention* (Wiley, 2000).

Jackie Ellis, Ph.D., M.S.W., L.C.S.W., has over 15 years of direct practice experience in mental health and public child welfare and currently serves as field liaison for students receiving Title IV-E Child Welfare Funding. Her current practice and research interests include equine-facilitated psychotherapy, human caring as a motivational factor in social work practice, intervention with abusing and neglecting families, and preparing social work students for practice in public child welfare.

Roberta R. Greene, M.S.W., Ph.D., is Professor of Social Work at the University of Indiana, Indianapolis. She is the former Dean of this School and also served as Associate Dean of the University of Georgia School of Social Work. She is a leading author in the areas of social work literature, multicultural issues, gerontology, and geriatric social work. Her books include *Social Work Case Management* (with B. S.

Vourlekis), *Human Behavior Theory: A Diversity Framework,* and *Human Behavior Theory and Social Work Practice* (with P. Ephross).

R. Kevin Grigsby, D.S.W., L.C.S.W., is Vice Dean for Faculty and Administrative Affairs and Professor of Behavioral Science at Pennsylvania State College of Medicine in Hershey, Pennsylvania. Dr. Grigsby has an extensive history of program planning, implementation, and evaluation in the area of innovative home- and community-based health and mental health services. His practice experience has been primarily in underserved rural and inner-city areas. His areas of practice expertise include children at imminent risk of out-of-home placement, perinatal intervention with substance-abusing women, children and adolescents in shelter care, home-based services to parents and children with HIV-related illnesses, and the use of advanced telecommunications technology in health services delivery.

June G. Hopps, Ph.D., is the Parham Professor of Family and Children's Studies, School of Social Work, University of Georgia. She is Dean Emerita of the Graduate School of Social Work, Boston College, and and Chair of the Board of Trustees, Spelman College. She is former Editor-in-Chief of the journal *Social Work* and Associate Editor-in-Chief for the *Encyclopedia of Social Work,* 19th ed. She is the author of numerous publications on social policy and on practice with overwhelmed clients.

Arthur M. Horne, Ph.D., is Professor in the Counseling Psychology Program and a faculty member of the certificate program in Marriage and Family Therapy at the University of Georgia. Dr. Horne is coauthor or coeditor of *Troubled Families, Family Counseling and Therapy, Group Counseling and Group Psychotherapy, Handbook of Counseling Boys and Adolescent Males, Treating Conduct and Oppositional Defiant Disordered Children,* and *Bully Busters.* He is the Principal Investigator of the Middle School Violence Prevention Program and the Coprincipal Investigator of ACT Early: Identifying and Assisting Youth at Risk.

Jeffrey J. Koob, M.S.W., L.C.S.W., Ph.D., is an Assistant Professor at California State University, Long Beach, Department of Social Work. He originally interned at the Brief Family Therapy Center in Milwaukee, Wisconsin, in 1985, when Steve de Shazer and Insoo Berg were writing and developing Solution-Focused Brief Therapy (SFBT). His research, teaching, and service are directed toward the application of SFBT to different populations and treatment settings.

Nancy P. Kropf, M.S.W., Ph.D., is Professor of Social Work and former Associate and Interim Dean at the University of Georgia. Her areas of research include caregiving relationships of older families and older people who have lifelong disabilities. She is currently President of the Association for Gerontology Education–Social Work (AGE–SW) and is a Hartford Geriatric Social Work Scholar. Her extensive publications include *Developmental Disabilities: Handbook of Interdisciplinary Practice* (with B. A. Thyer) and *Gerontological Social Work: Knowledge, Service Settings, and Special Populations* (with R. L. Schneider).

Ray H. MacNair, M.A., M.S.W., Ph.D., is former Director of M.S.W. Admissions at the University of Georgia School of Social Work. His practice specialties are community development, neighborhood organizing, affordable housing, social move-ment organizing, community-based research, and collaborative systems. His pub-lications include analysis of collaborative system styles, citizen participation, agency boundary maintenance, research on human service planning groups, the ecological theory of community practice, analysis of various forms of community practice research, and the impact of identities on social movement organizing.

Thomas V. Sayger, Ph.D., is a Professor and Co-Director of Training in Counseling Psychology at the University of Memphis. He is a licensed psychologist, member of the Division of Family Psychology of the American Psychological Association, and member of the Executive Board of the Council of Counseling Psychology Training Programs. Dr. Sayger's research and clinical practice focus on preven-tion, early intervention, and family–school collaborative programs for behavior-disordered children and their families.

Elizabeth O. Trawick, M.D., is a psychoanalyst in private practice in Beverly Hills, California. She has been interested in Object Relation/Kleinian theory for many years and treats children, adults, and families using these formulations. She is an Assistant Clinical Professor of Psychiatry at the University of California, Los An-geles. She is on the faculty of two psychoanalytic institutes and is the current pres-ident of the Los Angeles Psychoanalytic Society.

John B. Turner, D.S.W., is former Dean and Professor Emeritus, School of Social Work, University of North Carolina, Chapel Hill. He has also been Dean and Pro-fessor at the Mandel School of Applied Social Sciences, Case Western Reserve Uni-versity, Cleveland, Ohio. He taught at Atlanta University School of Social Work; the University of Georgia School of Social Work; Smith College, McGill University, and the University of Toronto Schools of Social Work; and also taught at schools of social work in Egypt. His practice and research interests include minority poor families and children, group work, community organization, and policy.

Joseph Walsh, Ph.D., L.C.S.W., is an Associate Professor of Social Work at Virginia Commonwealth University, where he teaches courses in clinical practice and human behavior, among others. Joe has been a clinical practitioner in the field of mental health since 1974, specializing in work with persons who have mental illness, and their families. He is the author of three books: *Endings in Clinical Practice, Clinical Case Management with Persons Having Mental Illness: A Relationship-based Perspective,* and *The Social Worker and Psychotropic Medication* (coathored with Kia J. Bentley).

Nancy R. Williams, Ph.D., is an Associate Professor of Social Work in the Univer-sity of Georgia's School of Social Work. She received her doctorate in Marriage and the Family from Florida State University and is licensed as both a Clinical Social Worker and Marriage and Family Therapist. She has over 25 years of direct prac-tice experience in the mental health/human services field, working with individ-uals, groups, couples, and families. Her current research areas include resilience development in trauma survivors, conflict resolution skill development, and inte-grative psychoeducational groups for couples.

Outline of Approaches

Note: Numbers in the table body are page references.

Part I

Theory Base and Contextual Practice: Metatheories for Working with Families at Four Levels of Need

Working with families is so important that a family focus is now a major priority for the helping professions. Yet existing approaches to this field tend to emphasize only one model for practice, assuming that this one model fits all types of family problems. But the differences in types of family issues and problems are extensive. These differences indicate a need for multiple methods from which the family practitioner may select and apply an approach on the basis of how well it fits with the needs and issues that a specific family is currently facing.

This section begins with Kilpatrick's analysis of types, or levels, of family needs and functioning. To start where the family is, it is essential that the practitioner first assess the family's needs. The theoretical framework of an ecosystems and social constructionism perspective utilized in this book is set forth in Chapter 2 by Holland and Kilpatrick. In Chapter 3, by Hopps and Kilpatrick, the contexts of helping are explored, focusing on the helping relationship/therapeutic alliance and on client diversity. Ethnic sensitive practice, gender issues, powerlessness, poverty, and changing family structures are discussed. In Chapter 4, Kilpatrick, Becvar, and Holland deal with ethically informed and spiritually sensitive practice when working with families.

The chapters in this first section set the stage for those that follow. The specific approaches to working with families at various levels of need flow from this theoretical and philosophical base and build on it.

1

Levels of Family Need

Allie C. Kilpatrick, Ph.D.

Helping professionals see families who are on many different levels of need and whose circumstances, problems, and skills are varied. For a practitioner to use only one model of assessment and intervention is like the saying, "If the only tool you have is a hammer, everything looks like a nail." The situation is required to fit the helper's model even when there is no workable fit. Thus the helper's need is met, rather than the clients' needs. This chapter describes four levels of family need and explores various methods of assessment and interventions that are relevant at each level.

In her 1945 social work classic, *Common Human Needs,* Charlotte Towle wrote about needs in relation to factors that affect human development. She contended that the following elements are essential if persons are to develop into maturity and be motivated toward social goals: physical welfare, such as food, shelter, and health care; opportunity for emotional and intellectual growth; relationships with others; and provision for spiritual needs. She points out that needs are relative to a person's age and life situation. Most human needs are typically met within a family structure or in relationship with others.

Abraham Maslow (1970) developed a hierarchy of needs that supports Towle's thinking and expands our understanding of human development. According to his hierarchy, a person must satisfy primary physiological needs before social needs can be considered. He included five levels of need: physical and life-sustaining needs (the need for food, water, air, warmth, sexual gratification, elimination of bodily wastes, and so on); physical safety (the need for protection from physical attack and disease); love (the need to be cherished, supported, and aided by others); self-esteem (the need to have a sense of personal worth and value, to respect and value one's self); and self-actualization (the need to be creative and productive, and to attain worthwhile objectives). We must remember, however, that often a lower-level need cannot be satisfied without a relationship with another person, as, for example, a young child's need for food.

Building on these two formulations of needs, family problems encountered in helping situations may be seen as clustered around various levels of need based on the primary need at that time. These range from the basic survival needs to concerns about the self-actualization of family members and spiritual needs. Weltner (1985, 1986) views functional levels of families' needs from the analogy of building a house, which draws our attention to the necessity of addressing the most basic level of needs before moving to higher levels of need. Figure 1.1 illustrates the four levels of family need that will be utilized in this book.

Level I

The most basic level of family need has to do with the essential requisites for survival and well-being. These include the family's needs for food, shelter, protection from danger, health care, and minimums of nurturance. Referring to the house analogy, Level I would be the basement and refers to issues of life and death (see Figure 1.1).

Some families experience crises, such as a job loss or major illness that leaves them destitute. Other families who do not adequately meet these challenges are often considered neglectful and underorganized. These families lack a leadership and control structure that is needed in order to meet basic nurturing and protection needs of members. In other words, there is insufficient parenting capacity. According to the Beavers Family Competence Scale (Beavers, Hulgus, & Hampson, 1988), these families are leaderless; no one has enough power to structure interactions. This situation was more descriptive of neglectful families in lower socioeconomic circumstances than of nonneglectful families in similar circumstances (Gaudin, Polansky, Kilpatrick, & Shilton, 1991).

Sometimes, families struggling with Level I problems show evidence that the parental coalition is weakened or undermined by a parent–child coalition; family closeness is amorphous and vague, with indistinct boundaries among members. Faced with such basic resource deprivations as food, shelter, protection, education, clothing, transportation, and medical care, these families are rarely able to provide one another with the necessary emotional nurturance (Epstein, Bishop, & Baldwin, 1982). Examples of typical problems may include an overwhelmed single mother (as is the case in most neglectful families); the incapacitation or dysfunction of the strongest family member by illness, alcohol, or drugs; and natural or emotional catastrophes and pervasive life stresses that have depleted physical and emotional resources.

Work with these families must build on basic strengths and resiliences—as is true at all levels—and focus on resources. For Level I families, Weltner (1985) suggests that the intervention should center on mobilizing support for the ineffective executive or parental system. Intervention could begin with a survey of potential resources from the community, including church groups or extended family (genograms and ecomaps are helpful; see Hartman & Laird, 1983), and then assess and build on family resilience and family strengths. Resilience, or the ability

Level IV
Fine art of living.
Focus on inner conflict,
problems, intimacy,
self-actualization,
insight, and yearnings.

Level III
Space (privacy and
access). Focus on
boundaries (individual,
family, and generational).

Level II
Limits and safety.
Focus on strengths,
controls, and patterns
of coping.

Level I
Food, shelter,
protection, medical
care, and minimal
nurturance. Focus on
strengths and resources.

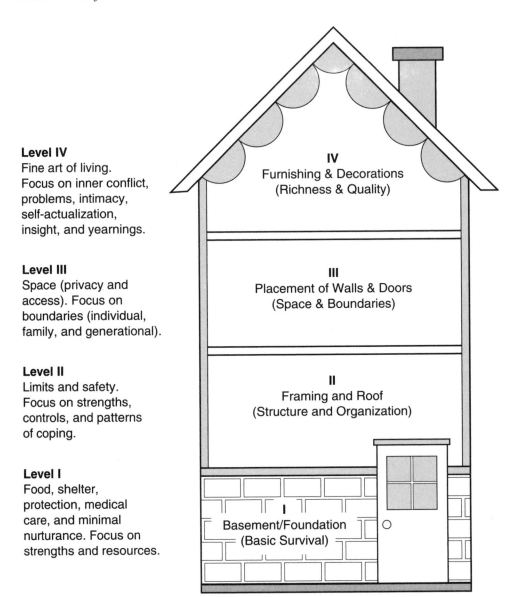

IV
Furnishing & Decorations
(Richness & Quality)

III
Placement of Walls & Doors
(Space & Boundaries)

II
Framing and Roof
(Structure and Organization)

I
Basement/Foundation
(Basic Survival)

FIGURE 1.1   *Levels of Family Needs: Issues and Relevant Interventions*
Source: Kilpatrick & Cleveland, 1993.

to withstand and rebound from crises and adversities, can be strengthened. Helping families to discover positive meanings in stress and distress is an important
ingredient in strength-based interventions. Wolin and Wolin (1993), for example,
highlight the "survivor's pride" (p. 8). This help could be offered to families

demonstrating resilience in some area. Case management and referral to medical, income maintenance, and legal resources; protective services and family preservation programs; and hospitalization in crises may be necessary. Advocacy and guidance may be indicated, depending on the situation. Guidance on the use of respite care, referral to substance-abuse counseling, child development and child care information, and budget and time management may be necessary. Often, an advocacy role with school, welfare, and correctional or juvenile justice systems is necessary. Table 1.1 illustrates some of the issues, relevant intervention strategies, and possible intervention techniques that could be applicable on this level.

The following brief case study is illustrative of a family with needs on Level I and typical interventions that could be used. The case study demonstrates the mobilization of resources through case management skills and building on strengths to meet family needs.

Mrs. M. came to the attention of Family Services after she called the hotline. She had not been feeling well for some time and had lost her job. After she was diagnosed with AIDS, which was given to her by her husband, he had left her. She had no source of income and was being evicted from her apartment in the housing project. She had two daughters, ages two and four, and they were without food. Family Services was able to meet her immediate needs by helping with food and paying the rent. They then referred her to Family Support Services. The worker there, using case management, helped her to obtain treatment for AIDS. After assessing her potential resources and strengths, and with some encouragement from the worker, Mrs. M. agreed to contact some family members for help with the children. In the meantime, with education and support from the worker, the mother was able to provide more security, nurturing, and support for the children. With Mrs. M's approval and cooperation, the worker helped to locate her husband. After counseling with them both, he agreed to obtain medical treatment and to return home.

Level II

With Level II families, the basic needs of minimal safety, stability, and nurturance have been met, and maintaining authority and setting limits are the prominent issues. In the house analogy in Figure 1.1, Level II refers to the framing and roof of the house and represents the family's structure and organization. The parental system is unable to set and maintain sufficient limits for one or more family members, and this inability threatens the stability of the whole family system. This failure could involve either a lack of clear expectations or a lack of power to enforce the expectations.

Other examples could include families where the children are out of control, with acting-out teenagers and parents who are involved in substance abuse or excessive gambling, or parents are otherwise failing to maintain key structures for the family. Marital conflict may appear to be out of control and threaten dissolution of

TABLE 1.1   Family Assessment and Intervention

Level	Issue	Intervention Strategy	Intervention Technique

I	• Is executive capacity sufficient to manage all basic nurturant needs?
	• Food, shelter, protection, medical care, minimal nurturance.
	• Resilience of individual and family.
		• Focus on strengths, not problems.
		• Survey and mobilize available support to bolster executive capacity.
		• Build family resilience.
		• Promote positive response to stress.
			• Family preservation.
			• Case management.
			• Marshal more troops from:
			  Nuclear family.
			  Extended family.
			  Community.
			• Professional as convener, advocate, teacher, role model.

II	• Is there sufficient authority to provide minimal structure, limits, and safety?	• Focus on strengths.
		• Develop a coalition of those in charge against those needing control.
		• Increase clarity of expectation.
			• Develop parental coalitions.
			• Set limits.
			• Clear communication.
			• Social learning skills.
			  Written contracts.
			  Behavioral reinforcers.
			  Task assignments.

III	• Are there clear and appropriate boundaries?
	  Family.
	  Individual.
	  Generational.
		• Focus on problems.
		• Clarify the "ideal" family structure in conformity with ethnic or family expectations.
		• Have generational clarity.
			• Defend family and individual boundaries.
			• Balance triangles.
			• Rebuild alliances.
			• Develop generational boundaries.
			• Promote communication skills.

IV	• Are there problems of inner conflict or problems with intimacy? • Are family members self-actualizing?	• Focus on problems. • Clarify and resolve legacies and historical trauma. • Promote insight. • Focus on yearnings and spiritual needs.	• Narrative interventions. • Family sculpture. • Object relations interventions. • Resolution of three-generational issues. • Spiritual growth.

Source: Adapted from Weltner, 1985, p. 49.

the family unit. Violence in the family may be a threat, but members are not seen as needing immediate protection.

Again, interventions would begin with a survey of strengths, resiliences, and resources. In order to have the authority to deal with the situation and to offer sufficient hope, the practitioner must be in charge of structuring the sessions. Structural interventions enable the spouses to develop a coalition strong enough to demonstrate sufficient authority for the family to gain control of threatening or destructive behaviors.

Weltner (1986) points out that the focus of treatment in such situations must be to "develop a coalition of those in charge against those needing control" (p. 53). Family mapping of coalitions (Minuchin, 1974; Hartman & Laird, 1983) could be helpful with these families. Social learning and behavioral techniques with structural considerations may prove empowering to family members. Paquin and Bushorn (1991) show how behavioral techniques can help clarify the family's expectations for the behavior of each of its members and help them recognize their potential for modifying the behaviors of other family members.

The case study given below is typical of Level II family needs. As in Level I, interventions would begin with a survey of strengths, resilence, and resources.

Jose, age ten, was referred to the school social worker for disrupting the classroom, fighting with the other boys, and failing to do homework. His father was the head of household in this single-parent, Hispanic family. His mother had died of cancer when Jose was seven. He had two older sisters in high school who were going through turbulent teenage years.

After talking with Jose, his teachers, and then his father, the social worker began working with the teachers on some social learning and behavior techniques to modify Jose's behavior in the classroom. Jose's father was unable to come to the school during the day because he could not get off from work. The worker talked with him by phone in the evening and found that Jose was alone at home after school, with little or no supervision or structure from his sisters. His father worked long hours and was so tired at night that he just wanted to sit and drink beer. The children usually ate junk food for dinner on their own.

The worker scheduled an appointment to see all of them together in the evening. The mother's sister who lived nearby was also there. After discussing the concerns all of them were seeing in the family, they agreed that the aunt would work with the girls to help them take more responsibility for supervising Jose and helping him with his homework. She would also help them to prepare more nourishing meals at night. The father agreed to spend more time with Jose, especially on weekends. They related that they had all become more disorganized since the mother had died. Jose in particular had gradually become more aggressive and less interested in school. The worker suggested a referral to the mental health clinic so that Jose, as well as the rest of the family, could do their grief work concerning the mother. They all agreed to go. Within a few months, Jose's behavior and grades improved and he was taking more interest in school.

Although a wide variety of techniques may be used, both Level I and Level II interventions are essentially structural (Weltner, 1985) and ecosystems oriented. The goal is to mobilize all of the resources available, to modify the organizational patterns of the family, and to increase and test the strength of the parental or executive system. It is important to remember that children such as Jose have a readiness to fall in line. They are often aware of how much their own and their family's lives suffer as a result of their lack of discipline and control.

Level III

Level III focuses on space, with privacy and access as the issues. Using the house analogy in Figure 1.1, this level is concerned with the inner architecture. Although the foundation, walls, and roof are satisfactory, the arrangements of inner space, or the placement of walls and doors, are not. Level III families are complicated, and they have a structure and style that is often perceived as working. They may draw on and express a three-generational legacy, not a set of inherited deficiencies (Weltner, 1985). As pointed out by Aponte (2003), Levels I and II families usually are underorganized, lack family structure, and do not transmit adequate patterns of coping. By contrast, Level III and IV families have a rich mixture of coping mechanisms. Weltner (1985) describes these coping mechanisms as their characteristic defenses, the culture to which they are committed and which they attempt to pass on to and through their children.

If work with such families involves changing ingrained patterns, we can anticipate some struggle. Therefore, our techniques need to encompass and adapt to such struggles. The Beavers Interactional Competence Scale (Beavers et al., 1988) rates these families as having marked or moderate dominance (control is close to absolute, with little or no negotiation; dominance and submission are the rule) while family members are isolated and distanced from one another.

Level III interventions involve processes of reshaping the internal architecture of the family so that everyone has appropriate space, access, and privacy. Interventions with these families must challenge the existing family structure and confront the family's tendency to remain in current patterns of behavior. Examination of the communication and power structures around the presenting problem may be useful. Differentiation and individuation of family members from each other and the emotional system, flexibility, and clear generational boundaries are essential.

The following case study summarizes a case presented by Pippin and Callaway (1999) and is illustrative of the needs of families in Level III. Although a family systems approach is taken in this case, other Level III families' needs could be approached through solution-focused family interventions.

> Bill, Sr., and Carmen have two children, Bill, Jr., age 14, and Sonia, age 12. Bill, Jr., has always been difficult to manage. At this time he is sullen and negative at home, his school grades are low, and his parents fear that he is involved with alcohol and marijuana. Sonia seems to be a model child. Carmen is quiet, has an overinvolved relationship with Sonia, but appears to be bonded with Bill, Jr. Bill, Sr., is a successful surgeon. At home he exerts absolute authoritarian control. Both parents describe their own parents' relationships as conflictual and their own relationship as conflictual.
>
> There are three significant intergenerational triangles. First, Bill, Jr., and his mother are allied against his father. Next, Carmen and her mother have an overinvolved relationship which is repeated in Carmen's relationship with her own daughter. The third significant triangle is that of Bill, Sr., Carmen, and Bill, Jr., which is the same as Bill, Sr., had in his family of origin. The significance of these

triangles is the degree of fusion. Members in this three-generational family are so deeply enmeshed that inevitable growth and change with age is viewed with terror.

The overarching goal of treatment with this Level III family is realignment of the family system and establishment of boundaries. A second overall goal is to identify and ameliorate the sources of chronic anxiety within the family system that undermine individual growth and autonomy. The parental subsystem must be strengthened to become a supporting team in the management of the children.

Level IV

In Level IV families, basic needs are met, and structural boundaries are relatively clear and satisfactory. Presenting problems often focus on a desire for greater intimacy, greater sense of self, or more autonomy. The concern of Level IV families is the fine art of living fully and growing toward actualization of each member's potential. In relation to the house analogy, this level of functioning represents decorations, pictures, rugs, and lamps. Here the richness and quality of individuals and family life become the focus of interventions. Although some of these issues may have been discussed at earlier levels, it is on Level IV that such issues as inner conflicts, intimacy, self-realization, insight, and spiritual yearnings become the primary focus and are explored in depth.

Genograms extending over three or four or more generations are useful on this level in showing transgenerational patterns. Family sculpting may also be used. A focus on narrative interventions and rewriting one's own story are especially applicable on this level of family functioning. Object relations family interventions may be particularly helpful with these families, who desire insight into patterns and intergenerational functioning. Some families or individuals may want to focus on clarifying personal values, meanings, and spirituality, or they may wish to deal with existential issues. Helping professionals must be open to pursuing such issues, be comfortable in discussing them, and be able to assist families in clarifying their values and discovering the transcendent aspects of their being without imposing personal conclusions on them. Referrals to church-related counseling centers may be indicated.

Following is a family situation that may be a typical example for Level IV families:

A middle-class couple with several children entered treatment with the complaint by the wife of vague feelings of depression and loneliness. She and her husband began to do extended family work with some emphasis on object relations. Working through some of their earlier relationships and projection processes and contacts with family made the wife feel more connected and less lonely. The couple was able to weather the terminal illness of her mother in a relatively calm fashion, without the wife's becoming too depressed during the grief-work period. The loss of her mother opened up the desires of both members of the couple to focus more on inner awareness and spiritual growth. Building on insights gained and ongoing contacts with extended family, both were able to rewrite their own life story to some degree.

Intervention Criteria

Once the primary, current level of need is assessed, then an opening for intervention must be determined. Do you start with the family, the couple, or an individual? Do you deal with what people do, what they think and feel, or what has happened in the past? Do you assume health or pathology? Is the primary need for maintenance of functioning or problem resolution? These questions are addressed by an intervention choice points grid developed by Pinsof (1991, 1995), shown in Figure 1.2.

The "Contexts" columns in the table refer to the people who are involved in the problem maintenance structure. This could be the family (including the extended family and the community), the couple in the same generation (allowing for alternate lifestyles), or an individual. The "Orientations" headings refer to three intervention choices.

The *behavioral/interactional choice* has to do with what people do, their actions, and changing this. It involves surface behavior and is visual. Social learning, strategic, functional, and structural techniques may be used here.

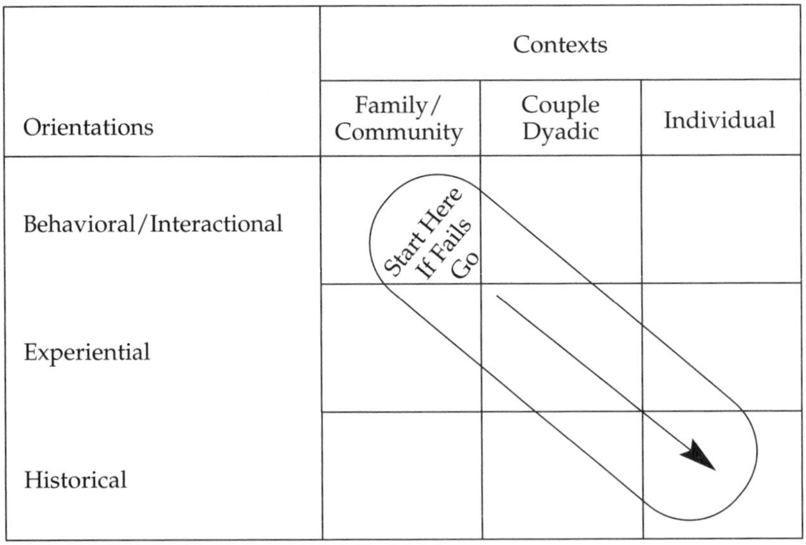

	Contexts		
Orientations	Family/Community	Couple Dyadic	Individual
Behavioral/Interactional			
Experiential			
Historical			

FIGURE 1.2 *Intervention Choice Points*

Source: Adapted from Pinsof, 1991.

The *experiential choice* makes use of cognition, affect, communication, and interpersonal relationships—what people think and feel. It involves meaning and uses auditory senses—listening. Both of these first two choices focus on the here and now.

The *historical choice* is the third intervention. It adds the dimension of time and addresses what has happened in the past. Family-of-origin work and psychodynamic or psychoanalytic methods may be used.

This model assumes that the people involved are healthy and that the problem can be resolved at a direct behavioral level. Therefore, in order to choose how to intervene, your decision points should progress from upper left to lower right, as shown in Figure 1.2. In other words, begin with the context of the family and the behavioral orientation. If the approach in this cell does not work, proceed down the cells diagonally to working with the couple experientially. If this approach does not work, then go to the individual and work with historical material. The progression is problem or failure driven in that, if a more direct approach is not successful, you proceed to another, less direct approach. It is also circular in that you continue to deal with meaning and behavior, and link what you are doing to the presenting problem. There is an explicit contract between the practitioner and the family to address the problem, so there must be a link between the presenting problem and what the practitioner does. This helps to keep the practitioner honest.

The essence of the choice framework is that working with families is a process of discovery, a "peeling of the onion." Is the problem simple and superficial or deep and complex? The family is assumed to be healthy and to have a simple, superficial problem that can be addressed at the family-unit level with behavioral interventions until it is proven that the problem exists at deeper levels. Therefore, practice begins with simple, cost-effective interventions. The goal is to teach the family to learn from the practitioner how to solve problems for themselves. This process may involve internalizing the approach of the practitioner so the family can assume what the practitioner would say or do and thus work things out for themselves.

Once a family's basic survival needs are met, this choice framework can provide a guide for work at the four levels of need within the house metaphor. The three orientations of the Pinsof choice points grid are then applicable at the intersection of the levels of the family need, as shown in Figure 1.3. The overlay of these two grids provides a practical guide for choosing the most applicable treatment model and the individual, couple, or family focus based on the assessment of family need.

A caveat is that these guidelines are rough frameworks into which families may not easily fit. There may be characteristics of several levels of need, as well as orientations. Professional judgment is required to decide the more relevant point of entry and intervention. The key question for the family practitioner is: What specific therapeutic intervention produces specific change in specific families under specific conditions?

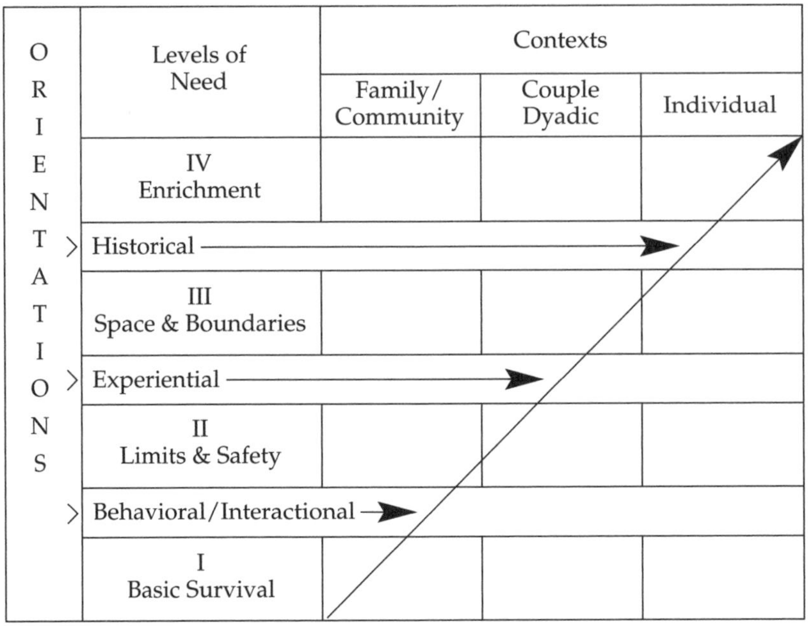

O R I E N T A T I O N S	Levels of Need	Contexts		
		Family/ Community	Couple Dyadic	Individual
	IV Enrichment			
> Historical ————————————————▶				
	III Space & Boundaries			
> Experiential ————————————▶				
	II Limits & Safety			
> Behavioral/Interactional ▶				
	I Basic Survival			

FIGURE 1.3 *Intervention Choice Points by Level of Need*

Summary

Needs and problems of families are quite varied. It is helpful to view families through the lenses of their particular level of need in order to assess strengths and resiliences and provide relevant interventions. Problems encountered in practice with families tend to cluster into four levels of need, from very basic to very high. Lower-level needs must be met before higher-level needs are addressed. Four levels of family need are described, ranging from basic survival to self-actualization. An analogy of building a house is used to illustrate the basic assumptions. In the first two levels, strengths are emphasized. On the higher two levels, problem areas are addressed directly. Working with these types of problems requires purposive selection among methods of practice and the application of appropriate interventions according to situation and needs of the specific family. Issues on each level, relevant intervention strategies, and possible techniques are identified.

Remember that these levels are not discrete. Family need is a continuum and rarely shows categorical typologies. Some characteristics are found in several levels. In the assessment process, the level that is most characteristic of the needs experienced by a particular family at that point in time must be assessed. In Levels III and IV particularly, the most crucially felt need of a given family could vary between the two levels, depending on whether there is a specific problem or crisis that needs to be addressed at that time or if the need is more toward growth.

Interventions that are particularly appropriate at a given level may also be used at some other levels, given certain conditions. An intervention choice point grid provides a guide that can be used in connection with the levels of need to decide the context and orientation for intervention. The application of specific methods of interventions with other levels of need is discussed in each chapter in Parts Two through Five with discussion and caveats.

Discussion Questions

1. Describe the four levels for assessing family needs and give some relevant intervention strategies and techniques that may be useful for each of these levels.

2. On which level would families involved with addiction issues likely be found, and where would be the most likely point for intervention?

3. What are some challenges or obstacles that would keep families' basic needs at a low level? What are some strengths, skills, or actions that would raise families' basic needs to a higher level?

4. What do the decorations in Weltner's "house" represent? At what level of need are the families who are concerned with these decorations? How would a therapist help them?

5. Formulate a case study to illustrate Level IV families.

6. Is the determination of family need level the responsibility of the clinician, or is it a joint effort involving the clients? What happens in the event of a disagreement on levels of need?

7. Apply all concepts discussed in this chapter to the choice point grid (Figure 1.2), utilizing families with whom you are working or know.

8. Select an incident from your childhood. Identify and describe the level of need of your family at that time. Choose a point of intervention in terms of context and orientation, and explain your rationale.

Internet Resources

www.parenting.com/parenting
www.questia.com/library/psychology/relationships-and-the-family

Suggested Readings

Beavers, W. R., & Hampson, R. B. (1990). *Successful families*. New York: Norton.
Family competence is seen as ranging from healthy family functioning to severely dysfunctional and is viewed along a progressive continuum. The approach focuses on assessment and intervention and stems from years of clinical, observational, and empirical work.

Minuchin, S., & Montalvo, B. (1967). Techniques for working with disorganized low socioeconomic families. *American Journal of Orthopsychiatry, 37,* 380–387.

Minuchin, S., Montalvo, B., Guerney, B. G., Rosman, B. L., & Schumer, F. (1967). *Families of the
slums.* New York: Basic Books.

These two books focus on the structure and dynamics of poor and disorganized families and
give specific techniques for working with them. They are based on a research study of families with more than one delinquent child and are especially helpful when working with
Level I families.

Towle, C. (1945). *Common human needs.* Washington, DC: National Association of Social Workers.

This book is one of the classics in social work. It discusses in great detail the human needs
that are common to all. It is one of the few books that urges provision for spiritual needs.

Weltner, J. S. (1986). A matchmaker's guide to family therapy. *Family Therapy Networker, 10*(2),
51–55.

This is an easy-to-read summary of the levels of functioning as seen by Weltner. It will give
more detail than is given in this chapter for those who wish to explore the concept further.

References

Aponte, H. J. (2003). Structural family interventions. In A. Kilpatrick & T. Holland (Eds.), *Working with families: An integrative model by level of need* (3rd ed.). Boston: Allyn & Bacon.

Beavers, W. R., Hulgus, Y. F., & Hampson, R. B. (1988). *Beavers system model of family functioning:
Family competence and family style evaluation manual.* Dallas: University of Texas Health Science
Center.

Epstein, N. B., Bishop, D. S., & Baldwin, L. M. (1982). McMaster model of family functioning: A
view of the normal family. In F. Walsh (Ed.), *Normal family processes.* New York: Guilford.

Gaudin, J., Polansky, N. A., Kilpatrick, A. C., & Shilton, P. (1991). *Structure and functioning in neglectful families.* Paper presented at the Ninth National Conference on Child Abuse and Neglect, Denver, CO.

Hartman, A., & Laird, J. (1983). *Family-centered social work practice.* New York: Free Press.

Kilpatrick, A., & Cleveland, P. (1993). Unpublished course material, University of Georgia School
of Social Work.

Maslow, A. (1970). *Motivation and personality.* New York: Harper & Row.

Minuchin, S. (1974). *Families and family therapy.* Cambridge, MA: Harvard University Press.

Paquin, G. W., & Bushorn, R. J. (1991). Family treatment assessment for novices. *Families in Society: The Journal of Contemporary Human Services, 72*(6), 353–359.

Pinsof, W. (1991). An integrated approach to chronic marital conflict. *The Learning Edge Series*
(Video). Washington, DC: American Association for Marriage and Family Therapy.

Pinsof, W. (1995). *Integrative problem centered therapy: A synthesis of biological, individual, and family
therapies.* New York: Basic Books.

Pippin, J. A., & Callaway, J. (1999). Family systems interventions. In A. C. Kilpatrick & T. P. Holland, *Working with families: An intergrative model by level of need.* Boston: Allyn & Bacon.

Towle, C. (1945). *Common human needs.* Washington, DC: National Association of Social Workers.

Weltner, J. S. (1985). Matchmaking: Choosing the appropriate therapy for families at various levels of pathology. In M. P. Mirkin & S. L. Koman (Eds.), *Handbook of adolescents and family therapy* (pp. 39–50). New York: Gardner Press.

Weltner, J. S. (1986). A matchmaker's guide to family therapy. *Family Therapy Networker, 10*(2), 51–55.

Wolin, S. J., & Wolin, S. (1993). *The resilient self.* New York: Villard Books.

2

An Ecological Systems–Social Constructionism Approach to Family Practice

Thomas P. Holland, Ph.D., and Allie C. Kilpatrick, Ph.D.

This chapter presents an overall framework within which the integrative model to family practice by level of need takes place. For family practice to be more applicable to the families served by helping professionals, we are adapting the comprehensive theories or metatheories of ecological systems and social constructionism for this framework. Each meta- or comprehensive theory offers a way of looking at the world, and each is inclusive of other methods (Breunlin, Schwartz, & Kune-Karrer, 1992; Payne, 1991). The description of these metatheories, their divergences and convergences, and how they blend to form a firm foundation for an integrated approach to family practice is now presented.

Ecological Systems Perspective

The ecological systems (ecosystems) perspective is a framework for assessment and interventions. It has been a dominant theoretical approach for viewing human behavior in the social environment. The environment is all-inclusive of micro- to macro-level systems and resources required for meeting family needs. The interface between people and their environment is seen as bidirectional and interactional, meaning that people affect the environment and in turn the environment affects people. The focus for the practitioner is to assess and intervene in all relevant factors at all levels of systems. This allows the practitioner to view situations holistically in assessment and interventions. It also stimulates the use of a broad repertoire of interventions that are suitable for the varying needs of particular family situations. Because it can encompass any relevant treatment model, the eco-systems approach can serve as a unifying perspective in family practice (Long & Holle, 1997; Meyer, 1988). It makes clear the need to see people and their environments within their historic and cultural contexts, in relationships to each other, and as continually influencing each other.

The Ecological View

The ecological perspective is based in the metaphor of biological organisms that live and adapt in a complex network of environmental forces. Von Bertalanffy (1968) believed that living organisms are organized wholes, not just the sum of their separate parts, and that they are essentially open systems, maintaining themselves with continuous inputs from and outputs to their environments.

The ecological perspective rests on an evolutionary, adaptive view of human beings in continuous transaction with their environment, with both the person and the environment continuously changing and accommodating each other (Brower, 1988). The key assumptions of an ecological perspective emphasize that people and environments are holistic and transactional. This approach makes clear the need to see people and their environments within their historic and cultural contexts, in relationships to one another, and as continually influencing one another, as described by Germain and Gitterman (1995).

Because ecologists were among the first systems thinkers, the perspective is also systemic. Germain and Gitterman give seven major concepts of the eco-systems perspective that are applicable to working with families. These are reciprocal exchanges, life stress, coping, habitat, niche, relatedness, and adaptations.

1. Transactions are understood as continuous reciprocal exchanges in the person–environment system. Through these exchanges, each shapes, changes, or otherwise influences the other over time. People's needs and predicaments are viewed as outcomes of person–environment exchanges, not just as the products of personality or environment alone (except in those cases where a specific problem may be an outcome of environmental or societal processes alone).

2. *Life stress* can refer to either a positive or a negative person–environment relationship (Lazarus, 1980). Germain and Gitterman (1987) cite Cox's explanation that stress can be seen as positive when an environmental demand, process, or event is experienced as a challenge and is therefore associated with positive feelings, a higher level of self-esteem, and the anticipation of mastery. Stress can be seen as negative when "actual or perceived environmental demands, harms, losses, or conflicts (or the future threat of any of these) exceed the actual or perceived capacity for dealing with them" (p. 488). They state that life stress and challenge express forms of person–environment relationships because they include both the external demand and the accompanying physiological or emotional stress at a subjective level.

3. The concept of **coping** refers to the special adaptations that are made in response to internal stress. Lazarus (1980) states that two major functions of coping are problem solving and managing negative feelings, and that these are interdependent. Each of these coping adaptations needs personal, familial, and environmental resources and relationships. When coping efforts are working, the demand or threat that causes the stress may be reduced or eliminated, and thus a crisis is avoided. If coping efforts are not successful, disruption in social functioning may result in various areas. Stress and coping are both transactional. Therefore, they help the practitioner to maintain a focus on both people and environments.

4. Habitat refers to the place where a person or family lives. Germain (1985) states:

> In the case of human beings, the physical and social settings within a cultural context are the habitat. Physical settings such as dwellings, buildings, rural villages and urban layouts must support the social settings of family life, social life, work life, religious life, and so on, in ways that fit with life styles, age, gender, and culture. Habitats that do not support the health and social functioning of individuals and families are likely to produce or to contribute to feelings of isolation, disorientation, and despair. Such stressful feelings may interfere further with the basic functions of family and community life. (p. 41)

Here again, many impoverished rural and urban communities around the world do not have the resources of habitats that support healthy social functioning and overall human well-being.

5. A **niche** is perceived as the result of one's accommodation to the environment. It refers to the status that is occupied by a member of the community. Niches are defined differently in different societies and in different historical eras. In our society today, one aspect of a good niche is a set of rights, including the rights of equal opportunity to educational and economic resources. However, devalued personal or cultural characteristics, such as color, ethnicity, gender, age, affinity/sexual orientation, disability, poverty, and other types of oppression, force millions of people to occupy niches that are incongruent with human needs and well-being (Germain, 1985).

6. The concept of **relatedness,** based on attachment theory (Bowlby, 1973), incorporates ideas about emotional and social loneliness and isolation (Weiss, 1973). Many research studies demonstrate the important influences of supportive networks of relatives, friends, neighbors, work colleagues, and pets in helping people cope with painful life stresses (Cobb, 1976; Gaudin, 1993, 1999). This aspect of the ecological perspective suggests the entry points in social networks for professionals to help people work out adaptive social arrangements in family, group, community, and institutional life.

7. It is important to remember that **adaptations,** as used in the ecological perspective, are active, dynamic, and often creative processes. People and their environments create an ecosystem in which each shapes the other. Thus people are not mere reactors to environmental forces. Sometimes they change environments to allow themselves to meet their physical and psychological needs. An example is a recent sit-in by handicapped students at a major university for better accessibility to buildings. They must then adapt to the changes they have induced. At other times, people change themselves to conform or adjust to environmental impera- tives or to satisfy needs and reach goals (Germain & Gitterman, 1980, 1995).

The Family Systems View

Systems theory was developed to go beyond mechanistic biology to include the interfunctioning of parts that make up whole systems. It goes beyond static con- cepts to take account of the temporal quality of life and the omnipresence of change. Among the key assumptions of this theory that are particularly relevant to family systems are wholeness, feedback, equifinality, and circular causality (Watzlawick, Beavin, & Jackson, 1967).

Wholeness.   Because systems behave as wholes, change in any one part will cause change in other parts and throughout the entire system. When this assump- tion is applied to family systems, it means that a family is not simply a collection of individuals but a coherent composite whose components behave as an ir- reducible unit. Therefore, the behavior of each individual in the family is related to and dependent on the behavior of all the others. For this reason, improvements or regressions in one family member prompt repercussions—positive and negative— in other family members (Goldenberg & Goldenberg, 1991; Nichols & Schwartz, 1991; Watzlawick et al., 1967).

Feedback.   Open systems are regulated by feedback loops or inputs from family members and from the environment. These inputs are acted on and modified by the family system. Feedback can be either positive or negative. Negative feedback contributes to homeostasis by the process of self-regulation and plays an impor- tant role in maintaining the stability of relationships. It reduces the tendency to- ward deviation from the family norms. On the other hand, positive feedback leads to change when it is used by the family system to amplify a pattern. For learning and growth to occur, families must incorporate positive feedback. All families to- gether must use some degree of both forms of feedback in order to adapt while maintaining their equilibrium in the face of developmental and environmental stresses (Goldenberg & Goldenberg, 1991; Simon, Stierlin, & Wynne, 1985; Wat- zlawick et al., 1967).

Equifinality.   **Equifinality** means that the same result may be reached from dif- ferent beginnings (Von Bertalanffy, 1968). In open systems, different initial condi- tions may lead to the same final result, and different outcomes may be produced from the same causes. The primary principle here is that, in order to understand families, it is more important to consider the ongoing organization of their inter- actions, not just the genesis or the product of these interactions (Simon et al., 1985; Watzlawick et al., 1967).

Circular Causality.   **Circular causality** means that systems are constantly modified by recursive circular feedback from multiple sources within and outside of the system. Events are related through a series of interacting loops or repeating cycles. In other words, there is no simple, linear cause and effect; events and behaviors interacting with one another over a period of time produce the effects (Nichols & Schwartz, 1991).

Applications to Family Practice

The use of the ecosystems metatheory in working with families supports adherence to certain principles that are consistent with this perspective.

1. This perspective requires professionals to carry out their practice according to the needs of a particular family, rather than viewing all family needs in terms of a single preferred treatment.

2. This perspective supports a variety of practice roles and tasks. It can serve as a base for internal and external changes, legislative advocacy, policy and planning, program development, primary prevention activities, research, and administration.

3. The practitioner's attention must encompass three interdependent realms or contexts in which human growth, development, and social functioning take place. **Life transitions** encompass developmental changes, such as puberty, aging, role changes, loss, or other crisis events faced by families. **Interpersonal processes** include patterns of relationship and communication in dyads, families, groups, social networks, communities or neighborhoods, and organizations. **Environmental properties** include the aspects of social and physical settings—their formal and informal resources and deficits—as they affect families (Germain & Gitterman, 1987). The use of genograms and ecomaps (Hartman & Laird, 1983; Mattaini, 1997) can facilitate the focus on these contents.

4. The focus is on strengths, not deficits, on solutions, not problems, and on the potential for continued family and individual growth and needed social change.

5. Assessment and intervention from an ecological systems perspective require knowledge of the diverse systems involved in interactions between people and their environments (Hefferman, Shuttlesworth, & Ambrosina, 1988). The different levels of systems, shown in Figure 2.1, are helpful in the assessment process around a given problem situation.

- In this model, the **microsystem** represents the individual in family and group settings that incorporate the day-to-day environment.

- The **mesosystem** incorporates the interactions of individuals, families, and groups within the person's microsystem.

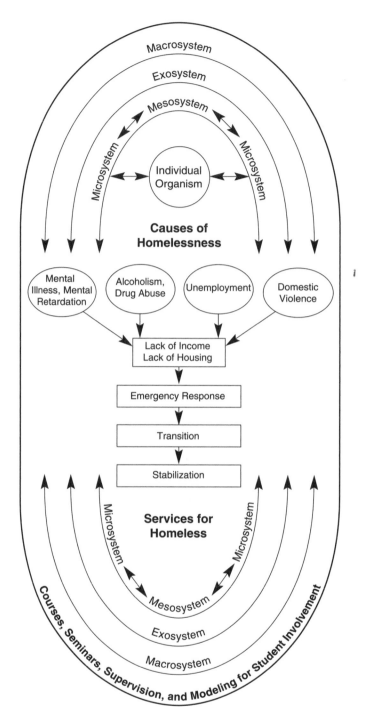

FIGURE 2.1 *An Ecosystems Model for Student Involvement with Homeless Families*

Source: From Cleveland & Kilpatrick, 1990.

- The **exosystem** represents the social structures, both formal and informal, that influence, delimit, or constrain what goes on there. It also includes community-level factors that have an impact on the way the person functions.

- The **macrosystem** involves societal forces and subsumes cultural and societal values, attitudes, and beliefs that influence the micro- and exosystems.

The example of homelessness shown in Figure 2.1 illustrates the use of the figure in helping students learn the ecosystems model. First, we look at the causes of homelessness, which may be apparent in several levels of systems. For example, mental illness, alcoholism, unemployment, and domestic violence may have precipitated the loss of income and housing. Any of these causes could be interrelated at micro-, meso-, exo-, or macrosystem levels. Services for homeless families must also be provided at several system levels. Individual/family counseling at the micro- and mesosystem levels is indicated in the emergency and transition levels. Resources at the exosystem level for temporary shelter and other transition services are needed. Changes in public attitudes and policy concerning employment opportunities, emergency responses, and causes of homelessness may take place at the macrosystem level.

The key assumptions in family systems theory of wholeness, feedback, equifinality, and circular causality are applied at the micro- and mesosystem levels. The ecosystems perspectives of reciprocal exchanges, life stress, coping, habitat, niche, and relatedness are applicable at the exo- and macrosystem levels.

Consideration should be given to the interplay of influences on all four levels during the assessment and intervention processes with families. This interplay helps in understanding the causes of a particular problem situation and also in the provision of services for such problems. Information concerning other problem areas can be used to fill in the blanks in the model to make the ecosystems theory more visible. Effective case management skills are important to applying this framework with some families.

By utilizing knowledge of all levels of the ecosystems perspective, the practitioner is better equipped to assess and provide services for families in accordance with the presenting problems and the family's current level of need. This application requires flexibility, creativity, and mobility outside the office and into the home and community.

A summary of how practitioners can implement this ecosystems perspective in their work is offered by Greene and Ephross (1991, p. 293).

- View the person/family/environment as inseparable.
- See the family practitioner as an equal partner in the helping process.
- Examine transactions between the person/family/environment by assessing all levels of systems affecting adaptiveness.
- Assess life situations and transitions that induce high stress levels.

- Attempt to enhance a person/family's personal and interpersonal competence through positive relationships and life experiences.
- Seek interventions that extend the "goodness of fit" among the person/family and the environment at all system levels.
- Focus on mutually sought solutions and person/family empowerment.

Caveats in Using the Ecosystems Metatheory

Although ecosystems theory offers a wealth of ideas about families and family practice, the family practitioner must be aware of some possible pitfalls in its use. One issue is that this perspective may lead to a conservative stance of valuing the status quo and avoiding real change. Influences that upset the homeostasis of a system may be framed as problems or forms of deviance, leading to responses that assess them not on their own merits but in terms of reducing or limiting their threats to existing relational patterns. Conflict may be seen as a negative influence, disrupting systemic balance; conformity may be assumed to be good. The underlying concern of treatment can be on ways to reduce tensions in the system and return it to stability as soon as possible.

A second issue is that ecosystems theory emphasizes how people adapt to environmental structures that exercise social control. Existing circumstances tend to be accepted as givens, and the focus may become how to adjust participants within those limits, rather than questioning the limits or valuing disruptions positively. Professionals may be in the role of experts in diagnosing sources of tension and in finding ways to enable participants to adapt in order to return to equilibrium. Thus, reducing tensions and reestablishing harmony may become goals of intervention. Successful adjustment of individuals within existing social norms may be assumed to be the highest good, and individuality, creativity, and autonomy become subordinate to the needs of the system.

Third, one may conclude that use of this metatheory requires many different interventive skills that practitioners are required to master in order to address the entire range of needs on all system levels. This conclusion, of course, is unrealistic. Metatheories provide a comprehensive theoretical framework within which the domain-specific theories and interventions are integrated and purposefully utilized to meet specific needs in a specific situation with specific persons. We support Wakefield's (1996) belief that ecosystems theory is not sufficient in itself and that practitioners should have skills in domain-specific interventions like those presented in this book. We disagree, however, with his contention that an ecosystems theory base is not clinically useful. Myriads of professionals have attested to the usefulness of the metatheory as presented here and supplemented by specific interventive methods to meet varying levels of need.

If family practitioners can avoid such pitfalls and heed these caveats, then effective applications of ecosystems theory may be made to practice. The key points of this section on ecosystems theory are summarized in Table 2.1.

TABLE 2.1   Key Principles of Ecological Systems Perspective

Ecological View

Transactions are continuous, reciprocal exchanges.
Life stresses are either positive or negative person–environment relationships.
Coping refers to problem solving and managing negative feelings.
Habitat is the physical and social setting within cultural contexts.
Niche is the result of one's accommodation to the environment.
Relatedness involves supportive networks and attachments.

Systems View

Wholeness—change in one part causes changes throughout system.
Feedback—regulates system by inputs from family and environment.
Equifinality—there is more than one way to get to a final goal.
Circular causality—not linear cause and effect, but interactions.

Practice Focus

Recognize diverse needs of families on varying levels.
Explore various practice roles involved in ecosystems dual focus.
Attend to life cycle transitions, interpersonal processes, and environmental settings.
Focus on strengths, not deficits; solutions, not problems.
Assess ecosystems at four levels (micro-, meso-, exo-, macro-).

Pitfalls

Focusing on personal adaptations to the exclusion of social change.
Valuing homeostasis as the goal.
Individuality, creativity, and autonomy becoming subordinate to the system.

Social Constructionist Perspective

A more recent arrival on the family practice scene, the social constructionist approach, is based on the metaphor of literature. Human actions and relationships are seen in terms of organized efforts to create meaning out of personal experiences. These efforts are like composing narratives, stories that people write about themselves. Experiences of the objective and the subjective realms are selectively arranged on the basis of assumed themes, which organize, structure, and give meaningfulness to the person or family (Berger & Luckmann, 1966; Hoffman, 1988, 1990; Sarbin, 1986; Von Glasersfeld, 1987).

Stories are crucial means that people in every culture use to create meaning and purpose in life. In all communities and families, stories appear in a variety of forms, including anecdotes, myths and fables, plays and movies, novels and poems, histories and biographies, case studies, and others. Much of our development as social beings occurs through listening to and understanding narratives, the stories that people around us tell about their own and others' lives. Reminiscences by the elderly represent important efforts to articulate meaning in their lives, and encouraging such reflections has been recognized as an important component of practice with the aged. Stories constitute the basic structures all persons use in order to make sense of their lives, and hence understanding narratives is fundamental to the practice of social work with families (Goldstein, 1988; Scott, 1989).

The social constructionism perspective on human behavior emphasizes the textual structure of everyday life, especially how people develop meaning in the diverse events of their day-to-day experience. Behavior is seen through the analogy of a story that a person is creating and telling about what that person is doing and how such tasks and experiences are organized into a meaningful whole (Holland, 1991; O'Hanlon & Weiner-Davis, 1988). One's present, dominant story can be empowering, or it can undermine meaningful relationships and effective social functioning (Polkinghorne, 1988).

A fundamental assumption of social constructionism is that reality is constructed or generated by participants, rather than being objective, external, or given. Our efforts to make sense of inner and outer experience involve trying to formulate some coherence and meaning from streams of events (Ricoeur, 1981). In order to create this formulation, we draw on our culture's storehouse of themes and attributions, handed down by our relatives and community leaders. Persons interpret events and experiences on the basis of cultural patterns, preformulated clusters of meaning that serve to enable the person to make sense of perceptions. All of these constructed meanings depend for their existence on the minds of the persons carrying and using them. No one's beliefs or conclusions are more "real" than another's, and all participate in editing, revising, and continuing the stories of meaning that they share.

Such contexts of meaning take on a narrative form, linking past, present, and anticipated future, involving movement toward or away from goals. Or the form may emphasize blockage or no change (Gergen, 1982). Story patterns involving interrupted movement toward a desired goal, followed by an inescapable defeat, constitute the theme of tragedy, whereas patterns involving movement away from a desired goal, followed by unexpected success, constitute the romantic theme. Other themes in many cultures include the use of a journey as a metaphor for life experiences, eventual retribution for injustices, and struggles between light and darkness or hope and despair.

A further component of social constructionism is the assumption that themes and clusters of assumed reality (cultures) cannot be controlled from the outside. They are not amenable to reconstruction through objective or instrumental manipulation by any outside technical expert, because they are formulations of the participants themselves. Participants may observe their own patterns and explore alternatives for themselves, allowing them to understand their experiences in new ways and hence respond differently than in the past. All that an outsider can do is to reflect themes in use and offer participants alternative themes for their consideration in making meaning out of their experiences. Outsiders (including practitioners) can attempt to create a context that invites participants to pursue such observations, reflections, and developments for themselves, but they cannot directly change the participants' themes or actions.

Applications to Family Practice

The social constructionist metatheory has extensive applicability for practice with families and for the role of the practitioner. In this chapter, the basic overarching principles that are consistent with this perspective are presented. More specific methods and techniques are found in Chapters 9 and 11, where solution-focused and narrative family interventions are discussed.

1. It is assumed that all interpretations and meanings are created by the participants, so there is no outside, "right" standard by which to diagnose or modify. Because everyone, including the professional, is engaged in developing meanings in order to deal with experience, the helping relationship is essentially a process of joint work on the themes brought by the family and the professional. In this shared work, the relationship is between equals and is nonhierarchical, and the power or right to assert interpretations is equally shared (Gergen & McNamee, 1992; Simon et al., 1985; Whitaker & Bumberry, 1988).

2. The professional respects the family's right to make use of its own themes and seeks to understand their origin and application. Together, the family and the professional explore the implications of the assumptions, directions, and anticipated ends of the family's dominant story.

3. We can nurture the development of such supportive, rather than paternalistic, relationships with families by reminding ourselves of the importance of trying to understand what a particular person's experiences seem like from the person's own perspective and by attempting to appreciate life and its problems as they are construed in the person's subjective experience (Goldstein, 1988). What families often need is not so much expert advice, technical fixes, or precise data as a responsive listener to their efforts to make sense out of their experiences and overt, caring encouragement to resume their roles as the capable authors of their own stories (Gergen & McNamee, 1992). The social constructionism approach to family practice emphasizes the client's *strengths*, rather than pathology or deficits; emphasizes *exceptions*, or times when the problem was not present; and builds on those times when something the client tried *did* work effectively. The relationship between family and professional is one of joint exploration and coauthorship, not a hierarchy in which one person has solutions to the other's deficits (Link & Sullivan, 1989).

Caveats in Using the Social Constructionist Metatheory

Social constructionism has prompted a shift in the attention of family practitioners from actions to meanings, from expertise to collaboration, and from diagnosis of problems to mutual creation of solutions. However, the spread of interest in social constructionism ought not be accepted as an unmixed blessing. Implications of its own story about how families and family interventions operate should be examined critically.

The first caveat regarding social constructionism is its assumption of relativism regarding all meanings. The theory holds that there is no reality "out there" and that meanings are strictly constructed by participants. If that is the case, then any interpretation would be as good as any other, from inclusive themes to destructive ones. The theory provides no explicit grounds for precluding various interpretations of experience, including illusions or sadism. Families trying to deny their pain would have a legitimate base for doing so with the maximum possible comfort, a condition about which the theory provides no evident guidance (Becvar & Becvar, 1988; Nichols & Schwartz, 1991). Although social constructionism does not necessarily lead to coauthorship of denials or destructive interpretations, nothing within the theory clearly precludes such possibilities.

A related problem with social constructionism is its inattention to the evident differences in power among family members and between families and communities. Dominant members of a family may impose their preferred interpretations on subordinate members, denying them the legitimacy of their own meanings and undermining their well-being. Likewise, community prejudice and discrimination may lead to denial of basic resources and opportunities for some families, particularly minorities, thus limiting their life chances and well-being regardless of the family's constructions or reconstructions. Again, nothing in social constructionism necessarily supports such abuses of power, but nothing in the theory draws explicit attention to them or provides explicit ways of dealing with them.

Underneath these problems lies a logical dilemma that confronts social constructionism: If there is no external reality, then that principle would preclude the assertion that the components of constructionism itself are true representations of anything, including its descriptions of how people deal with problems, develop meaning, undergo change, or do therapy (Held, 1990). In short, if we cannot know reality, then we cannot assert anything about it. Social constructionism can't have it both ways.

A likely response of advocates of social constructionism to such concerns may be that all of our perceptions of reality are incomplete. The theory is intended to be a metamodel for practice, rather than an assertion about ontological reality. Such defenses are hardly sufficient, because any theory would hasten to take refuge inside such permissiveness. So although social constructionism suggests many useful ideas for family practice, it continues to face difficult challenges in its formulation and refinement. The concern for family practitioners is to emphasize

TABLE 2.2   Key Principles of the Social Constructionist Perspective

Stories and Personal Meaning

Stories transmit meaning.

Their creation formulates coherent sequences.

They shape one's identity.

They organize values and explain choices.

They are organized by plots and themes.

They involve choosing from alternative interpretations.

Family functioning depends on shared meanings.

Meanings cannot be controlled from outside.

Emphasis shifts from actions to meanings, from expertise to collaboration, from diagnosis of problems to mutual creation of solutions.

Practice Focus

Nonhierarchical relationship.

Shared explorations.

Offer new meanings and assumptions.

Bring families' themes and values to awareness.

Be coauthor of a living story with them.

Nurture supportive, not paternalistic, relationships.

Pitfalls

Seeing any interpretation as being as good as any other.

Inattention to power differences in family and community regarding interpretations.

Assuming that social constructionism has all the answers and that they are the best.

---

the strengths of this metamodel and avoid its pitfalls. The key points of this section on social constructionism are summarized in Table 2.2.

Comparing and Integrating the Metatheories

Both of these approaches to family practice are comprehensive theories or metatheories, and both offer ways of looking at the world, particularly with regard to individual and social change (Payne, 1991). Each is inclusive in the sense that it accepts perspectives and methods drawn from other theories. We now look at a comparison of the two metatheories.

Both ecosystems and constructionism assume that a family is a group of persons involved in sustained, intimate interaction with one another. The interaction among these members becomes patterned or regularized on the basis of mutually shared expectations, meanings, and responses. Similarity or congruences among the meanings and expectations of members are the basis for stability and satisfaction, whereas incongruences lead to dissatisfaction and conflict. Creative explorations of alternative, more congruent shared meanings are the main concern of practice.

The two metatheories converge on a number of aspects and dimensions of family practice. The time focus of both is on the present and the anticipated future, rather than on the past. The context of each is the family as a group, not individuals. The goals emphasized by both perspectives involve enabling the family to identify and develop creative alternatives to unsatisfying patterns, rather than correcting past deficits. The role of the practitioner called for by both is to be a peer as much as possible in the process of mutual reflection and exploration of alternatives and change, not to be analytical, instructive, or prescriptive. The style of intervention emphasized by each is exploratory, nondirective, less structured, seeking exceptions to problems, and not corrective, analytical, or educational.

Both metatheories interpret experience in symbolic or metaphorical terms, not as literal or as problems to be controlled. Their treatment of "resistance" is one protective of the core meanings and relationships among family members, not one that works in terms of lack of motivation or dysfunction. The criteria for success of intervention emphasized by both are mutual acceptability, satisfaction, and meaningfulness among family members, not logical, objective, or behavioral measures. The key similarities between these perspectives are summarized in Table 2.3.

The two metatheories diverge somewhat in their emphases within the treatment process. The ecosystems perspective focuses attention on breakdowns in family equilibrium needing negotiation to reestablish homeostasis or mutually satisfactory exchanges. Constructionism treats family issues in terms of breakdowns in shared meaning that need reconstruction into new and more satisfying shared meanings.

Both the ecosystems and social constructionism approaches to family practice provide broad perspectives on how to understand and deal with family issues. The ecosystems model focuses primarily on the transactions of the family within the larger social environment, whereas the social constructionist model emphasizes the meanings that families and their members formulate out of those streams of events.

Both approaches are based on specialized bodies of knowledge. The ecosystems theory emphasizes knowledge of the diverse transactions among people and their environments. Means of strengthening the effectiveness of those interactions are major concerns of practice. Social constructionism focuses on how people find meaning in the diverse experiences of their daily lives; treatment involves the development of meanings that are more empowering for families. The key divergences between these perspectives are summarized in Table 2.4.

TABLE 2.3   Convergences in Ecosystems and Constructionism

Dimension	*Comment*
Time	Both are focused on the present and the anticipated future, rather than on the past.
Goals	Both seek to identify and develop creative alternatives, rather than to correct past deficits.
Style of intervention	Both are exploratory, nondirective, less structured, seek exceptions to problems; not corrective, analytical, or educational.
Context	Both focus on the family as a system, not on individuals.
Role of practitioner	A peer as much as possible in the process of mutual reflection and exploration of alternatives; not analytical, instructive, or prescriptive.
Interpretation of experience	Symbolic or metaphorical; not literal or in terms of problems to be controlled.
Understanding of "resistance"	Protective of the core meanings and relationships among members; not focused on lack of motivation or dysfunction.
Criteria for success	Mutual acceptability, satisfaction, and meaningfulness to participants; not logical, objective, or behavioral.

TABLE 2.4   Comparisons in Ecosystems and Constructionism

Criteria
1. Explicit knowledge base: How clear and extensive is the grounding of the approach in theory and research?
2. Focus of attention: How are family issues defined?
3. Change process: Does the approach explain how family change occurs?
4. Guidelines for intervention: Does the approach delineate actions of the practitioner?
5. Values: What values are emphasized?

Ecosystems	*Social Constructionism*
1. Moderate	Limited
2. Disruption of equilibrium	Meaninglessness
3. Negotiation of new homeostasis	Construction of new meanings
4. As expert	As coauthor
5. Harmony	Meaningfulness

Although neither approach is a complete practice model in itself, both theories have spawned a variety of specific methods and techniques for application in professional practice with families (Meyer, 1988; Rosen, 1988). For example, the life model of social work practice is based in ecosystems theory (Germain & Gitterman, 1980), as are the family-centered approach (Hartman & Laird, 1983) and the competence approach (Maluccio, 1981). The narrative approach to family practice (White & Epston, 1990) and the solution-focused approach (O'Hanlon & Weiner-Davis, 1988) are based in social constructionism. These and other practice models provide the specificity needed in working directly with families.

Summary

This chapter offers a comprehensive framework for assessing and working with families at each of the four levels of family need presented in the previous chapter. The ecosystems–social constructionism approach to family practice is a combination of two metatheories that complement each other to form a broad theoretical base for family assessment and practice. This approach offers a way of looking at the world and particularly at personal and social change.

The two metatheories each have specific strengths that inform family practice. However, limits of each are discussed. The family practitioner should be aware of these limitations, as they have definite implications for practice. There are areas in which the two theories diverge that supplement each other and fill in particular gaps. There are more similarities that emerge as the theories are analyzed by specific dimensions. These convergences enable the practitioner to draw on the two metatheories in creating a meaningful approach to assessing and working with families.

The following sections of this book provide specific practice methods that can be used in working with families. Each is applied to one of the four levels of family need within the overall framework of the linked ecosystems–social constructionism approach.

Discussion Questions

1. Discuss the key assumptions of the systems view and apply these to a family.

2. Select a presenting problem and design an intervention utilizing the social constructionist perspective on human behavior.

3. Why is it important for practitioners to view a client system holistically?

4. How could the combined ecosystems–social constructionist approach be utilized with lower-functioning clients? Does the use of social constructionist theory imply that clients must be verbally skilled?

5. Discuss how the two metatheories diverge in their emphasis within the treatment process and the ways in which the integration of these two metatheories could be helpful in working with families.

6. Discuss how the theories of social constructionism and ecosystems can be combined to address the problems of families in poverty.

7. Prepare a narrative about your life or an important episode in your life according to the concepts of the social constructionist approach.

8. What biases do you have that would limit your use of social constructionist theory in working with families?

Internet Resources

Family Systems

http://psychematters.com/family.htm
www.aamft.org
www.aft.org.uk/mainpages/links.html
www.thebowencenter.org/pages/theory.html
www.behavenet.com/capsules/treatments/famsys/familysystems.htm
http://en.wikipedia.org/wiki/family_systems_therapy
www.addictionalternatives.com/philosophy/familysystems.htm

Social Constructionism

www.narrativeapproaches.com
www.narrativepsych.com
www.massey.ac.nz/~alock/virtualnarrativ.htm

Suggested Readings

Coles, R. (1989). *The call of stories: Teaching and the moral imagination.* Boston: Houghton Mifflin.
  The training of child psychiatrists has been immensely enriched by the work of Robert Coles, whose volume leads the reader through the author's experiences of working with his learning from the children in his practice as well as from the students in his classes. This book demonstrates the wide applicability of the narrative framework for practice and for education in the helping professions.

Greene, R. R., & Ephross, P. H. (1991). *Human behavior theory and social work practice.* New York: Aldine de Gruyter.
  This book gives a good overview of the ecosystems perspective within a human behavior framework. Applications to practice are made.

Hoffman, L. (1990). Constructing realities: An art of lenses. *Family Process, 29*(1), 1–12.
  Social construction theory is used to move toward a more collaborative and unconcealed therapeutic stance. This theory plus a second-order view and sensitivity to gender issues are the three "lenses" used for constructing realities.

Polkinghorne, D. E. (1988). *Narrative knowing and the human sciences.* Albany: State University of New York Press.
Using literary criticism, philosophy, history, and recent developments in the social sciences, this volume shows how to use research information organized by the narrative form—such information as clinical case histories, biographies, and personal stories. The relationships between narrative formats and classical empirical research designs are examined, and suggestions for studying human behavior from a narrative framework are set forth.

Sarup, M. (1989). *An introductory guide to poststructuralism and postmodernism.* Athens: University of Georgia Press.
Three of the most influential figures in recent literary criticism—Jacques Lacan, Jacques Derrida, and Michel Foucault—have had extensive influence on the way we think about meaning in our experiences. This book traces the rise of narrative approaches to thought, radically opposed to the Enlightenment tenets of progress and scientific truth, and explores some implications of this perspective for the future of human social life.

Wakefield, J. C. (1988). Psychotherapy, distributive justice, and social work, Parts 1 & 2. *Social Science Review, 62*(2,3), 187–210, 353–382.
Wakefield argues that social work's organizing value is minimal distributive justice, in which all people would have a minimally acceptable level of basic economic, social, and psychological goods. This concept seems to build on an ecosystems framework and then utilize varying methods and interventive skills for meeting specific levels of needs.

References

Becvar, D. S., & Becvar, R. J. (1988). *Family therapy: A systemic integration.* Boston: Allyn & Bacon.
Berger, P., & Luckmann, T. (1966). *The social construction of reality.* Garden City, NY: Doubleday.
Bowlby, J. (1973). Affectional bonds: Their nature and origin. In R. S. Weiss (Ed.), *Loneliness: The experience of emotional and social isolation* (pp. 38–52). Cambridge, MA: MIT Press.
Breunlin, D. C., Schwartz, R. C., & Kune-Karrer, B. M. (1992). *Metaframeworks: Transcending the models of family therapy.* San Francisco: Jossey-Bass.
Brower, A. M. (September 1988). Can the ecological model guide social work practice? *Social Service Review, 62*(3), 411–429.
Cleveland, P. H., & Kilpatrick, A. C. (1990). *Social work students' involvement with the homeless: An international model.* Paper presented at the International Congress of Schools of Social Work, Lima, Peru.
Cobb, S. (1976). Social support as a moderator of life stress. *Psychosomatic Medicine, 38*(5), 300–314.
Gaudin, J. M., Jr. (1993). *Child neglect: A guide for intervention.* Washington, DC: National Center on Child Abuse and Neglect.
Gaudin, J. M., Jr. (1999). Child neglect: Short-term and long-term outcomes. In H. Dubowitz (Ed.), *Neglected children: Research, practice, and policy* (pp. 89–108). Thousand Oaks, CA: Sage.
Gergen, K. J. (1982). *Toward transformation in social knowledge.* New York: Springer-Verlag.
Gergen, K. J., & McNamee, S. (1992). *Social constructionism in therapeutic process.* London: Sage.
Germain, C. B. (1985). The place of community within an ecological approach to social work practice. In S. H. Taylor & R. W. Roberts (Eds.), *Theories and practice of community social work* (pp. 30–55). New York: Columbia University Press.
Germain, C. B., & Gitterman, A. (1980). *The life model of social work practice.* New York: Columbia University Press.

Germain, C. B., & Gitterman, A. (1987). Ecological perspective. In A. Minahan et al. (Eds.), *Encyclopedia of social work* (18th ed., pp. 488–499). Silver Spring, MD: National Association of Social Workers.

Germain, C. B., & Gitterman, A. (1995). Ecological perspective. In R. L. Edwards (Ed. in Chief), *Encyclopedia of social work* (19th ed., pp. 816–824). Washington, DC: National Association of Social Workers.

Goldenberg, I., & Goldenberg, H. (1991). *Family therapy: An overview* (p. 38). Monterey, CA: Brooks-Cole Publishing.

Goldstein, H. (1988). Humanistic alternatives to the limits of scientific knowledge. *Social Thought, 14*(1), 47–58.

Greene, R. R., & Ephross, P. H. (1991). *Human behavior theory and social work practice.* New York: Aldine de Gruyter.

Hartman, A., & Laird, J. (1983). *Family centered social work practice.* New York: Free Press.

Hefferman, J., Shuttlesworth, G., & Ambrosina, R. (1988). A systems/ecological perspective. In *Social work and social welfare: An introduction.* St. Paul, MN: West Publishing.

Held, B. S. (1990). What's in a name: Some confusions and concerns about Constructivism. *Journal of Marital and Family Therapy, 16*, 179–186.

Hoffman, L. (1988). A constructivist position for family therapy. *The Irish Journal of Psychology, 9*, 110–129.

Hoffman, L. (1990). Constructing realities: An art of lenses. *Family Process, 29*(1), 1–12.

Holland, T. P. (1991). Narrative, knowledge, and professional practice. *Social Thought, 17*(1), 32–40.

Lazarus, R. S. (1980). The stress and coping paradigm. In L. A. Bond & J. C. Rosen (Eds.), *Competence and coping during adulthood* (pp. 28–74). Hanover, NH: University Press of New England.

Link, R. J., & Sullivan, M. (1989). Vital connections: Using literature to illustrate social work issues. *Journal of Social Work Education, 25*(3), 192–230.

Long, D. D., & Holle, M. C. (1997). *Macro systems in the social environment.* Itasca, IL: Peacock.

Maluccio, A. N. (1981). *Promoting competence in clients.* New York: Free Press.

Mattaini, M. A. (1997). *Visual ecoscan for clinical practice.* Silver Spring, MD: NASW Press.

Meyer, C. H. (1988). The ecosystems perspective. In R. A. Dorfman (Ed.), *Paradigms of clinical social work.* New York: Brunner/Mazel.

Nichols, M. P., & Schwartz, R. C. (1991). *Family therapy: Concepts and methods* (1st and 2nd eds.). Boston: Allyn & Bacon.

O'Hanlon, W. H., & Weiner-Davis, M. (1988). *In search of solutions: A new direction in psychotherapy.* New York: Norton.

Payne, M. (1991). *Modern social work theory: A critical introduction.* Chicago: Lyceum.

Polkinghorne, D. E. (1988). *Narrative knowing and the human sciences.* Albany: State University of New York Press.

Ricoeur, P. (1981). *Hermeneutics and the human sciences.* Cambridge, UK: Cambridge University Press.

Rosen, H. (1988). The constructivist-developmental paradigm. In R. A. Dorfman (Ed.), *Paradigms of clinical social work* (pp. 317–355). New York: Brunner/Mazel.

Sarbin, T. R. (1986). *Narrative psychology: The storied nature of human conduct.* New York: Praeger.

Scott, D. (1989). Meaning construction and social work practice. *Social Service Review, 63*(1), 39–51.

Simon, F. B., Stierlin, H., & Wynne, L. (1985). *The language of family therapy.* New York: Family Process Press.

Von Bertalanffy, L. (1968). *General systems theory.* New York: Braziller.

Von Glasersfeld, E. (1987). The control of perception and the construction of reality. *Dialectica, 33*, 37–50.

Wakefield, J. C. (1996). Does social work need the ecosystems perspective? Parts 1 & 2. *Social Service Review, 70*(1,2), 1–32, 183–213.

Watzlawick, P., Beavin, J. H., & Jackson, D. D. (1967). *Pragmatics of human communication: A study of interactional patterns, pathologies and paradoxes.* New York: Norton.

Weiss, R. S. (Ed.) (1973). *Loneliness: The experience of emotional and social isolation.* Cambridge, MA: MIT Press.

Whitaker, C. A., & Bumberry, W. M. (1988). *Dancing with the family.* New York: Brunner/Mazel.

White, M., & Epston, D. (1990). *Narrative means to therapeutic ends.* New York: Norton.

3

Contexts of Helping: Commonalities and Human Diversities

June G. Hopps, Ph.D., and Allie C. Kilpatrick, Ph.D., with assistance from Jillian Nelson, M.S.W. candidate, University of Georgia

Four levels of family need applicable to assessing and working with families have been presented. Following the assessment of the primary level of need, intervention procedures are planned based on this information. The metatheories of ecological systems and social constructionism are utilized as comprehensive perspectives within which to undertake the assessment and interventions with each family.

Another important consideration in the context of family practice is the acknowledgment of both commonalities and diversity. It is crucial that the family practitioner have knowledge, awareness, and skill in developing the necessary core and common conditions of the helping relationship or therapeutic alliance and in dealing with human diversity.

Practitioners share many more commonalities than differences with families. These commonalities can serve as the foundation for building the therapeutic alliance and also for exploring differences. Errors in professional judgment that should be avoided are the tendencies (1) to see differences or commonalities when they are *not* there or (2) to not see differences or commonalities when they *are*

Chapter reviewed by Robbie W. Tourse, Ph.D., Boston College, and Ollie Christain, Ph.D., Southern University.

present. This chapter seeks to explore and balance these two concepts of commonalities and differences.

The Helping Relationship/Therapeutic Alliance

The metatheories of ecosystems and social constructionism that provide the basis for the integrative approach to family practice emphasize the principles of respect, responsive listening, caring encouragement, nonhierarchical relationships, shared power, and equality of meanings as commonalities in working with families. Closely related to these principles is the "I–Thou" relationship described by Buber (1958), in which there is an emphasis on what takes place between people—for our purposes, especially between the practitioner and the family. The goal is for each to relate to the other in a way that acknowledges the other's internal life, without any possibility of one being exploited by the other. The interaction is a dialogue. The focus or emphasis is on the interchange between them and the experience of mutual confirmation that can occur.

Historically, the concept of the helping relationship has permeated work with people since the early days of social casework and psychoanalysis. Biestek (1957) traced the development of this concept in social casework from Mary Richmond in 1899 through 1951. He then developed his legendary seven principles of relationship, which started with the client's needs expressed to the practitioner as the first direction of the interaction, the response of the caseworker to the client's needs as the second direction, then the client's awareness of the caseworker's responsiveness as the third direction. Based on the needs of the client, the seven principles were then articulated as individualization, purposeful expression of feelings, controlled emotional involvement, acceptance, nonjudgmental attitude, self-determination, and confidentiality.

We have adapted Biestek's (1957) formulation to include terms relating his concepts to working with families (see Table 3.1 by Kilpatrick, 1995). These principles are relevant today and applicable to the family as the client system, although none are absolute. For example, the principle of confidentiality is limited by rights of other individuals, the practitioner, the community, and society. Such behaviors as abuse are legally required to be reported.

The personal characteristics and behaviors displayed by practitioners are intrinsically related to the formation of working and maintenance relationships. The research of Rogers, Gendlin, Kiesler, and Truax (1969) and Truax and Carkhuff (1967) presented evidence suggesting that therapists' ability to function in three core emotional and interpersonal dimensions has a significant influence on effectiveness. These core characteristics are **empathy,** the ability to accurately perceive what people are experiencing and to communicate that perception to them; **respect,** positive regard and the indication of a deep and honest acceptance of the worth of persons apart from behaviors; and **genuineness,** the ability to be honest with him- or herself and with others. Horvath (2000) agrees with this premise and supports the importance of the practitioner's relatedness to the client in the work-

TABLE 3.1 Seven Principles in the Helping Relationship

First Direction: The Need of the Family	Second Direction: The Response of the Practitioner	Third Direction: The Awareness of the Client/Family	The Name of the Principle
1. To be treated as individuals			1. Individualization
2. To express feelings			2. Purposeful expression of feelings
3. To get empathic responses to problems	The practitioner is sensitive to, understands, and appropriately responds to these needs.	The client/family is somehow aware of the practitioner's sensitivity, understanding, and response.	3. Controlled emotional involvement
4. To be recognized as people of worth			4. Acceptance
5. Not to be judged			5. Nonjudgmental attitude
6. To make own choices and decisions			6. Self-determination
7. To keep secrets about self and family			7. Confidentiality

Source: From Kilpatrick (1995).

ing alliance. An additional core condition of **warmth** (treating people in a way that makes them feel safe, accepted, and understood) was added by Goldstein (1975), who observed that, without warmth, the practitioner may be "technically correct but therapeutically impotent" (p. 31). These four core characteristics are necessary conditions for ensuring that no harm is done and for developing a therapeutic climate within which family work may be conducted.

Most family practitioners consider the relationship between the family and the practitioner to be an essential ingredient of the therapeutic process. However, little systematic attention has been given to examining the function of the therapeutic alliance in working with families. Minuchin (1974) has talked about the necessity for the therapist to "join" the family, and Davatz (1981) has emphasized the importance of "connecting" with family members. Pinsof and Catherall (1986) state that the therapeutic alliance may be the primary mediating variable that determines the outcome of discrete interventions. They assert that adding the alliance concept to the theoretical base of family therapy illuminates and brings into focus a critical aspect of therapy that has existed in a theoretical twilight (p. 138). Pinsof (1994) builds on previous definitions to define the alliance.

The therapeutic alliance consists of those aspects of the relationship between and within the therapist and patient systems that pertain to their capacity to mutually invest in and collaborate on the tasks and goals of therapy. (p. 7)

The major difference between this definition and preceding ones is that it tries to account for the social field in which the alliance occurs. There is an alliance between two systems—not just two people, regardless of the number of people directly involved in the sessions. The client system consists of all the human systems that are or may be involved in the maintenance or resolution of the presenting problem. The therapist system consists of all the people involved in treating the client system. In other words, the systems consist of all the people who can influence the change process. In working with families, the therapeutic alliance exists on at least three levels: the individual alliance with each family member, the subsystem alliance with each of the multiperson subsystems such as parents and children, and the whole system alliance with the whole family system (Pinsof, 1995; Pinsof & Catherall, 1986). The alliance the practitioner has with one or two family members influences the alliance with other family members in a circular, reciprocal fashion. Therefore, no single alliance with dyads or triads can be considered in isolation.

Any individual is affected by the way in which relevant members of his or her social field feel about the practitioner or interventions. If a spouse is resentful of the therapeutic process, then this resentment may be a significant mediating factor in the outcome. On the other hand, a supportive spouse or family system may greatly facilitate the outcome of the process.

Horvath (2000) and Florsheim, Shotorbani, Guest-Warnick, Barratt, and Hwang (2000) indicate that studies over time have proven that the therapeutic alliance is an important element in the helping encounter, regardless of the theoretical perspective utilized in treatment. Kivlighan and Shaughnessy (2000) confirmed in their research the importance of the overall strength of the therapeutic alliance. Their study also supported the notion of an alliance rupture's being part of developing a successful working relationship with clients—"perhaps a general pattern of initial engagement followed by conflict and then reengagement characterizes successful treatment" (p. 370).

A significant contribution to understanding the therapeutic alliance has been the development of three systemically oriented scales to measure the alliance in individual, couple, and family work (Pinsof, 1994; Pinsof & Catherall, 1986). Each measures the content dimensions of tasks, goals, and bonds as they relate to the therapeutic alliance. None of this research, however, definitively addresses client diversity and its impact and influence on the therapeutic alliance.

Client Diversity

This nation is witnessing large-scale immigration, both legal and illegal, and this is reflected in the diversity found among clients and families. A practitioner may encounter differences in cultures, ethnicity, race, social class, religious affiliations, regional identities, gender, age, disability, affinity and sexual orientation, and other factors that can significantly affect and define our lives. Some of those that are most relevant to practice with families are now addressed more specifically. They include issues of ethnic sensitive practice, multiculturalism and cultural democracy, political orientation, sexual orientation, power and powerlessness, poverty, and family structures.

Ethnic Sensitive Practice, Multiculturalism, and Cultural Democracy

The ethnic sensitive practice model, which is based on an ethnocultural perspective, proffers that core concepts of ethnicity, social class, and oppression are integrated within an organizing framework of intervention principles (Anderson, 2003). The model assumes that ethnic groups' cultural differences lead to unique realities for members that can be more clearly understood via knowledge of those differences (p. 44). An important component is giving attention to the oppression of members of racial and ethnic groups and choosing relevant practice models for that family's needs at that point in time. Practitioners should know that unwillingness to challenge and address oppression in large societal systems is akin to aiding families in adjusting to their oppressors. Oppression can never be accepted as normal. Some assumptions of ethnic sensitive practice are that (1) history affects the generation and solution of problems; (2) the present is more important that the past or the future; (3) nonconscious phenomena affect family functioning; and (4) although ethnicity can be a source of strain, discordance, and strife, it can also be a source of cohesion, identity, and strength (Schlesinger & Devore, 1995).

A multicultural perspective is another component of ethnic sensitive practice, and it necessitates practitioners learning to value and embrace the unique attributes and nuances of cultures other than their own. Philip Fellin (as cited in Lum, 2003) notes several principles of multiculturalism:

1. A multicultural perspective should be inclusive of all subcultural groups, viewed as distinct groups that are interdependent with mainstream U.S. culture.
2. A multicultural perspective should recognize that all people in U.S. society identify with "multiple cultures," with varying degrees of affiliation and society involvement.
3. A multicultural perspective should recognize that all members of U.S. society engage in various types of relationships within their various cultures, and in relation to a mainstream U.S. culture. Biculturalism, acculturation, amalgamation, and assimilation, as forms of attachment and social relationships with these cultures, are proposed as options for members of U.S. society.
4. A multicultural perspective would recognize the changing nature of U.S. society, as it is continually influenced by all of its subcultures, and by national demographic, social, and institutional trends (pp. 271–272).

A key to effective practice is the practitioners' capacity to understand culture and power and the connection between the two. They need to demonstrate knowledge of a client or group's culture in addition to a willingness to help clients respect their own culture and that of others.

> Practitioners' knowledge of their own culture should include the capacity to take responsibility for managing any biases, prejudices, learned misinformation, and distorted attitudes and stereotypes held about clients. Each client must be given the opportunity to demonstrate his or her own strengths. The flexibility in thinking and behavior that such a stance requires means that extra steps, extra efforts, and extra time will be needed to understand differences presented by a client. This means using a way of thinking that involves application of general knowledge about various cultural groups to a specific client. A two-level process, which involves a look at the specifics within the general and vice-versa while managing the complexities involved, is a key to empowering. (Hopps & Morris, 2000, p. 89)

Efforts at problem resolution must be in tune with ethnically distinctive values and community customs. Such practice involves the concept of the "dual perspective," a conscious and systematic process of perceiving, understanding, and comparing simultaneously the values, attitudes, and behavior of the larger societal system with those of the family's immediate community system. It recognizes that all clients are a part of two systems: the dominant or sustaining system, which is the source of power and economic resources, and the nurturing system, composed of the physical and social environment of the family and community (Norton, 1998).

> The dual perspective should not be interpreted as being a concept for use only with minorities; it can be applied to all people. It should direct attention to the "common human needs of people" and the degree to which they are not within the nurturing society and within the major society. (Anderson, 2003, p. 83)

The dual system faced by all individuals is noted in Figure 3.1.

In her discussion of the dual perspective, Arline Prigoff (2003) reviews the San Antonio Model (SAM), which highlights a Cultural Assessment Grid. In utilizing the grid, clients and practitioners are able to isolate elements of both clients and environmental systems that can be viewed as being resources in resolution of clients' problems (see Types I and II in Figure 3.2) or as contributors to problems (see Types III and IV).

If the dual perspective is followed in tandem with the grid, it becomes an effective tool in discerning elements of the environment and their impact on clients. For example, the dominant sustaining system can be hostile to cultural diversity and thus corresponds more closely with Type IV, whereas the sustaining system of people of color corresponds more with Type II. What this shows is how the two systems can act as positive nurturing forces or as negative and nonsustaining.

Ethnic and class history and traditions often involve institutional sources of oppression. Therefore, practice with families must pay simultaneous attention to family and community/systemic concerns.

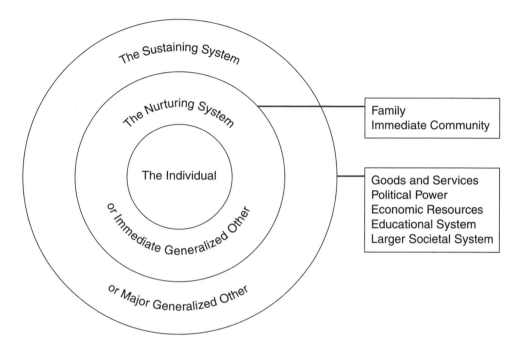

FIGURE 3.1 *The Dual System of All Individuals*
Source: From Norton, 1998; Anderson, 2003.

Thus, for example, we find victims of poverty and oppression caught up in a systemic process of powerlessness in which the failure of the larger society system to provide needed resources operates in a circular feedback process that entraps victims and puts in motion a malignant process. The failure of the larger system to provide necessary supports creates powerlessness in communities. And the more powerlessness in a community due to lack of resources and nutritive supplies, the more powerless are the families within, hindered from meeting the needs of their members and in organizing to improve the community so that it can provide them with more support. And the more powerless the families in efforts to protect their members from the stress of community failure and efforts to change its destructiveness, the more powerless are the individual members, blocked in attempts to acquire skills, develop self-esteem, and strengthen family. (Solomon, 1976)

Ethnic sensitive work often requires the practitioner to think in terms of a multisystem, interactive approach, as distinct from an isolated, linear approach, to intervention. Many client families are challenged by complex, multiple problems (substance abuse, unemployment, underemployment, and language barriers) that demand concurrent, targeted units of intervention. What this means is that practitioners must be knowledgeable not only about clinical/group processes but also about policies and operations of other resources, such as health care, employment and training, social security, and substance abuse counseling, so that they can help

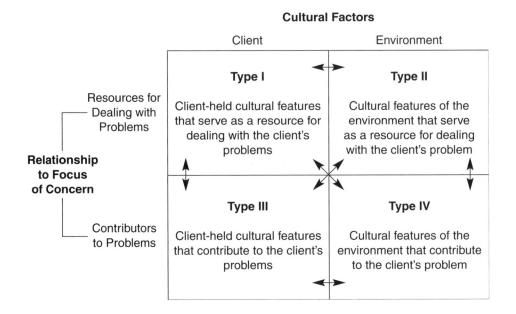

FIGURE 3.2   *Cultural Assessment Grid*

Source: From Anderson & Carter, 2003.

connect families to needed services. When services are not available or not available in a timely fashion, the therapist must assume an advocacy role. Increasing specialization in many agencies can become a barrier to the multisystem, interactive approaches that many families need. This is also the case with managed care, which requires the segmenting of problems (Hopps, Pinderhughes, & Shankar, 1995).

Gender Justice

Family practitioners are challenged by new levels of awareness regarding gender. The subtext is a priority now for the profession, due largely to advances in feminist theory and thought, broader concepts of masculinity, and the triumphant legal, economic, political, and emancipatory achievements of the civil rights movement, the women's movement, and gay liberation. Gender is at the core of an ideological analysis that facilitates examination of assumptions regarding principles of hierarchy, domination, and power of one sex over another (Hooyman, 1995).

Currently, postmodern feminism is struggling with defining its purpose and roles and is being challenged to address a number of issues, including but not limited to (1) demystifying the notion of exclusive consciousness of women as women and (2) recognizing the risks of universalizing women for the sake of solidarity. Although the latter is a needed component of change, it may also minimize individual women's uniqueness. The feminists' theme of a "universal civilizing mission" both undergirded and aided their claim to legitimacy. What this meant was that feminists felt they could address needs and interests of all women. Consequently, some women, mostly the white, western, middle class cohort, are being challenged by those who are not members of this cohort (poor women, women of color), who also assert that in times of "multiple contested oppressions" (i.e., class and race), gender might not be the deepest, most unyielding area of oppression. Unlike in the past, feminists are increasingly able to differentiate many facets of women's identities, including not only gender but race, ethnicity, class, religion, sexual orientation, physical and mental being, and personal political orientation or political sense of self. Thus postmodern feminism is compatible with social work in that it (1) respects diversity and (2) emphasizes context, which corresponds with one of the profession's foundations, person-in-environment (Forcey & Nash, 1998).

For the future, feminists must acknowledge that although there is power in viewing "women as women" and speaking as a united front in pursuit of positive social change, there is a risk of minimizing distinctiveness among women. What is needed is the capacity to handle this politically sensitive issue in such a way that it does not sacrifice women's differences or interdependence but rather enhances the thrust of empowerment for all women (Forcey & Nash, 1998).

Even with their power and authority attenuated via the influence of women, many men continued to resist new sex role definitions, clinging to traditional perspectives of manhood. But time marched forward, and with women gaining economic and political power, which translated into new status arrangements, men began adapting to change and examined opportunities to get in touch with their own masculine potential. Women proffered that patriarchy diminishes feminine characteristics—tenderness, love, and relatedness—in all people. Men, too, challenged patriarchy and stunted, insecure masculinity, which, they argued, contributes to problems related to inhibited intimacy, homophobia, need to dominate or be dominated, and violence directed toward both men and women (Chestang, 1995; Lichtenberg, 1995).

The task ahead: Both men and women should move beyond old barriers and hostilities, seek ways to explore their fullness and maturity, and relate to their common humanity (Keen, 1991). Stories and narratives of failed expectations, tolerance and intolerance, and growth should be shared in the safe zone of mutual respect, appreciation for personal struggle, and empathy. Given new growth, both men and women should also join with other worldwide organizations in fighting servitude, sexism, and homophobia. There is much work to do on the road to personal and community empowerment.

Another development to which therapists must be prepared to relate is the growing, increasingly open, politically and economically significant population of not only gays and lesbians but also transgenderists and bisexuals (although less is known about the latter two). The gay movement commenced with the Stonewall rebellion in 1969 and paralleled both the black power and women's movements. Hostility to this population originated with rampant and strongly held belief systems in heterocentrism, heterosexism, and homophobia, which throughout history oppressed those who could not or did not "own" a heterosexual identity. Such belief systems provided the undergirding for sociological, economic, political, and psychological factors that affected the development, sexual identity, resilience, and coping resources of this population. Gay people were victimized in colonial times, when sodomy was a crime punishable by death, and today they still constitute the largest hate crimes victim group, suffering beatings, torture, and death in addition to discrimination in employment, access to housing, social service, and health care (Appleby, Colon, & Hamilton, 2001).

Although diverse, gays and lesbians are thought to experience similar affirmative processes, namely,

> identification and confrontation of sexual difference; socialization in the gay and lesbian communities; self-identification or coming out to self and others; sexual experimentation; development of a sexual identity; nurturance of sexual and intimate relationships; formation of families . . . and life long contribution to profession and communities while under psychological and social duress. (Appleby et al., 2001, p. 149)

Indeed, practitioners must be able to work with families as a member transitions through these phases. They must be prepared to help the families find coping energy and perseverance when one (or more) of their members is confronted by and must work through internalized homophobia, a normative aspect of affirmative psychology that can occur at an early age with the incorporation of unavoidable noxious, negative attitudes and societal stigma into one's self-image.

It is not unusual for lesbians and gays to defend against internalized homophobia by denying who they are, distrusting and expressing anger and contempt for those who elect to be open and visible about their sexuality, becoming fearful, and withdrawing from families and associates. Many experience difficulties with intimacy, affectional relationships, and sexual functioning. They may avoid managing alcoholism, drug use, safe sex, and for AIDS and become overwhelmed with fragmentation in their lives, consequently exhibiting features of a borderline personality (Appleby et al., 2001).

Coping with stigma, discrimination, abuse, acts of violence, and internalized self-hatred as they do, suicide is no stranger to those who are sexually divergent. Family therapists must be at the forefront of efforts to minimize the influence of heterosexism, heterocentrism, homophobia, and other sexist attitudes in their practice and take the lead in helping to eradicate these "-isms" in social services where health and mental health services may be denied to the client and family. Therapists must also be mindful that families dealing with issues of sexual diversity can suffer trauma, stigma, isolation, and discrimination but that these forces are even greater in families of color.

Power, Powerlessness, and Power Needs of the Practitioner

Some groups in society are oppressed because of their race and ethnicity, gender, sexual orientation, income, age, or a combination of these. Other client groups with mental, developmental, or physical disabilities may also experience powerlessness.

Power is defined as the capacity to gain whatever resources are necessary to remove oneself from a condition of oppression, to guarantee one's ability to perform, and to affect not only one's own circumstances but also more general circumstances outside one's intimate surroundings (Goodrich, 1991, p. 10). Power thus involves the capacity to influence for one's own benefit the forces that affect one's life space; powerlessness is the inability to exert such influence (Pinderhughes, 1995).

Power as a construct is useful in understanding the relationship between the majority group and people of color and other ethnic groups, women, gays, and lesbians, as well as their interaction and role in the maintenance of majority–minority status, including discrimination, racism, and sexism. A dominant group requires and holds onto its resources and power by excluding and marginalizing low-status or different groups, making it difficult for them to access and acquire what they need; and by developing expectations that influence opportunities and outcomes for life chances of both the dominant group and those bestowed with less power (Hopps et al., 1995; Pinderhughes, 1995).

Indeed, overwhelmed and less powerful people may react to their role, status, and position by means that are truly unhealthy, unsafe, and unproductive. Pinderhughes (1995, pp. 290–291), states:

> For example, as individuals, minority people of color react to being tension relievers, anxiety reducers, and victims in the social system by behaviors that aim to provide them a sense of power. Many of them struggle not to accept the projections of the powerful that they are incompetent, dumb, crazy, a stud, sexual, or dependent. Considerable effort is expended to ward off a sense of powerlessness. People adopt behaviors in which they identify with the aggressor (which leads to feelings of self-hatred); are guarded (seen by the powerful as being paranoid); strike out (seen by the powerful as being violent); and are oppositional, passive-aggressive, or autonomous (seen by the powerful as being stubborn). It is important to consider that the dependency response to conditions of powerlessness does not mean ethnic minorities and people of color desire it; instead, they may adopt dependency to get a sense of power or to be close to persons who actually have power (McClelland, 1975). They may also try to get a sense of power by assuming the negative attributions of the dominant society in an exaggerated way, for example, by being a superstud, super dumb, or super-dependent. Although reactive, these behaviors, which Chestang (1976) identified as paradoxical mechanisms, also have meaning because they facilitate a feeling that one is the initiator.

These reactive behaviors often inhibit individuals and families from taking proactive steps to improve their social functioning, social standing, and rejection of designated, assigned positions. Just as not being able to exercise influence over life's chances can be painful, having such influence can be rewarding. Even so, those with power can exhibit fear of losing status and control and become fearful of those with little power. They may also experience guilt over their own privileged position; exhibit control needs; demonstrate a lack of tolerance, respect, and compassion for those who are different; and express affinity for those like themselves. Although guilty because of the reality of power, some might be willing to give a little, but few would give it up. Thus this power conundrum is at the crux of the struggle faced by people of color, women (though they have moved well ahead of people of color), new immigrants, and gays and lesbians in relation to the dominant group (Hopps et al., 1995; Pinderhughes, 1995).

Therapists must know that power is embodied in the professional role, which is endowed with knowledge and skills and emboldened by license to assess, intervene, and evaluate family functioning. Thus there is a power differential between the practitioner and the family. The realistic needs of some poor, minority families are so great and resources so slim that therapists may easily become overwhelmed and anxious and fall prey to self-comforting behaviors in efforts to reduce their stress and anxiety (Hopps et al., 1995). Therapists must assess and be realistic about their personal needs and never think of manipulating the helping/treatment encounter to meet their own status and power needs.

Poverty, Children, and Persistent Poverty

Poverty is a matter of the differentiated distribution of goods and privileges. In the preface to *The Power to Care*, Wilson states:

> In an industrial society groups are stratified in terms of the material assets or resources they control, the benefits and privileges they receive from these resources, the culture experiences they have accumulated from historical and existing economic and political arrangement and the influence they yield because of those arrangements. Accordingly, group variation in resources, lifestyles and life chances is related to these variations. (Hopps et al., 1995, p. vii)

Poverty is a major factor in the lives of too many families. It takes the form not only of a lack of sufficient income but also of the lifestyle that follows from that fact. The government defines the poverty level, using factors such as income before taxes, excluding capital gains and noncash benefits, and family composition and size. The poverty threshold for a family of four was $11,611 in 1987, $12,674 in 1989, $13,359 in 1990, $17,761 in 2000, and $18,811 in 2003 (U.S. Census Bureau, 2004). These families also depend heavily on other benefits, such as food stamps, rent supplements, and public housing. There is a strong correlation between poverty and single-parent households, which are mostly female; more than 50 percent of families in poverty are headed by females, whereas 22 percent are male headed, and 10 percent have two parents. One child in five is poor; under six years of age, one in four; and for African Americans, one in two. Persistent poverty is defined as a problem faced by families impoverished for 8 out of 10 years. In this cohort, African Americans and female-headed families are dominant (Hopps et al., 1995).

Poverty is a diversity issue that directly affects many families. Poverty and lack of housing have given rise to unprecedented rates of homelessness. Families with children are the fastest-growing homeless population. Practitioners must be acutely aware that these families in poverty have needs that are at Levels I and II of family functioning. These needs must be addressed before needs at Levels III and IV can be given adequate attention.

Family Structures

The family, society's most basic institution, has changed. Hopps and Morris state:

> The two-parent family in which the husband is the breadwinner and the wife the homemaker is not only no longer the norm but for many, neither a hope nor an ideal. "Alternative" styles now dominate, including the two-parent home, two-earner family, the single-parent family (due to divorce or out-of-wedlock births), the blended family, the gay or lesbian family, and the common law marriage with family. Even though the rate of increase in these pluralistic styles has slowed, their members indicate that people are significantly less affected either by traditional norms or by social stigma, and create family structures that suit their individual needs. Many others now simply defer marriage or remain single. (2000, p. 7)

Changes in the role and function of the family have occurred, with much less time and energy allocated for nurturance and caregiving. Women are no longer as available for these roles as in the past, although they are in the paid labor force as disproportionately low-wage workers (and are expected to constitute nearly 65 percent of the labor force at the middle of this decade). Groups that are particularly vulnerable because of the shifting economy and its impact on families are the young, the elderly, and single parents (Hopps & Morris, 2000).

Families who have been marginalized because of their racial or ethnic identity have experienced a drastically sharp transition from the two-parent to the one-parent family, and a most devastating challenge for them is poverty, as noted earlier. In instances in which a single mother heads a family with children, the potential for poverty becomes substantial: one in two, versus one in four if the head of the household is male. Practitioners must be knowledgeable about contraception, abstention, and sex education, placing before families options for delayed births, because the birthrate for unmarried African American women has arguably been viewed as a main cause of poverty. Now that rate is at its lowest in 40 years; currently, the increase in the rate of children born to unmarried white women resembles that of three to four decades ago for African American women (National Center for Health Statistics, 2003).

An integral part of the evolving family structure landscape is the growing presence of the same-sex couple and family. Gay unions and marriage discussion has centered on political and economic rights. But couples often want to establish families. With growing numbers of children worldwide who are without parents—owing to a host of circumstances, including drugs, poverty, AIDS/HIV, political unrest, and famine—gay and lesbian couples are able to adopt children and thereby fulfill parenting instincts and desires. Same-sex parents are often victims of prejudice and stereotypes, and their parenting capabilities often are questioned. However, to date, research on gay/lesbian parenting has found no evidence that their children's psychosocial development is compromised. Additionally, the home environment of same-sex couples is as supportive and enabling of their children's psychosocial development as that of heterosexual couples (Patterson, 1995).

If practitioners are to help families address and overcome the shift in family structure, they must find a way to incorporate resources relevant to education, including English-language classes, job training, work preparation, day care, transportation, and health care in their repertoire of referral services and be prepared to be assertive in connecting families to these resources. Families learn to model practitioners who advocate on their behalf, thus becoming empowered.

Summary

Within an ecosystems–social constructionism perspective, there exist many commonalities and differences of which we must be aware as we work with families who are functioning at various levels. Our common humanness unites us and is a foundation on which to build a therapeutic alliance. Differences and diversity issues must be recognized, with the goal of developing mutual respect and appreciation for differences. Thus the focus is on commonalities that unite us, not differences that divide us. The *helping relationship* or *therapeutic alliance* is a necessary condition for assuming that no harm is done and for developing a climate within which work can be done on problems that families bring to practitioners. The core needs of clients and the core conditions of the professional relationship of empathy, respect, genuineness, and warmth are commonalities for all our work with families. The therapeutic alliance consisting of the practitioner and client systems accounts for the social field in which the alliance occurs. *Diversity issues* include valuing multiculturalism and engaging in ethnically sensitive practice. A cultural-assessment grid is noted for use in developing ethnically sensitive practice. Ways that diversity issues interfere with the provision of social justice and contribute to oppression must be addressed.

Research addresses various dimensions of the therapeutic alliance but has not focused on diversity as a significant variable in the helping relationship. Given the growing presence of people of color and the many cultural differences that exist, attention must be given to this topic.

In the forefront of family practice today are issues of gender and justice, not just women's issues. Consciousness raising over the past few decades has served to focus our attention more on the oppressiveness of patriarchy, thus precipitating changes in both genders. However, oppression is felt by other groups as well, because of race, ethnicity, sexual preference, income, age, and the like. A major factor in oppression is access to the basic economic resources that are necessary for the well-being of any family. Practitioners must be especially sensitive to those families who are functioning at Levels I and II. Closely tied in with oppression is poverty, which is an especially crucial issue for people of color and single-parent families with children. These varying family structures—such as single-parent families but including also blended, childless, same-sex, multigenerational, and other families—may be especially vulnerable. Family practitioners must be sensitive to the different family structures and also realize the impact of ecosystem factors on them.

Discussion Questions

1. How does the addition of the concept "alliance" alter the previous understanding of the helping relationship?

2. How can new levels of awareness regarding gender and sexual diversity influence the therapeutic alliance on the three levels of individual, subsystem (parents or children), and whole family system?

3. Using a family from your practice, assess the manner in which you engaged or joined the client. Extend this discussion of the therapeutic alliance through all the contexts of helping.

4. What efforts can be made to show value and appreciation of the diverse culture of the families with whom we work?

5. Explain and discuss issues of power, powerlessness, and empowerment in a family from your practice. Identify any power needs that you might have experienced and how you managed them.

6. Discuss how you would assess a young, same-sex couple that applied to your agency for adoption of children.

Internet Resources

http://ethics.acusd.edu/Applied/race
http://dir.yahoo.com/Society_and_Culture/Issues_and_Causes/Multiculturalism/
www.canadianheritage.gc.ca/progs/multi/what-multi_e.cfm
www.diversity-oneness.com/index00.shtml

Suggested Readings

Anderson, J., & Carter, R. W. (Eds.). (2000). *Diversity persepctives for social work practice.* Boston: Allyn & Bacon.

Biestek, F. P. (1957). *The casework relationship.* Chicago: Loyola University Press.
This is a classic on the therapeutic relationship and should be required reading for all helping professionals. A chapter is devoted to each of the seven principles of the helping relationship.

Boyd-Franklin, N. (1989). *Black families in therapy: A multisystems approach.* New York: Guilford Press.
The author dispels myths, focuses on strengths, and sets African-American families in context. She gives major treatment interventions in a multisystemic approach and discusses diversity of family structures.

Brown, L. S., & Ballou, M. (Eds.). (1992). *Personality and psychopathology: Feminist reappraisals.* New York: Guilford Press.
  Synthesizing over 20 years of feminist thinking, this book gives original critiques of primary psychological theories and their accompanying definitions of pathology. The authors challenge previous theories of how healthy personalities develop and point out the need to keep any theory of personality relevant to women's lives.

Edwards, R. L. (Ed. in Chief). (1995). *Encyclopedia of social work* (19th ed., Vols. 1–3). Washington, DC: National Association of Social Workers.
  This most recent encyclopedia provides an objective overview of social work in the United States. It contains 10 articles specifically on the family, another on marriage and partners, and many others on methods of practice and diversity issues. It is highly recommended as a state-of-the-art reference book.

Hopps, J. G., Pinderhughes, E., & Shankar, R. (1995). *The power to care: Clinical practice effectiveness with overwhelmed clients.* New York: Free Press.
  This book contains important discussions on diversity, power, powerlessness and oppression, poverty, and clinical practice with overwhelmed clients.

Jordan, J. V., Kaplan, A. G., Miller, J. B., Stiver, I. P., & Surrey, J. L. (1991). *Women's growth in connection.* New York: Guilford Press.
  This book offers a new perspective on women's development and women's ways of being in the world. The authors are clinicians, supervisors, and teachers who have been searching for therapeutic models that are based on and reflect the lives of women rather than male models. It discusses women's meaning systems, values, and organization of experiences.

Pinsof, W. F., & Catherall, D. R. (1986). The integrative psychotherapy alliance: Family, couple and individual therapy scales. *Journal of Marital and Family Therapy, 12*(2), 137–151.
  This article introduces the therapeutic alliance concept into the family and marital therapy domain. It conceptualizes individual, couple, and family therapy as occurring within the same systemic framework. Three new scales that measure the alliance in individual, couple, and family therapy are discussed.

References

Anderson, J. (2003). Strengths perspective. In J. Anderson & R. W. Carter (Eds.), *Diversity perspectives for social work practice* (1st ed., pp. 11–20). Boston: Allyn & Bacon.
Appleby, G. A., Colon, E., & Hamilton, J. (2001). *Diversity, oppression and social functioning: Person-in-environment assessment and intervention.* Boston: Allyn & Bacon.
Biestek, F. P. (1957). *The casework relationship.* Chicago: Loyola University Press.
Buber, M. (1958). *I and thou* (2nd rev. ed.). New York: Charles Scribner's Sons.
Chestang, L. (1976). *The diverse society.* Washington, DC: National Association of Social Workers.
Chestang, L. (1995). Men: Direct practice. In R. L. Edwards (Ed. in Chief), *Encyclopedia of social work* (19th ed.). Washington, DC: National Association of Social Work.
Davatz, U. (1981). Establishing a therapeutic alliance in family systems therapy. In A. S. Gurman (Ed.), *Questions and answers in the practice of family therapy.* New York: Brunner/Mazel.
Devore, W., & Schlesinger, G. (1999). *Ethnic sensitive practice.* Boston: Allyn & Bacon.
Florsheim, P., Shotorbani, S., Guest-Warnick, G., Barratt, T., & Hwang, W-C. (2000). Role of the working alliance in the treatment of delinquent boys in community-based programs. *Journal of Clinical Child Psychology, 29*(1), 94–107.
Forcey, L. R., & Nash, M. (1998). Women & therapy: Rethinking feminist theory and social work therapy. *Woman & Therapy, 21*(4), 85–100. Retrieved August 23, 2004, from ProQuest database.
Goldstein, A. (1975). Relationship enhancement methods. In F. Kanfer & A. Goldstein (Eds.), *Helping people change: A textbook of methods.* New York: Pergamon Press.
Goodrich, T. J., (Ed.). (1991). *Women and power.* (p. 10). New York: Norton.
Hooyman, N. (1995). Diversity and population at risk: Women. In F. Reamer (Ed.). *The foundation of social work knowledge.* New York: Columbia University Press.

Hopps, J. G., Pinderhughes, E., & Shankar, R. (1995). *The power to care: Clinical practice effectiveness with overwhelmed clients.* New York: Free Press.

Hopps, J. G., & Morris, R. (Eds.). (2000). *Social work at the millennium: Critical reflections on the future of social work.* New York: Free Press.

Horvath, A. O. (2000). The therapeutic relationship: From transference to alliance. *Journal of Clinical Psychology: Millenium Issue: The Therapeutic Alliance, 56*(2), 163–173.

Hulbert, A. (2004, March 12). What do we know about the effects of same-sex parenting? *The Gay Science.* Retrieved October 17, 2004, from http://slate.msn.com/id.2097048.

Keen, S. (1991). *Fire in the belly: On being a man.* New York: Bantam Books.

Kilpatrick, A. (1995). Contexts of helping. In A. Kilpatrick and T. Holland, *Working with Families* (p. 39). Boston: Allyn & Bacon.

Kivlighan, D. M., Jr., & Shaughnessy, P. (2000). Patterns of working alliance development: A typology of client's working alliance ratings. *Journal of Counseling Psychology, 47*(3), 362–371.

Lichtenberg, P. (1995). Men: Overview. In R. L. Edwards (Ed. in Chief), *Encyclopedia of social work* (19th ed.). Washington, DC: National Association of Social Work.

Lum, D. (2003). People of color (ethnic minority) framework. In J. Anderson & R. W. Carter (Eds.), *Diversity perspectives for social work practice* (1st ed., pp. 61–76). Boston: Allyn & Bacon.

McClelland, D. (1975). Wrong, power. *Power, the inner experience.* New York: Wiley.

Minuchin, S. (1974). *Families and family therapy.* Cambridge, MA: Harvard University Press.

National Center for Health Statistics. (2003). *Births: Final data for 2002.* (DHHS Publication No. PHS 2004-1120). Hyattsville, MD: Government Printing Office. Retrieved November 10, 2004, from www.cdc.gov/nchs/data/nvsr/nvsr52/nvsr52_10.pdf.

Norton, D. (1998). *The dual perspective.* New York: Council on Social Work Education.

Patterson, C. J. (1995). Summary of Research Findings. In American Psychological Association (1995). *Lesbian and Gay Parenting: A Resource for Psychologists.* Washington, DC: Author. Retrieved October 17, 2004, from www.apa.org/pi/parent.html.

Pinderhughes, E. (1995). Diversity and population at risk: Ethnic minorities and people of color. In F. Reamer (Ed)., *The foundation of social work knowledge.* New York: Columbia University Press.

Pinsof, W. F. (1994). An integrative systems perspective on the therapeutic alliance: Theoretical, clinical and research implications. In A. Horvath & L. Greenberg (Eds.), *The working alliance: Theory, research and practice.* New York: Wiley.

Pinsof, W. F. (1995). *Integrative problem-centered therapy: A synthesis of family, individual, and biological therapies.* New York: Basic Books.

Pinsof, W. F., & Catherall, D. R. (1986). The integrative psychotherapy alliance: Family, couple and individual therapy scales. *Journal of Marital and Family Therapy, 12*(2), 137–151.

Prigoff, A. W. (2003). Dual perspective framework. In J. Anderson & R. W. Carter (Eds.), *Diversity perspectives for social work practice* (1st ed., pp. 77–92). Boston: Allyn & Bacon.

Rogers, C., Gendlin, E. T., Kiesler, D. L., & Truax, C. B. (1969). *The therapeutic relationship and its impact.* Madison: University of Wisconsin Press.

Schlesinger, E. G., & Devore, W. (1995). Ethnic-sensitive practice. In R. L. Edwards (Ed. in Chief), *Encyclopedia of social work* (19th ed., pp. 902–908). Washington, DC: National Association of Social Workers.

Solomon, B. (1976). Social work in a multi-ethnic society. In M. Solemeyer (Ed.), *Cross-cultural perspectives in social work practice and evaluation* (pp. 167–176). New York: Council on Social Work Education.

Transcript of Bush statement regarding support for an amendment to the U.S. Constitution to ban same-sex marriage. (2004, February 24). Retrieved October 17, 2004, from www.cnn.com/2004/ALLPOLITICS/02/24/elec04.prez.bush.transcript/index.html.

Truax, C. B., & Carkhuff, R. R. (1967). *Toward effective counseling and psychotherapy: Training and practice.* Chicago: Aldine de Gruyter.

U.S. Census Bureau. (2004). *Poverty Thresholds: Preliminary estimate of poverty thresholds for 2003.* Washington, DC: U.S. Department of Commerce. Retrieved November 10, 2004, from www.census.gov/hhes/poverty/threshld/03prelim.html.

4

Ethically Informed and Spiritually Sensitive Practice

Allie C. Kilpatrick, Ph.D., Dorothy S. Becvar, Ph.D., and Thomas P. Holland, Ph.D.

The entire therapeutic venture is fundamentally an exercise in ethics, involving the inventing, shaping, and reformulating of codes for living together (Efran, Lukens, & Lukens, 1988). Thus, in addition to the need for adherence to professional codes of ethics, there also must be recognition that family interventions constitute a dialogue whose goal is the creation of a context in which accommodation of the needs and desires of all the participants is facilitated. Fundamental to this context is the dimension of spirituality. Indeed, although often little recognized, some form of spirituality is a commonality in humanity (Becvar, 2001). At varying times in a person's life, this aspect of being may seek expression and, even when implicit, it inevitably influences beliefs and behaviors. This chapter provides suggestions for creating a practice that is well informed relative to ethical issues and is sensitive to the role of spirituality in the lives of both professionals and clients.

Ethically Informed Practice

Most professional groups that work with families have their own codes of ethics by which members are expected to abide. It is essential that students and practitioners know and practice according to these codes. Among the ethical issues discussed in the following section are some of the more complex issues we confront in family practice, as well as several models for dealing with them.

Ethical Practice

Working with families requires awareness of several important areas of ethical considerations and challenges. These involve tensions related to separating interventions from the larger ecosystems, focusing on individual or family welfare, using informed consent, respecting confidentiality, avoiding deception and manipulation, and deciding who should be included in therapy.

1. *Separating Interventions from the Larger Social, Cultural and Political Ecosystems.* For many years, family therapists have spoken of problems as being symptoms of family system dysfunction rather than manifestations of individual illness. Interventions have been focused on first-order change (individual behavior change within an unchanged system) or second-order change (changes within the system itself and the rules governing it) (Watzlawick, Weakland, & Fisch, 1974). However, as noted by Doherty and Boss (1991), we do not always consider the wider implications of the community, social, cultural, and political systems in the creation of problems or the ripples our interventions may produce in this larger pond on either level of change.

An illustration of how both society and the practitioner's interventions may play roles in exacerbating problems for clients can be seen in work with abusive families. For many years, society tolerated abusive behavior toward women and children. Now, society has changed, and practitioners label such behaviors as "bad" or "mad." If abusive behavior is part of a family's heritage, however, then their forebears, too, now may be seen as being bad. Further, if practitioners tell clients that the negative consequences of the abuse will likely remain with them all their lives, then they probably will, inasmuch as people participate in the creation of their own reality based, at least in part, on perceptions such as these shared by professionals (Becvar, 2001; Becvar & Becvar, 2003).

Appropriate rules of conduct evolve in a society, and practitioners contribute to defining acceptable and unacceptable behaviors and problems. We also play a role in defining what constitutes an ethical issue. Perhaps the ethical imperatives here are to avoid narrowing the range of focus to the point where there is little we see that is not illness, thus limiting preventive activities (Becvar & Becvar, 2003; Becvar, Becvar, & Bender, 1982) and ensuring that we do no harm. But we must be careful not to create more problems than our interventions solve and not to ignore ethical dilemmas that arise in our practice concerning such issues of social justice as institutional racism, societal gender bias, or accessibility to resources.

2. *Individual or Family Welfare.* In a survey of members of the American Association for Marriage and Family Therapy (Green & Hansen, 1989), the ethical dilemma rated as the second most frequently encountered and the second most important was the tension between "family versus individual needs" (second only to "reporting child abuse"). Practitioners are concerned with protecting the rights and promoting the welfare of all clients. When there are multiple clients, an intervention that serves one person's best interests may be counterproductive for another person. The ethical imperative here is to attempt to balance therapeutic responsibility toward individuals and the family as a unit (Doherty & Boss, 1991).

The basic philosophy of Western medicine and the medical code of ethics imply that a clinician's primary loyalty is to the patient as an individual; broader issues of public welfare are relegated to public health. By contrast, in the Eastern European tradition, the clinician's first obligation is to the community, and secondarily to the individual. Another aspect of this dilemma emerges from the fact that society also defines the roles of men and women. Practitioners have been guilty of subordinating rights of women and children to the family good, even when it is to the detriment of the former. It is not surprising that the issue of individual versus family rights was first raised by feminists, who have argued convincingly that balancing individual and family welfare requires practitioners to see beyond the therapy room to the family context (Doherty & Boss, 1991).

3. *Informed Consent.* The idea of informed consent involves "a knowledgeable decision based on adequate information about the therapy, the available alternatives, and the collateral risks" (Bray, Shepherd, & Hays, 1985, p. 53). State laws and professional association codes of ethics have made informed-consent procedures standard practice. Disclosure documents are often read by family members before they see the practitioner (Huber & Baruth, 1987). In order to make informed choices, clients should have information about the therapy setting, their rights and responsibilities, therapist credentials and competence, complaint procedures, the content and process of the professional relationship, the potential risks and benefits of change, limits of confidentiality, record keeping procedures and fees (Burkemper, 2004).

4. *Confidentiality.* With the passage of the Health Insurance Privacy and Portability Act (HIPPA), guidelines regarding the preservation of client confidentiality unless the client has granted permission to reveal personal information have become even stricter than previously was the case. At the same time, practitioners continue to have the right to disclose information when necessary to prevent a serious threat to the health of a client and/or to the safety of another person or the general public. Examples of the latter include incest, child abuse, or dangers such as those addressed by the Tarasoff decision (Health Insurance Privacy and Portability Act, 2002).

In addition, when working with families the practitioner may not reveal information unless all parties to the therapy have given their consent. In other words, even if one member of the family gives written permission to share information with a third party, the practitioner may not do so unless everyone who participated also gives written permission. The exception, of course, is when parents or legal guardians sign for children who are minors.

Another ethical challenge also may emerge relative to the relationships of family members with one another and how to handle secrets. Whether the practitioner is willing to keep private revelations fully confidential, allow no confidentiality among family members, or a balance between the two, the practitioner's position must be clearly communicated to the family as early as possible in the therapeutic encounter. This position must reflect the American Association for Marriage and Family Therapy (AAMFT) Code of Ethics (2001), which requires written permission to reveal one individual's confidence to other members of the client system in the context of therapy. The ethical imperative is to disclose the practitioner's policy on confidentiality as part of initial informed consent for treatment (Doherty & Boss, 1991).

   5. *Avoiding Deception and Manipulation.* According to Doherty and Boss (1991), the issue of deception is, along with gender bias, a central ethical issue in contemporary family practice. According to some theories, manipulation should be avoided at all costs. Others state that manipulation is unavoidable (Watzlawick et al., 1974). For example, all practitioners influence clients by sharing or withholding their thoughts and feelings concerning the client.

   Given the universality of the influence of practitioners on clients and the continual decisions made by the practitioner about what to disclose, the issue is not the nature of the intervention but whether any concealment involved is ethical and whether the therapist remains trustworthy (Doherty & Boss, 1991). The practitioner must not deceive the family about the practitioner's beliefs or intentions or conceal family realities about which the family deserves to know.

   6. *Participation.* Ethical issues arise around the coercion of reluctant adults or children in the family, especially when it violates the autonomy of a skeptical family member. Refusing to see the family unless all members are present could also be coercive to willing members, who may feel obligated to make successful efforts to engage the other members. Doherty and Boss (1991) assert that refusing treatment if family members do not participate would be unethical in public mental health centers, which are often the last resort for troubled families.

   Handling the ethical issues we have discussed builds on the principles of relationship, ecosystems, and social constructionism that were discussed in earlier chapters. These principles consistently focus on the integrity of practitioners in respectful, genuine, and caring relationships with families and with themselves. Underlying these principles are the basic ethical values of respecting autonomy, acting fairly and justly, promoting benefits and limiting harm. Guiding their application may be ethical theories such as utilitarianism, which emphasizes seeking outcomes that maximize positive changes and minimize negative ones. Another is duty theory, which emphasizes the ethical principles and obligations one has, such as telling the truth, deciding fairly, and keeping promises. Another is virtue theory, which looks at the motives and intentions of the actor. Professional codes of ethics tend to be constructed on the basis of duty theory, setting forth a variety of principles the clinician is obligated to follow. Because practitioners may encounter the challenge of competing principles, many ethicists advocate consideration of motivations and results as well as obligations.

Guides for Decision Making

The variety of ethical issues faced by family practitioners may be examined in terms of several underlying dimensions. Woody (1990, p. 135) proposes a pragmatic approach to dealing with ethical concerns in family practice, drawing on theories of ethics, codes of professional conduct, practice theories, sociological context, and the professional identity. These components serve as five decision-making bases for practitioners to use for a comprehensive analysis aimed at preventing ethical problems and reaching defensible ethical decisions. The assumption is that practitioners draw from several bases in the process of weighing competing values and coming to a decision, and use both intuitive and critical thinking.

Another perspective on the ways in which family practitioners deal with ethical issues was drawn from qualitative research by Holland and Kilpatrick (1991). They developed a three-dimensional framework based on their findings from a **grounded theory** study of practitioners and how they defined and made ethical decisions. Holland and Kilpatrick's model of clinical judgment has been refined since publication and now consists of three bipolar dimensions: the focus of decisions, ranging from means to ends; the interpersonal orientation, ranging from autonomy to mutuality; and the locus of authority, ranging from internalized to externalized.

The first dimension focuses directly on the practitioner's decisions and identifies a tension between pursuing solutions that maximize benefits regardless of risk versus complying with principles and procedures that are seen to reflect the values of the profession. The issue of deception and manipulation may be involved here.

The second dimension examines the interpersonal orientation in the decision-making process. It reflects practitioners' struggles between the protection of individual freedom and self-determination, and the responsibility of mutual caring, which urges active intervention in the service of protection and improvement for the good of all. Here, the issues of separating interventions from the larger ecosystem and focusing on individual family welfare come into play.

The third dimension involves the source of authority in the decision-making process. It focuses on the grounds for making these decisions and represents the conflict of allegiance to values that lie within the individual or the client/worker relationship and the obligation to comply with external sources, such as agency policy or existing norms. Issues of informed consent and confidentiality are applicable here (see Figure 4.1).

Crossing these three dimensions permits examination of each area in relation to the other two, which yields a comprehensive look at one's ethical orientation. Such a perspective suggests looking for interactions across these three dimensions in specific practice situations. A professional or a family may have a pattern of dealing with ethical problems that emphasizes following standard policies and procedures, exercising centralized control, and protecting the security of his or her position or the internal stability of the family. Another's approach to ethical dilemmas may emphasize a pattern that seeks to distribute

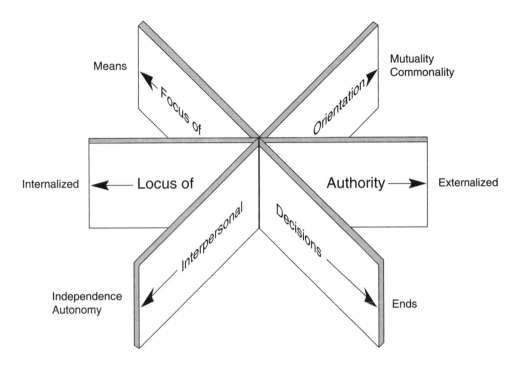

FIGURE 4.1 *Dimensions of Ethical Judgment*

power more broadly, to emphasize attainment of ends at the expense of following standard procedural rules, and to advance individual autonomy. Posing these dimensions in terms of polar extremes does not entail their opposition or mutual exclusion. One may attempt to balance them by seeking both group stability and individual flexibility, by encouraging both productivity and cohesiveness, and by being both nurturing and powerful. The importance of balance along each of the dimensions may be highlighted by the extreme forms that any of these values can take if unchecked.

In addressing ethical problems, dimensions such as these should be thoughtfully considered. Before trying to apply them to a decision or dilemma in practice, it is important to be aware of one's own values, prior socialization, and influences from others involved in the situation. Stereotypes and biases can influence judgment, especially if they are not explicitly recognized. In addition, the professional must take into consideration the cultural perspectives of the clients, which may vary from his or her own. If circumstances allow, one should not take up complex problems when fatigued, ill, or unduly influenced by pressures from others. If the professional has a personal stake in the outcome of the decision, a trusted but disinterested outside party should be invited into the deliberations to guard against self-interest bias.

Understanding the facts of the situation is essential, even though one cannot know everything about it. Reasonably complete information bearing on the case should be known and considered. Likewise, the professional is responsible for identifying the relevant technical and professional issues present and the possible choices available, including what options are feasible and what the relevant research indicates about them. Codes of professional ethics provide important guidance regarding choices and principles to follow.

The ethical dimensions of the situation must be identified explicitly and weighed reflectively. The decision maker specifies, evaluates, and measures the possible courses of action and the potential consequences of each. Who is involved, and what is at stake for each of them? Identify the duties, obligations, and interests of each party in the situation. What are the alternative courses of action (including doing nothing)? Then one weighs the principles involved in each alternative and their probable results. This includes consideration of the costs and benefits of alternatives, their long- and short-term effects, resources required and limitations on them, prior commitments and other constraints, justice and fairness for all parties involved, and possible need for reparations for those who may suffer losses.

Based on such considerations, it is often possible to identify one or two main courses of action. These should be examined for universality and consistency: Would it be appropriate for anyone in a similar situation to apply these principles and come to the same conclusion? If no alternative passes these tests, then one may select the option that results in the least undesirable net consequences. If others have not already been engaged in the deliberations, it is often helpful to test out conclusions and check for biases (remembering to safeguard the confidentiality of clients). These steps of ethical decision making are illustrated in Figures 4.2 and 4.3.

Codes of Ethics

Any profession has the responsibility to articulate its basic values and ethics through principles and standards that are relevant to all professional functions, settings, and populations served. These codes of ethics, to which we now turn our attention, serve to guide decision making and conduct relative to practice in general and, more specifically, when ethical issues arise. As discussed previously, ethical decision making is a process. Keeping in mind the guides for decision making and the dimensions for clinical judgment, we note that all professions that include working with families have their own codes of ethics. For illustrative purposes, the codes of ethics for the National Association of Social Workers (NASW) and the AAMFT are discussed. (See Internet Resources at the end of this chapter for various codes of ethics).

NASW Code of Ethics (1999).   The broad ethical principles in the code of ethics of the NASW are based on social work's core values of service, social justice,

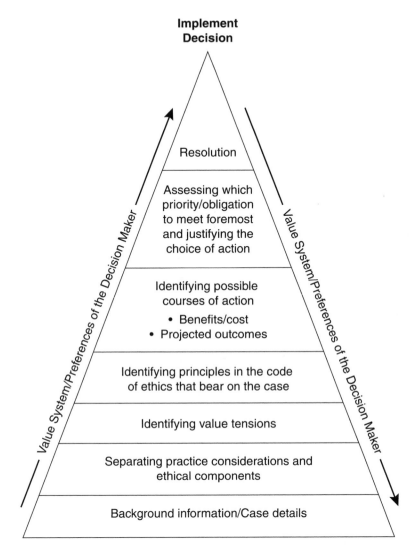

FIGURE 4.2 *Framework to Analyze Ethical Dilemmas*

Source: Mattison, 2000, Ethical decision making: The person in the process. *Social Work* 45(3), 206. Copyright 2000, National Association of Social Workers, Inc., *Social Work.*

dignity and worth of the person, importance of human relationships, integrity, and competence. The code was updated in 1999 and serves the following six purposes: It identifies core values of social work; summarizes broad ethical principles reflecting these values and sets standards; identifies relevant considerations and

Engage in Reflection and Self-Awareness

Be aware of one's ethical preferences
Develop a conscious awareness of one's value patterning

Analyze Current Ethical Dilemma

Begin by isolating the ethical components

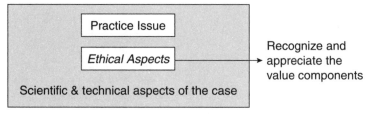

Practice Issue

Ethical Aspects ————————→ Recognize and
appreciate the
value components

Scientific & technical aspects of the case

Continue the Process of Reflection and Self-Awareness

Acknowledge which factors are influencing the decision

Client Factors	Personal
Organization	Professional

Follow Systematic Steps in the Decision-Making Process/Select a Resolution

Use an analytic guide to structure the decision-making process

Reflect on the Choice of Action

Measure the current ethical choice against others from the past
Sharpen and modify conscious awareness of one's value patterning

FIGURE 4.3   *Cycle of Reflection*

Source: Mattison, 2000, p. 210. Copyright 2000, National Association of Social Workers, Inc., *Social Work.*

conflicts; provides ethical standards for which the profession is accountable; socializes new practitioners to social work's mission, values, ethical principles, and ethical standards; and articulates standards used to assess unethical conduct.

The code sets forth standards to which all social workers should adhere and that are relevant to the professional activities of all social workers. The standards include the categories of social workers' ethical responsibilities to clients, to colleagues, in practice settings, as professionals, to the social work profession, and to the broader society.

The longest and most in-depth standard is the first one, the responsibility to clients. It covers the following: the commitment to clients, which is the primary obligation; self-determination of clients; the provision of valid informed consent to clients; the necessity of competence in providing services; the understanding of cultural competence, oppression, and social diversity; sensitivity to conflicts of interest, including dual relationships; the limits of privacy and confidentiality; guidelines for client access to records; sexual relationships with clients, which are strictly forbidden; rules for physical contact; prohibition of sexual harassment; ban on derogatory language; appropriate payment for services; dealing with clients who lack decision-making capacity; interruption of services; and termination of services. Special attention must be paid to each of these as practitioners discharge their professional responsibilities to clients in a respectful, caring manner.

AAMFT Code of Ethics (2001).   The revised code of ethics of the AAMFT, effective July 1, 2001, is binding on members in all categories, including students, clinical members, and Approved Supervisors; also included are applicants for both membership and for the Approved Supervisor designation. It is similar in many respects to the NASW code. Eight categories are addressed. These include responsibility to clients; confidentiality; professional competence and integrity; responsibility to students and supervisees; responsibility to research participants; responsibility to the profession; financial arrangements; and advertising.

The code requires that marriage and family therapists report any alleged unethical behavior of colleagues so that the profession can be self-regulating and can maintain the highest standards of ethical practice. Reports should be made to the AAMFT Ethics Committee and/or to state or provincial regulatory bodies as appropriate.

Other professionals who work with families, such as psychologists, counselors, chaplains, and nurses, have their own codes of ethics. State and provincial licensing boards also have their own codes. In some cases, these boards may have an umbrella code that covers several helping professions. All family practitioners are required to know the relevant codes that govern their practice. Although a code of ethics cannot guarantee ethical behavior, it provides an important set of guidelines. Ultimately, however, the ethical behavior of practitioners must come from their personal commitment to engage in informed ethical practice. Similarly, to practice in a manner that is spiritually sensitive requires knowledge of this dimension and a commitment to be aware of it and act in a responsible manner.

Spiritually Sensitive Practice

The 1996 Joint World Congress of the International Federation of Social Workers and the International Association of Schools of Social Work in Hong Kong heard the proclamation that there is a quiet revolution taking place in social work and other professions that is challenging the reliance solely on a traditional scientific-theory basis in favor of a more inclusive view of the human condition. The suggestion was made that social work's biopsychosocial paradigm be expanded to a bio-psychosocial-spiritual-cosmic paradigm as the integral basis for all courses taught (Schwartz & McGehee, 1996).

Because the majority of the world's families adopt some identifiable form of expression for their spirituality (Campbell & Moyers, 1988), it seems logical that practitioners should attend to the spiritual belief systems of clients if they are to understand fully the families with whom they work. To ignore this dimension may be to decrease the potential for effective practice (Kahle & Robbins, 2004). What is more, a paradigmatic shift in our views of spirituality, described as an ecosystemic revolution (Fox, 1983), has been occurring in the wake of a widespread increase in spiritual pluralism.

For the last several years, spirituality has experienced renewed attention in many secular domains. Thus we see an increase in attention to the subject of spirituality in bookstores, various professional conferences, popular magazines such as *Time* and *Newsweek,* and countless non-church-related associations, such as *Celestine Prophecy, A Course in Miracles,* Readings of Edgar Cayce, Angels, and so on. Spirituality is becoming part of the mental set of our times. In 1996 the 25-volume *World Spirituality* series released its 22nd volume, Peter Van Ness's *Spirituality and the Secular Quest,* which focuses on spirituality outside the church. Secular spirituality has been defined as "perceiving oneself to be connected to a larger whole through some unitive and transcending principle and living one's life accordingly" (Reed, 1997, p. 45). Also in the secular domain, a recent issue of *Time* magazine (Kluger, 2004) states that some scientists claim to have found the God gene and that our DNA compels us to seek a higher power.

The mental health professions also have begun to acknowledge and accommodate recent change in attitudes toward spirituality. Since 1994 the Council on Social Work Education has required that all master's degree programs in social work provide practice content that includes approaches and skills for clients from varying religious and spiritual backgrounds. And the social work profession recently has been described as "undergoing a resurgence of interest regarding the issue of spirituality in social work" (Rice, 2002, p. 303).

Past Barriers and Future Directions

In the past there have been several barriers to addressing the spiritual dimension with families. One is that, in order to become more scientific, we assumed we must separate ourselves from nonscientific spiritual constructs. The spiritual dimension is seen as esoteric and unobservable (Cornett, 1992), allowing the entrance of bias and subjectivity. Although subjective constructs such as spiritual power, psychic energy, and divine intervention are hard to observe and measure from a social constructionist perspective (Prest & Keller, 1993), we recognize that subjectivity is inevitable. Further, as Cornett notes, the failure to integrate spirituality into our clinical thinking represents an impoverishment in our practice.

A second barrier has been fears about the imposition of a particular frame of reference on clients. Effective practice is predicated on a nonimposing, nonjudgmental practitioner stance. Our spiritual commitments are better expressed through caring behavior. However, rather than attempting to monitor appropriately our spiritual expression in clinical work as we monitor other areas, many practitioners have simply discounted the need to explore the spiritual aspect of clients' lives, often with the assumption that these aspects are conflict-free, functional, or comfortable (Cornett, 1992). Rigid conceptions of spirituality and biases against formal institutions have also been barriers (Prest & Keller, 1993).

The last decade has seen a gradual breakdown of these barriers, with an increase in attention to the spiritual dimension in people's lives, as well as permission to include religious and spiritual issues in therapeutic conversations (Becvar, 1997a, 1997b; Frame, 2000). However, several areas relevant to ethical issues have accompanied this shift. These include the fact that a focus on spirituality in therapy is rarely included in professional training programs (Bowman, 1989); that there are many potential pitfalls requiring attention when including such a focus (Benningfield, 1997); that professionals must respect the autonomy of clients, safeguard their welfare, protect them from harm, and treat them in a just and honest manner when dealing with spiritual issues (Haug, 1998); and that therapists must recognize the limits of the knowledge it is possible to have relative to spirituality (Becvar, 2001). Thus the mandate for the future relative to the ability to practice in a spiritually sensitive manner is attention to each of these dimensions.

Definition of Spirituality

A definition of spirituality needs to encompass the person's understanding of and response to meaning in life (Cornett, 1992). It must include faith and values as spiritual dimensions (Kilpatrick & Holland, 1990), as well as the process of conceptualizing the individual's connection with others, the world, and the Creator (Campbell & Moyers, 1988). Spiritual expression could also be defined as the individual's response to the events in life over which he or she has no control. Canda (1988) gives an encompassing definition as follows:

> The gestalt of the total process of human life and development relates to the person's search for a sense of meaning and totally fulfilling relationships between oneself, other people and the encompassing universe and ontological ground of existence, whether a person understands this in terms that are theistic, atheistic, nontheistic, or any combination of these.

Canda and Furman (1999, pp. 44–45) note that definitions of spirituality in the social work literature include the following six attributes:

1. An essential or holistic quality of a person that is considered inherently valuable or sacred and irreducible.
2. An aspect of a person or group dealing with a search for meaning, moral frameworks, and relationships with others, including ultimate reality or life after life.
3. Particular experiences of a transpersonal nature.
4. A developmental process of moving toward a sense of wholeness in oneself and with others.
5. Participation in spiritual support groups that may or may not be formally religious.
6. Engagement in particular beliefs and behaviors, such as prayer or meditation, in a spiritual or religious context.

Implementation

As we think about acknowledging spirituality in practice, it is important to be aware that conflicts in values and the search for direction, meaning, integration, and faith underlie many of the problems presented by clients. What is more, despite the difficulties in dealing with such elusive and complex issues, few areas are more important than these. Even in poor communities, according to Aponte (1994), the challenge to the family is not only about bread or basic resources but about the spirit. We must encourage a sense of dignity, purpose, and future in families that have given up hope, meaning, and self-worth, and have succumbed to a sense of despair. Here, optimism and hope are the core elements in building the resilience so necessary when working with Level I family needs.

Practitioners might begin to address this realm by including in the initial assessment questions about the clients' belief system, asking, for example, "Where are you on religion or spirituality?" or "How important is or what role does religion or spirituality play in your life?" Practitioners might also ask about the spiritual resources clients have available to them—both personal, such as prayer or meditation, and professional, such as a member of the clergy or spiritual guide.

At the same time, it is important that practitioners have an understanding and awareness of their own spirituality in order to be helpful to family members in their pilgrimage of life. Indeed, like other personal issues, the spirituality of practitioners can be an obstacle or an asset. Thus each of us must be sensitive to our own biases in order to avoid value imposition or an inappropriate intrusion on the therapy process.

Effective practice also includes recognizing clients' desires and readiness to deal with spiritual concerns, accepting them, and being as comfortable with discussing this dimension as with discussing the physical, emotional, and intellectual dimensions of practice (May, 1982). Further, whatever clients' belief systems may be, a spiritual orientation on the part of the practitioner would focus on helping clients to define meaning in life and achieve ultimate satisfaction and thus may also participate in the facilitation of deeper levels of healing (Becvar, 1997a). Indeed, as Bardill (1997) states, a failure to account for the spiritual reality in practice means that a powerful reality of life has been ignored.

Hodge (2001) presents a multidimensional framework for spiritual assessment. The two components are a narrative spiritual history outline and an interpretive anthropological framework, as shown in Table 4.1. Using this assessment

TABLE 4.1 Framework for Spiritual Assessment

Initial Narrative Framework

1. Describe the religious/spiritual tradition you grew up in. How did your family express its spiritual beliefs? How important was spirituality to your family? extended family?

2. What sort of personal experiences (practices) stand out to you during your years at home? What made these experiences special? How have they informed your later life?

3. How have you changed or matured from those experiences? How would you describe your current spiritual or religious orientation? Is your spirituality a personal strength? If so, how?

Interpretive Anthropological Framework

1. *Affect.* What aspects of your spiritual life give you pleasure? What role does your spirituality play in handling life's sorrows? enhancing life's joys? coping with life's pain? How does your spirituality give you hope for the future? What do you wish to accomplish in the future?

2. *Behavior.* Are there particular spiritual rituals or practices that help you deal with life's obstacles? What is your level of involvement in faith-based communities? How are they supportive? Are there spiritually encouraging individuals that you maintain contact with?

3. *Cognition.* What are your current religious/spiritual beliefs? What are they based on? What beliefs do you find particularly meaningful? What does your faith say about personal trials? How does this belief help you overcome obstacles? How do your beliefs affect your health practices?

4. *Communion.* Describe your relationship to the Ultimate. What has been your experience of the Ultimate? How does the Ultimate communicate with you? How have these experiences encouraged you? Have there been times of deep spiritual intimacy? How does your relationship help you face life challenges? How would the Ultimate describe you?

5. *Conscience.* How do you determine right and wrong? What are your key values? How does your spirituality help you deal with guilt (sin)? What role does forgiveness play in your life?

6. *Intuition.* To what extent do you experience intuitive hunches (flashes of creative insight, premonitions, spiritual insights)? Have these insights been a strength in your life? If so, how?

Source: D. R. Hodge, 2001. Spiritual assessment: A review of major qualitative methods and a new framework for assessing spirituality. *Social Work* 46(3), 208. Copyright © 2001, National Association of Social Workers, Inc., *Social Work.*

tool could help "elicit what may be the most untapped strength among consumers, their spirituality" (p. 211). At the same time, Hodge (2003) also notes that no single assessment instrument is right for all clients and that practitioners should be familiar with several in order to be able to respond appropriately in each individual situation.

Having ascertained the degree of importance attributed by their clients to the realm of spirituality, practitioners may then include this aspect of life as a regular part of the therapeutic conversation. They also may wish to consult with or refer clients to others who have greater expertise in this area. In addition, they may engage in self-disclosure as appropriate, sharing the ways in which spirituality has helped them in their own journey toward health and healing.

At the same time, practitioners also must be able to accept the fact that for many clients such explicit discussions may be neither desirable nor useful. Even though spirituality is an important part of their life, some clients may not see it as relevant to the problems at hand. Some may feel it is just too personal or simply may feel uncomfortable discussing this topic with a therapist. Other clients may express lack of belief in any kind of spirituality. Some also may have experienced trauma in the context of their faith tradition (Hickson & Phelps, 1997). Nevertheless, a spiritual orientation on the part of the professional, which includes a nonjudgmental attitude as well as a focus on such issues as clients' values and their search for meaning and purpose in life, may participate in the creation of both a more effective therapeutic encounter and a more meaningful reality for clients (Becvar, 1997a). In addition, Canda and Furman (1999, p. 291) list the following as specific examples of spiritually oriented helping activities:

Active imagination
Art, music, dance, and poetry therapies
Assessing spiritual emergencies
Assessing spiritual propensity
Biofeedback
Caring for the body
Cooperation with clergy, religious communities, and spiritual support groups
Cooperation with traditional healers
Creating a spiritual development timeline and narrative
Developing and using multicultural teams
Developing mutually beneficial human–nature relationships
Developing and participating in rituals and ceremonies
Dialoguing across spiritual perspectives
Differentiating between spiritual emergencies and psychopathology
Dissolving inner chatter and distractions
Distinguishing between religious visions and hallucinations or delusions
Dream interpretation
Exploring family patterns of meaning and ritual
Exploring sacred stories, symbols, and teachings
Family brainstorming

Focused relaxing
Forgiveness
Guided visualization
Intentional breathing
Journaling and diary keeping
Meditation and prayer
Mindful paying attention
Nature retreats
Physical disciplines for spiritual cultivation, such as hatha yoga or t'ai chi
Reading scripture and inspirational materials
Reflecting on beliefs regarding death and afterlife
Reflecting on the helpful or harmful impact of religious participation
Win-win solution making

Regardless of the activities chosen, however, the intentional use of spirituality in practice is unique, not because of words or actions, but because of our assumptions about how these words or actions interface with the transcendent dimension. According to Anderson and Worthen (1997), three assumptions are basic to a spiritual perspective. These are (1) an awareness that God or a divine being exists, (2) a recognition that humans have an innate yearning for a connection with this being, and (3) a belief that this being is actively interested in humans and acts on our relationships to promote beneficial change. Working from these assumptions, practitioners share their own spiritual selves, and then the range of available resources and possibilities for change expands for all.

Accordingly, the practitioner is kind and operates from a place of integrity. Compassion for clients is expressed through a nonjudgmental stance, focused attention, and the creation of meaningful relationships. Humility and respect for everyone involved in the process also characterize spiritually sensitive practice. For example, despite the fact that certain client behaviors are socially unacceptable, the practitioner attempts to focus on understanding the context of clients and their behavior rather than on a blaming or demeaning attitude. Questions such as "How did you learn that it was okay to hit/abuse your spouse?" provide important information about areas in which further learning may be useful and help to move in the direction of potential solutions And, as clients are able to experience a respectful process, they may find themselves open to growth and change.

Growth and change in other areas may be facilitated through questions aimed directly at understanding the degree of meaning and purpose in the lives of clients:

- Are you doing the work you want to be doing?
- Are you satisfied with the education you have obtained?
- Is there any way in which you would like to increase your education or training?
- What are the ways in which you express your creativity?

- Do you have any special talents or skills that you haven't fully developed or expressed?
- Assuming that money and other responsibilities were no object, what would you do with your life if you could do what you truly wanted?
- What would you like to have accomplished by the time you reach age 70 in order to feel that your life has been meaningful?
- Have you developed your spiritual life to the extent that you desire?
- What are your most important values?
- What gives your life the most meaning?
- Is there anything you deeply value that you have not yet fully experienced or realized in your life?

The transpersonal or spiritual dimension is one of empowerment by the energies and wisdom that flow from a greater wholeness attained as we recognize that life does indeed have meaning and purpose. It is the bedrock of empowerment for the practitioner and families, and for national and international practice. Indeed, recent research (Faver, 2004) suggests that the ability of professionals to provide care is sustained by a sense of connectedness to a sacred source, to work, to supportive communities, and to clients, a phenomenon defined as relational spirituality. Instead of relegating issues of value to the private sphere, spiritually sensitive practice acknowledges that a transcendent dimension permeates all aspects of life, linking each individual with each other and with the community or public sphere. Such linkages typically prompt spiritual people into actions of concern for others (Elkins, 1990), especially the poor and the vulnerable. Although these persons may not always have spoken with one voice on every issue, they have affirmed in numerous ways their shared faith that the spiritual dimension of life leads to a transcendence of individualism and to a life of commitment and service to others (Leiby, 1985; Peck, 1987).

The convenient popular dichotomy between public and private morality works against the integration of our communities as well as our personal and professional lives. Our shared public interests rely in large part on the development of private virtue. Both private and public order depend on the availability of material resources and fair systems for their allocation to all. Therefore, a commitment to values of social justice and to the difficult tasks of implementing such values in our economic and political systems is essential (Siporin, 1986). Our spiritual heritage further emphasizes that individual self-actualization is gained through committed relationships with others, through investing our own resources and our very selves in furthering the good of others (Kilpatrick & Holland, 1990).

Recognition of the spiritual foundations of our lives and our professional practice leads to a number of implications regarding the client, the practitioner, their relationship, and the social context of the profession. Consistent with our social constructionist framework, clients are acknowledged as our peers. We recognize that they are human beings, too, and that, just as we have professional expertise, they are the experts on their personal lives and families. Exploration of spiritual issues is undertaken with respect for the individual's, couple's, or family's spiritual framework and with the understanding that their belief systems represent their view of reality, which is just as valid for them as ours is for us.

The spiritual, social, emotional, and material or physical dimensions of life are all necessary for our growth and well-being. Thus each should be considered in the therapeutic relationship. A biopsychosocial-spiritual model of human functioning makes spiritual issues a legitimate focus for practitioners and provides for a more complete understanding of the strengths, resources, weaknesses, and problems of families. Policies and services that provide accessibility to support in all of these areas are essential for human well-being. Increased openness to addressing relevant spiritual beliefs and metaphors could often provide the practitioner with an important avenue to effective interventions that have great potential for the facilitation of growth and change.

Ethical Challenges

As indicated in the first half of this chapter, practice that is ethically informed is essential. Thus, as one attempts to practice in a spiritually sensitive manner, it also is important to be cognizant of the potential dilemmas and ethical issues that may emerge in this realm for both professionals and clients. We will consider these under two headings: conflicts arising from religious/spiritual beliefs and limits of competence/lack of training.

Conflicts Arising from Religious/Spiritual Beliefs

Given the ethical imperatives to avoid discrimination and foster client self-determination, professionals must be able to recognize when a conflict in religious or spiritual values and practices precludes their ability to practice in an unbiased manner and support the rights of clients to make decisions for themselves. Differences in beliefs around issues and behaviors such as abortion, birth control, cohabitation, divorce, homosexuality, and sex before marriage, which often emerge from an individual's religious/spiritual belief system, may challenge the ability of the professional to work effectively with certain clients. In such situations, professionals are advised to seek supervision and/or to make appropriate referrals (Becvar, 2001).

Limits of Competence/Lack of Training

Given that attention to and permission to include the religious/spiritual dimension in clinical practice are relatively recent occurrences, it is not common for professionals to have had extensive training in this area unless they attended seminary-based programs (Becvar, 1997a). Although schools of social work are now often including at least one course on the topic in their curricula, sensitivity to the limits of one's competence is essential in order to prevent an ethics code violation. Being prepared adequately to accommodate issues and needs in this realm may require additional supervision or training through workshops or advanced study as well as finding consultants who might advise them when the need arises. Such training would help the social worker learn how to prevent personal issues from intruding inappropriately as well as ways to engage effectively with spiritual and religious issues as they emerge, either implicitly or explicitly, in the practice setting.

Summary

Ethics and spirituality are very personal matters that are the blueprints for inventing, shaping, and reformulating the way we are with ourselves and how we relate to others. And both are an inevitable part of the therapy context.

This chapter described how ethical issues influence what we are able to do with families and the ways in which practitioners must be informed in this area. Pertinent ethical issues raised in this chapter include separating interventions from the larger ecosystems; focusing on individual or family welfare; using informed consent; respecting confidentiality; issues regarding who participates in the treatment sessions; and avoiding deception and manipulation. Several models for decision making were presented, including an overview of grounds for making a decision bases, dimensions of clinical judgment, and codes of ethics. These provide guidelines for making ethically informed decisions in practice.

A final context to be considered is that of spiritually sensitive family practice. Although previously a much-neglected area, spirituality is now recognized as an important aspect of people's lives as well as of the therapy process. Many of the barriers to addressing families' spiritual concerns now have been overcome, and there is much support for working in a spiritually sensitive manner. Aspects of spirituality include faith, values, how a person understands and responds to meaning in life, and each person's connection with others and the world, as well as a recognition of a transcendent dimension. Several suggestions for including spirituality in the therapeutic conversation were provided. Increased openness in dealing with families' relevant spiritual beliefs may enrich and enhance practice. Spirituality is a resource to draw on not only from within the individual or family but also by utilizing churches within the ecosystem and the values underlying each person's or system's construction of reality. At the same time, it is important that practitioners recognize potential ethical conflicts that may arise relative to differences in value systems or limits of competence.

Discussion Questions

1. Describe and discuss ethical issues that may arise in an intervention with a family with a strong patriarchal tradition.

2. Regarding the ethical dilemma of meeting family versus individual needs, how would you balance the therapeutic responsibility toward both?

3. How do you effectively work with clients who present spiritual ideas that are different from, or even conflicting with, your own?

4. How can you assess when a client or family is ready to or needs to discuss spiritual issues?

5. What are some ethical issues of which to be aware when including spirituality in the therapeutic conversation?

Internet Resources

Ethics

http://ethics.acusd.edu
www.ethics.org
www.globalethics.org
www.ethics.ubc.ca
http://pages.prodigy.net/lizmitchell/volksware/ethics.htm

Professional Codes of Ethics

www.socialworkers.org/pubs/code/code.asp
www.aamft.org/resources/LRMPlan/Ethics/ethicscode2001.asp
www.amhca.org/code
www.nbcc.org/pdfs/ethics/NBCC-CodeofEthics.pdf

Spirituality

www.oamft.on.ca/featdec03.htm
http://sehd.binghamton.edu/affprogram/sssw
     Society for Spirituality and Social Work
www.cswe.org/spirituality/
     CSWE Social Work and Spirituality Resources
www.socwel.ku.edu/canda/
     Ed Canda's Home Page
http://kidshealth.org/parent/positive/family/spirituality.html

Suggested Readings

Assagioli, T. (1990). *Psychosynthesis. A manual of principles and techniques.* Wellingborough, UK: Crucible Press.
    The author defines and maps the geography of spiritual transformation through psychosynthesis. Psychological disturbances may serve as precursors to a more ethically and spiritually refined outlook. The process of spiritual development is described in four critical phases.

Becvar, D. S. (1997). *Soul healing: A spiritual orientation in counseling and therapy.* New York: Basic Books.
    This groundbreaking book shows how a spiritual orientation (which can encompass the full range of belief systems) can be used to facilitate healing at the deepest level.

Doherty, W. J., & Boss, P. G. (1991). Values and ethics in family therapy. In A. S. Gurman and D. P. Kniskern (Eds.), *Handbook of family therapy* (Vol. 2, pp. 606–637). New York: Brunner/Mazel. Of special interest in this chapter is the discussion of personal and cultural values in family therapy, ideological issues, ethical issues, and gender and ethics in family therapy. Future directions are also discussed.

Dykstra, C., & Parks, L. (1986). *Faith development and Fowler.* Birmingham, AL: Religious Education Press.
Fowler presents an overview of his faith development theory, and then other authors evaluate the theory and discuss how it can be enhanced.

Huber, C. H. (1993). *Ethical, legal and professional issues in the practice of marriage and family therapy* (2nd ed.). New York: Merrill.
A new edition of a very popular text used in many marriage and family therapy professional issues courses. Several chapters are devoted to ethical issues, the professional codes of ethics, and their implications for working with families.

Kilpatrick, A. C., & Holland, T. P. (1990). Spiritual dimensions of practice. *The Clinical Supervisor, 8*(2), 125–140.
This article places values and faith in a historical context within the profession of social work, presents developmental stages of faith, and gives some practical ways that students and practitioners can think about the spiritual dimensions of professional practice.

Mattison, M. (2000). Ethical decision making: The person in the process. *Social Work, 45*(3), 201–212.
Reflective self-awareness can alert the decision maker to the ways assumptions and values influence thinking about ethical dilemmas.

May, G. (1982). *Will and spirit: A contemplative psychology.* San Francisco: Harper.
Within Maslow's hierarchy of needs, May found that spirituality can be found at both ends of the continuum. He states: "It emerges at the bottom, when physiological needs for survival cannot be met and physical existence is threatened. It also arises when most other needs have been taken care of and one has the luxury to ask, 'What's it all for?' or 'Is this all there is?' Thus, it is in relative affluence or in utter desolation that human spiritual longing most obviously becomes prominent." (p. 91)

References

AAMFT Code of Ethics. (2001). Washington, DC: American Association for Marriage and Family Therapy.

Anderson, D. A., & Worthen, D. (1997). Exploring a fourth dimension: Spirituality as a resource for the couple therapist. *Journal of Marital and Family Therapy, 23*(1), 12.

Aponte, H. (1994). *Bread and spirit: Therapy with the new poor.* New York: Norton.

Bardill, D. R. (1997). *The relational model for family therapy: Living in the four realities.* New York: Haworth Press.

Becvar, D. S. (1997a). *Soul healing: A spiritual orientation in counseling and therapy.* New York: Basic Books.

Becvar, D. S. (Ed.). (1997b). *The family, spirituality and social work.* New York: Haworth Press.

Becvar, D. S. (2001). Moral values, spirituality and sexuality. In R. H. Woody & J. D. Woody (Eds.), *Ethics in marriage and family therapy.* Washington, DC: AAMFT.

Becvar, D. S., & Becvar, R. J. (2003). *Family therapy: A systemic integration* (6th ed.). Boston: Allyn & Bacon.

Becvar, R. J., Becvar, D. S., & Bender, A. E. (1982). Let us first do no harm. *Journal of Marital and Family Therapy, 8*(4), 385–391.

Benningfield, M. (1997). Addressing spiritual/religious issues in therapy: Potential problems and complication. In D. Becvar (Ed.), *The family, spirituality and social work* (pp. 25–42). New York: Haworth Press.

Bowman, E. S. (1989). Understanding and responding to religious material in the therapy of multiple personality disorder. *Dissociation, 2*(4), 231–238.

Bray, J. H., Shepherd, J. N., & Hays, J. R. (1985). Legal and ethical issues in informed consent to psychotherapy. *American Journal of Family Therapy, 23,* 50–60.

Burkemper, E. M. (2004). Informed consent in social work ethics education: Guiding student education with an informed consent template. *Journal of Teaching in Social Work, 24*(1,2), 141–160.

Campbell, I., & Moyers, B. (1988). *The power of myth.* New York: Doubleday.

Canda, E. (1988). Spirituality, religious diversity and social work practice. *Social Casework, 69*(4). 238–247.

Canda, E. R., & Furman, L. D. (1999). *Spiritual diversity in social work practice.* New York: Free Press.

Cornett, C. (1992). Toward a more comprehensive personology: Integrating a spiritual perspective into social work practice. *Social Work, 37*(2), 101–102.

Council on Social Work Education. (1994). *Curriculum policy statement for master's degree programs in social work education.* VA: Author.

Doherty, W. J., & Boss, P. G. (1991). Values and ethics in family therapy. In A. S. Gurman & D. P. Kniskern (Eds.), *Handbook of family therapy* (Vol. 11, pp. 606–637). New York: Brunner/Mazel.

Efran, J. A., Lukens, R., & Lukens, M. D. (1988). Constructivism: What's in it for you? *The Family Therapy Networker, 12*(5), 27–35.

Elkins, D. (1990, June). On being spiritual without necessarily being religious. *Association for Humanistic Psychology Perspective,* 4–5.

Faver, C. A. (2004). Relational spirituality in social caregiving. *Social Work, 49*(2), 241–249.

Fox, M. (1983). *Original blessing.* Santa Fe, NM: Bear & Co.

Frame, M. W. (2000). Spiritual and religious issues in counseling: Ethical considerations. *Family Journal: Counseling & Therapy for Couples and Families, 81*(1), 72–74.

Green, S. L., & Hansen, J. C. (1989). Ethical dilemmas faced by family therapists. *Journal of Marital and Family Therapy, 15*(2), 149–158.

Haug, I. (1998). Including a spiritual dimension in family therapy: Ethical considerations. *Contemporary Family Therapy, 20*(2), 181–194.

Health Insurance Privacy and Portability Act (HIPPA). (2002). Student training in preparation for compliance University of South Dakota School of Medicine. Retrieved from http://med.usd.edu/medicaleducation/USDSM_HIPPA.htm

Hickson, J., & Phelps, A. (1997). Women's spirituality: A proposed practice model. In D. Becvar (Ed.), *The family, spirituality and social work* (pp. 43–57). New York: Haworth Press.

Hodge, D. R. (2001). Spiritual assessment: A review of major qualitative methods and a new framework for assessing spirituality. *Social Work, 46*(3), 203–214.

Hodge, D. R. (2003). Assessing client spirituality: Understanding the advantages of utilizing different assessment approaches. *Society for Spirituality and Social Work Forum, 10*(1), 8–10.

Holland, T. P., & Kilpatrick, A. C. (1991). Ethical issues in social work: Toward a grounded theory of professional ethics. *Social Work, 36*(2), 138–144.

Huber, C. H., & Baruth, L. G. (1993). *Ethical, legal and professional issues in the practice of marriage and family therapy* (2nd ed.). Columbus, OH: Merrill.

Kahle, P. A., & Robbins, J. M. (2004). *The power of spirituality in therapy: Integrating spiritual and religious beliefs in mental health.* New York: Haworth Press.

Kilpatrick. A. C., & Holland, T. P. (1990). Spiritual dimensions of practice. *The Clinical Supervisor, 8*(2), 125–140.

Kluger, J. (2004, October 25). "Is God in our genes?" *Time,* 62–72.

Leiby, J. (1985). The moral foundations of social welfare and social work. *Social Work, 30,* 32–33.

Mattison, M. (2000). Ethical decision making: The person in the process. *Social Work, 45*(3), 201–210.

May, G. (1982). *Will and spirit: A contemplative psychology.* San Francisco: Harper.

NASW Code of Ethics. (1999). Washington, DC. National Association of Social Workers.

Peck, M. S. (1987). *The different drum.* New York: Simon & Schuster.

Prest, L. A., & Keller, J. F. (1993). Spirituality and family therapy: Spiritual beliefs, myths, and metaphors. *Journal of Marital and Family Therapy, 19*(2), 137–148.

Reed, H. (1997, January/February). Finding the sacred in the profane. *Venture Inward* (magazine of the Association for Research and Enlightenment, Inc./The Edgar Cayce Foundation/Atlantic University).

Rice, S. (2002). Magic happens: Revisiting the spirituality and social work debate. *Australian Social Work, 55*(4), 303–312.

Schwartz, M., & McGehee, E. (1996, July). Bipsychosocial-spiritual-cosmic paradigm in social work education In *Proceedings,* Joint World Congress of the International Federation of Social Workers and the International Association of Schools of Social Work, Hong Kong.

Siporin, M. (1986) Contribution of religious values to social work and the law. *Social Thought, 13,* 35–50.

Van Ness, P. (1996). *Spirituality and the secular quest.* In *World spirituality* (Vol. 22). New York: Crossroad.

Watzlawick, P., Weakland, J. H., & Fisch, R. (1974). *Change: Principles of problem formation and problem resolution.* New York: Norton.

Woody, I. D. (1990). Resolving ethical concerns in clinical practice: Toward a pragmatic model. *Journal of Marital and Family Therapy, 16*(2), 133–150.

Part II

First Level of Family Need: Basic Survival

Level I families are dealing with basic survival needs, such as food, clothing, shelter, protection, medical care, and minimal nurturance. A primary issue is whether there is good enough parenting capacity to support and protect the family's members. Families on this level may have presenting problems of pervasive life stresses, illness of a primary caretaker, economic deprivation, alcoholism, mental illness, or homelessness. We present two approaches that may be helpful to families who have Level I needs.

The first approach is designed to meet basic needs in neglectful families. In Chapter 5, Ellis and Grigsby discuss a new model of family preservation. The second approach focuses on ways to assist families and enable them to cope with illnesses (both physical and mental), disabilities, or other primary stressors. In Chapter 6, Greene and Kropf discuss the issues of family case management. They present a coordinated, congruent, and collaborative approach that can be used with both chronic and short-term problem situations. Cases presented are applicable across diverse racial and ethnic groups.

5

Interventions with Level I, Neglectful Families: A New Model of Family Preservation

Jackie Ellis, L.C.S.W., and R. Kevin Grigsby, D.S.W.

Mary Jones (age 22), a single mother of two (Alex, age 6, and Katie, age 6 months), was reported to the Department of Family and Children Services (DFCS) by the school social worker after Alex had been absent from school for three weeks. This was unusual, as Alex had previously had good attendance, was doing well academically, and seemed to enjoy school. The school social worker also expressed concern that for the last few weeks Alex attended school, she frequently appeared tired, was socially withdrawn, and sometimes fell asleep during class. Following this initial report, a second report received two days later from Katie's pediatrician indicated that Ms. Jones had failed to keep a follow-up appointment for Katie after bringing the child in for an ear infection. While attempting to contact Ms. Jones, the caseworker learned that the family had recently been evicted by the local Housing Authority because of an incident of domestic violence between Ms. Jones and her current boyfriend, Tom. Although Tom was arrested, the Housing Authority's strict policy concerning domestic violence resulted in Ms. Jones' eviction. Ms. Jones had moved into a mobile home owned by her uncle and located in a rural area of the county. On arrival at the new residence, the caseworker observed Alex playing in the yard. It was a cold day, and Alex was not appropriately dressed for the weather, wearing a short-sleeved shirt and sandals. The child's clothing appeared dirty and her hair was matted and uncombed. After a long delay, Ms. Jones answered the door holding Katie, who was wearing only a diaper. Katie's face and hands were dirty, and Ms. Jones appeared unable to comfort the crying child. The mobile home was sparsely furnished, and the family appeared to be living in only the kitchen/living room area. A blanket covered the door to the hallway. Although Ms.

Jones had been employed at a minimum-wage job before Katie's birth, she indicated that her only sources of income now were Temporary Assistance for Needy Families (TANF), at $280 per month, and food stamps, at $371 per month, which had to support herself and her children. Ms. Jones explained that she had been unable to locate affordable housing and had no choice but to move into the mobile home after being evicted by the Housing Authority about three weeks before. Since then, she had experienced "one problem after another." Because the central heating system for the mobile home was not working, Ms. Jones was using a kerosene heater to heat two rooms. She'd also had problems with broken water pipes, which her uncle had repaired yesterday. Although Ms. Jones was thankful her uncle had provided her with a place to stay, she had no transportation and no phone, and she was now out of touch with her only friend (another young mother who lived at the Housing Authority). Ms. Jones stated that she just did not have the energy to deal with all the problems. When the caseworker began to talk about the reports received by DFCS, Ms. Jones became tearful, reported feeling hopeless, and begged the caseworker not to take her children.

The Jones family is typical of many Level I families reported to public child welfare agencies for child neglect. Weltner (1982) described Level I families as having an "ineffective executive system" (p. 43); that is, parents struggle to meet the basic needs of their children for food, clothing, shelter, medical care, safety, and nurturance. These "multiproblem" families challenge even the most skilled practitioner. Level I families create a sense of urgency among workers, who often report feeling as if they are working harder than the family to remedy problems; the worker seems to experience the crisis more than the family does. Polansky, Chalmers, Williams, and Buttenweiser (1981) coined the term "apathy-futility syndrome" to describe neglectful mothers characterized by emotional numbness, loneliness, reluctance to discuss feelings, lack of competence in many areas of living, poor problem-solving skills, and a pervasive conviction that nothing is worth doing. Confronted with failure upon failure, the sense of hopelessness experienced by family members is pervasive (Kinney, Haapala, Booth, & Leavitt, 1990). Regrettably, intervention strategies with Level I neglectful families remain less well-developed than interventions with other forms of child maltreatment; "neglect has proved to be a particularly intractable problem in studies of child welfare interventions" (Fraser, Nelson, & Rivard, 1997, p. 147).

Yet "continuity of relationships, surroundings, and environmental influence are essential for healthy child development" (Goldstein, Freud, & Solnit, 1973, p. 31). As children develop in the context of relationship with their primary caregivers, supporting this relationship is of primary importance, as disruptions or termination of the caretaker–child relationship may lead to additional problems for the child. This chapter attempts to integrate theoretical and empirical knowledge from the area of child neglect with the knowledge base of family preservation services (FPS) to develop a model of intervention tailored to Level I neglectful families. First, child neglect is defined, and Belsky's (1993) developmental-ecological model provides a theoretical framework for understanding the etiology of child neglect. The chapter then explores the components of existing FPS and concludes with suggestions for modifying this model of service delivery—tailoring FPS to meet the needs of Level I neglectful families.

Needs of Neglectful Families

Neglect is defined as acts of omission on the part of a parent or caretaker that result in physical, emotional, social, or cognitive harm, or risk of harm, to a child. DePanfilis and Salus (1992) identified three broad categories of neglect: physical— failure or delay in providing adequate food, clothing, shelter, or medical care, inadequate personal hygiene, inadequate supervision; educational—failure to comply with state regulations for school attendance or lack of cooperation or involvement in the educational process; and emotional—failure to provide nurturance and affection, inadequate socialization. Neglect is the most frequently occurring form of child abuse, affects multiple children within families, and may be either chronic or short-term/situational (Nelson, Saunders, & Landsman, 1993). In 2002, 896,000 children were victims of child maltreatment; 60 percent of these victims experienced neglect; 19 percent experienced physical abuse; and 10 percent experienced sexual abuse (USDHHS, 2004). When compared to victims of physical abuse, children who experienced neglect were 46 percent more likely to experience recurrence (USDHHS, 2004). "The consequences of neglect to children are at least as serious as the consequences of abuse" (Smith & Fong, 2004, p. 1). Summarizing research on the long-term consequences of neglect, Gaudin (1999) identified all of the following: attachment problems; low self-esteem; difficulty coping with frustration; deficits in expressive and receptive language; intellectual and academic deficits; and impaired social relations. More child fatalities are attributed to neglect than to other forms of child maltreatment. In 2002, an estimated 1,400 children in the United States died from abuse and neglect: 38 percent were related to neglect, 30 percent were related to physical abuse, and 30 percent were related to combinations of types of maltreatment (USDHHS, 2004).

Assessment

"Most researchers and clinicians agree that child neglect is determined by multiple forces at work in the individual, family, neighborhood, and society" (DePanfilis, 1996, p. 37). Belsky's (1993) developmental–ecological model provides an excellent theoretical framework for understanding the role of potentiating and supportive factors across multiple contexts in the etiology of child maltreatment. This model attributes maltreatment to the interaction of factors within three contexts: the developmental–psychological context, the immediate context or parent–child interaction, and the societal context.

The developmental–psychological context includes individual parental and child factors. Child factors associated with maltreatment include premature births and congenital physical or developmental disabilities (Thomlison, 1997). As suggested in the model, parental history of maltreatment (Pianta, Egeland, & Erickson, 1989), depression, and high levels of stress (Ethier, Lacharite, & Couture, 1995; Pianta et al.) are examples of parental factors associated with child neglect. Faulty information processing has also been identified as a parental factor contributing to neglect; Crittenden (1999) theorized that neglectful parents process both cognitive and affective information in "distorted and limited ways" (p. 66).

The immediate context refers to interaction between parents and children and is especially important in cases of child neglect. For example, Crittenden (1981, 1985) observed neglectful mothers to be unresponsive to the needs of their infants, neither initiating interaction nor responding to the child's initiatives. Neglectful families report higher levels of unresolved conflict and demonstrate less warmth and empathy toward one another (Gaudin, Polansky, Kilpatrick, & Shilton, 1996). The social context is also important in understanding the etiology of neglect; neglectful families tend to be socially isolated (Polansky, Ammons, & Gaudin, 1985), receive less help from friends and relatives (Polansky et al., 1981), and lack the social skills to engage in reciprocal relationships (Polansky, Gaudin, Ammons, & Davis, 1985).

Within the broader societal context, the relationship between child poverty and neglect assumes central importance. Table 5.1 provides a number of startling facts concerning American children and poverty. Other potentiating factors in the social context include social policy that ignores the basic needs of families, the

TABLE 5.1 *American Children and Poverty*

- In 1993, families whose annual income was less than $15,000 were 44 more times likely to neglect their children than similar families whose annual incomes were greater than $30,000 (Sedlak & Broadhurst, 1996).
- In 1998, 18.7 percent of American children—13.3 million children—were poor (NCCP, 2000).
- Despite enormous wealth in our country, our child poverty rate is among the highest in the developed world; higher than child poverty rates in the United Kingdom, France, Germany, Spain, Canada, Australia, Ireland, Israel, or Italy (Annie E. Casey Foundation, 2003).
- The federal poverty level for a family of three (2002) was $15,020; for a family of four, $18,100 (USDHHS, 2002).
- In 2002, 37 percent of American children—more than 26 million—lived in low-income (double the federal poverty level) families. These families faced material hardships similar to families living in poverty (NCCP, 2004).
- Among children living in low-income families, 56 percent have at least one parent who works full-time and year-round (NCCP, 2004).
- With welfare reform, the ranks of the working poor are growing. The numbers of poor children living in families who have income from earnings but no income from public assistance has grown from 4.4 million in 1976 to 6.9 million in 2001 (Annie E. Casey Foundation, 2003).

resulting poverty, devaluing of the role of child-care providers, societal willing-ness to tolerate high levels of violence, and societal sanctioning of corporal pun-ishment. Potentiating factors have a cumulative effect: when several factors within or across contexts interact, the probability of maltreatment increases. However, the impact of risk factors may be constrained by buffers or supportive factors (Belsky & Vondra, 1989). Examples of supportive factors that might serve to mitigate the risk factors for neglect among young, single mothers include the psychological well-being of the mother (e.g., adequate self-esteem and self-efficacy), economic security, postnatal home visiting services, and a social network of supportive friends and relatives (Thomlison, 1997). In summary, neglect, like other forms of child maltreatment, is determined through the interaction of risk factors and buffers operating at multiple levels.

Consider the client in the example, Ms. Jones: Which factors within each of Belsky's three contexts (developmental–psychological, parent–child interaction, and societal) seem to influence Ms. Jones' ability to care for her children? Now let us consider a model of intervention designed to address factors at multiple levels that appear to contribute to child neglect: family preservation.

Goals: Defining Family Preservation

Family preservation has been multiply defined as a goal of social policy, a philos-ophy, and an intervention model (Courtney, 1997; Nelson, 1997; Wells & Tracy, 1996). In response to the growing numbers of children in foster care, associated in-creases in cost, and concerns about the psychological and emotional toll of "foster care drift," the Adoption Assistance and Child Welfare Act of 1980 [PL 96-272] re-quired that child welfare agencies make "reasonable efforts" to prevent out-of-home placement and to reunite families. Efforts by public child welfare agencies to provide services designed to prevent unnecessary out-of-home placement of children are often equated with family preservation. Critics of family preservation as a policy-level goal have argued that by allowing children to remain in the care of maltreating parents, family preservation compromises child safety (Gelles, 1993). Furthermore, experts in the field of child welfare have suggested that the outcome goal of placement prevention is too narrow and should be expanded to include child well-being and family functioning (Cash & Berry, 2003; Maluccio & Whittaker, 1997).

Basic Tenets

The philosophy of family preservation is built on the core belief that in most cases, it is best for children to grow up in their natural families. "Children who are sepa-rated from their families can miss out on significant portions of family history which makes it difficult for them to ever regain their original sense of belonging and continuity" (Kinney et al., 1990, p. 34). Family preservation requires a nonjudgmental, compassionate understanding of family problems based on the belief that *everyone* needs help sometimes. All families have strengths, and the power for change resides within the family. When treated with dignity and respect, family members may be successfully engaged as colleagues in the intervention process.

Throughout the 1980s and early 1990s, family preservation programs proliferated. Many were based on the popular Homebuilders model (Kinney et al., 1990), which reported high success rates in preventing out-of-home placements and was avidly marketed by the Edna McConnell Clark Foundation (Adams, 1994). As an intervention model, FPS differ significantly from traditional child welfare services (CWS). Fraser et al. (1997) identified several distinguishing characteristics of FPS; these are contrasted with CWS in Table 5.2.

Multiple theoretical perspectives inform FPS. Barth (1990) posits four major theories on which FPS draw: crisis intervention theory, family systems theory, social learning theory, and ecological theory. Although each of these theories may be integral to the delivery of FPS, they do not appear to completely describe the theoretical framework on which intensive FPS are constructed. Grigsby (1993) argues that social attachment theory also informs FPS. FPS "promote the maintenance of parent-child and other attachment relationships as these relationships provide the context for the child's growth and development" (Grigsby, p. 22). More recently, Staudt and Drake (2002a) have questioned the relevance of crisis intervention theory in FPS (see Modification of Structural Components section this chapter). Just as there is usually no single cause or condition that leads to the problems experienced by Level I neglectful families, no single theory appears to offer a complete explanation of families' problems or plan for intervention. Therefore, it is important that the practitioner assigned to work with Level I families have an

TABLE 5.2 *Comparison of Family Preservation Services and Traditional Child Welfare Services*

Family Preservation Services	Traditional Child Welfare Services
• Targeted to families with children at risk of out-of-home placement	• Targeted to families in which allegations of maltreatment have been substantiated
• Family Centered	• Child Centered
• Strengths based	• Focus on deficits and risk
• Services primarily delivered in clients' homes	• Combination of in-home and office-based services
• Predetermined, brief duration of services (usually ranging from one to four months)	• Open-ended duration of services (usually several months to a year)
• Frequent contact, sometimes daily	• Limited contact, usually two to three times per month
• Flexible scheduling, including evening and weekend visits; emergency/on-call services available 24 hours a day, 7 days a week	• Services available during business hours, 8 a.m. to 5 p.m.
• Mix of concrete and psychological services tailored to meet the needs of the family	• Case management services
• Small caseloads, usually 2–6 families	• Large caseloads, often 25–40 families

understanding of a range of theories: strict adherence or commitment to a single theoretical perspective may lead to a struggle to fit the family to a theory, rather than making use of theory as a guide.

Application of Research on Family Preservation

Is the FPS model of intervention effective in safely preventing out-of-home placement for high-risk children? Do FPS work? Does empirical support for FPS exist? A review of the literature concerning the effectiveness of FPS fails to answer these questions clearly. Blythe, Salley, and Jayaratne (1994) conducted a comprehensive review of outcomes of 12 FPS programs using brief, intensive interventions and targeting families with children at imminent risk of removal. They concluded that these studies "as a whole provide some support for the effectiveness of family preservation services, with some notable exceptions that suggest the opposite" (p. 233). A second and frequently cited meta-analysis of placement prevention among nine child welfare family preservation programs (Fraser et al., 1997) found positive treatment effects in six programs; however, only two of these studies produced large treatment effects. Finally, a recent review of family preservations outcomes (Lindsey, Martin, & Doh, 2002) examined research results published between 1970 and 2000 of 36 families. Among these studies, those employing the most rigorous designs (i.e., adequate samples and experimental designs), failed to produce statistically significant differences between groups. In other words, placement rates among families who received FPS were not significantly different from those receiving traditional CWS. However, when outcomes other than avoidance of out-of-home placement have been considered, FPS have demonstrated success in improving family functioning (McCroskey & Meezan, 1997) and in promoting family reunification (Fraser, Walton, Lewis, Pecora, & Walton, 1996).

Despite equivocal results of the cited meta-analyses, experts in the field of child welfare cite serious methodological flaws (e.g., the lack of targeting of services, treatment integrity, adequacy of outcome measures, reliability and validity of tools used to measure outcomes, and appropriateness of data analysis procedures) in many of the family preservation outcome studies (Epstein, 1997; Fraser et al., 1997; Maluccio & Whittaker, 1997; Staudt & Drake, 2002b). Evolving models of FPS merit further study; future research is indicated to evaluate outcomes including not only placement prevention, but child well-being and family functioning (Besharov, 1994; Courtney, 1997; Kelly & Blythe, 2000; Wells & Tracy, 1996). Examining the current level of knowledge development in family preservation, Staudt and Drake (2002b) concluded that "it is premature to conclude that family preservation is ineffective" (p. 646).

The professional literature suggests that newly developing models of FPS should be targeted to specific types of maltreating families (Courtney, 1997; Fraser et al., 1997). Even among particular subtypes of maltreating families, the factors leading to maltreatment and effective intervention strategies vary with each family (DiLeonardi, 1993). Comparing chronically neglectful families (i.e., families known to child welfare agencies for three or more years) to families with either newly confirmed cases of neglect or cases in which neglect was unsubstantiated,

Nelson et al. (1993) found that chronically neglectful families were larger/had more children, were more likely to have experienced out-of-home placement of a child, had more inappropriate expectations of their children and lacked knowledge of child development, were more likely to experience unemployment, had less education, and had caregivers who were more likely to experience chronic mental illness and depression. Understandably, intervention models like Homebuilders, which are based on crisis intervention theory and characterized by brevity and intensity, have been less successful in preventing out-of-home placement among neglectful families (Bath & Haapala, 1993; Berry, 1993; Cash & Berry, 2003; Nelson & Landsman, 1992; Yaun & Struckman-Johnson, 1991). The proposed model for intervening in neglectful Level I families who have come to the attention of public child welfare agencies due to child neglect (tertiary intervention) combines the philosophy of the family preservation movement and evidenced-based intervention techniques for alleviating child neglect.

Intervention Approach: Preserving Neglectful Level I Families

Effective models of intervention to preserve neglectful families require modification and expansion of existing models of FPS. Although evolving models of FPS should continue to share the philosophical and theoretical basis of FPS described earlier in this chapter, research concerning child neglect suggests modification of several structural components and outcome measures, as well as the importance of particular interventions and techniques when targeting neglectful families. In response to the backlash against FPS, it is suggested that the goals of family preservation and child safety are complementary (Maluccio, Pine, & Warsh, 1994) and that "with the appropriate resources and supports, it is possible to both preserve families and to protect children in most cases" (Nelson, 1997, p. 103).

Modification of Structural Components

The proposed model diverges from existing models of FPS with respect to three structural components: (1) duration of services, (2) intensity of services, and (3) the mix of services. Neglectful families often experience multiple, chronic problems, problems that require long-term intervention (Berry, Charlson, & Dawson, 2003; Dawson & Berry, 2002; Fraser et al., 1997). Reviewing demonstration projects targeting neglectful families, Dore (1993) found the average length of service to be 18 months. Because many neglectful parents possess limited relational skills and have had discouraging experiences with professional helpers, developing a therapeutic alliance with these parents often requires more time than afforded by brief models of FPS (Dore & Alexander, 1996). Borrowing from Besharov (1994), "long-term family preservation" services (p. 452) better describes the duration of services required to preserve neglectful families.

Informed by crisis intervention theory (Golan, 1978), extant FPS have been characterized by brevity and intensity of services. Crisis theory assumes that a time-limited (usually four to six weeks), active state of disequilibrium created by a crisis event provides a window of opportunity for change. The goal of crisis intervention is return to a precrisis level of functioning. As discussed by Staudt and Drake (2002a), the notion of crisis intervention lacks applicability to many families receiving FPS, particularly chronically neglectful families. Controlled studies provide only mixed empirical support that a crisis is generated by the threat of out-of-home placement of children; out-of-home placement is a low-occurrence event in both experimental and control groups; and the goal of returning chronically neglectful families to a precrisis state of functioning is clearly wrongheaded. This is not to say that neglectful families do not experience crises. If neglect is due to recent, situational factors, crisis intervention theory might serve as a theoretical guide. Thus, both the duration and intensity of FPS should be guided by the number, severity, and chronicity of potentiating and supportive factors.

A final structural component to be considered in the development of new models of FPS for neglectful families concerns the mix of services. As in prior models of FPS, a mix of concrete and psychological services is suggested; however, unlike previous models of FPS that were primarily home-based, services should also include a mix of in-home and community-based services. While in-home services offer a number of advantages (e.g., they are less threatening for clients, offer an opportunity to observe family interaction in a natural environment, and provide the optimal situation for practicing newly learned skills), community-based groups have proven effective in reducing the social isolation often experienced by neglectful families, and they offer opportunities for socialization, support, education, and parenting-skill development (DePanfilis, 1996; DiLeonardi, 1993; Gaudin, 1988; Gaudin, 1993). Because neglectful parents often lack social skills and may feel ill-at-ease in groups, care must be taken to engage parents through providing child care, transportation, refreshments, and social activities; providing structured activities that reduce anxiety; and limiting heterogeneity and size of groups (Gaudin, 1993). Additionally, group interventions should be preceded by the development of a therapeutic alliance with the social worker (DePanfilis, 1996), who might then attend initial group activities with clients to decrease anxiety and provide reassurance.

Engagement

The importance and difficulty of engaging neglectful families should not be underestimated. Often, these families are suspicious of anyone who is offering to help, and many have had prior negative experiences with formal systems (DePanfilis, 1999). Challenged by the multitude of complex problems present among neglectful families, practitioners may be tempted to place blame on parents. A caveat is in order: *The last thing these families need is another outsider to tell them what they are doing wrong!* In general, engaging the family in the helping relationship is sometimes the most difficult part of the intervention process.

The social work tenet of "starting where the client is" offers the practitioner and the family an opportunity to begin. The intervention may begin by asking the family what is important to them. Many families expect that someone is going to tell them, or even demand, that they "do something," as this is the typical intervention to which they are accustomed. Research has demonstrated the importance of client collaboration in FPS (Littell & Tajima, 2000). Collaboration, or client involvement in treatment planning, (1) helps workers tailor intervention to fit the needs of the family and (2) influences caregiver compliance with program expectations (e.g., working cooperatively with providers, keeping scheduled appointments, and completing assigned tasks), which is linked to child welfare outcomes such as subsequent reports of maltreatment and out-of-home placement. Because neglectful parents often have difficulty sustaining supportive interpersonal relationships, helpers must be able to build trust, allay fears and suspicions, demonstrate acceptance and empathy, and affirm clients' competence (Dore & Alexander, 1996). In order to successfully intervene with Level I families, families must be treated as "experts" on their own family and as equals in a partnership aimed at building on families' strengths in order to improve overall functioning.

Multidimensional, Strengths-Based Assessment

Comprehensive assessment of neglectful families should examine both contributing and protective factors in each of the three contexts described in Belsky's (1993) developmental–ecological model. Research on neglectful parents indicates several individual factors within the developmental–psychological context that should be assessed: depression, parental stress, and substance abuse (Berry et al., 2003; Dawson & Berry, 2002; DePanfilis, 1996, 1999; Dore, 1993). Rapid assessment measures that might be used to assess these factors include the Beck Depression Inventory (Beck, Rush, Shaw, & Emery, 1979); Parenting Stress Index (Abidin, 1990); and the Chemical Use, Abuse, and Dependency Scale (McGovern & Morrison, 1992). The remedial needs of each child in the family should also be assessed; "neglected children may require individual attention to help them overcome serious deficits in cognitive, academic, and social skills" (DePanfilis, 1999, p. 237). For example, therapeutic child care for young children might be used to "provide stimulation, cultural enrichment, and development of motor skills and social skills" (Gaudin, 1993, p. 42). Developmental remediation for older children might include tutorial programs to improve academic deficits and social skills development classes (Gaudin, 1993).

Crittenden's (1999) theory of distorted processing of cognitive and affective information among neglectful parents suggests the need to assess parents' abilities to process information. *Effective processing* of cognitive information refers to parents' abilities to link action to outcomes; *x* behavior results in *y* outcome. *Affective processing* refers to parents' abilities to experience and respond to feeling states that motivate protective and affectionate behavior. Stated somewhat differently, effective cognitive and affective processing allow parents to correctly interpret and respond to the child's physical, social, and emotional needs.

Assessment of the immediate context, or parent–child interaction, should be guided by family systems theory (Minuchin, 1974) and include evaluation of the functioning of executive subsystem with attention to clarity of roles, boundaries, and communication patterns. Well-functioning executive subsystems may be found in both single and two-parent families and are characterized by parental ability to provide for the basic material needs of children as well as by the ability to nurture, protect, educate, and socialize children.

Finally, assessment of the social context should include examination of the families' formal and informal support network. *Social support* refers to "social relationships that result in beneficial emotional or behavioral effects" for family members (DePanfilis, 1996, p. 39). Dimensions of social support that should be assessed include the duration, stability, consistency, accessibility, frequency, closeness, and degree of reciprocity of relationships (DePanfilis, 1996). At the broadest level, assessment should factor in society's response to problems faced by low income families, such as poverty and the inability of many working parents to earn a living wage; limited affordable, quality day care; lack of safe, affordable housing; and lack of universal heath care.

Too often practitioners working with Level I families become overwhelmed with the multitude of problems and infectious sense of helplessness encountered. Yet all families have strengths, and a comprehensive assessment should seek to discover strengths in the individual, interactional, and social contexts described in Belsky's (1993) model. In assessing strengths, practitioners must also ask questions about their own special abilities in working with a particular family (Sandau-Beckler, Salcido, Beckler, Mannes, & Beck, 2002); what strengths does the practitioner have to offer? For example, what skills does the practitioner have in establishing partnerships with families, in instilling hope? Strengths-based assessments might include the following types of questions regarding Level I neglectful families:

- What parenting challenges have parents successfully negotiated?
- When do parents know they are doing a good job with their children?
- How do family members express affection and support for one another?
- When and how does the family celebrate the accomplishments of members?
- How does the family have fun together?
- Who in the extended family or community can be counted on for support?
- What resources/services have been helpful to the family in the past; in what way were they helpful?
- What are the family's hopes and dreams?
- What skills has the family used to overcome barriers to services?
- How might community resources be mobilized to meet the current needs of the family?

Cognitive Behavioral Interventions

Among experts in the area of child neglect, there is high degree of consensus regarding the use of cognitive behavioral interventions (Berry, et al., 2003; Crittenden, 1999; Dawson & Berry, 2002; DePanfilis, 1996, 1999; Gaudin, Wodarski, Arkinson,

& Avery, 1990–1991). Focusing on skills development rather than insight, parent-education training helps parents understand and respond appropriately to the developmental needs of their children. A variety of techniques, such as verbal instruction, positive reinforcement, modeling, and coaching, may be used. Role playing and behavioral rehearsal may also be used to help neglectful parents reduce social isolation through the development of social skills. Cognitive behavioral interventions may also be used to treat depression, reduce stress, and increase problem-solving and coping skills. Finally, cognitive restructuring may be used to help parents "gain awareness of dysfunctional and self-defeating thoughts and misconceptions that impair functioning and replace them with beliefs and behaviors that lead to enhanced functioning used when caregivers are feeling overwhelmed and powerless" (DePanfilis, 1999, p. 225).

Advocacy

Many Level I neglectful families have been repeatedly victimized by unscrupulous landlords, salespersons, and even human service providers. Parents may lack information about community resources or be hesitant to access services because of past negative experiences. Application processes that involve reading and completing complicated forms; verifying income, rent, and other expenditures; waiting in crowded offices for hours with small children; and dealing with agency personnel who treat clients disrespectfully pose barriers to services. Intervention should help clients develop a working knowledge of available resources and the skills to advocate for themselves. Additionally, family preservation practitioners should develop collaborative relationships with community agencies and resources to help other providers understand the needs of Level I neglectful families, coordinate service delivery, and neutralize organizational barriers to service delivery. Finally, practitioners who are truly concerned about impoverished families must advocate for family-centered social policy. More than a decade ago, Dore (1993) stated, "Family preservation will truly occur when many families with children no longer struggle to exist at less than subsistence level, when poor parents are freed from anxiety and depression generated by raising children in hostile environments, and when it is widely acknowledged that the real cause of family breakdown is the failure of our society to value and support the parenting role" (p. 553).

Evaluation of Effectiveness

Evaluation of the effectiveness of intervention with Level I neglectful families must be expanded to include a number of outcomes beyond prevention of out-of-home placement of children. Ideally, evaluation should include measures of outcomes at several points in time; for example, preintervention, at six months, at termination, and possibly one year posttermination. Although outcome goals will vary based on the needs of individual families, the literature suggests that outcomes include improved family functioning, child well-being, and social support.

Measures of family functioning used in previous studies of FPS include the Index of Family Relations (Hudson, 1982); the Family Assessment Form (McCrosky & Meezan, 1997); and the North Carolina Family Assessment Form (Reed-Ashcraft, Kirk, & Fraser, 2001). Used widely in child welfare research, several subscales of the Child Well Being Scales (Magura & Moses, 1986) are particularly well suited as outcome measures for neglectful families. Subscales measure actual or potential unmet needs related to physical health care, nutrition/diet, clothing, personal hygiene, supervision, parenting, and household sanitation and safety. The Eco Map (Hartman, 1978) or the Social Network Map (Tracy & Whittaker, 1990) might be used to measure changes in social support/isolation.

Application to Families on Levels II, III, and IV

In general, Level II families may be approached in a manner similar to the approach used with the Level I family. The issues of authority and limits that are omnipresent in the Level I family are the prominent issues in the Level II family as well. Clinicians comment that the Level I family is often a family with young children, whereas the Level II family is a family with older, adolescent children. The Level II family is characterized by a lack of control in the family system caused by a dysfunctional executive system. A "strengths perspective" that begins with an inventory of available support and strengths is often the first step in engaging the family. Intervention should build on strengths to preserve and sustain the family while the executive capacity is strengthened. Although a good deal of nurturing and advocacy may be necessary in the Level I family, concentration on role modeling and the development of conflict resolution skills may be more appropriate when working with the Level II family.

Whereas the Level I and Level II families appear to have many similarities, families on Levels III and IV are quite different from their lower-level counterparts. In general, the Level I and Level II families are cognizant that things are not working well. In the parlance of family therapists, issues appear largely structural; the executive system of the family is unable to meet the functional demands of adequately caring for children. Aponte (1976) has described families like this as "underorganized," or lacking adequate coping patterns. In contrast, Level III and Level IV families have organized, well-established patterns of behavior to deal with problems that arise within the family. Although some of these patterns are adaptive and functional, others are maladaptive and often resistant to change. Intervention with families at Level III centers around clarification of generational boundaries and appropriate parent–child differentiation (Weltner, 1985). In Level IV families, the task of the practitioner may be focused on the development of an "inner 'richness'— insight, more sensitive awareness of the relational world, and understanding of the legacies and heritage" (Weltner, 1985, p. 47), rather than on the more basic functions of food, shelter, safety, and authority. Thus, the application of the principles and techniques described earlier for working with the Level I family have limited utility with and relevance to work with families on Levels III and IV.

Ethical Challenges

The primary ethical challenges in working with Level I neglecting families are:

1. Balancing individual needs with those of the family.
2. Knowing when a situation crosses the line between poor care and harm.
3. Balancing clinical judgments with family judgments regarding whether to remove or return a child.
4. Using the most effective means to meet the basic needs of the child, utilizing evaluation research.

Each of these challenges deserves careful consideration when using family preservation models for neglectful families.

Summary

Level I neglectful families present a tremendous challenge to our public child welfare system. The most frequently occurring form of child maltreatment, neglect, has serious long-term consequences for child victims. Belsky's (1993) developmental–ecological model provides a framework for understanding neglect as the result of the interaction of potentiating and supporting factors in the developmental–psychological, immediate, and social contexts. However, neither traditional child welfare services nor existing models of FPS have proven particularly effective models of intervention with neglectful families.

New models of intervention for preserving Level I neglectful families should combine empirical knowledge of existing FPS and knowledge of successful practices in ameliorating child neglect. The proposed model of FPS, tailored to Level I neglectful families, differs from existing models in the duration of services, the mix of services, and the emphasis on cognitive–behavioral intervention. This model also emphasizes the engagement process; multidimensional, strengths-based assessment; and advocacy.

Discussion Questions

1. How does the delivery of FPS differ from other models of intervention?
2. Are Alex and Katie Jones being neglected? What subtypes of neglect are present?
3. Why is it especially important to use a strengths approach when working with Level I neglectful families?
4. What strengths can be identified in the Jones family? How might you build on these strengths?
5. What further information is needed to complete a multidimensional, strengths-based assessment of the Jones family?

6. Should family preservation be a goal of child welfare policy? Should child welfare policy encompass other goals?

Internet Resources

www.familypreservation.com
http://aspe.hhs.gov/hsp/cyp/fplitrev.htm
www.nccpr.org
www.casanet.org/library/family-preservation/famprev.htm
http://library.adoption.com/Crisis-Intervention/Family-Preservation-Services/article/5257/1.html

Suggested Readings

Berry, M., Renae, C., Dawson, K. (2003). Promising practices in understanding and treating child neglect. *Child and Family Social Work, 8,* 13–24.
This article identifies the primary problems contributing to neglect and discusses promising practices and model programs for alleviating these problems.

Bricker-Jenkins, M. (1999). Hidden treasures: Unlocking strengths in public social services. In D. Saleebey (Ed.), *The strengths perspective in social work practice* (pp. 133–150). New York: Longman.
The authors profile the characteristics of public service practitioners who are effective with clients, in the community, in the workplace, and within themselves (i.e., in their interior life).

DePanfilis, D. (1996). Social isolation of neglectful families: A review of social support assessment and intervention models. *Child Maltreatment, 1,* 37–52.
This article reviews social support interventions designed to reduce social isolation among neglectful families.

Dubowitz, H. (Ed.) (1999). *Neglected children: Research, practice, and policy.* Thousand Oaks, CA: Sage.
A synthesis of current knowledge of child neglect, this book addresses a broad range of topics related to neglect, including causes and contributing factors, cultural competency, parental substance abuse, fatal child neglect, risk assessment, policy issues, intervention, and prevention.

Kinney, J., Haapala, D., & Booth, C. (1991). Getting off to a good start. In J. Kinney, D. Haapala, & C. Booth, *Keeping families together: The homebuilders model* (pp. 55–70). New York: Aldine de Gruyter.
This chapter provides practical suggestions for establishing trust and forming partnerships with multiproblem families.

Lutzker, J. R., & Bigelow, K. M. (2002). *Reducing child maltreatment: A guidebook for parent services.* New York: Guilford Press.
This text describes a 15-week, ecobehavioral treatment model for families at risk of child maltreatment. *Project Safe Care* focuses on intervention in three key areas that are relevant to neglectful Level I families: home safety, infant and child health care, and parent–child interaction.

References

Abidin, R. R. (1990). *Parenting Stress Index.* Charlottesville, VA: Pediatric Psychology Press.
Adams, P. (1994). Marketing social change: The case of family preservation. *Children and Youth Services Review, 16,* 417–431.

Adoption Assistance and Child Welfare Act of 1980. PL 96–272. US Code 101, 102.

Aponte, H. (1976). Underorganization in the poor family. In P. Guerin (Ed.), *Family therapy: Theory and practice.* New York: Gardner Press.

Annie E. Casey Foundation (2003). *Kids count data book.* Baltimore, MD: Author.

Barth, R. P. (1990). Theories guiding home-based, intensive family preservation services. In J. K. Whittaker, J. Kinney, E. M. Tracy, & C. Booth (Eds.), *Reaching high-risk families: Intensive family preservation in human services* (pp. 89–112). New York: Aldine de Gruyter.

Bath, H. I., & Haapala, D. A. (1993). Intensive family preservation services with abused and neglected children: An examination of group differences. *Child Abuse and Neglect, 17,* 213–225.

Beck, A. T., Rush, A. J., Shaw, B. F., & Emery, G. (1979). *Cognitive therapy of depression.* New York: Guilford Press.

Belsky, J. (1993). Etiology of child maltreatment: A developmental-ecological analysis. *Psychological Bulletin, 114*(3), 413–434.

Belsky, J., & Vondra, J. (1989). Lessons from child abuse: The determinants of parenting. In D. Cicchetti & V. Carlson (Eds.), *Child maltreatment: Theory and research on the causes and consequences of child abuse and neglect* (pp. 53–202). New York: Cambridge University Press.

Berry, M. (1993). The relative effectiveness of family preservation services with neglectful families. In E. S. Morton & R. K. Grigsby (Eds.), *Advancing family preservation practice* (pp. 70–98). Newbury Park, CA: Sage.

Berry, M., Charlson, R., & Dawson, K. (2003). Promising practices in understanding and treating child neglect. *Child and Family Social Work, 8,* 13–24.

Besharov, D. (1994). Looking beyond 30, 60, and 90 days. *Children and Youth Services Review, 16,* 445–451.

Blythe, B. J., Salley, M. P., & Jayaratne, S. (1994). A review of intensive family preservation services. *Social Work Research, 18,* 213–224.

Cash, S. J., & Berry, M. (2003). The impact of family preservation services on child and family well-being. *Journal of Social Service Research, 29*(3), 1–26.

Courtney, M. E. (1997). Reconsidering family preservation: A review of *Putting families first. Children and Youth Services Review, 19,* 61–76.

Crittenden, P. M. (1981). Abusing, neglecting, problematic, and adequate dyads: Differentiating by patterns of interaction. *Merrill-Palmer Quarterly, 27,* 1–18.

Crittenden, P. M. (1985). Maltreated infants: Vulnerability and resilience. *Journal of Child Psychology and Psychiatry, 26,* 85–96.

Crittenden, P. M. (1999). Child neglect: cases and contributors. In H. Dubowitz (Ed.), *Neglected children: Research, practice, and policy* (pp. 47–68). Thousand Oaks, CA: Sage.

Dawson, K., & Berry, M. (2002). Engaging families in child welfare services: An evidence-based approach to best practice. *Child Welfare, 81,* 293–318.

DePanfilis, D. (1996). Social isolation of neglectful families: A review of social support assessment and intervention models. *Child Maltreatment, 1,* 37–52.

DePanfilis, D. (1999). Intervening with families when children are neglected. In H. Dubowitz (Ed.), *Neglected children: Research, practice, and policy* (pp. 211–236). Thousand Oaks, CA: Sage.

DePanfilis, D., & Salus, M. (1992). *A coordinated response to child abuse and neglect: A basic manual.* Washington, DC: U.S. Department of Health and Human Services.

DiLeonardi, J. W. (1993). Families in poverty and chronic neglect of children. *Families in Society, 74,* 557–562.

Dore, M. M. (1993). Family preservation and poor families: When "homebuilding" is not enough. *Families in Society, 74,* 545–556.

Dore, M. M., & Alexander, L. B. (1996). Preserving families at risk of child abuse and neglect: The role of the helping alliance. *Child Abuse and Neglect, 20,* 349–361.

Epstein, W. M. (1997). Social science, child welfare, and family preservation: A failure of rationality in public policy. *Children and Youth Services Review, 19,* 41–60.

Ethier, L. S., Lacharite, C., & Couture, G. (1995). Childhood adversity, parental stress, and depression of negligent mothers. *Child Abuse and Neglect, 19,* 619–632.

Fraser, M. W., Nelson, K. E., & Rivard, J. (1997). Effectiveness of family preservation services. *Social Work Research, 21,* 138–153.

Fraser, M. W., Walton, E., Lewis, R. E., Pecora, P. J., & Walton, W. K. (1996). An experiment in family reunification: Correlates of outcomes at one-year follow-up. *Children and Youth Services Review, 18,* 335–361.

Gaudin, J. M., Jr. (1988). Treatment of families who neglect their children. In E. Nunally, C. S. Chilman, & F. M. Cox (Eds.), *Mental illness, delinquency, addictions, and neglect* (pp. 167–188). Newbury Park, CA: Sage.

Gaudin, J. M., Jr. (1993). *Child neglect: A guide for intervention.* Washington, DC: National Center on Child Abuse and Neglect.

Gaudin, J. M., Jr. (1999). Child neglect: Short-term and long-term outcomes. In H. Dubowitz (Ed.), *Neglected children: Research, practice, and policy* (pp. 89–108). Thousand Oaks, CA: Sage.

Gaudin, J. M., Jr., Polansky, N. A., Kilpatrick, A. C., Shilton, P. (1996). Family functioning in neglectful families. *Child Abuse and Neglect, 20,* 363–377.

Gaudin, J. M., Jr., Wodarski, J. S., Arkinson, M. K., & Avery, L. S. (1990–1991). Remedying child neglect: Effectiveness of social network interventions. *Journal of Applied Social Sciences, 15*(1), 97–123.

Gelles, R. J. (1993). Family reunification/family preservation: Are children really being protected? *Journal of Interpersonal Violence, 8,* 557–562.

Golan, N. (1978). *Treatment in crisis situations.* New York: Free Press.

Goldstein, J., Freud, A., & Solnit, A. J. (1973). *Beyond the best interests of the child.* New York: Free Press.

Grigsby, R. K. (1993). Theories that guide intensive family preservation: A second look. In E. S. Morton and R. K. Grigsby (Eds.), *Advancing family preservation practice* (pp. 16–27). Newbury Park, CA: Sage.

Hartman, A. (1978). Diagrammatic assessment of family relationships. *Social Casework, 59,* 465–476.

Hudson, W. W. (1982). *The clinical measurement package: A field manual.* Homewood, IL: Dorsey Press.

Kelly, S., & Blythe, B. J. (2000). Family preservation: A potential not yet realized. *Child Welfare, 79,* 29–42.

Kinney, J., Haapala, D., Booth, C., & Leavitt, S. (1990). The homebuilders model. In J. K. Whittaker, J. Kinney, E. M. Tracy, & C. Booth (Eds.), *Reaching high-risk families: Intensive family preservation in human services.* New York: Aldine de Gruyter.

Lindsey, D., Martin, S., & Doh, J. (2002). The failure of intensive casework services to reduce foster care placements: An examination of family preservation studies. *Children and Youth Services Review, 24,* 743–775.

Littell, J. H., & Tajima, E. A. (2000). A multilevel model of client participation in intensive family preservation services. *Social Service Review, 74,* 405–435.

Magura, S., & Moses, B. S. (1986). *Outcome measures for child welfare services: Theory and applications.* Washington, DC: Child Welfare League of America.

Maluccio, A. N., Pine, B. A., & Warsh, R. (1994). Protecting children by preserving their families. *Children and Youth Services Review, 16,* 295–307.

Maluccio, A. N., & Whittaker, J. K. (1997). Learning from the "Family Preservation" Initiative. *Children and Youth Services Review, 19,* 5–16.

McCroskey, J., & Meezan, W. (1997). Family preservation and family functioning. Washington, DC: CWLA Press.

McGovern, M. P., & Morrison, D. H. (1992). The Chemical Use, Abuse and Dependency Scale (CURD): Rationale, reliability, and validity. *Journal of Substance Abuse Treatment, 9,* 27–38.

Minuchin, S. (1974). *Families and family therapy.* Cambridge, MA: Harvard University Press.

National Center for Children in Poverty (2000). *Child poverty in the states: Levels and trends from 1979 to 1998.* Retrieved July 5, 2004, from www.ncgp.ora/media/cpr00b-text.pdf.

National Center for Children in Poverty (2004). *Low income children in the United States.* Retrieved July 5, 2004, from www.nccp.org/pub-cpfD4.html.

Nelson, K. E. (1997). Family preservation—What is it? *Children and Youth Services Review, 19,* 101–118.

Nelson, K. E., & Landsman, M. J. (1992). *Alternative models of family preservation: Family-based services in context.* Springfield, IL: Charles C. Thomas.

Nelson, K. E., Saunders, E. J., Landsman, M. J. (1993). Chronic child neglect in perspective. *Social Work, 38,* 661–671.

Pianta, R., Egeland, B., & Erickson, M. F. (1989). The antecedents of maltreatment: Results of the Mother-Child Interaction Project. In D. Cicchetti & V. Carlson (Eds.), *Child maltreatment: Theory and research on the causes and consequences of child abuse and neglect* (pp. 203–253). New York: Cambridge University Press.

Polansky, N., Ammons, P., & Gaudin, J. (1985). Loneliness and isolation in child neglect. *Social Casework, 66,* 38–47.

Polansky, N. A., Chalmers, M. A., Williams, D. P., & Buttenweiser, E. W. (1981). *Damaged parents: An anatomy of neglect.* Chicago: University of Chicago Press.

Polansky, N. A., Gaudin, J. M., Ammons, P. W., & Davis, K. B. (1985). The psychological ecology of the neglectful mother. *Child Abuse & Neglect, 9,* 265–275.

Reed-Ashcraft, K., Kirk, R. S., & Fraser, M. W. (2001). The reliability and validity of the North Carolina Family Assessment Scale. *Research on Social Work Practice, 11,* 503–520.

Sandau-Beckler, P., Salcido, R., Beckler, M. J., Mannes, M., & Beck, M. (2002). Infusing family-centered values into child protection practice. *Children and Youth Services Review, 24,* 719–741.

Sedlak, A. J., & Broadhurst, D. D. (1996). *Third national incidence study of child abuse and neglect: Final report.* Washington, DC: U.S. Department of Health and Human Services.

Smith, M. G., & Fong, R. (2004). *The children of neglect: When no one cares.* New York: Brunner/Mazel.

Staudt, M., & Drake, B. (2002a). Intensive family preservation services: Where's the crisis? *Children and Youth Services Review, 24,* 777–795.

Staudt, M., & Drake, B. (2002b). Research on services to preserve maltreating families. *Children and Youth Services Review, 24,* 645–652.

Thomlison, B. (1997). Risk and protective factors in child maltreatment. In M. W. Fraser (Ed.), *Risk and resilience in childhood: An ecological perspective* (pp. 50–72). Washington DC: NASW Press.

Tracy, E. M., & Whittaker, J. K. (1990). The social network map: Some further refinements on administration. *Families in Society, 7,* 461–470.

U.S. Department of Health and Human Services. (2005). *The 2005 HHS Poverty Guidelines.* Retrieved May 3, 2005, from www.aspe.hhs.gov/poverty/05poverty.html

U.S. Department of Health and Human Services. (2004). *Child Maltreatment 2002.* Washington, DC: U.S. Department of Health and Human Services, Administration for Children and Families.

Wells, K., & Tracy, E. (1996). Reorienting intensive family preservation services in relation to public child welfare practice. *Child Welfare, 6,* 667–692.

Weltner, J. S. (1982). A structural approach to the single-parent family. *Family Process, 21,* 203–210.

Weltner, J. S. (1985). Matchmaking: Choosing the appropriate therapy for families at various levels of pathology. In M. P. Mirkin & S. L. Koman (Eds.), *Handbook of adolescents and family therapy* (pp. 39–50). New York: Gardner Press.

Yuan, Y. T., & Struckman-Johnson, D. L. (1991). Placement outcomes for neglected children with prior placements in family preservation programs. In K. Wells & D. E. Biegel (Eds.), *Family preservation services: Research and evaluation* (pp. 92–118). Newbury Park, CA: Sage.

6

A Family Case Management Approach for Level I Needs

Roberta R. Greene, Ph.D., and Nancy P. Kropf, Ph.D.

Case management is a process for assisting families who have multiple service needs. In reality, it may be appropriate for families who have Level I through IV needs whenever they experience multiple complex difficulties that require a range of services from numerous providers. The goals of family case management are to mobilize a family's strengths, to marshal resources, and to maximize family functional capacity. This chapter discusses family-centered case management and focuses on the Level I family.

Family Needs

Throughout the life of the family, members must negotiate changes, shifts, and alterations in their relationships with one another. This movement through the life cycle, known as "family development," requires that families establish, maintain, and adapt to new roles. In making these life transitions, the family builds on strengths and must meet stressful challenges.

Case management can help families cope with and adjust to the stress related to unexpected, or nonnormative, situations. An example of a Level I situation that requires reorganization in the family system is a severe illness of a member. For example, Kaplan (1992) has suggested that case management for families with children with HIV infection demands attention to the special developmental needs of the child over a period of years. Case management has also been found to be effective in promoting apnea monitor usage in families where newborns are at risk for sudden infant death syndrome (Baker & Thyer, 1999). Other Level I needs experienced by families include homelessness, chronic mental illness, or a developmental disability of a family member. In addition, people isolated and debilitated by crack cocaine or HIV require assertive outreach services (Greene, 2000a).

Case management services can also help families adapt to normative transition phases across the life span. Structural changes that occur at family transition points, such as births, reaching adulthood, or retirement, also can disturb the family's balance. For example, a case manager can play an important role in helping a young single mother with family and household responsibilities. (East, 1999; Sun, 2000). A case manager can be instrumental in identifying and linking a new mother with emotional, financial, and medical support for her new role as a caregiver to a young infant.

Case managers need to understand that the family is a social unit that faces a series of developmental tasks. These tasks vary along the parameters of cultural differences but at the same time have universal roots (Minuchin, 1974). The stages of the life cycle have been defined for "intact nuclear families in contemporary Western societies" (Tseng & Hsu, 1991, p. 8) as the unattached young adult, the formation of the dyadic relationship, the family with young children, the family with adolescents, the family launching children, the family with older members, and the family in later years (Becvar & Becvar, 1996; Goldenberg & Goldenberg, 1980; Rhodes, 1980).

However, the structure and development of the family may vary because of diverse needs and interests (Greene & Riley, in press). Groze and Rosenthal (1991) have described the adaptability of families who have adopted special-needs children; Weston (1991), the relationship of gay men and lesbian women in their chosen families; and Kuhn (1990), the normative family crises of confronting dementia in an older family member. McGoldrick (1989) has pointed out that, although women play a central role in families, only recently has there been the idea that they may have a "life cycle apart from their roles as wife and mothers" (p. 200).

Family developmental patterns may be affected by the geographical origin and birthplace of the members, and where they are in the cycle of acculturation to mainstream U.S. society. Ho (1987) has proposed that practitioners should be aware that behaviors differ depending on whether a family and its members are foreign or native born and on the degree to which they are bicultural. Falicov and Karrer (1980) have concluded that studies of the family life cycle should take into consideration the effects of cultural variables such as social class, ethnicity, and religion. For example, in Hispanic American families, individual needs are viewed as secondary compared with those of the family system (Jordan, Lewellan, & Vandiver, 1994). When making application to family assessment, it would therefore be more appropriate for the case manager to think of several "typical" family life cycles.

Family Case Assessment

An important principle in family case management is that a biopsychosocial change in any one member affects the balance of the whole family group. Greene

(2000b) has pointed out that most elderly clients come to the attention of an agency at a time of crisis. At that time, the question, Who is the client? must be asked. The answer is that the crisis involves the entire family. Consequently, the case manager's assessment and treatment interventions must consider both the elderly person's biopsychosocial needs and the family's role allocations and adapting and coping capacity.

The following case example involves a family with a member who has a chronic mental illness (Kelly & Kropf, 1995). The son, who is now in middle adulthood, is being cared for by his aging parents. This case clearly illustrates the usefulness of addressing the issues and needs from a whole-family perspective.

Philip Jordan is a 40-year-old, single male diagnosed with schizophrenia. He lives at home with his 75-year-old parents in a small southern town where his father is a retired pastor from the local Baptist church. Philip, who has a 22-year history of mental illness, has experienced many psychiatric hospitalizations but has remained out of the hospital for the past two years. Currently he has a flat affect, depressed mood, and mild paranoid ideation concerning his parents. He reports bizarre hallucinations involving religious themes and sexual thoughts.

At the time of his first psychotic break, Philip's parents were in their late fifties. His parents blamed themselves for Philip's illness and prayed for him to be "cured and return to being normal." Instead of regaining his emotional health, Philip's condition has worsened over time. His father retired prematurely, believing that if he devoted all his time to caring for his son, Philip would improve. However, the retirement has caused the parents to be estranged from their supports and has placed a financial burden on the family.

The family went to the local mental health center to discuss their situation. Their family physician had suggested that they contact the mental health program, because Philip's mother's health had been deteriorating. The parents had begun to realize that their advancing age was creating difficulties in providing care for their son. They were also concerned about Philip's lack of social contacts and the family's worsening financial circumstances due to additional medical expenses.

The mental health center intake worker gathered extensive information about family functioning. Philip's physical, emotional, and social functioning and medication management were discussed. Beyond Philip's functioning, information was acquired about the other family members. This included the parents' own health status, their knowledge of mental illness, their social support system, and their feelings of competence in managing Philip's caregiving needs in this life stage. Spiritual issues were also explored with the family and were especially significant because religious participation was such an important aspect of family life in early phases. Based on a model developed for older adults (Hays, Meador, Branch, & George, 2001), information about the family's spiritual history was gathered, including their practices, social participation, and social support.

As a part of this family-focused assessment, the parents discussed the stress of this caregiving role and effects on their physical and emotional health. Of particular concern was the evaluation of functional areas in which competence may be furthered or fostered (Bandura, 1997). His father spoke about his disappointment over his early retirement, subsequent financial worries, and loss of status in the community. He also reported that he struggled with the idea that Philip was God's way of testing his faith. In particular, he seemed to miss the fellowship that came from being with other members of the congregation. Mrs. Jordan discussed her worries about Philip's future care and her worsening hypertension and digestive problems. Through her discussion with Philip, the case manager also became aware of his anxiety over the health of his parents and fears about his own future. The interviews with the total family unit allowed the case manager to form a holistic impression about past functioning of the family, their present situation, and future needs.

Treatment Goals

Building on the assessment data, the case manager and family discussed service goals that were formalized into a service contract. The plan included goals that addressed the individual members, the parents as a couple, and the family as a household unit. Additionally, the plan overtly specified the relationship between the mental health service personnel and the family.

The contract addressed the issues of independence, family functioning, and spirituality that had been discussed by the family during the assessment. For Philip, goals were constructed to assist with vocational training and placement. This plan was intended to decrease Philip's isolation, provide him with structured time during the day, and allow him to contribute to the household finances. To provide the parents with a temporary break, the family decided to have Philip begin taking respite care weekends at a group home. This plan also allowed Philip to experience a residential situation before a family crisis could force him to do so.

Other goals were constructed that related to the parents' issues. They were interested in becoming involved in a psychoeducational group sponsored by the mental health center to learn more about schizophrenia and behavior management. They were also interested in attending an upcoming session on estate planning led by a local attorney. In addition, the case manager discussed spiritual needs within the family, such as reconnecting to their family of faith.

The role of the case manager with the parents was to provide information about resources that they might use to assist in their relationship to Philip. They were also assured that their service plan would be periodically reviewed and that the family would have a voice in formulating future goals.

The case manager and family discussed future plans for Philip. The short-term goals were to have the family begin the process of exploring and considering options for Philip's future care. As an initial step in this process, they prepared a plan that helped the family specify and clarify values and preferences as a part of the process of determining what type of future care arrangements were best suited for a person with a disability (Mount & Zwernik, 1988). Intermediate goals for the family were to visit the group homes in their county, discuss Philip's care with other relevant family members (one other son who lived out of state), begin to use respite care to familiarize Philip with residential living experiences, and work with an attorney who could explicate financial issues relevant to the eventuality of parental death. These steps were all part of a long-range goal of helping the family make arrangements for the time when the parents could no longer continue as care providers.

Treatment Approach: A Generalist Model of Case Management

A variety of case management models exist, and the choice of using a particular approach depends on numerous factors, including the target client group, staff capabilities, financial resources of the agency, and organizational structure. Rothman (1992) describes four models, each having a different structure or focus. In the generalist model, one case manager performs a variety of roles to facilitate a client's movement through the service delivery system (Robinson, 2000). The generalist case management model most closely resembles traditional social casework (Levine & Fleming, 1984).

A second approach is the case management team, in which a multidisciplinary group functions as the case management system for a client. Each team member is responsible for performing a specialized function (social work, physical therapy, speech therapy, psychology).

A third model, the therapist case manager, is used extensively in the mental health system. This approach infuses a therapeutic relationship into the case manager role.

The final model, one of supportive care, is based on the natural environment of the client (neighborhood, cultural group). In this model, case management is provided to the client through the natural helping network.

In order to be effective practitioners, generalist case managers must have a broad perspective on human services, one that moves beyond the boundaries of the social welfare agencies in which they work. The use of a social system model can assist the case manager in practice with actual clients. Kuhn (1974) identified three elements of a social system. Dattalo (1992) has taken each and operationalized it in the case management process (see Figure 6.1). The first is the detector function, which is an information-gathering phase. The case manager gathers information about both the client problem and resources and service options. The second element is the selector function, in which information is screened for use in the treatment process. The case manager uses theoretical frameworks and practice principles to organize information in understanding client preferences, values, and behaviors. The final function, the effector function, is the "doing function." After gathering information about the problem and possible solutions, the case manager constructs a plan of action about treatment goals.

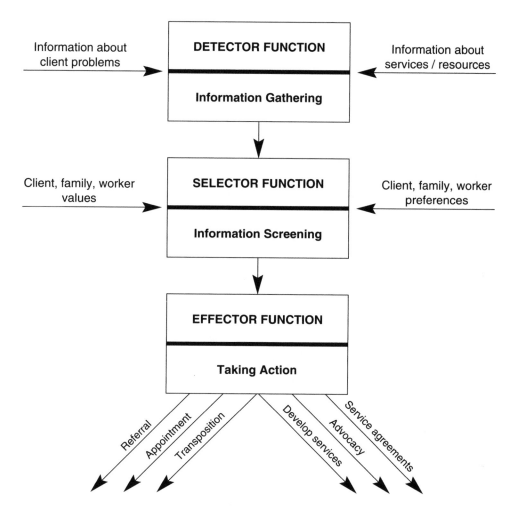

FIGURE 6.1 *Kuhn's Social System Model*

Source: R. L. Schnieder and Nancy P. Kropf, eds., *Gerontological Social Work* (Chicago: Nelson-Hall, 1992), p. 141.

Key Features of Case Management

Another way of examining the process is to outline the key features of case management. This practice approach is aimed at ensuring that clients with complex, multiple problems and service needs receive all services in a timely and appropriate way. This process has traditionally required that the case manager conduct a skillful assessment of the client's functional capacity and support network and plan, advocate for, and obtain a range of suitable community-based services encompassing economic, health and medical, social, and personal care needs (Table 6.1). Such screening takes on more importance when case managers work

TABLE 6.1   Key Features of Social Work Case Management Practice

Social work case management practice

- is a process based on a trusting and enabling client–social worker relationship.
- utilizes the social work dual focus of understanding the person in the environment working with populations at risk.
- aims to ensure a continuum of care to clients who have complex, multiple problems and disabilities.
- attempts to intervene clinically to ameliorate the emotional problems accompanying illness or loss of function.
- utilizes the social work skills of brokering and advocacy as a boundary-spanning approach to service delivery.
- targets clients who require a range of community-based or long-term care services, encompassing economic, health/medical, social, and personal care needs.
- aims to provide services in the least restrictive environment.
- requires the assessment of the client's functional capacity and support network in determining the level of care.
- affirms the traditional social work values of self-determination and the worth and dignity of the individual and the concept of mutual responsibility in decision making.

Source: B. S. Vourlekis & R. R. Greene (Eds.), *Social work case management* (New York: Aldine de Gruyter, 1992). Copyright © 1992 by Aldine Publishers. Reprinted by permission of AldineTransaction, a division of Transaction Publishers.

with clients who are at high risk, such as those with catastrophic conditions and costly injury or illness.

Community-based case-managed services have been used in all fields of practice, including child welfare, aging, and mental health. Although the presenting problem of the person at risk may vary, the purpose of a case management system is to provide the client with service options along a continuum of care. The concept of a continuum of care suggests that clients may need any one of a comprehensive range of services, depending on each person's ability to function relatively independently. Clients who have greater impairments and lower levels of functioning require more structured environments and higher levels of care.

Case managers increasingly use a strengths perspective practice model (Kisthardt, 1992; Kisthardt & Rapp, 1992; Myers, Kropf, & Robinson, in press; Saleebey, 1992; Sun, 2000; Whitley, White, Kelley, & Yorker, 1999). The strengths perspective documents a client family's present daily living situation and determines what they want to change, achieve, or maintain. The strengths perspective also rests on an empowerment theme that seeks ways for clients to set their own agendas and further engage with others in their environment (Rose, 1992). For example, Kisthardt (1992) has suggested that people who have persistent mental illness not be labeled as being "resistant to treatment" or "lacking in social skills."

Rather, clients should be understood as unique, complex individuals, coping with social pressures as well as their "talents, desires, and hopes" (p. 61).

Case management reflects the historic struggle to effect change in the person, the environment, or both (Greene, 1992). In this approach, the case manager assesses the client within the context of his or her environment and provides both direct and indirect service. Direct service is based on a mutually trusting, therapeutic client–social worker relationship in which the case manager evaluates the client's circumstances and intervenes to ameliorate emotional problems accompanying illness or loss of functioning. The emotional problems and the stress associated with loss of functional capacity require that the case manager combine intrapsychic and interpersonal strategies with environmental interventions. Such indirect service involves community-based strategies for resource allocation and advocacy on behalf of the client at risk.

Far too often, clients with many service needs can become "disconnected" from narrowly defined programs, such as those that provide only housing, cash, or nutritional supports (Rubin, 1987). Key features of the case manager's role are responsibility for the development of a mutually agreeable care plan that offers continuity in services and assisting the client in mediating systems problems that create disruption in service delivery (Roberts-DeGennaro, 1987). Because the case manager needs to understand how systems work and how to access them, and often must coordinate the work of multiple service providers by intervening across service systems' boundaries, case management has been called a boundary-spanning approach (Hearn, 1969; Rubin, 1987). Key aspects of a boundary-spanning approach are developing resource systems, linking clients to resource systems, and making systems more accessible and responsible. Central to carrying out this social work approach are advocacy, or negotiating for the equitable distribution of resources, and brokerage, or locating and obtaining needed resources.

Interventions: Family Case Management

Family services and case management have long been important components of social work practice. Family-focused social work, with its mission to resolve family social and emotional difficulties, can be traced to the Charity Organization Societies (COS) of the 1880s. During those early years, pioneer social workers were noted for meeting with families in their homes to discuss their difficulties and to assess the need for financial relief and other tangible assistance (Hartman & Laird, 1987; Richmond, 1917). Because the Charity Organization Society social workers also were concerned with the lack of coordination among services and fund-raising activities, case management shares similar roots with COS as one of the profession's earliest means of linking clients to service delivery systems (Rubin, 1987; Weil, Karis & Associates, 1985). These common beginnings reflect a strong interest in the family as the focus of intervention, an emphasis on a systematic approach to information collection and assessment, a belief in the value of equity in resource allocation, and an emphasis on case coordination. Although case management and family-centered practice share a surprising amount of common ground, little has been written about the relationship of these core practice functions.

Although most people in need of case management assistance are receiving the bulk of their care from families and other primary groups, the role of the family in the case management process is ill defined. Although practitioners increasingly have come to appreciate the value of natural helpers, or what Pincus and Minahan (1973) termed "informal resource systems" (p. 15), case management systems are designed largely for the individual client (Caragonne, 1980; Moore, 1990).

Nonetheless, when discussing case management services, some theorists have considered the individual client's resources and natural supports. For example, the National Association of Social Workers (NASW) (1999) *Standards and Guidelines for the Functionally Impaired* has defined the family as critical to the assessment process. Bertsche and Horejsi (1980) have suggested that the family be involved in the initial interview, the formulation of the psychosocial assessment, the decision-making process related to the care plan, followup of service delivery problems, and counseling and emotional support. They go on to describe the case manager's role vis-à-vis the family as a "liaison . . . to help the client make his or her preferences known and secure the services needed" (p. 97).

In addition, Moore (1990) has suggested that a key case manager role is to integrate formal and informal services provided by the family and other primary groups. He noted that health and social services, families, and formal organizations have complementary goals and that the coordination of shared resources is necessary. According to Nelson (1982), the goal of coordination is to achieve a fit between formal services and primary-group caregiving, not to substitute for family care. Moore (1990) has maintained that it is often the practitioner who acts as a facilitator among the client, the family, and formal caregivers. In addition, Cantor, Rehr, and Trotz (1981) have suggested that, wherever possible, members of the family should be the case managers and that professionals should offer training to support this family responsibility. In this way, the service package is designed to support the family and to maximize its caregiving potential.

Principles for Family-Focused Case Management

Although the family case management literature is limited, the literature on family-centered practice is rich and often consistent with a systems perspective. This perspective generally views the family as promoting positive interdependence and problem resolution and uses intervention strategies aimed at developing the family as a system of mutual aid. By moving the family to "center stage," the family social work literature recognizes the family as the "primary social service institution" and network for planning and problem solving (Hartman, 1981, p. 7). From a family systems perspective, interventions and case management care plans are designed to preserve and enhance functioning and to modify dysfunctional family patterns (Greene, 1999) (Table 6.2).

As no two families are alike, once the case manager has reached out to the family as a unit, it is necessary to assess the family as a group that makes up a causal network. Systems theory suggests that to understand a family, each member should not be viewed in isolation. Rather, it is necessary to examine the relationships among family members, and any one individual's behavior is considered as the consequences of the total situation (Shafer, 1969).

In case management with families, for the social worker to be able to achieve the most effective and culturally sound plan of care, it is important to recognize differences in family forms. For example, persons with AIDS (PWAs) who also are gay or lesbian may want to receive care in conjunction either with their family of origin or their family of choice. Therefore, it is critical for the case manager to establish a helping relationship unique to that particular family.

Application to Families on This Level of Need

Families in need of case management services have a range of needs for flexibility, adaptability, and goal achievement. Although some families may be relatively

TABLE 6.2   Key Features of Family-Focused Social Work Case Management

Family-focused social work requires that the case manager

- identify the family as the unit of attention.
- assess the frail or impaired person's biopsychosocial functioning and needs within a culturally sound family context.
- write a mutually agreed-upon family care plan.
- refer client systems to services and entitlements not available within the natural support system.
- implement and coordinate the work that is done with the family.
- determine what services need to be coordinated on behalf of the family.
- intervene clinically to ameliorate family emotional problems and stress accompanying illness or loss of functioning.
- determine how the impaired person and family will interact with formal care providers.
- integrate formal and informal services provided by the family and other primary groups.
- offer or advocate for particular services that the informal support network is not able to offer.
- contact client networks and service providers to determine the quality of service provision.
- mediate conflicts between the family and service providers to empower the family when they are not successful.
- collect information and data to augment the advocacy and evaluation efforts to ensure quality of care.

Source: Greene, 1999.

high functioning, other families experience high levels of tension, use outside resources poorly, and tend to have insufficient organization to meet their goals. These are examples of Level I and II needs where attention to basic resources is indicated (financial, medical), and structural and organizational changes are required within the family. These families may appear disordered and often require many services and clinical interventions.

Because most programs have limited resources, case finding is critical in providing case management services. This process involves delineating a target population and determining who is especially suited to receive a service because their informal support network is unable to provide a particular resource. Some families may require case management briefly during a transition in development, such as discharge from a hospital after an acute illness. Other families may need ongoing services, with the goal of maintaining functioning or preventing regression to the greatest possible extent.

Interventions

The purpose of case management is to provide the client system—in this case, the family—with service options that promote group and individual functioning. To accomplish this task, Dattalo (1992) has identified three sets of roles that a case manager performs:

1. Counselor roles that are client focused, such as being an educator and enabler.
2. Coordinator roles, matching clients with services; as such, serving as a service broker and developing information about the resource network.
3. Advocacy roles that focus on the service system, such as being a mediator and community organizer.

Using these role clusters, the case manager can establish interventions with the family to help them engage in the service system, provide support once services have been initiated, and address shortcomings in the way services are organized. Specific interventions used by case managers in working with families include building positive relationships with the family system, completing a comprehensive assessment, structuring a case plan, linking the family to needed services, monitoring service delivery, and serving as an advocate.

Building Relationships

In all practice situations, building positive relationships with clients is an important initial component. In family case management, the practitioner has the task of promoting alliances to engage all members of the family system in the service contract. Relationship building with a family may include a number of tasks for the case manager, including education about the expectations and responsibilities of the client role and the practitioner roles, assurance about the nature and use of information shared between the family and practitioner, and listening and discussing the perceptions of the family toward using services.

Because of the stigma that is a result of a psychiatric diagnosis, building a positive relationship with families who care for a member with chronic mental illness, such as the Jordan family, is critical. Even mental health professionals may blame the family for their family member's pathology (Fadden, Bebbington, & Kuipers, 1987; Lefley, 1989). This situation has caused antagonistic relationships between families and the mental health system. Establishing rapport and trust, an important phase of any helping relationship, is especially crucial with these families (Cummings & Kropf, 2000).

Completing a Comprehensive Assessment

Case managers use a format for examining the person who is frail or impaired within a family context. The NASW standards (1999) suggest that assessment and practice must be done with cultural competence and respect for the social diversity of their clientele. Because the family is a unit or interdependent group, it is necessary to assess how a change in one member's functioning affects role expectations throughout the family system (Greene, 1999).

In order to gather this tremendous amount of information, data should be collected from a variety of sources. These include records from other formal service providers in addition to information from the family members themselves. Within a family case management situation, perspectives and experiences of all members of the system must be incorporated. With the Jordan family, for example, the case manager examined the concerns of the aging parents and incorporated their needs into the family service plan. The focus of service provision is broader than just identifying Philip's needs. Frequently, different family members will claim different views about their service needs. In these situations, the case manager will spend time exploring, clarifying, and negotiating these issues with the various family members.

Structuring a Case Plan

A thorough assessment of a family provides the foundation for a case plan. A service plan is based on a psychosocial study of the client and his or her family. It is a mutually agreed-upon blueprint for deciding what services need to be mobilized on behalf of the impaired person and family (Naleppa & Reid, 1998). It also involves the way in which the family will interact with formal care providers and the cost of that care.

In constructing a case plan, the case manager builds on the informal support network of the family. An ecomap can be used to graphically portray the supports used by the family and the quality of the established relationships. Additional resources, such as available community resources, can be added to the ecomap to demonstrate how the case plan will increase support of the family.

Linking Clients to Services

Linking involves referring or transferring client systems to services and entitlements that are indicated in the family care plan as being necessary and available. This process includes identifying available services and gathering information about service access issues. The case manager can also be involved in helping families learn about other resources and transition into another type of service program. Case managers can enable clients to use available resources by demonstrating how to take appropriate and effective action; for example, how to seek out and join a caregiver support group.

Monitoring Service

The relative success of case management practice is based on seeing whether work among the various services involved in a case is performed in a harmonious fashion (Greene, 1992). The case manager is the coordinator of this effort, making certain that information is exchanged among the numerous service providers who may be involved with a family. Monitoring service delivery to determine if client systems are receiving allocated resources requires that the case manager keep in ongoing contact with the client and his or her network and service providers. Where the family is not successful, it may mean mediating conflicts between the family and service providers. This may also mean that troubleshooting can fill much of the case manager's day (Steinberg & Carter, 1983).

In working with families, monitoring service delivery is intertwined with a dynamic assessment process. Changes that affect the family system precipitate changes in service needs for the family. In the Jordan family, for example, Mrs. Jordan suffered a stroke a few months after the family visited the mental health center. Mrs. Jordan's illness had a dramatic impact on the family's ability to carry out their service goals. The case manager maintained a key role in making certain that services were not disrupted during this family emergency. The case manager was also pivotal in helping the family receive resources, such as homemaker services and transportation, that lapsed as a result of the mother's illness.

Advocacy

Advocacy is a social work intervention strategy that is concerned with poor or inequitable distribution of resources. Data collected from the client system can be used by the family or case manager to augment the advocacy effort to ensure the quality of care.

The Jordan family exemplifies a situation that is becoming an increasing concern in mental health—older parents who provide care to a chronically disabled son or daughter. At this life stage, the older family is concerned with the ability to continue to provide extended care for a person who has a chronic mental illness. Case managers who work with older families may need to advocate for services that are specific to issues faced by older families (Cummings & Kropf, 2000). Examples of advocacy efforts include establishing legal/residential workshops specifically oriented to late-life caregivers, structuring an emergency respite care program to be used in instances of health crises experienced by care providers, and exploring the concept of "retirement" for older people who have chronic psychiatric disabilities.

Evaluation

Evaluation of services and service delivery systems is necessary for accountability to the client system, to the funding source, and to policymakers (Greene, 1992). Measures of quality delivered to the client system help ensure that service conforms to acceptable methods of practice. Case managers engage in effort on two levels: evaluating the progress of the family in the established treatment goals and evaluating the comprehensive quality of available services.

The evaluation of the family's advancement involves measuring progress toward treatment goals. Case plans that are constructed using behavioral objectives and time frames lend themselves to the evaluation phase. Consider the following goal for Mr. and Mrs. Jordan:

Goal
Become involved in a support group for caregivers of people with chronic mental illness.

Objective 1
Contact the support group leader to discuss the content and structure of group. Completed in one week.

Objective 2
Contact neighbors, friends, relatives to identify a companion for Philip so parents can attend meeting. Completed in two weeks.

Objective 3
Parents attend first support group meeting. Completed in one month.

Using these types of behavioral objectives within specified time frames, the case manager can help the family partialize and evaluate progress. Points of inertia, or inactivity in the family, can suggest to the case manager areas where additional support is needed. For example, the inability of the Jordans to accomplish objective 2 suggests that they may lack social support or that they have difficulty asking for support from others. This discovery led to enhancing the treatment plan to address this issue with the family.

Evaluating progress with a family is an empowering experience in itself. Families that cannot partialize problems may feel immobilized and overwhelmed. The case manager can motivate families by presenting them with their own progress.

In addition to evaluation of the client systems, case managers are also involved in evaluating service networks. This level of evaluation can be structured around these basic questions (Dattalo, 1992):

1. What services are available for the families?
2. How accessible are these services?
3. Are there services that are available but not used by families?
4. What needs are unmet by available services?
5. Who are potential providers of needed but unmet services?

By answering these questions, case managers gain a comprehensive understanding of how services are able to meet the needs of the families whom they serve.

Application to Families at Other Levels of Need

Case management may be used with families operating at Levels III and IV. These families appear to have a high level of organization and are well prepared or differentiated in meeting their tasks (Goldenberg & Goldenberg, 2003). Very often, however, the resources secured by the case manager make the critical difference, restoring the functional capacity of the family group in crisis.

In working with clients, regardless of their level of need, the case manager must be acutely aware of the psychosocial effects of the problem situation. For example, families who are dealing with economic survival issues may require help understanding their feelings of fear and anger. Living from day to day can be stressful, and children in particular may experience great anxiety. Such families may benefit from structural family interventions that work to realign hierarchical power positions: Do the parents continue to be seen as providers? Who are the breadwinners (Levels I and II of family functioning)?

The case included in this chapter, which discussed a family with a member who is chronically mentally ill, provides an example of how the case manager will have to fill a number of different roles. He or she needs to build a relationship with and seek resources for the identified client: the member with the mental illness. The practitioner also may examine how other family members are adjusting to the member who is mentally ill, as well as explore what intimacy, conflict, and self-realization issues may warrant attention (Level IV of family need). In addition, families who are highly functioning may have their equilibrium severely disrupted when important resources are not available.

The key to appropriate choices of intervention rests with assessment of family need. The selection of an intervention model from among an eclectic array is made carefully and is often a blend of approaches, depending on the particular constellation of family issues.

Ethical Challenges

By definition, case management involves access to and rationing and distribution of health and social service resources. With the graying of the American population, the number of individuals needing case management services will increase dramatically. At the same time, case managers will need to "make do" with the amount of money budgeted for their total caseload. Such budget constraints create an informal rationing process at the "local" delivery level. In addition, financial constraints may hamper a social worker's outreach efforts to those invisible potential clients most in need. These ethical challenges necessitate explicit discussions among policymakers.

Summary

Although family-focused interventions and case coordination have existed simultaneously since the beginnings of social work practice, a family-centered approach to case management has not been widely addressed. This chapter has promoted an inclusive model of working with a family whose needs are primarily on Level I. The model of practice is built on the active premise that one person in the family does not "own a problem"—issues affect all members. The case of the Jordan family provided an example of how a case manager could take a whole-family approach within a mental health context. The service goals did not reduce the family to "identified client and parents" but defined the client system as the family unit.

The role of the case manager in family-focused practice is to meet family needs and promote family harmony. The case manager has the responsibility to empower family members to activate and augment their support network. Formal services are introduced where the support system cannot accomplish tasks and meet the family's needs. The case manager helps the family identify and clarify their service needs and construct a plan of action. The case manager is also responsible for determining that the plan is being implemented and for evaluating its success.

Discussion Questions

1. What are the overlapping features of individual- versus family-focused case management? How would the Jordan case study differ if the approach was individual-focused?

2. What are the advantages and disadvantages of having a single case manager, as opposed to team case management?

3. Describe the roles of a case manager using a family approach.

4. How do you maintain a trusting relationship in a case management role in difficult settings (such as public housing) when you feel you have done all you can to obtain trust?

5. How would a case manager address spirituality needs of families as part of treatment goals?

6. B. is a 28-year-old female with a history of substance abuse and incest as a child. She recently attempted suicide. Would the family case management approach be useful in working with this situation? What would be the short-term goals? long-term goals?

7. Identify a family from your practice whose primary needs are at Level I and with whom you think the case management approach would be particularly relevant. Briefly identify the family's current supports and needs, and give at least five specific ways in which you could potentially assist this family utilizing relevant family case management methods.

8. Is case management a type of family therapy? Why or why not?

9. Why would the case management approach be utilized with Level I and II families more often than with Level III and IV families?

Internet Resources _____

www.casemanagement.com
   An abundance of material on case management is available at this site.
www.maconcountyhealth.org/babylove/babylovecm.html
www.sinai.org/who/sci_programs/chicago_fam_case_mgmt.asp
   Increasingly, consumers can find information online about such care management resources as prenatal clinics and classes on child development.
www.help.org (search for elder care management)
   Care managers who provide elder care may also be found online.

Suggested Readings _____

Hartman, A., & Laird, J. (1983). *Family-centered social work practice.* New York: Free Press.
   This book offers a classic rationale for and discussion of family-focused social work practice. It offers a must-not-miss introduction to anyone interested in the field.

Hegar, R. L. (1992). Monitoring child welfare services. In B. S. Vourlekis and R. R. Greene (Eds.), *Social work case management.* New York: Aldine de Gruyter.
   This chapter of an edited text on case management focuses on case management in the child welfare area. It addresses such concepts as permanency planning, protective services, and family preservation.

Naleppa, M., & Reid, W. J. (1998). Task centered case management for the elderly: Developing a practice model. *Research on Social Work Practice, 8*(1), 63–85.
   This study employs a task-centered model of case management and evaluates collaboration between the older client and the case manager in achieving client goals.

O'Connor, G. (1988). Case management: System and practice. *Social Casework, 69,* 97–106.
   This journal article discusses the two levels of case management—the systems level, which deals with interagency connections and the continuum of care, and the practice level, which focuses on direct service to the client.

Robinson, M. (2000). Case management for gerontological social workers. In R. L. Schneider, N. P. Kropf, & A. Kisor (Eds.), *Gerontological social work: Knowledge, service settings and special populations* (2nd ed., pp. 136–166). Belmont, CA: Wadsworth.

Vourlekis, B. S., & Greene, R. R. (Eds.). (1992). *Social work case management.* New York: Aldine de Gruyter.

This book discusses the eight basic functions of case management through an examination of different fields of practice. There are chapters on private case management with the elderly, programs in child welfare, adult protective services, school social work, and pediatric AIDS.

Weil, M., & J. M. Karls & Associates. (1985). *Case management in human service practice.* San Francisco: Jossey-Bass.

The authors conceptualize eight basic case management functions. Chapters illustrate practice issues in several settings and fields of practice.

References

Baker, L. R., & Thyer, B. A. (1999). Family social work intervention to increase parental compliance with infant apnea monitor use in the home. *Journal of Family Social Work, 3*(3), 21–27.

Bandura, A. (1997). *Self efficacy: The exercise of control.* New York: W. H. Freeman.

Becvar, D. S., & Becvar, R. J. (1996). *Family therapy: A systematic integration* (3rd ed). Boston: Allyn & Bacon.

Bertsche, V. A., & Horejsi, C. R. (1980). Coordination of client services. *Social Work, 25*(2), 94–98.

Cantor, M., Rehr, H., & Trotz, V. (1981). Workshop II case management and family involvement. *The Mount Sinai Journal of Medicine, 48*(6), 566–568.

Caragonne, P. (1980). *An analysis of the function of the case manager in our mental health social service settings.* Austin: University of Texas School of Social Work.

Cummings, S., & Kropf, N. P. (2000). An infusion model for including content on elders with chronic mental illness in the curriculum. *Advances in Social Work, 1*(1), 93–103.

Dattalo, P. (1992). Case management for gerontological social workers. In R. L. Schneider & N. P. Kropf (Eds.), *Gerontological social work: Knowledge, service settings, and special populations* (pp. 138–170). Chicago: Nelson-Hall.

East, J. F. (1999). Hidden barriers to success for women in welfare reform. *Families in Society, 80,* 295–304.

Fadden, G., Bebbington, P., & Kuipers, L. (1987). The burden of care: The impact of functional psychiatric illness on the patient's family. *British Journal of Psychiatry, 150,* 285–292.

Falicov, C. J., & Karrer, B. M. (1980). Cultural variations in the family life cycle: The Mexican American family. In E. A. Carter and M. McGoldrick (Eds.), *The family cycle* (pp. 383–426). New York: Gardner Press.

Goldenberg, I., & Goldenberg, H. (2003). *Family therapy: An overview* (5th ed.). Monterey, CA: Brooks/Cole Publishing.

Greene, R. R. (1992). Case management: An arena for social work practice. In B. S. Vourlekis and R. R. Greene (Eds.), *Social work case management* (pp. 11–25). New York: Aldine de Gruyter.

Greene, R. R., (1999). *Human behavior theory and social work practice* (2nd ed.). New York: Aldine de Gruyter.

Greene, R. R. (2000a). Case management with older adults: Developing a new paradigm. Paper presented at the Indiana Social Services Administration, Division of Addiction and Mental Health Services, Building Case Management in the New Millennium.

Greene, R. R. (2000b). *Social work with the aged and their families* (2nd ed.) New York: Aldine de Gruyter.

Greene, R. R., & Riley, J. (in press). Family and group approaches to interventions with older adults and their caregivers. In B. Berkman & S. Ambruosco (Eds.), *The Oxford handbook of social work in aging.* New York: Oxford University Press.

Groze, V., & Rosenthal, J. A. (1991). A structural analyses of families adopting special needs children. *Families in Society, 72*(2), 469–482.

Hartman, A. (1981). The family: A central focus for practice. *Social Work*, 7–13.

Hartman, A., & Laird, J. (1987). Family practice. In A. Minahan et al. (Eds.), *Encyclopedia of social work* (18th ed., pp. 575–589). Washington, DC: National Association of Social Workers.

Hayes, J. C., Meador, R. G., Branch, P. S. & George, L. K. (2001) The Spiritual History Scale in four dimensions (SHS-4): Validity and reliability. *The Gerontologist, 41,* 239–249.

Hearn, G. (1969). Progress toward an holistic conception of social work. In G. Hearn (Ed.), *The general systems approach: Contributions toward an holistic conception of social work* (pp. 63–70). New York: Council on Social Work Education.

Ho, K. H. (1987). *Family therapy with ethnic minorities*. Newbury Park, CA: Sage.

Jordan, C., Lewellan, A., & Vandiver, V. (1994). A social work perspective of psychosocial rehabilitation: Psychoeducational models for minority families. *International Journal of Mental Health, 23*(4), 27–43.

Kaplan, M. (1992). Case planning for children with HIV/AIDS: A family perspective. In B. Vourlekis and R. Greene (Eds.), *Social work case management* (pp. 76–88). New York: Aldine de Gruyter.

Kelly, T., & Kropf, N. P. (1995). Stigmatized and perpetual parents: Older parents caring for adult children with life-long disabilities. *Journal of Gerontological Social Work, 24*(1,2), 3–16.

Kisthardt, W. E. (1992). A strengths model of case management: The principles and functions of a helping partnership with persons with persistent mental illness. In D. Saleebey (Ed.), *The strengths perspective in social work* (pp. 59–83). New York: Longman.

Kisthardt, W. E., & Rapp, C. (1992). Bridging the gap between policy and practice: Implementing a strengths perspective in case management. In S. M. Rose (Ed.), *Case management and social work practice* (pp. 112–125). New York: Longman.

Kuhn, A. (1974). *The logic of social systems: A unified deductive, system-based approach to social science.* San Francisco: Jossey-Bass.

Kuhn, D. R. (1990). The normative crises of families confronting dementia. *Families in Society, 71*(8), 451–460.

Lefley, H. P. (1989). Family burden and family stigma in major mental illness. *American Psychologist, 44,* 556–560.

Levine, I. S., & Fleming, M. (1984). *Human resource development: Issues in case management.* Baltimore: Center for Rehabilitation and Manpower Services, University of Maryland.

McGoldrick, M. J. (1989). Women through the life cycle. In M. McGoldrick and F. Walsh (Eds.), *Women in families: A framework for family therapy* (pp. 200–226). New York: Norton.

Minuchin, S. (1974). *Families and family therapy.* Cambridge, MA: Harvard University Press.

Moore, S. T. (1990). A social work practice model of case management: The case management grid. *Social Work, 35*(5), 444–448.

Mount, B., & Zwernik, K. (1988). *It's never too early, it's never too late: A booklet about personal futures planning* (Publication #421–88–109). St. Paul, MN: Metropolitan Council.

Myers, L., Kropf, N. P., & Robinson, M. (2002). Grandparents raising grandchildren: Case management in a rural setting. *Journal of Human Behavior in the Social Environment, 5*(1), 53–71.

Naleppa, M., & Reid, W. (1998). Task centered case management for the elderly: Developing a practice model. *Research on Social Work Practice, 8*(1), 63–85.

National Association of Social Workers (NASW). (1999). *NASW Code of Ethics.* Retrieved 2001 from www.naswdc.org/code.htm

Nelson, G. M. (1982). Support for the aged: Public and private responsibility. *Social Work, 27*(7), 137–143.

Pincus, A., & Minahan, A. (1973). *Social work practice: Model and method.* Itasca, IL: Peacock.

Rhodes, S. L. (1980). A developmental approach to the life cycle of the family. In M. Bloom (Ed.), *Life span development* (pp. 30–40). New York: Macmillan.

Richmond, M. (1917). *Social diagnoses.* New York: Russell Sage Foundation.

Roberts-DeGenarro, M. (1987). Developing case management as a practice model. *Social Casework, 68*(8), 466–470.

Robinson, M. (2000). Case management for social workers: A gerontological approach. In R. L. Schneider, N. P. Kropf, & A. J. Kisor (Eds.). *Gerontological social work: Knowledge, service settings, and special populations* (2nd ed., pp. 136–166). Belmont, CA: Wadsworth.

Rose, S. (1992). Case management: An advocacy/empowerment design. In S. M. Rose (Ed.), *Case management and social work practice* (pp. 271–298). New York: Longman.

Rothman, J. (1992). Guidelines for case management: Putting to professional use. Itasca, IL: Peacock.

Rubin, A. (1987). Case management. In A. Minahan et al. (Eds.), *Encyclopedia of social work* (pp. 212–222). Washington, DC: National Association of Social Workers.

Saleebey, D. (1992). *The strengths perspective in social work.* New York: Longman.

Shafer, C. M. (1969). Teaching social work practice in an integrated course: A general systems approach. In G. Hearn (Ed.), *The general systems approach: Contributions toward a holistic conception of social work* (pp. 26–36). New York: Council on Social Work Education.

Steinberg, R. M., & Carter, G. W. (1983). *Case management and the elderly.* Lexington, MA: D. C. Heath.

Sun, A. P. (2000). Helping substance-abusing mothers in the child welfare system: Turning crisis into opportunity. *Families in Society, 81*(2), 142–151.

Tseng, W. S., & Hsu, J. (1991). *Culture and family problems and therapy.* New York: Haworth Press.

Weil, M., & Karls, J. M., & Associates. (1985). *Case management in human service practice.* San Francisco: Jossey-Bass.

Weston, K. (1991). *Families we choose: Lesbians, gays, kinship.* New York: Columbia University Press.

Whitley, D. M., White, K. R., Kelley, S. J., & Yorker, B. (1999). Strengths based case management: The application to grandparents raising grandchildren. *Families in Society: The Journal of Contemporary Human Services, 80,* 110–119.

Part III

Second Level of Family Need: Structure, Limits, and Safety

Level II families have their basic survival needs met and are dealing primarily with issues of family structure, limits, and safety.

The first approach to working with families at this level is structural family interventions, discussed by Aponte in Chapter 7. It is based on family systems theory and has been used with a wide range of families in diverse racial, ethnic, and socioeconomic groups, as well as with single-parent and foster care families. It is one of the approaches that is used more internationally.

In Chapter 8, Horne and Sayger present the social learning family interventions approach to families who have needs on Level II. This approach deals with both internal and external or environmental factors that affect family needs and focuses on learning more effective social skills.

7

Structural Family Interventions

Harry J. Aponte, M.S.W.

Structural family therapy (SFT) is a systems based model that places a special focus on the internal organization of relationships within families vis-à-vis their functioning. It aims to solve problems of dysfunction by making changes in the underlying structure of personal relationships through intervening actively in client experiences.

Levels of Family Need

SFT arose to meet the needs of troubled inner-city youth and their families. The model was first presented in a book whose title spoke to the original target population, *Families of the Slums* (Minuchin, Montalvo, Guerney, Rosman, & Schumer, 1967). What most directly influenced the emerging character of this new model was the *underorganization* (Aponte, 1994b, pp. 13–31) of these families that had Level II needs. The structure of the family relationships lacked "the *constancy, differentiation,* and *flexibility* they need[ed] to meet the demands of life" (Aponte, 1994b, p. 17). The model sought to bring effective organization to the family so that its members could find better solutions to their problems.

Given that the original families were "products of slums" (Minuchin, Montalvo, et al., 1967, p. 6), it is no wonder that the model also lent itself from the very beginning to work with families that had Level I needs. Families needed to be able to organize themselves with effective authority and hierarchy, clear personal boundaries, and stable relationship alliances and possess communication skills to negotiate these structural components of their relationships. Because of the social conditions within which these disadvantaged families faced their problems, the model looked not only at the internal relationship context of the family but at the structure of the social environment within which these families struggled with life (Aponte, 1994b, pp. 13–31).

It was not long, however, before the original proponents of the model began to discover the relevance of relationship structure in families to other problems, such as anorexia nervosa (Minuchin, Rosman, & Baker, 1978). Predictably, families in which youngsters were starving themselves in order to manage their emotional distress and family conflicts did not tend to come from the lowest socioeconomic strata. For the most part they were middle-class families with Level III needs. The factor these families had in common with the lower-income families was the direct impact that a dysfunctional family structure had on the functioning of its members.

With time, moreover, the growing awareness of the crisis in values that the society is undergoing makes it apparent to some that it is not enough to speak only of structure and function in relation to people's life struggles. In the current cultural milieu, neither families nor their therapists share a common base of values on which they can base their efforts to solve problems. This awareness brought about an incorporation into the structural model of notions of values and spirituality (Aponte, 1994b; Aponte, 1996; Aponte, 2002a; Aponte, 2002b). The Level IV spiritual needs of life, relating to moral standards, philosophical perspective, and the social base of spirituality are all relevant to families in our current age, regardless of socioeconomic status (Aponte, 1999).

Assessment

The core focus of an assessment in SFT is how families are organized in relation to the problems they experience in the present. SFT views the past as "manifest in the present and . . . available to change by interventions that change the present" (Minuchin, 1974, p. 14). The assessment demands a clear identification of the focal issue, preferably in the operational terms in which it is currently manifested (Aponte & VanDeusen, 1981, p. 316). In SFT, enactment is the basic context in which family assessments take place (Aponte, 1994b, p. 21; Minuchin, 1974, p. 141). Structural therapists look to have families relive in the therapy the struggles they have at home. Witnessing and engaging with an actual interaction with its underlying relationship structure is a more reliable source of data than what people report about their lives.

The three underlying structural dimensions (Aponte & VanDeusen, 1981, pp. 312–313) that draw a structural therapist's attention are

1. *Boundaries:* What defines who is in or out of a family relationship vis-à-vis the focal issue, as well as what their roles are in this interaction;
2. *Alignment:* Who is with or against the other in the family transactions;
3. *Power:* What the relative influence is of each in the family interactions.

Therapists formulate their structural hypotheses at the level of the current boundary, alignment, and power organization of the family in relation to its problems (Aponte & VanDeusen, 1981, pp. 314–315; Minuchin, 1974, p. 130). They also formulate a second level of hypotheses, called functional hypotheses, that "speak to the *meaning* and *significance* of the current structure" (Aponte, 1994b, p. 36). The present structure of family relationships has a history and a purpose. Functional hypotheses describe the historical background of the family that brought it to the immediate difficulty, and the current motivations that drive family members to relate to each other as they do now around the current issue. Because structural therapists work through the interactions they witness in the present, their every action with families is intentionally based on hypotheses about what they are observing. In fact, SFT considers change-inducing interventions to be not just techniques but technical interventions ensconced in relationships "occurring through the process of the therapist's affiliation with the family" (Minuchin, 1974, p. 91). In other words, structural therapists promote change through specifically aimed techniques within strategically shaped relationships. Consequently, therapists' every action should flow from their diagnostic hypotheses, and these hypotheses should be confirmed or altered according to the therapeutic impact of therapists' actions (Aponte, 1994b, p. 38).

In an interview with the Gonzagas, a Mexican American family, a consultant was presented with a set of parents and five children, ages 4 to 16 (Aponte, 1994b, pp. 32–57). The identified patient was an 11-year-old boy, Pancho, who was having school problems. In the initial presentation of the case, the mother was outspoken and articulate about the problem. The father, a packer, had been described by the family's co-therapists as relatively uninvolved in raising the children and not active in the therapy, although he attended every session. The consultant began the session hypothesizing that the father's regular attendance indicated that, although silent, he cared about what was happening with the children. Yet, he hypothesized that in terms of *boundaries* the father was peripheral to the mother's handling of Pancho's school problems. The mother exercised the *power* of the executive parent in relation to this boy's school problems by being the one who communicated with the school and oversaw his school performance. However, in terms of a *alignment*, Pancho resisted her guidance. The consultant hypothesized that the boy was likely triangulated between parents who had a conflictual marriage. The consulting therapist had little family history to formulate his functional hypotheses but did speculate that this Latin-cultured father who had relatively limited education was not comfortable in the American world of professional agencies that are mostly populated by highly educated women.

Seeing how little control the mother had over Pancho, the consultant further hypothesized to himself that at the heart of her powerlessness was the lack of the father's support with the boys. To probe the father's willingness and ability to help his son, the consultant invited him to engage Pancho in a discussion about his difficulties, hoping for an *enactment* of the current father–son relationship. What emerged from the interaction was that the boy was frightened of his father, who was slow to dialogue but quick to hit. When the consultant gave the other two boys in the family the opportunity to join the discussion, the father was confronted by the 16-year-old's painful plea to have his father quit calling him a "liar" and to stop hitting him, because he felt humiliated and intimidated. The father came to the realization that he was important to his sons and that they needed him to treat them with both affection and respect. The father, with emotion, concluded that *he* was the problem in this situation and quietly said he understood the boys' reactions because he "too had a father." The consultant worked to bring the father into the parenting in a way that would convince him how needed he was by his wife and children. The original therapists were to follow up with the couple about their marital difficulties to help them work more cooperatively as parents.

Goals

SFT aims to engage clients in an active experience of change, beginning with the enactment in the therapeutic session. It seeks to engage family members around current, concrete issues. The approach looks to achieve palpable results by family members' exercising of their strengths in the here-and-now with the active, personal engagement of the therapist. This new experience is meant to form the basis for better future patterns of relating and solving problems.

Intervention Approach

There are basically seven principles of intervention that form the foundation of SFT.

A Focus on Concrete Issues

SFT focuses on the urgent issue that holds the family's attention and intensity of concern (Aponte, 1998b). With the Gonzaga family it was Pancho's school problems. The issue that forces a family's concern is the issue that will move a family to seek help. What hurts becomes the impulse for change.

When clients confront their roles in the solution of a problem, they face challenges to change and choices that demand much of them. These choices bear within them reasons to change that draw on spiritual and moral convictions. Clients' spirituality adds purpose and meaning to their need to solve problems. Structural therapists look for motivation to change that comes from the pain of life and the hope of personal betterment.

Location in the Present

For SFT, the current issue contains within it (1) the focal point of today's concern, (2) the dynamics immediately generating the distress, and (3) traces of the family's past experience that help explain the "why" of today's problem. In other words, today's issue carries with it the immediate pain urging relief, as well as the deeper structural and dynamic forces that are driving the problem. The present issue is alive with the emotions, history, and spirituality that give that experience its meaning and importance. The therapeutic process itself is considered by the practitioner to be yet another current context in which the issue is lived. The therapist's immediate task is to make the context of therapy a vital arena in which to engage the family and address the problem.

Mediation of the Client's Experience in Session

The principal field of intervention for SFT is the family's enactment of their issue in the session (Aponte & VanDeusen, 1981, p. 329; Minuchin and Fishman, 1981, pp. 78–97). The structural therapist looks to seize the moment when family members spontaneously enact their struggle in the session, or creates a situation that draws the family into their characteristic interaction around the issue. Talking about an issue draws from the intellect and memory. The drama, or enactment, of the struggle during a therapy session embodies all the affect and energy that drives the family's behavior. By becoming alive on the therapeutic stage, the issue becomes more readily understandable and accessible to the therapist. With the Gonzaga family, the consultant directly asked the father to talk with Pancho about how they relate around the boy's school problems. When Pancho told of his fear of his father, and the oldest brother spontaneously spoke of how hurt he was by the father's disrespect of him, the consultant held still and let the father respond with his own intensity to his sons. The situation became an opportunity to see how they interacted but also to suggest a new way for the father to engage with his boys. That enactment is both material for assessment and a chance to intervene.

Achieving Change through Restructured Relationships

The structural family therapist pays special attention to the structure of family relationships with respect to the focal issue. This transactional structure is the skeleton undergirding the dynamics that generate the family's problem. There are essentially two species of structural dysfunction: conflict driven and underorganized. The conflictual structure reflects competing interests among family members. The underorganized structure represents a lack of the stability, flexibility, or richness of development needed in family relationships to meet the challenges of the family's functions. Structural therapists intervene to resolve conflict, repair what is broken, and build new strength in the family's underlying structure.

As noted earlier, at least one perspective on the structural model has evolved to incorporate the spiritual dimension of life into a tricornered vision of human social functioning that includes structure, function, and values. People organize themselves psychologically and in relationships to carry out life's functions, but always in relation to their morals, ideals, and philosophy of life. This spiritual dimension can take a secular form without reference to a transcendent spiritual world, or it can be embodied in a formal religious belief system and faith community. In either case people's spiritual framework is vital to the process in which they choose how to think about and contend with life's challenges. In practice, the structural therapist who has a spiritually sensitive perspective brings to the therapeutic effort a recognition of moral choice, personal philosophy, and faith community in the dynamics that influence how people approach the solution of their problems (Aponte, 1996; Aponte, 1998b; Aponte, 2002a; Aponte, 2002b).

Building on Client Strengths

SFT centers the therapeutic process on the resources and power of the client to grow and change, whether within themselves or in their family relationships (Aponte, 1999). The model works through a "search for strength" (Minuchin & Colapinto, 1980). Structural therapists actively engage with families to block old, pathological transactional patterns (Aponte & VanDeusen, pp. 335–336) while also working to build on families' strengths to create new, effective solutions to life's problems. People's resources may reside within their characters, family relationships, and in their communities, including faith communities (Aponte, 1994b, pp. 58–82; Aponte, 1996).

The spiritual dimension of therapy pivots on the ultimate resource of positive, personal power for clients: free will, the seat of our moral choices. The personal power in freedom of the will that Frankl (1963) experienced in the Nazi concentration camps, the poor and disenfranchised can also discover within themselves in their distressed communities: "For the powerless and invisible, acting on the freedom to choose is to claim their potential and importance in the face of daunting circumstances" (Aponte, 1999, p. 82).

Speaking to client strength starts with relating to the personal value and dignity of clients and hinges ultimately on the acknowledgment of clients' personal power and responsibility to freely choose the actions that will determine their destiny. Clients' belief systems contain the strength, standards, and ideals behind their will to choose, and their families and faith communities are their most intimate social supports.

Aiming at Palpable Outcomes

While SFT looks into the underlying structure of people's actions and relationships, the model is practiced in real-life experience and aims for outcomes that make a significant difference in how people live. The initial formulation of the problem takes the form of action and interaction that makes clear the concern of the family (Aponte & VanDeusen, 1981, p. 316). The structural therapist then enters the family's struggle through the enactment, an actual reliving of the family drama in session, and follows up with interventions aimed at creating new transformative experiences during session. When the consultant had Mr. Gonzaga talking with his boys in session in ways that elicited mutuality instead of stifling through intimidation, both father and sons discovered a warm reciprocal affection. Structural therapists also assign tasks as homework (Minuchin, 1974, p. 151), moving the therapeutic experience back into the home, where the family drama normally takes place. Finally, when structural therapists formulate goals, they think in terms of day-to-day experiences that embody the structural and dynamic changes that family members tested in the therapist's office (Aponte, 1992b).

Understanding a problem and communicating effectively with regard to it are means to an end. Living life more successfully is the goal.

Intervention through the Practitioner's Active Involvement with the Family

Structural therapists actively engage with families to create experiences both among family members and between practitioner and family, as a means of generating change.

• Initially therapists look to join (Minuchin, 1974, pp. 133–137) families "in a carefully planned way" (Minuchin, 1974, p. 91). This is not only an effort to gain the trust of family members but a strategic therapeutic opportunity to relate in new ways that draw out new interactions within families.

• In more stubborn and chronic situations, practitioners may themselves engage with families with greater intensity (Minuchin, 1981, pp. 116–141) or intensify a conflictual interaction among family members (Aponte & VanDeusen, 1981, p. 335) in order to induce reactions that bring clients out from behind their defensive walls.

• Therapists may attempt to block (Aponte & VanDeusen, 1981, p. 335) or unbalance (Minuchin & Fishman, 1981, pp. 161–190) petrified patterns of interaction to challenge family members to adopt more functional modes of operating.

• On the other hand, when clients are more readily disposed to change, practitioners may facilitate healthier attitudes, behaviors, and patterns of interaction (Aponte & VanDeusen, 1981, p. 336) through what they simply encourage, point out, or suggest.

• Therapists may intentionally employ themselves in purposeful personal interactions with clients within their professional roles to coax different therapeutic experiences for clients (Aponte, 1992a). This use of self calls for therapists to be emotionally free to use their own person deliberately and more fully for therapeutic purposes. They must be able to utilize their personal assets as well as their flaws and life struggles to both identify with and differentiate themselves from clients. In SFT this active use of self is employed with specific strategic goals within the person-to-person interactions between client and therapist.

Evaluation

As noted earlier, the structural model grew out of research on the treatment of poor, underorganized families. The results of the research as published in *Families of the Slums* (Minuchin, Montalvo et al., 1967) demonstrated the effectiveness of interventions on the family structure underlying specific troubling issues. These interventions challenged old structures and created new ones through freshly constructed client experiences in session. The initial research on underorganized families was immediately followed by research with families with children suffering from psychosomatic conditions, most of whom were not economically or socially disadvantaged (Minuchin et al., 1978).

The impact of family structure on psychosomatic illness has been studied further (Kog, Vertommen, & Vandereycken, 1987; Northey, Griffin, & Krainz, 1998; Onnis, Tortolani, & Cancrini, 1986; Wood, Watkins, Boyle, Nogunera, Zimand, & Carroll, 1989), and SFT has been examined in application to such disparate topics as drug addiction (Allen-Eckert, Fon, Nichols, Watson, & Liddle, 2001; Stanton, Todd, & Associates, 1982), family therapy with children (Abelsohn & Saayman, 1991; Kerig, 1995), family and culture (Fisek, 1991; Jung, 1984; Santisteban et al., 1997), and business and industry (Deacon, 1996). There has also been exploration, within the framework of SFT, of the role of the wider system on the treatment of families (Peck, Sheinberg, & Akamatsu, 1995). The concept of structure in systems has broad application. However, research on structural interventions in family and social institutions should also take into account the personal, cultural, and social values of the observers, the practitioners, and the clients. Family and social structure cannot be studied or evaluated outside of the values that determine what is healthy or unhealthy and morally right or wrong.

Application to Families at Other Levels of Need

The structural model has clearly demonstrated its relevance to Levels I, II, and III needs. The theory and intervention techniques are well adapted to address concerns about concrete issues, hierarchical family structure, and personal boundary issues. While it is not specifically tailored to therapeutic foci about intimacy in relationships and personal self-actualization, SFT clearly addresses these issues as part of the work on relationships within families and couples. Individual self-actualization is integral to an understanding of the evolution of the individual's psychological structure in the contexts of family and society. Values and spirituality, which relate most strongly to Level IV concerns, have been a later addition to SFT for the understating of human relationships.

Ethical Challenges

Because of the active posture of the therapist, SFT faces two ethical challenges:

- The imposition of the therapist's values on clients.
- The blurring of boundaries between therapist and client.

In SFT, therapists actively engage in helping clients identify their issues, set goals, and determine the therapeutic approach to reach those goals. All this work is built on a value platform, the moral planks and ideals that set the foundation of values for the therapy. Ideally, these values are explicitly or implicitly agreed on by therapist and client without coercion or manipulation on the part of the therapist.

However, because of the active posture of the therapist, vigilance and sensitivity are required to make this a truly mutual process.

Again, because of the active engagement of the therapist with the client in every aspect of the therapeutic process, it can be all too easy for therapists to unilaterally manipulate the definition of the issues, decide goals for therapy, and set the course for change. This is the reason why it is so critical for structural therapists to do work on their own person (Aponte, 1992a; Aponte, 1994a; Aponte & Winter, 2000). Structural therapists, like other therapists who actively use themselves in therapy, should engage as part of their training in work on knowing their personal issues—their family history, their signature themes (persona struggles), and their political, social, and moral values. They should develop the ability to observe themselves in therapy, to be aware of their mental associations, memories, emotional reactions, and personal moral and spiritual dispositions. Finally, the goals are for them to utilize themselves, along with their personal reactions, in the therapeutic process in order to better assess and relate in a purposefully therapeutic manner to clients to clients and to implement their interventions.

Summary

Structural family therapy is not a single, tightly organized model of intervention with a unitary, orthodox theory. However, what is common among virtually all the approaches to the model is the emphasis on family structure, the clients' experience in the session, the here-and-now issues and their underlying dynamics, building on client strengths, aiming at real-life outcomes, and the active style of client engagement and intervention by practitioners. Some perspectives on the model emphasize technique over therapeutic relationship, whereas others stress the therapist's personal involvement. Structural therapists also differ in their views on normal family structure and in their opinions about the importance of spirituality to the work of therapy. These differences are incidental to the essence of the model, which focuses on actively addressing today's issues in session through the enactment of the structures of the underlying relationships. The model continues to be a dominant approach in the field of family therapy.

Moreover, amid today's eclecticism, it is rare to find practitioners who practice a single, orthodox approach to therapy. For example, structural therapists commonly utilize Bowen's thinking about the family of origin. From the earliest days, structuralists have employed strategic techniques. What structural therapists today ignore the psychoanalytic concept of the unconscious? On the other hand, SFT has influenced practitioners from other orientations. The insights of SFT about structure in family systems are no longer the exclusive concerns of the structural model. SFT has made its contributions to the field of family therapy and has learned from the contributions of other family-therapy models, as well as models of therapy for individuals—as it should be.

Discussion Questions

1. What are the essential components of the structural model?

2. How can elements of other models be utilized in SFT and components of SFT be incorporated into other models of family therapy?

3. How is SFT applicable to Level III and IV needs?

4. What are practical applications of spirituality to work with families in the structural model?

5. How does one incorporate the diversity of values and spirituality among practitioners and clients into the structural model?

Suggested Videotapes

A house divided: Structural family therapy with a black family. (1990). Golden Triad Films. (Golden Triad Films, 800-869-9454.)
Aponte works with an African American family in this complex family situation of a married couple who have children from previous marriages. The father was released from jail for this interview.

Tres madres: Structural family therapy with an Anglo/Hispanic family. (1990). Golden Triad Films. (Golden Triad Films, 800-869-9454)
Aponte works with a three-generation family that has both Anglo and Latino family members. The presenting issue is a very unhappy, sleepwalking little girl. The focus of the therapy is a young mother valiantly struggling to survive a dysfunctional family background, poverty, and cultural difficulties.

A daughter who needs a mother. (1991). AAMFT Master Series. (AAMFT, www.aamft.org)
Aponte works with an African American family in which the focus is on the relationship between a mother and her emotionally alienated adolescent daughter. The mother struggles with the effects of her own emotionally deprived childhood on her relationship with her daughter.

Williams family: Strength and vulnerability. (1995). Research and Education Foundation, AAMFT. (Child Development Media, #20929P-Vb-X, 800-405-8942)
This film features Aponte's interview with the family from Chapter 11 of his book *Bread and Spirit*. It reveals a family that has courageously overcome the overwhelming trials and tragedies of racism, sickle-cell anemia, drug addiction, and untimely, violent deaths. Their spirituality has been a key source of their strength.

Clinical application of forgiveness. (1996). National Conference on Forgiveness, University of Maryland. (Frederick A. DiBlasio, Ph.D., School of Social Work. University of Maryland at Baltimore, 410-706-7799)
This videotape shows the actual session that is discussed in Aponte's article "Love, the spiritual wellspring of forgiveness: An example of spirituality in therapy."

Family therapy with the experts: Structural therapy with Harry Aponte. (1998). Allyn & Bacon. (Allyn & Bacon, Order Video #3208L8, 800-278-3525)
This videotape is from the series Family Therapy with the Experts. It contains not only a full clinical session by Aponte demonstrating structural family therapy but also an interview in which he discusses the structural model.

Suggested Readings

Aponte, H. J. (1992). Training the person of the therapist in structural family therapy. *Journal of Marital and Family Therapy, 18*(3), 269–281.
This article attempts to apply the notion of the person-of-the-therapist to structural family therapy, and is the first effort to address more fully the use of self in this model.

Aponte, H. J. (1994). *Bread and spirit: Therapy with the new poor.* New York: Norton.
This book contains updates to Aponte's basic structural writings, along with some new material. The particular emphasis of the book is on therapy with disadvantaged families and the place of values and spirituality in this work.

Aponte, H. J. (1998). Love, the spiritual wellspring of forgiveness: An example of spirituality in therapy. *Journal of Family Therapy, 20*(1), 37–58.
Using the example of setting the value platform for a therapeutic contract, this article demonstrates a method for incorporating spirituality into therapy.

Aponte, H. J. (1999). The stresses of poverty and the comfort of spirituality. In F. Walsh (Ed.), *Spiritual resources in family therapy* (pp. 76–89). New York: Guilford Press.
This chapter in Froma Walsh's book is a more recent elaboration of the application of a spiritual perspective to therapy with a particular population.

Aponte, H. J. (2002). Spiritually sensitive psychotherapy. In R. F. Massey & S. D. Massey (Vol. Eds.) *Comprehensive handbook of psychotherapy: Vol. 3. Interpersonal/humanistic/existential approaches to psychotherapy* (pp. 279–302). New York: Wiley.

Minuchin, S. (1974). *Families and family therapy.* Cambridge, MA: Harvard University Press.
This book is the most complete representation of Minuchin's concept of structural family therapy.

Minuchin, S., & Fishman, H. C. (1981). *Family Therapy Techniques.* Cambridge, MA: Harvard University Press.
This book contains Minuchin and Fishman's most comprehensive compendium of structural family therapy's technical interventions.

References

Abelsohn, D., & Saayman, G. (1991). Adolescent adjustment to parental divorce: An investigation from the perspective of basic dimensions of structural family therapy theory. *Family Process, 30*(2), 177–191.

Allen-Eckert, H., Fon, E., Nichols, M. P., Watson, N., & Liddle, H. A. (2001). Development of the family therapy enactment rating scale. *Family Process, 40*(4), 469–478.

Aponte, H. J. (1992a). Training the person of the therapist in structural family therapy. *Journal of Marital and Family Therapy, 18*(3), 269–281.

Aponte, H. J. (1992b). The black sheep of the family: A structural approach to brief therapy. In S. H. Budman, M. F. Hoyt, & S. Friedman (Eds.), *The first session in brief therapy* (pp. 324–342). New York: Guilford Press.

Aponte, H. J. (1994a). How personal can training get? *Journal of Marital and Family Therapy, 20*(1), 3–15.

Aponte, H. J. (1994b). *Bread and spirit: Therapy with the new poor.* New York: Norton.

Aponte, H. J. (1996, Fall). Political bias, moral values, and spirituality in the training of psychotherapists. *Bulletin of the Menninger Clinic, 60*(4), 488–502.

Aponte, H. J. (1998a). Intimacy in the therapist-client relationship. In W. J. Matthews & J. H. Edgette (Eds.), *Current thinking and research in brief therapy: Solutions, strategies, narratives* (Vol. 2, pp. 3–27). Philadelphia: Taylor & Francis.

Aponte, H. J. (1998b). Love, the spiritual wellspring of forgiveness: An example of spirituality in therapy. *Journal of Family Therapy, 20*(1), 37–58.

Aponte, H. J. (1999). The stresses of poverty and the comfort of spirituality. In F. Walsh (Ed.), *Spiritual resources in family therapy* (pp. 76–89). New York: Guilford Press.

Aponte, H. J. (2002a). Spirituality: The heart of therapy. *The Journal of Family Psychotherapy 13*(1,2), 13–27.

Aponte, H. J. (2002b). Spiritually sensitive therapy. In R. F. Massey & S. D. Massey (Vol. Eds.), *Comprehensive handbook of psychotherapy: Vol. 3. Interpersonal/humanistic/existential approaches to psychotherapy* (pp. 279–302). New York: Wiley.

Aponte, H. J., & VanDeusen, J. M. (1981). Structural family therapy. In A. S. Gurman & D. P. Kniskern (Eds.), *Handbook of family therapy* (pp. 310–360). New York: Brunner/Mazel.

Aponte, H. J., & Winter, J. E. (2000). The person & practice of the therapist. In M. Baldwin (Ed.), *The use of self in therapy* (2nd ed.). New York: Haworth.

Deacon, S. (1996). Utilizing structural family therapy and systems theory in the business world. *Contemporary Family Therapy, 18*(4), 549–565.

Fisek, G. O. (1991). A cross-cultural examination of proximity and hierarchy: A dimension of family structure. *Family Process, 30,* 121–133.

Frankl, V. E. (1963). *Man's search for meaning.* New York: Washington Square Press.

Jung, M. (1984). Structural family therapy: Its application to Chinese families. *Family Process, 23*(3), 365–374.

Kerig, P. K. (1995). Triangles in the family circle: Effects of family structure on marriage, parenting, and child adjustment. *Journal of Family Psychology, 9*(1), 28–43.

Kog, E., Vertommen, H., & Vandereycken, W. (1987, June). Minuchin's psychosomatic family model revisited: A concept-validation study using a multitrait-multimethod approach. *Family Process, 26*(2), 235–253.

Minuchin, S. (1974). *Families and family therapy.* Cambridge, MA: Harvard University Press.

Minuchin, S., & Colapinto, J. (Eds.). (1980). *Taming Monsters* [Videotape]. Philadelphia Child Guidance Clinic.

Minuchin, S., & Fishman, H. C. (1981). *Family Therapy Techniques.* Cambridge, MA: Harvard University Press.

Minuchin, S., Montalvo, B., Guerney, B., Jr., Rosman, B., & Schumer, F. (1967). *Families of the slums.* New York: Basic Books.

Minuchin, S., Rosman, B., & Baker, L. (1978). *Psychosomatic families.* Cambridge, MA: Harvard University Press.

Northey, S., Griffin, W. A., & Krainz, S. (1998). A partial test of the psychosomatic family model: Marital interaction patterns in asthma and non-asthma families. *Journal of Family Psychology, 12*(2), 220–233.

Onnis, L., Tortolani, D., & Cancrini, L. (1986, March). Systemic research on chronicity factors in infantile asthma. *Family Process, 14*(2), 107–121.

Peck, J. S., Sheinberg, M., & Akamatsu, N. N. (1995). Forming a consortium: A design for interagency collaboration in the delivery of service following the disclosure of incest. *Family Process, 34*(2), 107–121.

Santisteban, D., Coatsworth, J. D., Perez-Vidal, A., Mitrani, V., Jean-Gilles, M., & Szapocznik, J. (1997). Brief, structural/strategic family therapy with African American and Hispanic high-risk youth. *Journal of Community Psychology, 25,* 453–471.

Stanton, M. D., Todd, T. C., & Associates. (1982). *The family therapy of drug abuse and addiction.* New York: Guilford Press.

Wood, B., Watkins, J. B., Boyle, J. T., Noguiera, J., Zimand, E., & Carroll, L. (1989, December). The psychosomatic family model: An empirical and theoretical analysis. *Family Process, 28*(4), 399–417.

8

Social Learning Family Interventions

Arthur M. Horne, Ph.D., and Thomas V. Sayger, Ph.D.

Family life has become increasingly stressful during the past century. There has been more isolation of family members due to the urbanization of society and a move toward small nuclear families instead of extended families. The urbanization process has led to a focus on work outside the home for most adults. Increased costs of living have resulted in more parents working longer hours out of the home, with fewer support systems available to provide parenting and child care. There is a significant level of violence in American society. This, coupled with drug and alcohol abuse, a concomitant increase in sexual experimentation among young people, and more teenage parenting and single-parent households, has resulted in a dramatic growth in the numbers of children and family members living below the poverty level and a corresponding increase in suicidal and homicidal behavior among young people. In many communities, gang membership has supplanted family membership as the primary source of identity.

Family Needs

Within American society there are substantial numbers of families that are functioning above the crisis level, the level at which families need support from the community for their very survival needs. Although the survival needs of these families have been met, they still have very real and serious problems. Examples of families with problems that fall within the second category of need include families with disruptive, acting-out children; families that are experiencing considerable disarray in the form of poor family organization and structure; families with difficulties in communicating and effective problem solving; families that have children in difficulty with school or community agencies; and families experiencing high levels of disruptive affect, as in violent anger or disabling depression.

Many of the families that have needs on Level II are there because of internal and external (environmental) factors that have affected them. These include the following child and family risk factors:

Child
Child perception that parents support fighting as a way of solving conflict
Expects success and no negative consequences for aggression
Lacks problem-solving skills
Attributes aggression where there is none
Holds beliefs that support violence
Depression
Drug and alcohol use
Low academic achievement
Weapon carrying
Negative parental relationships

Family
Lack of supervision
Lack of attachment
Lack of discipline or consequences
Negative relationships
Psychopathology of one or both parents
Antisocial behavior of family members
Susceptibility to stressors
Unemployment
Marital conflict
Divorce

School
Lack of supervision
Lack of attachment
Lack of discipline or consequences
Negative relationships

Families that have sought help have included ones like those in the following examples.

The McCallisters called the counseling center requesting to be seen because of a referral from the school psychologist. Their son Kevin had experienced high rates of behavioral conduct problems in school for a number of years. Now that he had reached sixth grade, he had become a serious enough problem to be perceived as a danger to other children. The father was a carpenter who worked long hours when employed and who had little time for the family. The mother, a waitress, worked afternoons and was seldom home when the children came home after school. Kevin, the oldest, had been a behavioral problem throughout his school career and had been referred for testing several times.

Each time he was evaluated, Kevin was identified as marginal in terms of special needs; consequently, he had not received any special placement. The two younger children, also boys, had behavioral problems but had not demonstrated the extent of physical aggression that Kevin had shown. The initial interview with the family indicated that the father was quite removed and distant from parenting, seeing the role of parenting as the mother's responsibility. He was angry that he had been called into the situation. The mother, who scored in the clinical range on a depression inventory, indicated that she loved the children but that they had been a disappointment, causing her more pain than pleasure. Kevin was antagonistic to being involved in treatment, whereas the two younger boys were curious and rambunctious.

The Washington family was referred because Selena Washington, a 15-year-old, had been caught shoplifting. She had a history of aggressive behavior, including attempting to extort money from children at school, threatening to hurt other children if they didn't pay her for "protection," and stealing items from school. Selena had been arrested at a convenience store and held overnight at a juvenile detention center. She had attended juvenile court, and the judge had ordered that Selena, her single-parent mother, and the siblings living at home participate in family counseling. Mrs. Washington was angry at the inconvenience, and Selena was quite rebellious. None of the family members indicated that they saw counseling as a positive experience. They indicated that they would participate in counseling only by showing up for the minimum number of times the judge had ordered.

The Prikosovics contacted the center and requested marriage counseling. They indicated that Mr. Prikosovic came from an Eastern European background, and Mrs. Prikosovic was of Irish heritage. They had been married for six years. Although the marriage had started out amicably, the last two years had been marked by conflict, arguments, and recently by physical aggression between the two of them. They had attempted religious counseling by their priest, but he had encouraged them to follow traditional roles of husband and wife, with the wife deferring to Mr. Prikosovic as the head of the household. Mrs. Prikosovic indicated that she had been willing to accept that role when they were first married, but that it was no longer tolerable for her. They both reported significant conflict in the area of sexuality within the marriage. There were no children.

Robert Verde, a recent university graduate, came for his first session at the center and reported that his lover had just left him for another man. Robert was very distraught and reported the possibility of inflicting personal harm on himself. He stated that he had experienced a number of lovers during his university education but that his recent partner had been with him for more than a year. They were very close and trusting with each other. Robert was devastated that his lover left him after such a close and involved relationship. Robert indicated that his family had not been told about the partnership because Robert did not want his fundamentally religious farming family to know he was gay.

Assessment and Treatment Goals

Each family described presented very real pain and need for assistance in addressing the pressing problems that they were experiencing in their lives. There are general goals that are established for all families receiving treatment.

1. Develop a sense of optimism and hope about their particular situation.
2. Appreciate the universality or general nature of their situation.
3. Become aware of the alternative ways of addressing the problems they are experiencing, so that they see more options available to them.
4. Learn more effective basic living skills: communication, problem solving, decision making, environmental interaction.
5. Develop independence in living skills.

The goals of treatment become focused as each family member presents his or her unique and individual issues.

The McCallisters

The McCallisters require a careful negotiation to determine the level of change and restructuring that would be acceptable and agreeable. Mr. McCallister has reported little interest in participating in treatment, seeing the problem as one primarily for the mother. Here, the therapist must make a decision about family responsibility and power: Should the therapist support the traditional roles that have been assigned and accepted by family members, or should there be a focus on realigning the roles and responsibilities of the parents? The goals for the McCallister family might include

- Empowering the mother to take greater control over how family members spend their time (father absent, chaotic family schedule).
- Teaching both parents more effective parenting skills.
- Helping the boys learn anger-control skills.
- Identifying problem-solving skills and, especially important, couples communication skills.

The Washingtons

The Washington family does not want to participate in treatment. A goal for this family would be to identify ways in which their family is functioning well and to help them see that they are not "bad" or "sick" but doing the best they can, given their economic and social circumstances. However, they need assistance in learning more effective ways of dealing with their environmental circumstances. Specific goals for the Washington family might include

- Empowering the mother to be able to take greater responsibility for the behavior of the children.
- Teaching the family effective disciplinary techniques.
- Helping the children learn self-control strategies that will help them stay out of trouble.
- Establishing better communication skills within the family.
- Addressing environmental issues (employment, leisure time).
- Working with school issues such that greater success is experienced in the school environment.

The Prikosovics

The Prikosovics have demonstrated difficulties in maintaining and enhancing intimacy. They need to learn more effective communication and basic problem-solving skills. They are experiencing an evolving and developing relationship but have become "stuck" at a level of development that is not acceptable and is, in fact, detrimental to their growing closer together. Goals might include

- Developing more effective problem-solving skills.
- Learning better communication skills.
- Addressing the beliefs or narratives they have about their relationship.
- Discussing the power and role relationships that have become troublesome.

Mr. Verde

Robert Verde is having difficulty managing his needs for intimacy and relationships in light of his homosexuality and negative social pressures. He needs assistance in learning to manage issues of intimacy (being discarded) and sexual orientation, developing personal strength to manage his loneliness, and learning communication skills, both to facilitate meeting other persons and to learn ways of talking with his family members. Goals might be

- Learning to develop the strength to manage developmental passages, such as the loss of a loved one.
- Developing effective coping skills to manage his loss and fear.
- Practicing communication skills that will allow greater means of meeting people and sharing with his current family and friends.
- Developing self-control skills to manage his life more effectively.

Consistent with other families at Level II, the four families in the case examples are experiencing difficulties with inefficient and ineffective family structures. In turn, these faulty structures inhibit the effective solving of current problems, confusion with family rules, roles, and responsibilities, exacerbating the low level of functioning. As a result, these kinds of confusion limit the families' capacity to overcome their life challenges and their feelings of insecurity, dissatisfaction, and discomfort with the level of intimacy within the family.

Social Learning Family Interventions

Several principles aid in our understanding of family needs and the contingencies on which current family interactions are based. The social learning family treatment approach, (Fleischman, Horne, & Arthur, 1983; Horne & Sayger, 1990, 2000; Tolan & Guerra, 1994) has been successfully employed with a variety of families and with many levels of family needs. This model enables the practitioner to utilize a well-structured series of intervention strategies, yet allows for the necessary flexibility when working with diverse, chaotic, and unique family systems. Because social learning family interventions allow for unique family structures and flexibility in implementing change according to the expressed needs of each family, this approach can be effective across racial and ethnic categories, and with varying gender roles and responsibilities. The effectiveness of social learning family interventions has been researched in a variety of clinical settings. It has been shown to be useful in the remediation of difficult child behavior problems, marital conflict, ineffective power structures and coalitions, and poor community–school–home relations (Horne, Glaser, & Calhoun, 1998; Sayger, Horne, & Glaser, 1993; Sayger, Horne, Walker, & Passmore, 1988; Szykula, Sayger, Morris, & Sudweeks, 1987).

Theoretical Base and Basic Tenets

Many theoretical approaches to family intervention have been utilized with Level II families, with varying degrees of success. All of these models attempt to approach clinical work with families from a positive viewpoint, and focus on the families' strengths and current abilities to cope with chaotic and challenging living environments. Clearly, no one theoretical approach provides the answer for all families experiencing difficulties; thus family practitioners must be clear about the needs of each family they plan to assist and how they will develop their intervention to meet those needs. An underlying knowledge of how one believes individuals and families develop and learn their behavioral patterns is the cornerstone for effectively implementing a family intervention.

For those clinicians who practice social learning family interventions, the following beliefs and assumptions about human/family development are the bases for intervention:

1. People learn within a social context through watching how other people in their environment behave, reacting to these behaviors, and interacting with those individuals in their social system (spouse, partner, child, parent, extended family members, teachers, coworkers).
2. The problem behaviors demonstrated by the individual or family are logical from a learning perspective, given the contingencies within that family's or person's environment and their personal beliefs.
3. People behave the way they do either because they have learned that behavior, or because they have not learned alternative, and often more positive, ways to behave.

4. People's beliefs and cognitive processes influence their affective and behavioral responses.
5. People attempt to maximize the rewards of their behavior while minimizing the costs. People are more likely to perform in ways that result in what they perceive to be the best outcome for them.
6. In order to change how someone else behaves, a person has to change the way he or she typically responds to that behavior.
7. The more consistent the consequence and the more immediately it occurs after the behavior, the faster the person will learn. Inconsistent consequences make learning harder, because people do not know what to expect.
8. Because people rarely learn from only one act of behaving and receiving a consequence, repeated trying or testing is a necessary part of learning.
9. The family is the expert on what is happening in their life, and each family is unique.

This framework is appropriate for families at the second level of functioning. The intervention focuses on the development of effective communication skills, establishes appropriate limits and levels of authority, encourages strong parental alliances, and aids families in the development and use of self-control and problem-solving skills. It also addresses the cognitive thought processes to replace dysfunctional thoughts with more facilitative thinking. In essence, social learning family interventions help family members learn not only how to survive family life but also how to make their family life healthier from a psychological perspective and more enjoyable in general.

Applications and Intervention Strategies

Social cognitive learning intervention strategies focus on families at Level II and fall into three general categories. First, cognitive restructuring addresses any disruptive or maladaptive thoughts that might result in painful or disturbing feelings and, consequently, maladaptive behaviors. Second, coping skills training, such as relaxation training, self-control strategies, behavior rehearsal, and modeling, addresses inappropriate learning experiences. Third, problem-solving skills training (behavioral contracts, negotiation, brainstorming) assists families in developing alternative strategies for resolving current and future conflicts or concerns. Perhaps the most important objective of intervention with Level II families is to focus on creating a structured learning environment in which family members can learn and practice new behaviors that alter their currently ineffective family structure.

Therapeutic Relationship.   The development of a positive therapeutic relationship is central to effective family intervention. The relationship between professional and client develops in much the same way as all social systems are formed, that is, through modeling appropriate social behavior, coaching the family members in effective social communication, and setting up positive consequences for establishing the therapeutic alliance. To accomplish these goals, the family practitioner must first help the family establish positive expectations for change. Level II families are characterized by a negative view of their chances for remediation. They feel that they have tried everything they know how to do, and nothing has worked. Thus it is important for the practitioner to communicate to each family that she or he believes that the family can successfully deal with its current problems. The process of preparing the family for success can be initiated by

1. *Defining all members in the family as being hurt by their circumstance.* Most families attempt to find someone or something to blame for their problems. Objects of blame may be the child, parent, judge, social service system, neighborhood, teacher, school, social caseworker, extended family members, or therapist. In defining all members in the family as being in pain, everyone acknowledges that each family member is affected by hurtful ways and that blaming will not solve the problem.

2. *Normalizing the family problems.* Families may communicate hopelessness or feelings of "Why me?" when they are first referred for treatment. It is important to inform the family in treatment that all families have problems, and although the family's current problems may seem to be overwhelming and uncontrollable, families in similar situations have been successful in overcoming their conflicts.

3. *Emphasizing the family's strengths and positive motivation.* Although many families may initially proclaim their reluctance to participate in treatment, the fact that they have attended a session shows that they still have some concern for their family and hold some hope for change.

4. *Communicating empathy.* The family must believe that the practitioner understands what it is like for the family to be experiencing these problems. Assuming the position that family members are the experts on their own family can assist the professional in communicating positively to the family that he or she is there to listen, understand, and help the family successfully overcome their concerns.

5. *Communicating hope.* Although the problems facing the family may be enormous and difficult, a positive attitude and an ability to see the hope and irony in the situation are necessary. Most families at Level II have forgotten how to laugh and enjoy themselves; thus the practitioner must attempt to make the treatment intervention enjoyable and even fun, without diminishing the seriousness of the problems being addressed.

Other relationship-building skills that the professional would utilize include

- Breaking complex problems into manageable units.
- Dealing with one issue or task at a time.
- Giving everyone a chance to participate.
- Teaching new skills in specific, nontechnical language.
- Modeling new skills.
- Personalizing in-session rehearsals.
- Predicting feelings and behavior changes.

- Soliciting and anticipating concerns.
- Encouraging client initiative and giving credit for positive changes.
- Determining reasons for client resistance.
- Checking for comprehension and understanding when teaching new skills.
- Sharing the treatment or session agenda.
- Gathering information about what family members do.
- Gathering information about cognitive and emotional reactions.
- Gathering information about behavioral sequences and patterns.

Structuring for Success. Structuring for success begins with the initial contact between the family and the practitioner. Not only does the professional want to be successful in assisting the family to function in a more effective manner, but the family must also establish a belief in their own ability to succeed. To establish this positive expectation for change and success, interventions begin with clearly and objectively defining the problem, establishing specific behavioral goals, emphasizing consistency and persistence in developing family routines, interacting with respect and dignity, emphasizing family strengths, and enhancing the couple's and/or the parent–child relationship. Families are encouraged to begin tracking the instances of problem behaviors in their family to determine patterns, sequences, frequency, intensity, and duration of the problems. Usually, families will discover that the incidence of problem behavior is less frequent than they had perceived, yet the discomfort, anger, pain, and disruption created by the behavior are no less real. However, in discovering that the behavior occurs less frequently, the family becomes more hopeful that positive change can be achieved, and thus their motivation and commitment to treatment will increase.

Self-Management Skills Training. Individuals who cannot gain and maintain control of their emotions and behaviors find it very difficult, if not impossible, to interact with family members in a positive and respectful manner. A study conducted by Morris et al. (1988) found that fathers of aggressive boys reported five times more negative thoughts about their families and eight times more negative thoughts about their child than did fathers of well-behaved boys. This finding further supports the belief that the maladaptive thought processes that family members have about their relatives must be altered if they hope to develop a more functional family environment. These self-control strategies might be utilized to assist family members in gaining and maintaining self-control:

1. *Relaxation Training.* Learning self control by learning to control bodily reactions through training in deep-breathing exercises, progressive muscle relaxation, or other relaxation strategies is very effective.

2. *Positive Reframing.* Individuals will typically react to behaviors based on some perception they have regarding the intent of that behavior. For instance, a parent who is constantly being interrupted by a child may assume that the child is being an ill-mannered pest. This belief might lead the parent to respond in a negative manner. However, if the child's reaction were reframed as an attempt to gain the parent's highly valued attention, the parent might respond more positively. Functioning under a more positive frame of reference, the parent can then teach the child more appropriate ways of gaining parental attention. This reframing can also be identified as an attempt to replace upsetting, and possibly irrational, thoughts with calming thoughts that allow the family members to interact in healthier ways.

3. *Child Self-Control Strategies.* The most effective way to implement and train children to use self-control strategies is by aiding the parent in instructing the child. The turtle technique (Schneider & Robin, 1976) assists younger children in gaining control over impulsive, aggressive, and disruptive behaviors and teaches children to slow down, "pull into their shell," calm down, and think of their behavioral goal. This strategy encourages the child to think before he or she acts.

4. *Disciplinary Strategies.* For families in which parental authority has been undermined, it becomes important to assist them in gaining control through consistent and effective disciplinary methods. Many Level II parents have relied on spanking, lecturing, or grounding to punish children for their misbehavior. These punishments are typically ineffective, particularly if the parents' authority is not secure or respected. Emphasizing modeling, direct instruction, and rehearsal to develop effective discipline, parents can be instructed in the development of strategies that allow the child to fully experience the consequences of his or her misbehavior. The following disciplinary strategies are often recommended:

Time-out. Time-out is useful for general child noncompliance or defiance, or when immediate cessation of the behavior is important. Short-term time-out is most effective with children younger than age 10 and requires the parent to send the child to a nonreinforcing environment for a specified length of time to "cool off" and gain self-control.

Premack Principle. Often referred to as "Grandma's law," the Premack principle requires the child to complete a desired or expected activity before doing something he or she prefers to do. A form of contract, this strategy is often misused and reversed, and therefore rendered ineffective. For example, the child must eat his or her vegetables before he or she has dessert; this is an appropriate contract. However, because the child is whining or yelling, many parents will allow the child to eat the dessert to make him or her quiet. Typically, the child will continue to refuse to eat his or her vegetables. In essence, the child has won the battle.

Natural and Logical Consequences. Particularly useful with irresponsible children, natural and logical consequences allow children to experience the consequences of their behavior; thus a child learns which behaviors have negative costs and which provide positive rewards.

Assigning Extra Chores. Effectively used with older children and adolescents, extra chores are assigned for children who lie, damage property, or steal. The child should be assigned to do one hour of work for each transgression. It is important that the chore be something that would not disrupt other family functions if not completed (such as cooking dinner). Additionally, the child is restricted from the telephone, friends, food, and fun until the work is completed. In instances of property damage or stealing, the child should also be expected to pay restitution.

Loss of Privileges. To be effective, the loss of a privilege must involve something the child values. For instance, telling the child that he or she cannot use the car on the weekend when he or she does not have a driver's license would not be effective. Also, parents must not go overboard. If the child loses a privilege for too long, he or she will soon find a replacement of equal or greater value, and the suspended privilege will lose its effectiveness. Loss of privileges is often effective when other disciplinary strategies have been unsuccessful.

Communication Skills Training.   Healthy and functional family communication begins with ensuring that the message that is intended to be sent is the message that is being heard. Family members must be specific and brief and utilize I-messages instead of you-messages if they hope to increase the effectiveness of their communication. Effective communication involves the following:

1. *Speaking your piece.* Individuals in the family must express their desires and opinions instead of relying on others to "read their mind."
2. *Finding out what others are thinking.* Many individuals make the mistake of believing they know what other family members are thinking. To be sure, family members must ask others what they are thinking.
3. *Showing others that they are being heard.* Maintaining good eye contact and otherwise indicating interest, and trying to understand what others are saying will communicate concern and commitment to clear communication.
4. *Asking questions when confused.* If family members do not understand what other members are trying to communicate, ask them for clarification.
5. *Stopping and letting others know when communication is breaking down.* During arguments, many things that are said in haste and anger may cause others to feel hurt or angry in return. It is best to stop the interaction before it progresses to this stage and to wait until a more calm and rational discussion can occur.

Other behaviors can derail communication and should be avoided. Such behaviors as put-downs, blaming, denial, defensiveness, mind reading, sidetracking, or giving up only lead to the demise of effective communication.

Problem-Solving Skills Training.   Most families at Level II are relatively unskilled problem solvers in many aspects of their lives. To overcome these deficiencies, interventions will assist family members in problem-solving exercises specifically designed to address the unique problems of each family. Basic to problem-solving skills training is the act of brainstorming alternative solutions for specific problems. An approach that seems particularly useful with such families is to ask these questions:

1. What is your goal? What would you like to see happen?
2. What are you doing to achieve this goal?
3. Is what you are doing helping you to achieve this goal?
4. If not, what are you going to do differently?

At first, most families will require a great deal of assistance to generate positive alternatives to their current behavior. However, through modeling this four-step process, the family will soon be able to generate many alternative solutions. The task for the practitioner then becomes helping the family evaluate the potential consequences for each solution and selecting and implementing the alternative that is deemed to be the most satisfactory in resolving the problem.

Evaluation of Effectiveness

Sayger et al. (1993); Sayger et al. (1988); Smith, Sayger, and Szykula (1999); and Szykula et al. (1987) have measured the effectiveness of social learning family interventions in a variety of settings with children with behavior disorders and their families. The results have been impressive, with significant decreases in negative child behaviors and corresponding increases in positive child behaviors both at home and in school. Sayger et al. (1988) also reported that these behavioral changes were maintained after a 9- to-12-month follow up. In a comparison of strategic and behavioral family therapies in an outpatient child psychiatric facility, Szykula et al. (1987) reported that 100 percent of the families participating in social learning family intervention demonstrated gains toward their treatment attainment goals, whereas 67 percent of those in the strategic family therapy group made gains toward treatment goals.

In a study of the impact of social learning family treatment for child conduct problems on the level of marital satisfaction of parents, Sayger et al. (1993) noted that those parents reporting low marital satisfaction prior to treatment reported scores in the maritally satisfied range after treatment.

Sayger, Szykula, and Sudweeks (1992) found that parents participating in social learning family interventions reported significantly more positive than negative side effects of their participation in treatment. These studies suggest that consumer satisfaction ratings show that family treatments are both efficacious and effective in the positive treatment of many aspects of poorly functioning families with problems ranging from marital conflict to child behavior problems.

Application to Families on Levels I, III, and IV

Social learning family treatment offers a structured approach to dealing with a variety of family concerns. As such, it can be effectively employed with families at all levels of functioning. Families functioning at Level I can benefit from the positive focus on structure, organization, and problem solving. Even with families at levels higher than Level I, instances may occur in which their safety and security are challenged through unemployment, death, divorce, or other life events. The need to define and develop a new family structure and organization can become a focus in treatment. Families at Level III can benefit from the focus on establishing clear boundaries and emphases on communication skills building. Level IV families can benefit as they develop self-knowledge and awareness regarding their behavior patterns, goals for the future, and general understanding of family systems and structures.

Ethical Challenges

Social learning family therapy has a strong research- and evidence-based background that demonstrates considerable effectiveness, particularly when working with families that have skills deficits; that is, those who do not have adequate skills for the family work that needs to occur. A challenge for the therapist, though, is to determine whether the skills are lacking because of lack of knowledge, lack of valuing of the skills, or other reasons, such as being incompatible with the cultural norms of the family being seen.

Social learning family therapy has an implied "value" of how families should function, and approaches family deficits as just that: deficits. In some cultural groups the specific approaches used in social learning therapy are not valued or endorsed; rather, they are seen as being "white" or "middle class" or incompatible in other ways.

Social learning family therapy is often seen as "easy" because it has been, to some extent, manualized; that is, described in manuals. Social learning is at times seen as something "anyone can do" because the manual tells them what to do, and so the ones who carry out the therapy are often poorly trained, particularly in the important clinical skills necessary to be effective with families in need of support and therapy.

Social learning family therapy is often seen as a "first step," as in "let's try to teach them some basic family skills and see if that works," rather than attempting to understand the dynamics of the family and how systemic issues may be functioning to continue the dysfunctional interactions among family members. Social learning family therapy may be effective with first order changes (behavioral) in the family using this approach, but to accomplish second order changes (rules/ systemic), the family dynamics must be incorporated into the process.

Summary

Social learning family interventions with Level II families focus on learning more effective social skills. People learn in social settings, with the family being the primary such setting. Through live and vicarious modeling, each member of the family learns to interact consistently with how other family members act, or "You attract more bees with honey than with vinegar" versus "Nastiness begets nastiness." People seek the maximum pleasure and least pain that they can experience in life, and as a result, often use aversive methods of interacting to obtain the greatest payoffs. Frequently, this tendency results in an environment focusing on aversive interactions, the abuse of members of the family, and a lack of family (community) happiness because individual desires at times take precedence over the best interests of the group.

Social learning family interventions present a relearning opportunity, helping family members learn to interact with one another in more pleasant, affirming, and respectful ways. Two primary contributions are teaching family members how to interact in positive rather than aversive ways, by showing respect and dignity for the members of the family; and a provision of structure and organization that brings order to chaos, predictability to uncertainty, trust rather than fear.

Although this approach is not proposed as the only intervention for all families, it has been demonstrated to be highly effective for assisting families experiencing considerable chaos, with clinicians using aversion to control family members. When families are functioning with inadequate or inappropriate social skills, social learning family interventions facilitate the learning of more adaptive and fulfilling ways of living together.

Discussion Questions

1. Identify the particular population that the social learning family intervention model has been used with the most. Why has this population been targeted? What is there about the social learning family intervention model that particularly lends itself to working with this population?

2. The authors provide evidence substantiating the efficacy of social learning family intervention. Describe why behavioral research methods have been especially applicable to this model of intervention, and discuss whether the information is useful for the clinical practitioner.

3. It often appears that clinicians are guided more by intuition and feel than by research supporting particular models. Family treatment adheres to a research model for evaluating the development and application of principles. Discuss why social learning family treatment makes use of this research model, whereas many other models do not.

4. The authors noted that the social learning family treatment model is not necessarily the only or the best intervention to use. Describe guidelines that could assist you in deciding whether the social learning family treatment model is applicable to a given case.

5. The authors address the "softer" clinical skills necessary to be effective with families. Discuss the importance of relationship skills to a program that is predominantly technique and intervention oriented.

6. Explain from an ethical/professional position how you can justify using or not using a model that is less appealing but more efficacious.

7. Identify the aspects of treatment that seem to be key for families at Level II.

Internet Resources

http://teachnet.edb.utexas.edu/~lynda_abbot/social.htm

Suggested Readings

Goldstein, A., & Huff, C. (1993). *The gang intervention handbook.* Champaign, IL: Research Press.
This handbook describes interventions useful for addressing gang problems, including two chapters describing family interventions.

Horne, A., & Sayger, T. V. (2000). Social learning family therapy. In A. Horne (Ed.), *Family counseling and therapy* (3rd ed.). Itasca, IL: Peacock.
This text presents an overview of models and theories of family therapy intervention. The chapter on social learning family therapy includes a historical foundation for the model and reviews the research supporting the model. The chapter also describes applications to marriage work.

McDonald, L., & Sayger, T. V. (1998). Impact of a family and school-based prevention program on protective factors for high-risk youth. In J. Valentine, J. A. DeJong, and N. J. Kennedy (Eds.), *Substance abuse prevention in multicultural communities* (pp. 61–85). New York: Haworth Press.
Presents research results from a drug abuse prevention program.

Sayger, T. V., & Heid, K. O. (1991). Counseling the impoverished rural client: Issues for family therapists. *The Psychotherapy Patient, 7,* 161–168.
Discusses the problems facing family therapists when working with the rural poor and possible strategies for family intervention.

Sayger, T. V., Szykula, S. A., & Laylander, J. A. (1991). Adolescent-focused family counseling: A comparison of behavioral and strategic approaches. *Journal of Family Psychotherapy, 2,* 57–79.
This article presents a hypothetical case and discusses the application of social learning and strategic family therapy in addressing the family issues.

References

Fleischman, M., Horne, A., & Arthur, J. (1983). *Troubled families: A treatment program.* Champaign, IL: Research Press.

Horne, A., Glaser, B., and Calhoun, G. (1998). Conduct disorders. In R. Ammerman, C. G. Last, & M. Hersen (Eds.), *Handbook of prescriptive treatments for children and adolescents* (2nd ed.). New York: Pergamon Press.

Horne, A. M., & Sayger, T. V. (1990). *Treating conduct and oppositional defiant disorders in children.* Elmsford, NY: Pergamon Press.

Horne, A., & Sayger, T. V. (2000). Social learning family therapy. In A. Horne (Ed.), *Family counseling and therapy* (3rd ed.). Itasca, IL: Peacock.

Morris, P. W., Horne, A. M., Jessell, J. C., Passmore, J. L., Walker, J. M., & Sayger, T. V. (1988). Behavioral and cognitive characteristics of fathers of aggressive and well-behaved boys. *Journal of Cognitive Psychotherapy: An International Quarterly, 2,* 251–265.

Sayger, T. V., Horne, A. M., & Glaser, B. A. (1993). Marital satisfaction and social learning family therapy for child conduct problems: Generalization of treatment effects. *Journal of Marital and Family Therapy, 19,* 393–402.

Sayger, T. V., Horne, A. M., Walker, J. M., & Passmore, J. L. (1988). Social learning family therapy with aggressive children: Treatment outcome and maintenance. *Journal of Family Psychology, 1,* 261–285.

Sayger, T. V., Szykula, S. A., & Sudweeks, C. (1992). Treatment side effects: Positive and negative attributes of child-focused family therapy. *Child and Family Behavior Therapy, 14,* 1–9.

Schneider, M., & Robin, A. (1976). The turtle technique: A method for the self control of impulsive behavior. In J. Krumboltz & C. Thoreson (Eds.), *Counseling methods.* New York: Holt, Rinehart & Winston.

Smith, W. J., Sayger, T. V., & Szykula, S. A. (1999). Child-focused family therapy: Behavioural family therapy versus brief family therapy. *Australian and New Zealand Journal of Family Therapy, 20,* 83–88.

Szykula, S. A., Sayger, T. V., Morris, S. B., & Sudweeks, C. (1987). Child-focused behavior and strategic therapies: Outcome comparisons. *Psychotherapy: Theory, Research, Practice and Training, 24*(3S), 546–551.

Tolan, P. H., & Guerra, N. G. (1994). What works in reducing adolescent violence: An empirical review of the field. Boulder: The Center for the Study and Prevention of Violence, University of Colorado.

Part IV

Third Level of Family Need: Boundaries and Control

Families with needs on Level III have their basic survival needs met and have achieved some success in dealing with the issues of family structure, limits, and safety. They have a structure and style that usually works for them. As a result, they are able to focus on more specific needs, such as clear and appropriate boundaries and control. In the house analogy for Level III, the primary focus is on the inner architecture, because the presence of the outer structure and basement are assumed.

In Chapter 9, Koob discusses solution-focused interventions, one of the brief intervention approaches appropriate for families at this level of need. The emphasis on health and strengths in this approach make it an especially useful model for families functioning at Level III. The second interactive approach for such families is presented by Walsh in Chapter 10. Family systems interventions draw heavily on Bowen's family theory, which is an intergenerational approach.

9

Solution-Focused Family Interventions

Jeffrey J. Koob, Ph.D.

Solution-focused brief therapy (SFBT) is, as the name implies, a postmodern intervention that focuses on solutions rather than problems. For example, if a child frowns, one could focus on the child's not frowning (problem-focused), or one could focus on the child's smiling (solution-focused). If the child smiles more, then by definition he or she frowns less. To obtain this dynamic interplay, however, certain assumptions must be made (de Shazer, 1985, 1988, 1994, 1997; de Shazer et al., 1986; O' Hanlon & Weiner-Davis, 1989).

Assumptions

1. *The Family Is the Expert.* Unlike problem-focused therapies, in which the therapist is viewed as the expert, SFBT therapists believe that families have the knowledge, resources, and strengths to find their own solutions. The therapist is there to help guide them toward those solutions. In other words, the therapist is the expert in knowing the therapeutic techniques; the family is the expert in defining their solution. In addition, because the therapist is not constructing the solution from his or her own cultural perspective, SFBT is sensitive to families' cultural identification, thus allowing cultural differences to help shape the solution.

2. *Problems and Solutions Are Not Connected.* If one can accept this assumption, issues of diagnosis and assessment become moot (although not to managed care). SFBT maintains that at one time a problem emerged due to an antecedent. It is unnecessary, however, to discover that antecedent or to help the client in gaining insight surrounding the antecedent. Rather, one can determine what clients would prefer to be doing instead of continuing the problem, and that exception becomes the solution. It is, in fact, unnecessary for the therapist to know the presenting problem; it is necessary, however, for the therapist to ask what the client would prefer to be experiencing instead of the problem.

3. *Make Unsolvable Problems Solvable.* Clients present the therapist with what, in their view, are unsolvable problems. The therapist's task, therefore, is to redefine or reframe the problem into solvable terms. Take, for example, a client saying, "I cannot be happy, because I am a depressed person." Now imagine a therapist asking, "Are there times when you are less depressed?" This represents a slight change in the definition, and this definition, unlike the client's, is amenable to change.

4. *Change Is Constant and Inevitable.* This questions the idea of a system struggling to maintain homeostasis. From this view, problems can be seen not only as necessary for change but as part of the change process. The notion is not to eliminate a problem so that the system can go back to a steady state; rather, it is to define the problem as part of the change process. This allows the system to become unstuck within the change process (problem) and prompts the system to complete the present change (solution). In other words, "Your child frowns because he or she is sad" (problem) becomes "Your child frowns as a means of communicating with you" (new definition). "How would you like your child to communicate with you?" (client as expert). "I would like my child to smile more" (solution).

5. *Only a Small Change Is Needed.* De Shazer (personal communication, September 15, 1985) uses the analogy of a person walking in the desert. He says that if the person makes a one-degree angle to the right, it will not seem like much at first, but as time passes the walker will end up miles away from the original destination. This implies that the therapist needs only to effect a small change in the system, not solve each problem individually or even attack the most serious problem, and that small change over time will snowball into dramatic changes.

6. *Keep It Brief.* Due to the focus on solutions rather than problems, the time spent in assessment, clinical diagnosis, and facilitating insight are frequently bypassed. Rather, with an emphasis on how a client would like life to be, the interaction becomes positive, motivating, and future oriented. This shift, however, from "problem talk" to "solution talk," must follow the client's lead, an issue that will be dealt with later in this chapter.

Typical Needs of Level III Families

Level III families tend to have "a structure and a style that is often perceived as working" (Weltner, 1985, p. 46). The analogy for this level is the inner architecture of the house. When one is working with the inner structure, the presence of the outer structure is assumed. In these families it is assumed that "there is sufficient strength and health to allow for resolution" (p. 47). This assumption is congruent with the use of a solution-focused approach to family treatment (Cleveland & Lindsey, 1999).

Assessment

A mother, daughter, and father present at an SFBT clinic (based on a case by Insoo Kim Berg, 1995). The clinician asks what prompted them to make an appointment. The mother explains rather emphatically that her daughter (who appears to the therapist as being in junior high) "needs to be in school." The mother further asserts that, if it were not for her daughter's boyfriend, her daughter would be in school. She concludes that her daughter "needs to be bad, because her boyfriend is bad." Rhetorically she asks, "Where has my little girl gone, and who is this stranger now living in the house?" The father and daughter sit quietly. The therapist agrees that it is difficult for mothers to lose their "little girls."

The daughter explains, "I know I should be in school." The therapist shows surprise and gives some praise that the daughter knows the importance of education. "Wow, how do you know this? Most children your age don't know this. Mom, did you know your daughter knew this?" The daughter further explains that perhaps if her mother were not so confrontational, she would feel less stressed and then be more comfortable about attending school.

The father diplomatically summarizes the interaction, suggesting, "If our daughter attended school, perhaps my wife would be less confrontational; if my wife were less confrontational, perhaps our daughter would attend school." The mother and daughter sit quietly.

The therapist asks about exceptions to the rule—times when the daughter does manage to get to school; times when the mother and daughter have a nonconfrontational conversation. Both mother and daughter agree that their relationship was nonconfrontational prior to the boyfriend. The daughter contends that she is able to get to school when there is a test. The therapist shows surprise, gives praise that she is able to do this, and asks the daughter to elaborate further.

Finally, the therapist asks each of them what is known as the miracle question; namely, "When you go to sleep tonight, imagine that a miracle happens, but because you were sleeping you were not aware of it. The miracle is that, when you wake up, you will no longer have the problem that brought you to therapy. Upon awaking, what will be the first sign to you that a miracle has happened?" For the mother, it is her daughter going to school and having meaningful conversations with her; for the daughter, it is hearing laughter in the house and everyone talking to one another in a tension-free environment; for the father, it is getting a job (he is currently unemployed and, to the therapist, looks depressed). The therapist then asks them to rate on a scale from 1 to 10, with 10 representing their miracle, how close they are to achieving that miracle.

The therapist takes a consulting break and returns to the family with a list of compliments, normalizations, reframes, and a task. The task is that each of them is to choose a special day in which they will pretend in turn that they have achieved their miracle. It will be the task of the other two to guess which day was the special day for each of them.

Theory Base and Basic Tenets

Beyond Milton Erickson

SFBT, similar to strategic (Haley, 1976), structural (Minuchin, 1974), and communication therapies (Satir, 1964), derives its roots from the teachings of Milton Erickson. All of these therapies have in common the use of joining, normalization, reframing, paradox, systems focus, nonpathologizing, a focus on small change, and a small number of sessions. SFBT, however, differs from these other therapies in two major aspects. Whereas in these other therapies the therapist is the expert who directs the client toward resolution of a problem, SFBT, on the other hand, views the client as the expert, with the therapist assisting the client in the construction of the solution (de Shazer 1985, 1988; O' Hanlon & Weiner-Davis, 1989; Walter & Pellar, 1992). In other words, clients possess all of the building materials (strengths), and the therapist first helps them decide what they want to build (solution) and then helps them to build it. De Shazer (personal communication, September 15, 1985) explains that one can follow in the footsteps of Milton Erickson or one can stand on his shoulders and see what lies beyond. In other words, one can improve on what Erickson started.

This notion of improvement lends a dynamic structure to SFBT. A group of students once asked de Shazer what they should read in order to prepare to learn SFBT. De Shazer said, "Read what I have yet to write" (personal communication, September 15, 1985). The best one can do, however, is to read what he has recently written. As an illustration, if one were to read de Shazer's earlier works (1985), in which he discusses skeleton keys, where one key (solution) can fit many different locks (problems), this would not be entirely consistent with his later works. De Shazer's (1997) more current idea, that problems and solutions are not related, may make the use of the key obsolete. In other words, SFBT is a continuously evolving treatment method in which some earlier tenets can later become obsolete.

Miracle Question Is the Heart

A tenet not likely to become obsolete is the miracle question. It could be said that the miracle question is the heart of SFBT. Remember the question: "When you go to sleep tonight, imagine that a miracle happens, but because you were sleeping you were not aware of it. The miracle is that, when you wake up, you will no longer have the problem that brought you to therapy. Upon awaking, what will be the first sign to you that a miracle has happened?"

The miracle question has strong theoretical underpinnings in the works of Polak (1973), Toffler (1974), and Frankl (1963). These researchers conclude that when people have a positive vision of their future, they will succeed, and without a vision, they will fail.

Polak sought to discover why some nations survive and others perish. He found that this had no relationship to the country's size, wealth, strategic location, or natural resources. Nations that had a powerful vision of their future (Constitution, Magna Carta, Declaration of Independence) survived; those without, perished.

Toffler's writings inspired teachers to discover which students excelled in life and which students failed. They found that high GPAs, high scores on standardized tests, and upbringing in advantaged families (with wealth, education, and resources) were not keys to success. Rather, they found that those students with positive visions of their future (strong goals for what they wanted to accomplish in their lives) were the students who would be successful.

Finally, Frankl found that prisoners who survived the concentration camp experience were not those who were the youngest and healthiest. Rather, he found it was those prisoners who had something important yet to accomplish in their lives who survived. They had positive visions of their future.

The purpose of the miracle question in SFBT is for the client, with the help of the therapist, to build a positive vision of the client's future. This is a future in which the presenting problems do not exist and in which they would derive additional positive experiences not present in their current lives. This positive vision of the future, therefore, becomes the motivating factor for clients to improve their lives. According to Polak, Toffler, and Frankl, without it, one will fail; with it, one will attain success.

Cup Is Half Full

When clients present with problems, these problems have become the major foci of their lives. They have for all intents and purposes stopped focusing on any positive experiences in their lives. SFBT therapists believe that a cup that is half empty is a cup that is half full. Clients have been focusing on the empty part; it is the work of the therapist to refocus their attention on the full part. Take for example the coping question: "Given all of these difficulties in your life, how are you able to cope?" This changes the focus from problem talk to solution talk (the positives in their lives). The formula first-session task from the case assessment is also an example of refocusing the client toward the positives (de Shazer & Molnar, 1984).

Language Constructs Reality

SFBT places a great deal of significance on the use of language. Sentences are constructed in such a way as to create an alternative future. For example, "When the problem is solved, what will you be doing differently?" *When* is used instead of *If* in order to suggest a positive future to the client. This use of language is consistent with Erickson's use of hypnotherapy. De Shazer, however, contends that this same suggestive state can be reached through the proper choice of words rather than through formal induction. In fact, de Shazer (1994) more recently wrote a book entitled *Words Were Originally Magic,* in which he described how the German philosopher Ludwig Wittgenstein (1974) unraveled Bertrand Russell's (1959) problems of philosophy (we can know nothing for sure) by focusing on words when used in context (creates meaning), and words when used out of context (creates problems), with context being the key. In other words, Russell's asking how we can "know" anything for sure takes the word *know* out of the context in which it is normally used. Wittgenstein argued that Russell makes the question unanswerable. Wittgenstein's asking if we "know" our name uses the word *know* in context and makes the question answerable. Example:

> *Therapist:* "How do things need to change in order to make you happy?"
>
> *Client:* "I can never be happy, because I am a *depressed person.*"
>
> *Therapist:* "Then what needs to happen to make you *less depressed*?"

Treatment Goals

In an ideal SFBT setting, the therapist meets with the family in front of a two-way mirror. The family signs consent forms, agreeing to be videotaped and observed by a two-member consulting team on the other side of the mirror. In the room is a telephone that can be used by the team to call the therapist with questions to ask the family. In addition, the family is informed that, after approximately 45 minutes, the therapist will leave the room, consult with the team, and return with some recommendations.

To illustrate a classical SFBT treatment process, a prototype can be illustrated in three sessions.

Session 1

The therapist is initially searching for the "customer" among the family in the session. This is the person who is most motivated toward change. Because motivation and other characteristics indicative of the client constitute 40 percent of why clients get better (Garfield, 1994), it is worth the small effort. It is, in fact, this person who will ensure that change in the system occurs. Often this is the person who initiates the phone call for treatment. It may be the person who speaks first in a session. One way to be sure is to ask the family, "Who is most concerned about resolving this problem? Who is second? Who is third?"

Next the therapist listens to the clients, using the basic counseling skills of establishing rapport, empathy, joining, reflection, and summarization, to name a few. As the therapist listens, however, he or she waits for an end to the different problems, repeats the list of all the difficulties, and then asks the client the coping question: "Given all of these problems [list them], how are you able to cope?" The purpose is to move from problem talk to solution talk. If clients change their tone to being more positive, are able to elaborate at least a few, if not several, strengths, and continue on this positive trend, the therapist has set the stage for change. If the client, however, cannot sustain solution talk and keeps going back to the problem, then the therapist goes back to the problem.

If solution talk is enabled, the therapist moves to the miracle question. When the first session is going well, much of the focus will be on the miracle. The therapist will encourage the family to expound on the miracle. For example, "After the miracle happens, what will you notice first? What will you notice next? What will your spouse notice?"

Once the miracle question is elaborated, the therapist asks the scaling question to gauge how close they are to achieving their miracle. If a client says they are at a 5, the therapist expresses praise in that they are halfway there. Next the therapist asks what has to happen for them to move from a 5 to a 6. If the client says that is too far a move, the therapist asks about moving from a 5 to a 5.1.

Finally, the therapist takes a consulting break, whether he or she has a team behind the two-way mirror or not, and comes back with a prescription (recommendation). The therapist starts with compliments, normalizations, and reframes. The formula first-session task is then prescribed: "When people enter therapy, they begin to change. There are things in your life, however, that you do not want to change because they are positive. So, between now and the next time we meet, pay attention to those positive things in your life, and we will discuss them next week."

Session 2

The therapist begins by repeating the first-session task and asking the clients what they found. When the clients mention positive changes, the therapist amplifies (encourages the clients to elaborate) these changes. For example, if the clients say they went to a movie, the therapist asks, "Is this a new behavior? How do you explain it? How were you able to do it? How can you continue to keep it happening?" If the clients say nothing is positive and puzzled prompting does not help ("Nothing!?" "Are you sure!?"), the therapist meticulously unravels every detail of the family's activities that occurred since leaving the therapist's office the week before. Positive changes will surface.

Assuming that this session focused primarily on positive changes, the therapist again asks the scaling question, comparing it to last week's. It usually goes up; at the worst, it stays the same. If it were to go down, the therapist would ask, "What did you do to keep it from going further down?"

Finally, the therapist takes a consulting break. When the therapist returns, the family is again given compliments, normalizations, and reframes. The formula second-session task is then prescribed: "Progress is often two steps forward and one step back. If you find yourself taking a step back this week, pay attention to what you do to keep moving forward again."

Session 3

The therapist begins by repeating the second-session task. If there were steps back, the therapist asks, "What did you do to move forward again? How were you able to do this? It must have been difficult, but somehow you were able to do it. How will you continue to do this in the future?" In this fashion, the therapist continues to address all of the steps back, one step at a time. For issues where steps back were not taken, or if no steps back were taken, the therapist asks how they were able not to take a step back. It may be possible to close the case at this time or at least extend the time of the next visit.

Epilogue

As a final note, this is a prototypical treatment process. If clients do not feel bad about what is happening in their lives, it is doubtful that they will be in therapy. If the therapist is not sensitive and empathetic to the client's feelings, the client will not return. Although SFBT therapists do not encourage problem talk ("Tell me more about how the problem is interfering with your life.") and elaboration of feelings ("Tell me more about how that made you feel."), it is a serious mistake to move from problem talk to solution talk until the client is ready. If these are feelings they have never expressed or stories they have never told, the SFBT does not move to solution talk until the client is ready. These are probably the most common reasons for a necessary and appropriate increase in sessions.

Application

Using this prototypical treatment process, this process can be customized for the previous family case assessment.

Session 1

In recalling the family case assessment, "How old is the daughter? What grade is she in at school? How many days a week does she miss school? How long have the parents been married? How long has the father been unemployed?" Some might argue that, for a family case assessment, the SFBT therapist missed a lot of critical information. However, if the family is the expert, how does it help the family if the therapist asks questions to which the family already knows the answers? In addition, because problems and solutions are not connected, why ask for information that is not relevant to the solution? These last two questions are consistent with an assessment by an SFBT therapist.

What the therapist does instead is attempt to find the customer. The customer is the person most concerned about the problem. It stands to reason, therefore, that the customer is the most motivated to solve the problem. The therapist helps join with the mother by allowing her to talk first, using her language ("little girl") and normalizing the situation ("difficult for mothers to lose their 'little girls' "). The normalization also begins to help make the unsolvable problem ("Where has my little girl gone?") a solvable problem (she is growing up). As long as the therapist joins with the mother, the mother will keep the family in therapy until it is mutually agreed to terminate.

After the mother has explained the situation, the daughter agrees that she should be in school. Because this is a solution introduced by the mother, the therapist encourages the daughter to discuss this further. In addition, the therapist wants the mother to hear why the daughter thinks she should be in school and the fact that the mother and daughter agree. Already the family has introduced some material that will become compliments during the recommendation or prescription segment. First, both the mother and the daughter agree on something. Second, the daughter is smart enough to realize that school is important. Third, the parents have raised an intelligent daughter.

When the father is asked for his perspective, he is able to briefly summarize the situation between the mother and the daughter. His awareness and diplomacy will also be material for compliments during the prescription segment.

Next the therapist asks about exceptions to the rule—times in the past or in the present when these problems did not exist or were easily solved. This is a source of solutions. It may be discovered that the family had solutions in the past but has forgotten them. Because the family is the expert, the therapist is using the resources of the family. In addition, exceptions to the rule tell the family how the circumstances need to be different in order for the solution to emerge (goes to school when she has a test). The daughter's ability to understand the importance of taking tests can also lead to a compliment during the prescription segment.

Because the family members are able to talk about positives in their lives and to voice positive things about one another, the therapist can introduce the miracle question. If the members reject the question ("Miracles don't happen." "I cannot think of anything."), then it may be that the question was asked too soon. The therapist needs to continue with problem talk. Another explanation is that a client does not entertain the possibility of miracles. In that case, the therapist could ask, "If you were very lucky" or "If you won the lottery," for example. Generally, the client's mood state is perhaps the best indicator of when it is time to ask the miracle question. In this case assessment, the family members are able to elaborate their miracle. If there are similarities in their miracles (the daughter's hearing laughter), this becomes a possible compliment for the prescription section.

To determine how close family members are to achieving their miracle, a scaling question is asked. If a family member says they are at a 5, the therapist expresses praise in that they are halfway there (all the numbers can be defined in a positive way). Even at a 1 (although there are techniques for never getting a 1 as a response), the clients can be told that they are on track toward their miracle or that they are in the game. Next, the therapist asks what has to happen for them to move from a 5 to a 6. If the clients say that is too far a move, the therapist asks about moving from a 5 to a 5.1. In the case assessment, the mother says she is at a 5, so the therapist expresses encouragement that the mother is halfway to her miracle; the daughter is at a 6, so the therapist expresses encouragement that she is over halfway there; the father is at a 5, so he is also encouraged. All of these rankings, of course, provide further material for the prescription section.

Finally, the therapist takes a consulting break, meets with the team to write a prescription, and then returns to the family to administer the prescription. This break is consistent with the suggestible state achieved in Ericksonian hypnotherapy. When the therapist leaves the room, the family is wondering what the therapist and the consulting team will have to say on their return. De Shazer (1985) believes that this puts the family in a susceptible state, thus making them more receptive to the prescription. Keeping in mind the case assessment, the prescription may sound like what follows (except that the client's names would be used).

Prescription

"Mother, the team agrees with you that it is difficult for a parent to see a daughter grow up and wonder where their little girl has gone. A child who was once easy to talk with becomes a daughter who now seems like a stranger. This must be very hard for you. The team is impressed with your hard effort and dedication to deal with this situation.

"Daughter, the team sees your difficulty in juggling school, family responsibilities, and a social life. It seems early for someone your age to try to do this on your own, but given how bright you are and your potential, we can see why you are trying. It seems that you must have inherited your hard effort and dedication from your mother.

"Father, your diplomatic way of looking at the situation between your wife and daughter is impressive. You manage to stay neutral, and by doing so, you may become the diplomat between your wife and daughter.

"Parents, the team congratulates you on raising such an intelligent daughter. She is aware of the importance of school. Few children her age are intelligent enough to understand how important school is to their future.

"All of you have formed miracles that consider not only your own happiness but the happiness of the other family members. Mother, your daughter's going to school; daughter, hearing laughter in the house; father, obtaining a job. All of these situations bring happiness to your family. In addition, all of you are already halfway or more to achieving your miracle. Although achieving miracles is not easy, this family possesses the capacity for hard work and the dedication that are needed to achieve miracles.

"Finally, we want to give each of you a homework assignment. Each of you chooses a special day in which you will pretend that you have moved up your scale one point. For mother and father, that means you have moved from a 5 to a 6; for daughter, that means you have moved from a 6 to a 7. You cannot tell the other two what day you have chosen as your special day. It will be the additional task of the other two to guess which day you chose as your special day."

Session 2

The therapist enters the room, sits down, and notices that the family members are smiling. The mother is dressed in more relaxed clothing than in the last session (jeans rather than suit); the daughter and husband are dressed more neatly (new jeans rather than ripped jeans).

The therapist starts by asking about the task. The mother begins by explaining how she got up in the morning, went to the kitchen to make breakfast, and had an enjoyable conversation with her husband and daughter, who in reality were still in bed. When the daughter came home late, she made believe that her daughter and boyfriend were out buying her a gift, and it caused them to be late. When she watched a movie, she told her daughter and husband all about it as if they were interested. The mother said that it was fun. The therapist praised the mother for her creativity. The daughter and father told similar stories, with the father "cracking jokes" and making the mother and daughter laugh (for real, not pretend). Not surprisingly, they were able to identify each family member's special day.

The mother and father went on a date that included dinner and a movie. The daughter smiled, turning to look at both of them, as they told their story. The therapist showed encouragement and asked, "Is that different for the two of you to go on a date? What did you both do to make it happen? How will you continue to keep it happening in the future?" After exhausting all the material regarding the date, the therapist asked, "Are there other positive changes that occurred in the past week?"

The daughter smiles and explains that she has gone to school every day. The therapist gives encouragement and asks, "Wow, how were you able to do that?" The daughter explains that she knows the importance of school.

The father explains that he is willing to take a temporary or part-time job until something better comes along. The therapist gives encouragement and asks, "Is that new for you? Your willingness to look for a part-time job until a full-time job comes along?" He states that, yes, it is new for him.

Finally, the therapist asks them to remember when they rated how close they were to achieving a miracle on a scale from 1 to 10. The therapist then says to the mother, "Last week you were at a 5—more than halfway to achieving your miracle. Where are you now?" The mother says that she is at a 6. The therapist gives encouragement, asks the father and daughter the same question, and finds that each has moved up their scales by one point.

Epilogue

The family was complimented and given the formula second-session task, regarding progress being two steps forward and one step back. At session 3 they continued to show improvement (school attendance, conversations, dates), so a fourth session was scheduled for two weeks later, at which time the therapy ended.

Application to Spirituality

Spirituality, morality, ethics, and *religion* commonly have different definitions, depending on who is using the word. In SFBT, these concepts become important to therapy only if they are important to the client. Because the therapist is attempting to learn the culture, the language, and the clients' vision of a positive future, the therapist learns the clients' view of these concepts only if the clients believe that they are necessary for a positive solution.

As an example, a client with HIV (the virus that can lead to AIDS) said, "I am so angry that I am going to f**k everyone at the bar." The client has introduced an ethical, moral, religious, or spiritual issue, depending on the client's definition. It relates to the "cup half empty" approach. The cup half empty for this client is to use his disease to harm others; the cup half full is to use his disease to help others. The SFBT therapist's response was "And how will this help you?" The client looked puzzled and said, "Well, it won't help me." This nonconfrontational stance tends to puzzle the client, who may have instead expected the therapist to take a confrontational posture. With nothing to fuel the anger, the anger dissipates. Seeing the cup half full and being nonconfrontational, therefore, are ways to deal with spiritual issues.

In a similar case, another client with HIV who was asked by the therapist, "And how will this help you?" instead replied, "I'll feel better." The therapist then asked, "When will you stop feeling better?" (future orientation). The client looked puzzled and said, "When I feel guilty for what I did." The therapist replied, "So what could you do instead—that, instead of making you feel guilty, it 'might' make you feel proud? And it would keep you feeling better?" The client said, "Help them not to make the same mistake that I did." *Might* is used as a hedging word, in order to suggest the word *proud* to the client, because the client had not used the word. It makes the client more amenable to the word. This future orientation is leading toward the miracle question, in which spiritual issues may play a part in the miracle construction.

Later, both clients spoke of getting involved in social change as a way of helping others affected by HIV and AIDS ("How will this help you?" became "How will this help others?"). The therapist complimented the clients on their evolving "social consciousness." One client responded that he had never considered himself "religious" (which he defined as following the teachings of an organized religion) but did consider himself "spiritual" (he defined this as believing that there is something out there greater than humanity). The therapist used this to compliment the client in the delivery of the prescription, stating, "As you find your body becoming less healthy, you will find your mind, on the other hand, becoming more healthy. Or, as you would say, more 'spiritual.' " (Both the therapist and the client were aware of the effect of the virus on the brain; therefore, "healthy mind" was not misconstrued to mean that the virus would leave the brain.)

This movement from expressing the desire to harm others toward a spiritual desire to help others assisted these clients in finding meaning in their lives. This meaning helped them deal with end-of-life issues.

Interventions

Joining

This is basically the therapist's means of establishing rapport with the family. Initially, the SFBT finds the customer and ensures that the therapist joins with the customer. Sometimes small talk is engaged in before the session begins, as a way of breaking down formality and giving an indirect compliment. For example, "People sometimes have difficulty finding us. Did you find our location OK?" "It is often difficult to park around here. Were you able to find a spot OK?" Using the client's language (actual phrases that they use) is critical to joining with the family. When the family hears their words, they know you are listening. An SFBT therapist takes the stance of being nonconfrontational. Therapists may say that they are confused or puzzled by some information that seems inconsistent, but an SFBT therapist never confronts. Finally, discarding the notion that clients "resist" (de Shazer, 1984) helps the therapist join with the clients. Berg (1995) states that even clients labeled as "involuntary" do not resist therapy. She contends that if they were "resisting" they would not be sitting in your office.

Normalizing

For clients, problems are issues that are not normal. It stands to reason, therefore, that if the therapist can suggest to the clients that the issue is normal, by definition it will cease to be a problem. For example, "How do you know this is rebellious behavior, and not just being a teenager?" Rebellious behavior is a problem; acting like a teenager is normal behavior.

Circular Question

People may act based on what they believe others think, rather than on what others are actually thinking. To unravel this mystery, an SFBT therapist might ask, "What do you think your mother thinks about your missing school?" The answer to this question helps the mother see how the daughter believes she views the situation. In our family case assessment, if the daughter were to say that she believes her mother sees her as stupid, this will likely lead to a compliment from the mother regarding the daughter's intelligence. It also helps to clear misunderstandings. A further level of difficulty to this type of questioning would be, "What do you think your mother thinks *you* think about your missing school?" In essence, these types of questions help members understand how it is that other family members act in certain ways.

Coping Question

This question helps the family move from problem talk to solution talk. At a point in the session when it seems that the client has described all of his or her problems, this question can be used—basically, "Given all of these problems [list all of them], how are you able to cope?" If the client is able to mention positive aspects and is able to sustain this positive direction, he or she is becoming ready for the miracle question. If, on the other hand, the client has little to say or says some positives but keeps going back to the problems, then the therapist needs to continue to listen to the problems until the client is ready. It may be that positives cannot be discussed until the second session. When the therapist gives the task, it should be directed toward looking for positives (formula first-session task). This sets the stage for asking the miracle question in session 2.

Miracle Question

This question, as stated earlier, provides the client with a positive vision of the future. This vision becomes a motivating factor and a description of when therapy has been successful (when the miracle is reached or the family agrees that they are close enough). One serious caution regarding the miracle question is that it must deal with the possible, never the improbable. For example, you would not say to an AIDS patient that the miracle is that he or she will no longer have AIDS. You would not say to a person in a wheelchair that the miracle is that he or she will be able to walk. Instead, you would say to each of these individuals that the miracle is that he or she will be able to *cope* with AIDS or *cope* with being in a wheelchair.

Scaling Question

This question is used to gauge a baseline and measure progress in a behavior, goal, or construct—essentially, "On a scale from 1 to 10, with 1 being that you are so depressed you can't even leave your house, given that you are at least at a 2 and that 10 would be that you are so happy that you don't need to see me anymore, how would you rate your level of happiness?" This example includes a means of not having the client say they are at a 1, and it changes the scale to one of happiness, which may not work for all clients (those who believe that they can never be happy). If a client says he or she is at a 1, you can mention how he or she is on the track to success or in the game for achieving happiness, for example. At 2, they are almost halfway to being halfway there; at 3 they are halfway to being halfway there; at 4 they are almost halfway there; at 5 they are halfway there; at 6 they are over halfway there; and so forth. Obviously, other comments can be made to represent the numbers. When a client gives a number on the scale, the therapist then asks what has to happen to move up one number. If a whole number is too large a move for the client, decimal places can be used (from a 5 to a 5.1). You will get an answer.

Exceptions to the Rule

This is a team search between the therapist and the client to discover solutions to a problem that either the client forgot or never considered using for a different problem. For example, "Was there a time in your life when this problem did not occur? When was the last time the problem did not happen? In the time that the problem has surfaced, has there been a time when you have been able to stop the problem from occurring? Have you had problems in the past that were similar to this problem? How were you able to stop those problems from happening?"

Formula Tasks

These are the tasks that are suggested at the end of an SFBT session as the final part of the prescription. The first session task tends to be, "When people enter therapy, they begin to change. There are things in your life, however, that you do not want to change because they are positive. So, between now and the next time we meet, pay attention to those positive things in your life, and we will discuss them next week." Other first-session tasks might include "Do not change anything" or "Do something different." All of these tasks accept the assumption that the client is the expert and therefore can find a solution to the problem. The traditional task encourages the family to make changes. "Do not change anything" is more vague and suggests that they can keep it from getting worse and therefore can at some point make it better. "Do something different" encourages the family to find a solution. Whatever it is that they do differently may in fact resolve the problem.

The second session task tends to be "Progress is often two steps forward and one step back. If you find yourself taking a step back this week, pay attention to what you do to keep moving forward again." Another possibility is "Pay attention to what you do when you overcome the urge to [engage in that behavior]." Both of these tasks are encouraging the client to pay close attention to the solution. The first option provides the additional value of normalizing or reframing relapse. If there is a step back, some families disregard any progress made at that point, thinking, "It's right back to the way it used to be." By acknowledging that we do take steps back, this is reframed as part of progress and as an acceptable route toward progress. In addition, sometimes families progress quickly, and members worry or express a fear of relapsing. This task helps them. As a variation on this task, the therapist may suggest that the family take a step back in the next week. This becomes a no-lose situation. If they take a step back, they are following the normal route toward progress; if they do not take a step back, that is certainly positive.

Sometimes when a family is asked to take a step back, they will argue with the therapist, adamantly stating that they refuse to take a step back. That is certainly a positive sign.

Hypnotic Situations

These are situations that make the family more susceptible to what the therapist suggests. Previously it was discussed how the consultation break serves to make the family more susceptible to the prescription—namely, they are wondering what the team has to say. During the compliment segment of the prescription, the therapist attempts to produce a "yes set." If the family nods and agrees to several compliments in a row, they are more likely to agree to the statement that follows. This may be a statement that the family has struggled to agree on during the session— for example, "Your daughter wants to go to school." Finally, the therapist may word a sentence in such a way that it comes out as a command rather than a suggestion—for example, "You may find that, as you look for exceptions, that you,

Matt, stop overeating, you will make the right choices for yourself." The italicized words are said as a statement while looking directly at the client. The sentence is clumsy and another sentence follows, so the statement (hypnotic suggestion) is more hidden to the client.

Hedging Words

Berg and DeJong (1996) suggest using "hedging" words. They contend that using words such as *seems, might,* or *perhaps* seed suggestions in one's mind that later grow to fruitful solutions. For example, "It seems that perhaps you might change too fast." Hedging words also allow the SFBT therapist to "back off" if the client rejects the suggestion. This allows the client to maintain their position as expert and keeps the therapist from creating a milieu of resistance.

The Team

When one has the luxury of working with a team, they become an invaluable source of intervention material. They may keep track of the client's pet phrases, possible compliments, and suggestions for a task. In addition, they can call you when you are meeting with a family and offer suggestions for change. Finally, they can allow the therapist to join with the family against the team—for example, "I agree with you. You should not take a step back. But the team thinks that you should." In this way the team can also parallel the struggles that the family is experiencing regarding the possibility of relapse.

Evaluation

Gingerich and Eisengart (2000) reviewed all of the controlled outcome studies on SFBT ($N = 15$) up to and including 1999. Although all of these 15 studies met criteria for controlled outcomes, 5 studies were determined to be superior to the other 10 in terms of degree of experimental control. Those 5 studies will be reported here.

Sundstrom (1993) randomly assigned 40 female college students who were suffering from depression to one of two groups: SFBT group ($N = 20$) or interpersonal psychotherapy for depression group (ITP; $N = 20$). Sundstrom found a statistically significant treatment effect for both groups from pre to post. Sunstrom did not, however, find any differences between groups. It was concluded, therefore, that SFBT is as effective as a well-established treatment for depression (ITP), but not superior to that treatment.

Zimmerman, Jacobsen, MacIntyre, and Watson (1996) compared 30 parents in an SFBT parenting group to 12 parents on a waiting list. Results indicated that there were more statistically significant differences in the SFBT group compared to the waiting-list group—namely, the SFBT group improved on parenting skills.

Cockburn, Thomas, and Cockburn (1997) randomly assigned 48 orthopedic patients to one of four groups: groups 1 and 3 were SFBT plus standard rehabilitation; groups 2 and 4 standard rehabilitation only. Results indicated that there were statistically significant differences between the two SFBT groups and the two comparison groups. The SFBT groups improved on their ability to cope with their disability. In addition, and more importantly, the SFBT groups were able to return to work in a shorter period of time.

Lindforss and Magnusson (1997) randomly assigned 60 serious criminals with high recidivism rates to one of two groups: an SFBT group ($N = 30$) or a control group ($N = 30$). Comparing the two groups on recidivism rates, results indicated that the SFBT group had a lower recidivism rate compared to the control group (statistically significant), in addition to less serious offenses and shorter sentences for the SFBT reoffending prisoners compared to the control reoffending prisoners.

Seagram (1997) matched 40 adolescent offenders on severity of antisocial behaviors to form two groups: an SFBT group ($N = 21$) and a standard institutional care group ($N = 19$). Seagram reported several statistically significant findings for the SFBT group compared to the comparison group—namely, the SFBT group improved in prosocial behaviors. Improvements, however, were only modest.

More recent studies on the effectiveness of SFBT have included children (Corcoran & Stephenson, 2000; Franklin, Biever, Moore, Clemons, & Scamardo, 2001), the elderly (Dahl, Bathel, & Carreon, 2000), married couples (Nelson & Kelley, 2001; Pomeroy, Green, & Van Laningham, 2002), and substance-abuse users (Molt & Gysin, 2003).

Corcoran and Stephenson used SFBT with 136 children, aged 5 to 17, who were referred for classroom behavioral problems. Results indicated positive changes on the Conners' Parent Rating Scale and mixed results on the Feelings, Attitudes, and Behaviors Scale for children. Franklin et al. (2001) obtained similar results with 7 children, aged 10 to 13, who were diagnosed with learning disabilities and classroom behavioral problems. Employing single system design techniques, results indicated positive changes on a range of behavioral problems measured by Conners' Teacher Rating Scales.

Dahl et al. (2000) used SFBT with 74 patients, aged 65 to 89, who were suffering from depression, anxiety, and marital problems. Results indicated positive outcomes on self-rating scores, motivational scores, Global Assessment of Functioning scale (GAF), and patient satisfaction.

Pomeroy et al. (2002) used SFBT with 12 HIV/AIDS, serodiscordant, heterosexual couples. Results indicated positive outcomes for increased marital satisfaction and decreased depression and anxiety. Nelson and Kelley (2001) obtained similar results with 5 couples (10 participants) who were attending group therapy. Employing single system design techniques, results indicated positive outcomes for increased marital satisfaction and goal attainment for 8 of the 10 participants.

Mott and Gysin (2003) transformed a residential substance abuse treatment center from a problem-focused approach to a solution-focused approach. Results indicated improved quality and effectiveness of substance-abuse treatment and improved staff morale.

Applications to Families on Levels I, II, and IV

Weltner's (1985) analogy for the issues of those families who might be considered at Level I is the basement of a house. These issues are life-and-death issues, such as housing and health care needs, and sufficient parenting to nurture and protect the family. The goal for intervention is to add resources. The Level II analogy is the framing and roof and refers to authority and limits within the family unit. At Level IV, the goal is "the development of an inner 'richness'—insight, more sensitive awareness of the relational world, an understanding of legacies and heritage" (p. 47). The utility of this approach in dealing with these issues has not been established. It is probable that this approach is more effectively used with issues at Level III than with those at Levels II and IV (Cleveland & Lindsey, 1999).

Ethical Challenges

Social work ethics speak to the elimination of oppression, sensitivity to human diversity, empowerment, confidentiality, and a strengths perspective, to name a few. When the therapist is the "expert," they use their cultural lens to assess, diagnose, and treat the problem; when the client is the "expert," these issues are not relevant to helping the client.

When the practitioner takes the stance of not being the expert or "not knowing," they put the client in the position of being the "expert." This does not mean an expert with regard to therapy, but rather an expert with regard to their contextual framework shaped by their human characteristics. It more closely resembles that of an anthropologist immersing themselves in a culture; that is, the therapist, from a position of "not knowing," must learn the solution from the client. This is accomplished through asking the right questions (i.e., through exception finding, miracle, scaling); that is, the practitioner is "expert" in asking the right questions, following the right leads (toward strengths), and ignoring the wrong leads (toward problems).

Social workers from a traditional perspective argue that ethically "one size does not fit all." Through their lens, they are correct. If the therapist is "expert," they must learn as many therapies and aspects of human diversity as possible to be effective. This could be quite a challenge. Social workers from a SFBT perspective, on the other hand, argue that you must learn the contextual framework of each client system you are seeing in therapy in order to be effective. After all, even two clients from the same culture are not likely to share the same contextual situation.

Finally, this traditional perspective of "one size does not fit all" argues that the practitioner can alter their treatment to be culturally sensitive, much as a tailor would alter a suit. SFBT, on the other hand, argues that we must be the tailor that asks the client, "What would you like to have made? What material shall we use? I will need to take your measurements." It is the shift from therapist as expert to client as expert that makes this situation possible. That shift, however, is a shift in paradigm.

Summary

Solution-focused brief therapy (SFBT) stands in contrast to mainstream approaches, with its rejection of insight, problem-focused, detailed assessments, and expert stance. Rather, SFBT learns the language, culture, and expertise of the clients in order to assist them in constructing a positive vision of their future. Once this vision is formed, it becomes the task of the therapist to help lead the clients toward that vision from a stance that is one step behind. SFBT is more than the sum of its techniques. Once you look through SFBT lenses and see that resistance does not exist, that the cup is always half full, and that change is constant, you can never see the world as it used to be. The significance of this change is that you do not use SFBT, you become SFBT. The caution, however, is not to accept SFBT until you are convinced that it is right for you.

Discussion Questions

1. How can treatment be successful if the therapist does not know what the problem is that brought the family to therapy?

2. Because we do not have a clinical diagnosis for "normal," how do we know when a family no longer needs therapy?

3. How does language change perception?

4. How does a belief that resistance does not exist help the family?

5. How does SFBT respect cultural differences?

Internet Resources

Brief Family Therapy Center, www.brief-therapy.org
   This is the official site of SFBT, operated by Steve de Shazer and Insoo Berg in Milwaukee, Wisconsin. It is a direct source of resources, seminars, and consulting services from de Shazer and Berg.
Brief Therapy Institute of Sydney, www.brieftherapysydney.com.au
   This is the most comprehensive source for SFBT sites. This information is consistent with the information in this chapter and the work of de Shazer and Berg.
Bill O' Hanlon, http://brieftherapy.com
   One of the most creative innovators of the SFBT approach, Mr. O'Hanlon is known for his engaging and entertaining workshop style. He also offers free handouts for those wanting to learn more about the approach.

Don Jackson's Perspective, www.brieftherapynetwork.com/how-to.html

Michele Weiner-Davis, www.weiner-davis.com

> Directly trained by de Shazer and Berg in the early '80s, Weiner-Davis has created a significant niche by her application of SFBT to marital therapy. She remains one of the most skilled clinicians in the SFBT technique.

Wally J. Gingerich, Ph.D., www.gingerich.net

> A professor of social work who offers courses in SFBT, Gingerich is a strong proponent of evidence-based practice. If empirical support of the model interests you, this is where you will find the most comprehensive evidence of the effectiveness of SFBT.

Suggested Readings

DeJong, P., & Berg, I. K. (2002). *Interviewing for solutions* (2nd ed.). Belmont, CA: Brooks/Cole.

> Excellent resource for teaching solution-focused brief therapy to practitioners. Particularly valuable because the authors use the model with clients who are generally considered to be multiproblem, difficult, and unmotivated. In addition, the book has a companion student workbook and an instructor's manual (sold separately).

de Shazer, S. (1997). *Putting difference to work.* New York: Norton.

> As with any of de Shazer's books, these are more for the theoretician than for the clinician. This one is selected only because it is more recent than the others. Again, if you are interested in the theory of solution-focused brief therapy, any of de Shazer's books would be the logical choice.

Miller, G. (1997). *Becoming miracle workers: Language and meaning in brief therapy.* New York: Norton.

> Written by an ethnomethodologist who for 12 years sat behind a team that sat behind the mirror watching the therapist. A clinician will see therapy through different eyes; but, be warned, it is possible that one will never look at therapy the same way again.

Walter, J. L., & Pellar, J. E. (1992). *Becoming solution-focused in brief therapy.* New York: Brunner/Mazel.

> If one is looking for an SFBT primer, this is it. The authors use common cases, explain the model clearly, and offer step-by-step instructions on how to do it.

References

Berg, I. K. (1995). *I'd hear laughter* [Film]. (Available from Brief Family Therapy Center, P. O. Box 13736, Milwaukee, WI 53213–0736).

Berg, I. K., & DeJong, P. (1996). Solution-building conversations: Co-constructing a sense of competence with clients. *Families in Society, 77,* 376–391.

Cleveland, P. H., & Lindsey, E. W. (1999). Solution-focused family interventions. In A. C. Kilpatrick & T. P. Holland (Eds.), *Working with families: An integrative model by level of need* (2nd ed., pp. 139–154). Boston, MA: Allyn and Bacon.

Cockburn, J. T., Thomas, F. N., & Cockburn, O. J. (1997). Solution-focused therapy and psychosocial adjustment to orthopedic rehabilitation in a work hardening program. *Journal of Occupational Rehabilitation, 7*(2), 97–106.

Corcoran, J., & Stephenson, M. (2000). The effectiveness of solution-focused therapy with child behavioral problems: A preliminary report. *Families in Society, 81*(5), 468–474.

Dahl, R., Bathel, D., & Carreon, C. (2000). The use of solution-focused therapy with an elderly population. *Journal of Systemic Therapies, 19*(4), 45–55.

de Shazer, S. (1984). The death of resistance. *Family Process, 23,* 11–17.

de Shazer, S. (1985). *Keys to solution in brief therapy.* New York: Norton.

de Shazer, S. (1988). *Clues: Investigating solutions in brief therapy.* New York: Norton.

de Shazer, S. (1994). *Words were originally magic.* New York: Norton.

de Shazer, S. (1997). *Putting difference to work.* New York: Norton.

de Shazer, S., Berg, I. K., Lipchik, E., Nunnally, E., Molnar, A., Gingerich, E., & Weiner-Davis, M. (1986). Brief treatment: Focused solution development. *Family Process, 25,* 207–222.

de Shazer, S., & Molnar, A. (1984). Four useful interventions in brief family treatment. *Journal of Marital and Family Treatment, 10*(3), 297–304.

Frankl, V. E. (1963). *Man's search for meaning.* Boston: Beacon Press.

Franklin, C., Biever, J., Moore, K., Clemons, D., & Scamardo, M. (2001). The effectiveness of solution-focused therapy with children in a school setting. *Research on Social Work Practice, 11*(4), 411–434.

Garfield, S. L. (1994). Research on client variables in psychotherapy. In A. E. Bergin & S. L. Garfield (Eds.), *Handbook of psychotherapy and behavior change* (4th ed., pp. 190–228). New York: Wiley.

Gingerich, W. J., & Eisengart, S. (2000). Solution-focused brief therapy: A review of the outcome research. *Family Process, 39*(4), 477–498.

Haley, J. (1976). *Problem solving therapies.* New York: Grune & Stratton.

Lindforss, L., & Magnusson, D. (1997). Solution-focused therapy in prison. *Contemporary Family Therapy, 19,* 89–103.

Minuchin, S. (1974). *Families and family therapy.* Cambridge, MA: Harvard University Press.

Mott, S., & Gysin, T. (2003). Postmodern ideas in substance abuse treatment. *Journal of Social Work Practice in the Addictions, 3*(3), 3–19.

Nelson, T. S., & Kelley, L. (2001). Solution-focused couples group. *Journal of Systemic Therapies, 20*(4), 47–66.

O'Hanlon, W. H., & Weiner-Davis, M. (1989). *In search of solutions.* New York: Norton.

Polak, F. (1973). *The image of the future.* San Francisco: Jossey-Bass.

Pomeroy, E. C., Green, D. L., & Van Laningham, L. (2002). Couples who care: The effectiveness of a psychoeducational group intervention for HIV serodiscordant couples. *Research on Social Work Practice, 12*(2), 238–252.

Russell, B. (1959). *The problems of philosophy.* Oxford: Oxford University Press.

Satir, V. (1964). *Conjoint family therapy.* Palo Alto, CA: Science and Behavior.

Seagram, B. C. (1997). *The efficacy of solution-focused therapy with young offenders.* Unpublished doctoral dissertation. York University, North York, Ontario, Canada.

Sundstrom, S. M. (1993). *Single-session psychotherapy for depression: Is it better to focus on problems or solutions?* Unpublished doctoral dissertation. Iowa State University, Ames.

Toffler, A. (1974). *Learning for tomorrow: The role of the future in education.* New York: Random House.

Walter, J. L., & Pellar, J. E. (1992). *Becoming solution-focused in brief therapy.* New York: Brunner/Mazel.

Weltner, J. (1985). Matchmaking: Choosing the appropriate treatment for families at various levels of pathology. In M. Marikin & S. Koman (Eds.), *Handbook of adolescents and family treatment.* New York: Gardner Press.

Wittgenstein, L. (1974). *Philosophical investigations.* Oxford: Basil Blackwell.

Zimmerman, T. S., Jacobsen, R. B., MacIntyre, M., & Watson, C. (1996). Solution-focused parenting groups: An empirical study. *Journal of Systemic Therapies, 15*(4), 12–25.

10

Family Systems Theory

Joseph Walsh, Ph.D.

Since its introduction in the 1960s and 1970s, family systems theory has thrived as an influential and widely utilized theory of family assessment and intervention. The theory provides a comprehensive conceptual framework for understanding how emotional ties within families of origin (including extended family members) influence the lives of individuals in ways they often fail to appreciate and may tend to minimize. The theory is sometimes called family emotional systems theory to underscore this point and to distinguish it from the generic family systems term. This theory is unique in its attention to multigenerational family processes and also in its prescriptions for working with individuals in a family context (Bowen, 1978; Kerr & Bowen, 1988).

Murray Bowen, creator of the theory, was trained as a psychoanalyst. This helps to explain why family systems theory has implications for the treatment of individuals as well as families. The nature of healthy human functioning in the theory includes the acquisition of a balance of emotion and reason. The concept of differentiation is used to characterize one's ability to achieve this balance. The concept also describes one's ability to function effectively both apart from and within the family of origin. Differentiation is made possible by a facilitative family environment in which the person can establish an identity related to, but also separate from, the identity of the nuclear family.

Within most cultures of American society, people typically accelerate the processes of physically and emotionally separating from their family of origin during late adolescence. This is a major life transition for those who leave and for those who stay behind. According to family systems theory, people who have achieved differentiation will be successful in this transition, and those who have not (or are enmeshed) will have difficulty. One's capacity to develop positive new relationships in adulthood is affected by learned patterns of managing family-of-origin relationships. In every case, positive or negative, the influence of the family is pervasive throughout life.

Needs Presented by Level III Families

As discussed in Chapter 1, families come to the attention of clinical practitioners for a variety of reasons. Their concerns may be related to a lack of material resources, family crisis or disorganization, relationship difficulties, or a desire for greater self-actualization. The concepts from family systems theory may be useful to the practitioner with families at *all* levels of need as a means of assessing the nature of family interactions. Understanding the quality of family relationships, a hallmark of this theory, may be significant in treatment planning regardless of the family's specific needs. The intervention strategies suggested by family systems theory, however, are not appropriate for all problem situations.

Family systems interventions are generally appropriate when the focus will be on the quality of nuclear or extended family interpersonal processes and on the desire for one or more family members to become more differentiated. Level III families often appear to be functioning well to the outside observer. It is their interpersonal lives, including issues of boundaries, enmeshment, and emotional distance, that are the sources of their problems. These processes may be evidenced in a variety of presenting problems that represent too much or too little investment of some members in family activities, relationships, and well-being. The practitioner will require some structural stability in the family to help members become aware of their patterns of behavior that may be contributing to problem situations.

Titelman (1998) edited a book that includes examples of a range of problems for which family systems interventions may be appropriate. These include family problems related to marital fusion, emotional dysfunction in children, a child with a medical problem, college students with adjustment problems, concerns about elderly members, depression, phobias and obsessive compulsive disorder, alcoholism, incest, divorce, and remarriage. More recently the theory and its interventions have been found useful for issues encountered in homelessness (Hertlein & Killmer, 2004), couples where battering has occurred (Stith, McCollum, Rosen, & Locke, 2003), and increasing the effectiveness of high school principals (Gottlieb, 2001).

Assessment

What follows are the major concepts of family systems theory that are central to the process of assessment. These are drawn primarily from Bowen (1978).

The Multigenerational Perspective

One of Bowen's greatest contributions to the field of family theory was his principle that individual personalities and patterns of interaction among family members have their origins in previous generations. Additionally, he demonstrated that extended family relationships might be as important to personal development as nuclear family relationships. In these ways Bowen foreshadowed recent developments in the field of family therapy, of moving beyond the nuclear family unit into a consideration of other influences on family life.

Bowen recommended a three-generation assessment of families, partly because of realistic limits on the availability of information and also because of his early career work with families who included a member with schizophrenia. His schizophrenia research in the late 1950s focused on 14 families whom he studied for time periods of six months to three years (Bowen, 1959; Dysinger & Bowen, 1959; Howells & Guirguis, 1985). Bowen concluded that the type of family anxiety that results in one member's developing schizophrenia required three generations to unfold. In his sample, the first generation's parents were relatively mature, but the child acquired their combined immaturity, manifested as anxiety and fusion, lack of a separate identity. The same process repeated in the next generation produced sufficient emotional fusion for schizophrenia to develop. Bowen is criticized for being one of a group of influential family theorists who produced literature blaming the development of schizophrenia on parents. It is now understood that schizophrenia is largely biological. Still, Bowen's work of that time was helpful to family therapists for understanding the manner in which anxiety can be passed down through generations.

The practitioner does not have to have information about three generations to effectively provide family interventions. Family structures are more diverse and fragmented today than they have ever been in American life. Clinical practitioners experience reconstituted families, dissolving families, single parent families, and gay and lesbian families. Geographic mobility is such that many people have limited awareness of their blood or territorial origins. It is always important to acquire as much information as possible about nuclear, extended, and cross-generation family relationships, but the practitioner can proceed with whatever data are available. In fact, the trend in family systems theory in the past 20 years has been developing strategies to work with families with a focus on only one generation (Titelman, 1998).

Differentiation of Self

Healthy or adaptive individual functioning is characterized by differentiation of self. This is a key concept in family systems theory that has two meanings. First, it represents a person's capacity to distinguish between and balance his or her thinking and feeling selves. Both aspects of experience are important. The thinking process represents one's ability to detach from, or look objectively at, personal reactions or biases. Emotional processes provide important information about the significance of the situation. The "total" human experience involves both emotion and reason. While Bowen advocated for a balance of reason and emotion, he thought this was really not an attainable condition because emotional feeling, unlike intellect, was a pervasive life force. For that reason it must also be emphasized that differentiation is an ideal that can never be fully attained.

The term *differentiation* also refers to the ability of an individual to physically differentiate from his or her family of origin in a manner that preserves aspects of those emotional ties while not being constrained by them. Differentiation is thus a characteristic not of a person but of a relationship. The person develops the capacity to maintain a balance in being able to separate self and maintaining old and new emotional ties. It will be shown later that this idea has been amended by some feminist thinkers who perceive the self as being more connected than separate in nature (e.g., Knudson-Martin, 2002).

In some ways it is ironic that family systems theory provides such a rich understanding of the emotional lives of people within their families, because it emphasizes the importance of reason in the formulation of "health." Highly charged emotional interactions can cloud a person's ability to appropriately separate his or her feelings from those of others and to have an independent existence. Bowen felt that it was important for one's reasoning ability to develop so that it could keep emotional experience from becoming the only basis on which decisions are made.

Triangles

In family systems theory, the interpersonal triangle is the primary unit of analysis. All intimate relationships are inherently unstable; they require the availability of a third party to maintain their stability. On first glance this might seem to be a paradoxical notion, but it makes common sense. The price of intimacy in any relationship is the experience of occasional conflict. People cannot exist in harmony all the time. When in conflict, people usually rely on a third person (or different third persons, depending on the circumstances) for mediation, ventilation, or problem-solving assistance. (One author has written about the "pet-focused" family, in which the pet can become a part of the triangle in these same ways [Entin, 2001].) This is a natural, healthy process. Serious problems related to one's differentiation may develop, however, when he or she is drawn into certain types of triangles within the family. When a "weaker" (undifferentiated) person is drawn into a triangle in a way that does not facilitate the original two people's resolution of their conflict, the person may be deprived of the opportunity to become a unique individual. He or she may assume the ongoing role of helping the other two people avoid their problems with each other. For example, in one study of 150 families in Japan and the United States it was found that triangled daughters in both cultures had lower scores on a measure of ego development (Bell, Bell, & Nakata, 2001). Problematic triangulation in families occurs when conflicted adults draw in weaker family members, often the children, to maintain the stability of their relationship.

Anxiety and the Nuclear Family Emotional System

Anxiety is an unpleasant but normal and functional affect that provides people with warning signs for perceived threats (Marks, 1987). Its symptoms include tension and nervous system hyperactivity. An anxiety-producing situation may be perceived as an opportunity for growth or as a threat to well-being. Anxiety becomes problematic when it interferes with one's capacity for problem solving. The concept of anxiety is central to psychodynamic theory, and Bowen adapted it to family systems theory. Family systems feature levels of anxiety, just as individuals do.

The nuclear family emotional system includes four relationship patterns that may foster problem development (Georgetown Family Center, 2004). With marital conflict, each spouse projects his or her anxiety onto the other and attempts to control the other person. With the problematic emotional functioning of one spouse, the other spouse makes accommodations to preserve relationship harmony but may develop heightened anxiety as a result. If one or more children exhibit a physical or emotional functional impairment, the parents will focus their anxieties on that child, who in turn may become emotionally reactive to them. With emotional fusion, family members distance themselves from one another to reduce the intensity of their relationships, and they may become isolated in the process.

A family system that is characterized by psychological tension for any of the above reasons may produce an atmosphere of anxiety that is shared by all of its members. As described earlier, this system anxiety can be passed on and increased through generations. An individual who is not differentiated experiences relatively high levels of tension in family relationships and will tend to be drawn to friends, spouses, and partners with similar levels of anxiety.

Parental Projection

Psychological defenses are processes by which people protect themselves from intolerable anxiety by keeping unacceptable impulses out of their awareness (Goldstein, 1995). Defenses are positive coping mechanisms when they help the person function effectively and do not significantly distort reality. Projection is a common defense mechanism, in which one person attributes to someone else his or her unacceptable thoughts and feelings. The projector is not aware of having the feelings or thoughts but believes instead that the person on whom they are projected is experiencing them. For example, a wife may feel anger toward her husband for spending too little time in the household. If she is threatened by the idea of being angry with her spouse, she may project that feeling onto a child. She may decide that the child is angry with the father and report that "fact" to her husband.

Projection may involve significant distortions of others' feelings, attitudes, and behaviors. Parents often use the projection defense with their children as "targets," because children are vulnerable family members. Children tend to accept the pronouncements, insights, and beliefs of their parents. Within family systems, children may suffer if the parents project negative feelings and ideas onto them. They may believe that they possess the negative thoughts and feelings attributed to them, and behave as such. In family systems theory, parental projection is a major source of transmitted family anxiety.

Fusion and Emotional Cutoff

Emotional fusion is the opposite of differentiation of self. It is a shared state involving two or more people, the result of a triangulation in which one member sacrifices his or her striving toward differentiation in the service of balancing the relationship of two other people. When one person is emotionally fused with another, his or her emotional reactivity to the other person becomes strong. The person does not "think," but "feels," and does so in response to the emotional state of the other person. The feelings of the mother, for example, become those of the son. When she is happy, he is happy, and when she is sad, he is sad. The son does not have an emotional life apart from that of his mother. Neither person is consciously aware of this state because they lack the capacity to reason about or reflect on the situation. This happens because, for a significant length of time during childhood and adolescence, prior to having an opportunity to differentiate, the fused person began to serve an ongoing function within a triangle that served the needs of two other family members.

People tend not to have insight into the fact that they are fused, but they experience high levels of emotional reactivity to the other person and may attempt to extricate themselves from the relationship. A common strategy is the emotional cutoff, a person's attempts to emotionally distance him- or herself from certain members of the family or from the entire family. Emotional cutoff is the result of a person's inability to directly resolve issues of fusion, which in turn prevents him or her from forming a unique identity or satisfying relationships with others.

In situations in which the family is living together, emotional cutoff may be characterized by physical avoidance of another person or, more commonly, not discussing emotionally charged topics. For example, a son in conflict with his mother may be pleased to talk about what happened at school, but they may avoid discussing how they feel about each other or the family. This pattern can continue after the family member leaves home. The son and mother may enjoy each other's company to an extent but have superficial interactions. The son may look for substitute families at work, at college, or at church.

Emotional cutoff is often seen in physical distance. Adolescents may be eager to leave home as a solution to their family problems. Again, this may represent a normal family transition. However, when distance alone is seen as a solution to ongoing family tensions, the person may be disappointed. A first-year college student may feel that he can at last become his own person, when in fact his fusion with another family member prevents him from fully experiencing other people. An important aspect of emotional cutoff is that the person experiencing it is usually not aware of the strength of the pull of the primary relationship. The process is denied or minimized.

Other Concepts

Bowen believed that sibling position within a nuclear family is a partial predictor of a child's personality development. For example, oldest children tend to be more responsible and conservative, whereas younger children are more sociable and rebellious. These differences are due in part to the constellations of triangles that exist in families of different sizes. Research during the past 10 years, however, has tended to dispel the notion that personality types can be validly predicted on the basis of family position alone (Steelman, Powell, Werum, & Carter, 2002). There are many other variables to be considered, including gender, number of years between siblings, innate temperaments, and the nature of external environments. Still, being alert to the different triangulation possibilities for each sibling is useful in assessing family systems.

Societal emotional processes are the manner in which social systems can be conceptualized as analogous to those of the family with regard to the rules that govern interpersonal behavior within and among them. Family systems concepts may be helpful for understanding these other systems. For example, the social service delivery system itself has been described as one-third of a triangle, along with participating individual members and the family, with implications for the differentiation and fusion of participants (Moore, 1990). The church congregation has also been conceptualized as a family (Howe, 1998). Each member's relationship patterns acquired in the family of origin may be replicated with the congregation, and it is this body from which the individual must strive for appropriate differentiation. Although interesting, the concept of societal emotional processes is not yet as well developed as those concepts that are specific to the family unit.

The Genogram

A major tool for assessment is the multigenerational genogram. This is a visual representation on one sheet of paper of a family's composition, structure, member characteristics, and relationships (Kerr & Bowen, 1988; McGoldrick, Gerson, & Shellenberger, 1999). It typically covers a span of three generations. Information provided on a genogram includes basic facts about family members (such as dates of birth and death, marriages, moves, and illnesses); the primary characteristics and levels of functioning of each member (education, occupation, health status, talents, successes, and failures); and relationship patterns among members (closeness, conflicts, and cutoffs). Overall family characteristics that may be assessed include structure (roles, rules, and boundaries) and the impact of life events, life transitions, and relationship patterns across generations. The advantage of the genogram as an assessment tool is its presentation of complex family data on one page. It is also an excellent means of eliciting family medical information (Sawin & Harrigan, 1995).

Some practitioners may be reluctant to construct genograms at the level of detail suggested by family systems theory because it is time-consuming and may be annoying to clients who are eager to move into problem resolution activities (McGoldrick, 1996). Despite these concerns, it is important to understand that, in the first session, it engages all family members in the discussion and usually represents an interesting new way for them to think about the family system.

Assessment Questions

Having reviewed the core concepts of family systems theory and the nature of problems that it suggests, the following list of assessment questions for the clinical practitioner is offered:

- What are the family's current stresses? How are they expressed?
- What physical and emotional symptoms are evident in this family?
- How do the evident symptoms affect family relationships?
- What is the nature of this family's relationship system?
- How does the nuclear family interact with the extended family?
- How stable is the family now? How successfully does it handle anxiety?
- How well differentiated are the family members?
- What triangles exist in the family? Which are primary? Are they functional?
- Are any emotional cutoffs operating?
- How has the family handled stress historically?

Goals of the Intervention

The nature of change in family systems theory involves an opening up of the system (Kerr & Bowen, 1988). Presenting problems involve triangles, fusion, and emotional cutoff. Change requires detriangulation and new alliance building among members of the nuclear and extended family. The practitioner attends to the following goals:

- Lowering family system anxiety.
- Increasing the reflective capacity (insight) of all members.
- Promoting differentiation of self by emotionally realigning the family system (which includes the opening of closed relationships).
- Instilling in members sensitivity to the influences of multigenerational family patterns.
- Enhancing habits of problem sharing.
- Redressing inequalities within the family by inhibiting dominant members.

Intervention Approaches

Family systems therapists do not work with a set of explicit, concrete intervention techniques. The theory offers instead intervention strategies with which the practitioner can design techniques in accordance with a family's particular concerns (Bowen, 1978; Kerr & Bowen, 1988). These are summarized in the following section.

The Clinical Relationship

As a prerequisite to change, family members must experience the clinical setting as safe, comfortable, and relatively free of the anxiety that tends to characterize their natural environment. The practitioner acts as a coach. He or she remains on the sidelines of family interaction, asking questions and making suggestions that the family members discuss and enact with each other. The practitioner strives to be the focus of the family's attention and to set the tone of their exchanges. He or she must be calm, promote an unheated atmosphere, and maintain professional detachment. The purposes of this posture are to avoid emotional reactivity and negative triangulation with family members. The practitioner also serves as a model for rational interaction.

In the early stages of intervention, the practitioner may ask family members to talk directly to him or her about sensitive issues, rather than to one another, to minimize interpersonal tensions. If tensions are so high that productive interactions cannot proceed, the practitioner can use displacement stories as a means of taking the family's focus off itself and giving it some distance from its own concerns. This is a technique in which the practitioner provides an example of a hypothetical family with processes and problems similar to those of the actual family. The practitioner asks the actual family to share observations and suggest interventions.

The Genogram

By participating in the construction of the genogram, family members gain insight into their family processes. They learn about interpersonal patterns and how triangles operate within the family. With these insights family members learn to appreciate that their behavior is related to larger systemic processes and the ways in which those processes support or inhibit member functioning. The process normalizes some family problems, particularly those related to transitions. Family members may become able to identify their own strategies to enhance family functioning. The genogram often stimulates a process of life review among older adults. Another way in which the genogram serves as an effective early intervention is that, during the construction, each member is observing a diagram rather than looking at others. This brings a shared focus to the discussion and displaces any negative feelings onto an object rather than onto another person.

Detriangulation

This represents any strategy by which the practitioner disrupts one triangle and opens up the family members to new, more functional alliances or triangles. There are many ways in which the worker can detriangulate the family (Guerin, Fogarty, Fay, & Kautto, 1996). He or she can shift alliances with tasks to be performed within the session or when members are at home. Within the session, the practitioner might encourage role reversals, or situations in which members interact with each other in different ways. A child who is accustomed to complaining to his mother about the annoying behavior of a sibling might be asked to confront the sibling. When a couple is triangled with a child as a means of avoiding issues in their relationship, they might be instructed to spend a certain amount of time together talking about whatever is on their minds that day. If they need the assistance of a third party to bring an issue to resolution, they might be encouraged to talk with a different adult family member. In these ways members are guided into new functional attachments with nuclear or extended family members. Any strategy that contributes to members' opening up the family to new attachments can be pursued. The practitioner should always encourage the development of new attachments that have the possibility of promoting a member's differentiation.

Increasing Insight

Family systems theory shares with psychodynamic theory a belief that understanding can lead to change. The practitioner facilitates reflective discussions that promote insight about the effects of relationships on one's personality and behavior. Two techniques that promote insight are person–situation reflection, focused on the present, and developmental reflection, focused on the history of the person, the family, and its patterns (Woods & Hollis, 2000). Children and adolescents may appear to have a lesser capacity for reflection, but insight can be defined for them simply as understanding that one person's behavior always affects another person's feelings and behavior. Two related techniques that the practitioner might use are "externalizing the thinking," or helping each member put into words what is generally kept inside, and encouraging the "I" position. In the latter practice the practitioner asks each person to speak about his or her own thoughts and feelings, label them as such, and accept responsibility for them. This works against the tendencies of many clients to blame others for what they think and feel.

Education

Families often benefit from understanding that their patterns of interaction have sources in the family's history and that improving family life may involve "going backwards" to revisit relationships with various extended family members. This helps family members feel less confused and guilty about their behaviors. In teaching families about family system processes, the practitioner helps each member to observe the self within triangles and to examine behavior in terms of family themes. This also serves as a normalizing strategy for families who worry that they are uniquely dysfunctional or beyond help. The practitioner must decide when to integrate teaching moments with other interventions. The practitioner should always provide this information in terms that the family can understand.

Working with Individuals

This is a book about family intervention, but it must be mentioned that one of the strengths of family systems theory is its utility for working with any subset of a family or even with individual clients (McGoldrick & Carter, 2001). Family systems intervention requires an awareness, but not necessarily the presence, of all family members. In individual therapy, the practitioner can construct a genogram with the client and examine the client's behavior in terms of emerging family themes. The practitioner helps the client observe the self in triangles and then detriangulate by developing new or different relationships with family members who are available. The practitioner can also help the client develop insight and use this knowledge of the effects of family relationships to disrupt the repetitions of unsatisfactory relationship patterns with others.

Applications

Normal life transitions can create problems in functioning for individuals and families. Among family systems theorists, Carter and McGoldrick (1989) have identified six general stages of a family's lifespan, including young adulthood (between families), the young couple, families with young children, families with adolescents, families at midlife (including launching children), and families in later life. As families enter each new stage, they may experience difficulty coping with the challenges inherent in that stage. The following case provides an example of family stresses related to two lifespan stages—adolescence and the declining health of older members. Concepts from family systems theory are useful for understanding the heightened anxiety and emotional tumult that creeps into a family with aging or dying members (Bowen, 1991; Margles, 1995). The illustration includes excerpts from the social worker's dialogues with the family (indicators of many of the intervention strategies are included in parentheses).

The Charles Family

Dan Charles was a 16-year-old high school sophomore referred to the mental health center because of poor grades, negative attitudes about school and his peers, and reports by his parents of suicidal thinking. The Charles family (Figure 10.1) had moved from Ohio to Virginia six months earlier when Dan's father, Jeff (age 41), accepted new employment. According to Dan and his parents, Dan was unhappy about living in Virginia. He was irritable, argumentative, and in persistent power struggles with them. Dan usually stayed in the house when he was not in school and had made no friends. He complained about life in Virginia and said he wanted to move back home. Dan complained about his classmates and refused to participate in school activities. Dan's two younger siblings (Adam, 10, and Robyn, 8) resented Dan's anger and how he took it out on them. They enjoyed living in Virginia and had made new friends.

During the practitioner's assessment, however, other family issues emerged as significant to the present situation (Figure 10.1). She learned that Claudia (age 42), Dan's mother, was concerned about the health of her aging parents back in Ohio. Claudia's mother was in the middle stages of Alzheimer's disease, and her father was physically limited by congestive heart failure. For that reason, Claudia felt guilty about moving away from Ohio.

The practitioner met with the family 10 times over a period of four months, focusing on systems issues rather than the presenting problem of one member's maladjustment. She framed the family's functioning in a context of everyone's need to better adjust to the move, and the family was agreeable to working on this.

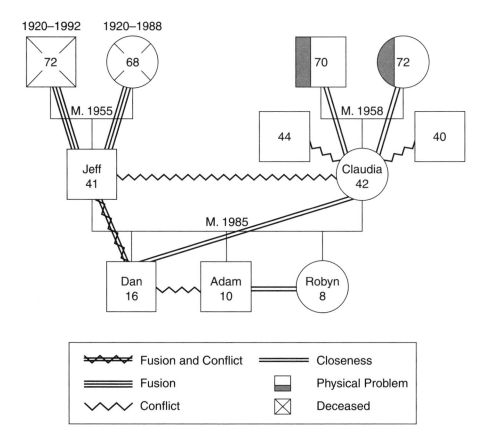

FIGURE 10.1   *The Charles Family*

Social worker (Reframing):   "Obviously, things have been tense in the home for all of you. But consider that you've had to move several times in the last few years, and there have been real worries about money and health. Considering all that, you've done well in some ways. I can see that you all care about each other, and that you'd all like the atmosphere at home to improve."

Jeff: "That's not quite true, though. We're not all trying [he looks at Dan]."

Social worker: "But you said he's been a good kid in the past. I wonder if you're all clear about what this experience has meant to him. Dan?"

Dan: "My folks should know."

Social worker: "Maybe they do, and maybe they don't. Perhaps you'll become able to tell them more about that."

One motivator for the family was that, because they were now rooted in a new location, they had few choices but to support one another. The practitioner introduced the theme of life-cycle stresses and complimented all of them on the good decisions they had made in their transition. Dan was pleased to have the focus taken off him.

> *Social worker (Education):* "All families go through transition periods. When there is a new child born, when a parent dies, when a child goes to school or moves away. Those things all have a big effect on everyone, even though you may not be aware of it at first. I think that, among other things, your family is in a transition period. Family members have to take some responsibility for themselves, of course, but I think you are all affected by these changes. Some of what you're concerned about is related to that. I hope you all recognize that and can maybe make some decisions about how to make this transition easier."

As they reviewed the genogram the practitioner suggested that they could help each other with their adjustment by dealing more directly with their feelings and interacting with each other in new ways. She included attention to the grandparents in this process. Recognizing the entire family's concern for the aging couple, she integrated strategies to see that all of their needs were addressed.

> *Social worker (Education, lowering system anxiety):* "It's clear to me that you share a sense of family, especially since you're all concerned about Claudia's parents. It has to be hard to be this far away from them. Again, I'm not sure if you are all aware of what each other are experiencing, not only with this move but with other challenges over the past few years, like the family finances. With people close to us, if we don't regularly 'check in' we may begin to make assumptions that aren't true. Or we may decide that not talking is the easiest way to avoid stress."

The social worker referred to the genogram as a means of encouraging the family members to consider the entire system.

> *Social worker (Use of the genogram):* "Genograms sometimes lay out family relationships in a way that is more clear than just talking about them. For example, Claudia, it looks like your brothers have put you in charge of your parents, even though they live closer. Is that accurate?"
>
> *Claudia:* "Men aren't as thoughtful that way. It's my job to make sure my folks get what they need and don't become isolated. You know what it's like for older folks—they get lonely, and then they give up and die."
>
> *Jeff:* "Men aren't thoughtful? You think I'm like your brothers?"

Dan: "Well, look (pointing at the genogram). It was just you and your parents. They took care of you. They died before you had to repay that."

Social worker: "Since we're all looking at the genogram, do any of you see anything interesting?"

Claudia: "Yes. I take care of my folks, and Jeff is used to being taken care of. So now he expects me to take care of him."

Jeff (defensively): "Claudia goes overboard worrying about her parents. She gives them more attention than she gives the rest of us. Shouldn't we be number one now?"

Social worker (Redirecting the interaction): "I suggest that all of you direct your comments to each other rather than to me. You're really speaking to each other. Don't worry about me, I'll follow along and participate."

Jeff and Claudia argued about this issue often. Jeff was the only child in his family of origin. He was born when his parents, now deceased, were in their forties. They had been quite doting, and Jeff was accustomed to being taken care of. Jeff seemed to want Claudia to attend to him in the ways she did for her parents. Claudia, being a natural peacemaker, tried to see Jeff's side of the issue. Still, she resented his insensitivity to her experiencing this midlife role reversal with her parents.

Claudia: "He just doesn't know what it's like for me."

Social worker (use of "I" statements): "I don't know if he does or not. It's important for you to make it clear to Jeff how you feel, Claudia. In fact, all of you should try to make clear how the behavior of you parents and brothers and sister makes you feel, both good and bad. You can best get your feelings across by using what are called 'I' statements. That is, always say, 'I feel this way' or 'I feel that way' when something happens."

Adam: "I don't get it."

Social worker: "For example, if your sister makes a lot of noise and keeps you from getting your homework done, you might say, 'I get mad when you make such a racket because I can't study,' instead of only saying something like, 'Stop making such a racket!'"

The practitioner suspected that Dan tended to be triangled with his parents as a diversion from their conflicts. When they were angry with each other they found fault with Dan and vented their feelings at him.

Claudia: "He used to be a good kid. But now, look. The rest of us are trying our hardest to make all these adjustments, and he goes off and sulks, not helping at all."

Social worker (use of 'I' statements): "Make sure you talk to Dan instead of to me. And tell him how his behavior makes you feel."

Claudia: "Okay. Dan, I feel frustrated when you go off by yourself when I'm trying to talk to you. I feel like you're mocking me. [To the social worker] Is that okay?"

The practitioner wondered if Dan willingly took on the role of troublemaker when his parents were in conflict. It was true that the recent move was hard on Dan, more so than the other children, due to his stage of life. But the combined family stress may have resulted in Dan's increased efforts to divert (a) his parents' attention from each other, (b) his mother from her guilt about not fulfilling her role in her nuclear family, and (c) his father's anger about his unmet needs to be cared for.

Social worker (Detriangluation discussion): "It's normal that there would be a lot of tension in a household after a major move. Dan, I know your parents are concerned about your welfare. I'm wondering, though, how you see them reacting to, for example, a failing grade at school or your staying in your room all day."

Dan: "Well, they yell. They yell at me. It can go on for days."

Social worker: "Are things pretty calm between them otherwise?"

Robyn: "Oh no."

Social worker: "What's that, Robyn?"

Robyn: "They yell at each other a lot."

Social worker: "You think so? Adam, what do you observe?"

Adam: "Yeah. That's just the way it is. But it's okay, it doesn't bother me much."

Social worker: "So things can get tense in the house. That's not necessarily a problem unless you lose sight of what you are really upset about."

Jeff: "I don't follow you."

Social worker: "Sometimes people use each other as outlets when they're upset but maybe not sure what, exactly, they're upset about. With all that's happened, is it possible that you take out some feelings on each other that might be related to your mixed feelings about moving?"

[And later] Social worker (Displacement): "Sometimes kids might become concerned about their parents arguing and actually do things to take the parents' attention away from each other, or give them something to agree on."

While the younger children did not seem to be as obviously affected by the family anxiety, the practitioner was concerned that their "staying out" of the situation put them at risk for emotional cutoff.

Robyn: "I'm doing fine. Nobody seems mad at me, except Dan sometimes. I can get away from it. It doesn't bother me, really. I can go to my room."

> *Social worker:*   "That helps, sure. And it's okay to have your private space. But I wonder if you are able to feel comfortable being around your parents and brothers. I hope you do, most of the time."

The practitioner eventually helped the family develop plans for groups of them to travel to Ohio every three weeks to look after Claudia's parents. These represented de-triangulation exercises and an effort to open up the nuclear family to the extended family system.

> *Social worker:*   "Claudia, you like to visit your parents. Have you considered taking other family members along?"
>
> *Claudia:*   "Not much. They're all trying to get adjusted here, and it's my problem, really."
>
> *Social worker:*   "But they might be interested in going along. Have you asked them?"
>
> *Claudia:*   "No. I've been preoccupied and . . . [hesitating] I thought Jeff might get annoyed and think I was trying to keep the kids from getting settled here."
>
> *Jeff:*   "Oh, come on, I'd never say that!"
>
> *Claudia:*   "You might think I was planning to get us all back home."
>
> *Social worker (Opening up the system to extended family members):*   "Jeff and Claudia, if you agree that you're going to live here, as you said before, and make the best of it, perhaps you don't have to have such doubts. These short trips can be a good way for you to connect with each other and stay connected to the grandparents."

The family decided that Claudia and two of the children might make one trip, enabling them to spend two full days together. Jeff and two of the children might travel to Ohio on another weekend. Jeff and Claudia could not take long trips together without the entire family, so the practitioner encouraged them to spend time together close to home but away from the children. Their lives had centered on the children for years. The couple reluctantly decided to meet once a week for lunch.

> *Jeff:*   "I'm not sure that lunch together can help. It seems kind of trite. We have most suppers together as it is."
>
> *Social worker:*   "With the kids, though."
>
> *Claudia:*   "Jeff, there's less of a chance we'll get upset if the kids aren't around, sulking."

Claudia felt good about this plan, and it lowered her anxiety. The practitioner helped the family appreciate Claudia's need to provide support to members of two generations. In the spirit of developing new family tasks Jeff and the children decided that they could undertake minor home renovation projects during the absences of the other members.

> *Social worker (Coaching):* "Jeff, you've mentioned that you and Dan don't spend time together anymore. What did you used to do?"
>
> *Jeff:* "We camped, played sports. I don't know, he's getting older, he doesn't do as much of that stuff anymore."
>
> *Dan:* "There's the carpentry stuff, too."
>
> *Jeff:* "Yeah, we used to work on the house some. Sanding the floors, building cabinets."
>
> *Social worker:* "Might you enjoy sanding floors together again?"
>
> *Jeff:* "Actually, there's a lot to do in the new place. But he won't help."
>
> *Dan:* "I might."

The practitioner hoped that this would both enhance their sense of mastery and positively change the nature of their relationships. In all of these strategies the practitioner was helping the family to form new alliances and to differentiate. The children, with the encouragement of the social worker, spent some of their time in Ohio talking with their grandparents about their mother and father's lives when they were younger. This strengthened their relationships with their grandparents.

Another effective intervention strategy was the practitioner's support of the family's following through with a vague desire to join a church in Virginia. The family had not been active in their church in Ohio but were more interested in doing so now, partly because of their relative social isolation. Claudia had become more conscious of her religious roots since her parents had become ill and were facing existential concerns more directly.

> *Social worker:* "I'm getting the feeling that there's a lot of . . . intensity to what happens in the house. Is there anything that you all do that involves other people? I know you don't have family in the area."
>
> *Claudia:* "We go to church. Sometimes. We haven't spent much time there, really."
>
> *Social worker:* "Did you ever? I mean, before you moved here?"
>
> *Jeff:* "Sure. I volunteered on Sundays, too, to clean up after services."
>
> *Social worker:* "Churches have family activities, too. Is there anything fun the kids might do there?"

The practitioner supported the idea, as it might provide the family with a bonding experience. This activity could also help them consider family functioning within a spiritual context. The family did participate in several church activity groups that helped them to initiate social ties. In the past their church affiliations had not provided them with a basis for family-focused activity, but it became more a part of their lives now.

When therapy ended, the family had made a better adjustment to life in Virginia. (Note that only the clinical social worker's *active* interventions were highlighted in this vignette, because of space limitations.) Relationships improved among the members, and Dan was feeling better about his parents, his siblings, and his school. Jeff had helped Claudia confront her brothers about their need to be more attentive to her parents, and Jeff and Dan continued to spend recreational time together. The family had talked about possibly moving Claudia's parents to Virginia if their health continued to deteriorate. They continued to make monthly trips to Ohio.

Evaluation of Effectiveness

There is no persuasive large-scale empirical evidence that family systems theory is an effective guide to intervention. This is not to say that it is not effective. Rather, it has not been the subject of outcome studies that go beyond case narratives. If this seems discouraging, it must be emphasized that evaluating the effectiveness of family theories is generally difficult, and family systems theory is among the most difficult to operationalize. Bowen did not believe that empirical study was an appropriate way to determine the usefulness of his theory. He believed that such methods overlooked its richness in focusing on limited variables. He believed that what people say they do is not always the same as what they do, so he did not put great faith in standardized clinical self-report measures (Georgetown Family Center, 2004).

Although family systems theory is rich in concepts to guide the conceptualization of family dynamics, its intervention techniques are not highly specific. Family systems practitioners can be creative in their intervention approaches and may operate differently in practice. One practitioner may tend to be didactic, another may be task focused, and a third may use reflective methods. As Frank and Frank (1993) postulate in their cross-cultural study of healing practices, it is the healer's possession of a guiding theoretical framework that is one significant predictor of effectiveness. In this sense, the attractiveness of this theory to clinical practitioners for over 30 years supports its utility.

Family systems theorists emphasize research on process rather than outcome, and on single cases or small samples. Such studies are currently in progress at the Georgetown Family Center (2004) and include the topics of families and cancer, families with substance-abusing adolescents, family processes in immigrant families, relationships and physiology, relationship processes and reproductive functioning, the process of differentiation, and the workplace as an emotional system. Previous center studies have focused on AIDS and the family (Maloney-Schara, 1990), aging and the family (Kerr, 1984), family violence, and managing diabetes. The theory is also used as a model for adolescent group work to promote member growth through differentiation (Nims, 1998).

The literature does include examples of tests of the utility of the theory's concepts, and several are presented here. Roberts (2003) tested 125 college undergraduates to examine whether level of differentiation (defined as moderate levels of autonomy and intimacy with the family of origin) was associated with life stressors and social resources. She found that higher levels of differentiation correlated with lower levels of perceived life stress and more social resources; further, lower social class status was significantly associated with more life stressors but not fewer social resources. The author concluded that social class influences the number of one's stressors but not one's social resources. Kim-Appel (2003) examined the relationship between differentiation and psychological symptom status (somatization, interpersonal problems, depression, anxiety, hostility, and a global symptom measure) in persons aged 62 and older. Her hypotheses were confirmed, as measures of differentiation correlated negatively with emotional reactivity and emotional cutoff and correlated positively with "I" position statements. She concluded that differentiation is significant to social functioning across the life span and that psychological intervention with older adults can productively utilize family systems concepts.

Several studies have focused on family of origin influences on career decision making. Dodge (2001) investigated the effects of differentiation (and, from another theory, the concept of personal authority) on career development outcomes for 243 college students. Each concept was positively associated with a sense of vocational identity and self-efficacy in career decision making. Further, family of origin conflict was inversely associated with low self-efficacy in career decision making, low individuation, and dysfunctional career thoughts. The author concluded that addressing family conflict in therapy could have a positive impact on career development in young adults. In another study of this type, 1,006 college students were surveyed using measures of fusion, triangulation, intimidation, anxiety, and career decision making (Larson & Wilson, 1998). Results indicated that anxiety (from fusion) inhibits career development, but triangulation is not related to career decision problems.

Larsen, Bensen, Wilson, & Medora (1998) studied the effects of the intergenerational transmission of anxiety on 977 late adolescents' attitudes about marriage. The participants' experiences of fusion and triangulation were found to be related to negative opinions about marriage. Timmer & Veroff (2000) studied the relationship of family of origin ties to marital happiness after four years of marriage for 199 Black and 173 White couples. One predictor of marital happiness for wives, particularly those from disrupted families, was closeness to the husbands' families of origin. When husbands' or wives' parents were divorced or separated, closeness to the husband's family reduced the risk of divorce. Avnir and Shor (1998) operationalized the concept of differentiation with a set of indicators so that the concept may be qualitatively assessed during family intervention.

The clinical practitioner can evaluate his or her own effectiveness with family systems theory through the application of single systems (comparing baseline and treatment measures) or pre-experimental (comparing pretreatment with posttreatment measures) measures. All that is required is a background in basic research methods. The practitioner can translate a family's goals into observable indicators that can be monitored. Coco and Courtney (1998) provide one example. They initiated and evaluated a family systems intervention for preventing adolescent runaway behavior using pre- and postintervention measures of family satisfaction and cohesion.

Application to Families at Other Levels of Need

Family systems theory interventions require that the client, whether an individual or a family, has the capacity to interact in an atmosphere of relative calm and be able to reflect on relationships with significant others. There must be a stable enough family structure that the practitioner can maintain a detachment from family processes. Because this is a historical approach to intervention, the ability to focus on several generations is desirable. Family systems theory would not be appropriate for *most* Level I and *many* Level II families. The practitioner's focus in Level I is meeting basic material and support needs. There is an urgency to those needs that suggests interventions that do not rely on sustained reflection. Nor is there time for multigenerational assessment in critical situations. Likewise, Level II families are often characterized by chaos that derives from structural instability. The high level of worker activity necessary to adjust the family structure is inconsistent with the family systems perspective.

Family systems theory might be appropriate for some families at other levels of need after their initial problems are resolved. After the Level I family acquires access to basic needs, its members may struggle with issues related to enmeshments or cutoff. A structural breakdown of a Level II family may be related to a triangulation in which an adolescent accedes to an inappropriate position of power. The practitioner's ability to assess those dynamics may be helpful in determining how to help the family organize problem-solving activities, strengthen certain subsystems, or plan for growth after the primary intervention ends.

Ethical Challenges

Clinical social workers routinely face ethical challenges in their work, regardless of their theoretical base. They are human beings first, with personal values and preferences, and they must always monitor how they adhere to the profession's ethical principles of challenging social injustice, respecting the dignity of each person (and family), supporting the importance of relationships, being trustworthy, and maintaining practice competence. Still, each theory reflects a unique orientation to practice, and social workers utilizing them may experience particular ethical challenges. Family emotional systems interventions may give rise to the five challenges listed below:

1. Because interventions are relatively nondirective, the social worker must be cautious of any tendencies to step into a more directive role, especially when confronting such issues as family violence or neglect.
2. The social worker must balance the risks and benefits of getting involved in any pressing external family issues such as advocacy for housing, employment, or health care. The theory recognizes the importance of societal processes on family functioning but does not extensively address how related goals can be incorporated into family intervention.
3. The theory warns against the practitioner becoming triangled with family members in a negative way. The social worker must monitor his or her tendency to "take sides" with or against some family member or subsystem, with regard to such issues as gender discrimination or ageism.
4. The social worker must continually assess his or her own level of differentiation, since he or she cannot help the family progress beyond that level. This does not require that the practitioner seek therapy, but he or she needs to use supervision in a way that promotes this process. This may be difficult in agencies where intensive supervision is not provided.
5. Because of the absence of clear indicators for termination, the practitioner needs to establish indicators for ending so that the intervention does not become too "diffuse." Several resources have recently become available on this topic (Walsh, 2003; Walsh & Harrigan, 2003).

Summary

Family systems theory is unique in its attention to overt and subtle emotional family processes that develop over several generations. It is an appropriate guide to assessments and interventions that focus on the quality of nuclear and extended family interpersonal processes and the desire for family members to become differentiated. The theory is an effective means of working on issues related to boundaries, enmeshment, and emotional distance. It is versatile in its applicability to individuals and subsets of families. Its potential for use across cultures has also been articulated, although not yet extensively (Hines, Garcia-Preto, McGoldrick, & Weltman, 1992).

Family systems theory has been criticized, however, for two related reasons (Bartle-Haring, 1997; Knudson-Martin, 1994; Levant & Silverstein, 2001). First, it has not adequately attended to variations in how men and women experience differentiation and fusion. The theory has incorporated a male bias in its valuing of reason over emotion and prioritization of separation over connection. Beginning with Gilligan (1982), developmental theories about women have considered their relational and communication styles to be different from those of men. Second, even with its attention to societal emotional processes, the theory has not been sufficiently contextual in its identification of males as the dominant cultural group and their uses of power in family systems. Although these criticisms are valid, they began to be addressed by theorists in the 1990s. Family issues of gender difference and power can be productively addressed in therapy (McGoldrick, 1996).

Level III families pose a challenge to clinical practitioners because they are well defended and cope well in many ways. They are also a challenge because of the potential vulnerability of the practitioner to the influence of his or her family issues on the clinical work. The struggles of the presenting family may resonate with the practitioner's family experiences, and he or she may be inclined to take sides or be blind to certain family dynamics. Titelman (1987) has written extensively about the practitioner's need to be sensitive to these forces and to utilize clinical supervision to maintain neutrality in the intervention process.

Discussion Questions

1. Imagine that a professional colleague asks you to describe family systems theory. What three core concepts would you emphasize, and why?

2. Describe a point of fusion you have observed in your work with an individual, a family, or a family subsystem. Describe one way that you might (or did) proceed to modify that relationship.

3. Why is the triangle considered to be the smallest stable relationship system? What does attention to this concept imply about family assessment and intervention strategies?

4. Describe how the genogram can serve as both an assessment tool and an intervention strategy.

5. What is the ideal position of the practitioner in family systems work, so that both engagement and therapeutic distance can be achieved?

6. One intervention strategy in family systems theory involves guiding members into new attachments with nuclear and extended family members. Why should extended family members be included in this process when possible?

7. Consider a case of family dissolution in which the primary issue in the three-member family is the adolescent child's adjustment to the divorce of her parents. Describe one possible intervention strategy if the child will be in joint custody but is disengaged from one parent.

8. You are working with a family in which the mother is dying of ovarian cancer. The two children are grown and live independently in the same city as the parents. The son, like the father, is highly involved in the mother's care. The daughter shows minimal concern with her mother's imminent death. How might you organize an intervention to help the mother communicate more openly with her daughter?

9. Consider a situation in which you are working with an individual adult client whose problem is related to an inability to risk intimacy (however you define it) in relationships with significant others. In the assessment you learn that this person was the hero child in a family where the father was an alcohol abuser. Describe one possible intervention strategy.

10. Consider a situation in which you are working with a single mother who is having trouble "letting go" of her 19-year-old daughter, who is moving toward independence in a normal way. There are two other children, aged 14 and 10. The mother fits the profile of the hero child in her own nuclear family, in which there was an alcoholic parent. Describe one possible intervention strategy for helping the mother "let go."

Internet Resources

Colucci-Coritt, M. (1999). *Feminist family therapy.*
www.mindymac.com/Feminist_Family_Therapy.htm
This essay includes a concise, useful reaction of some feminist thinkers to the prominent family systems theorists, including Murray Bowen.
Family Systems Theory. (2004).
http://plaza.ufl.edu/irma/paper2.html
This site provides links to ten other Web sites, all of which contain useful information about various aspects of family systems theory and its applications.
Georgetown Family Center. (2004). Bowen Center for the Study of the Family.
www.georgetownfamilycenter.org/index.html
This is the best Internet resource available for current information on family emotional systems theory, including research and training opportunities. The mission of this center is to lead the development of Bowen's theory into a science of human behavior and to assist individuals, families, communities, and organizations in solving problems through improving human relationships.
Multigenerational Family Processes. (2005).
www.ddstats.com/fs/content/module4.htm
The material in this module has been adapted from the works of a number of contributors, chief among them Murray Bowen and Ivan Boszormenyi-Nagy. It contains an overview of useful terms and major concepts from family systems theory.
Smartdraw. (2004).
www.smartdraw.com/specials/genealogy.asp
This site provides free genogram program downloads.
Wylie, M. S. (2004). *Family therapy's neglected prophet.*
www.bowentheory.com/familytherapysneglectedprophetwylie.htm
An excellent biographical overview of Bowen's life and career.

Suggested Readings

Bowen, M. (1978). *Family therapy in clinical practice.* New York: Jason Aronson.
This is the essential source of originator Murray Bowen's major writings on the topic of family systems theory.
Guerin, P. J., Fogarty, T. F., Fay, L. F., & Kautto, J. G. (1996). *Working with relationship triangles: The one-two-three of psychotherapy.* New York: Guilford Press.
This is the most recent book by Guerin, a major proponent of family systems theory, and his associates. With its focus on the triangle, the theory's primary unit of analysis, the book has a broad clinical application.
Kerr, M. E., & Bowen, M. (1988). *Family evaluation: An approach based on Bowen theory.* New York: Norton.

This book focuses on developments in family systems theory since the publication of Bowen's earlier volume (1978). Its coauthor, Michael Kerr, is widely acknowledged to be the theory's major proponent since Bowen's death.

McGoldrick, M., Gerson, R., & Shellenberger, S. (1999). *Genograms: Assessment and intervention* (2nd ed.). New York: Norton.
This is the most comprehensive source of information about genograms and their application in the professional literature. The book is readable and even entertaining in its selection of examples.

Titelman, P. (Ed.) (1998). *Clinical applications of Bowen family systems theory.* New York: Haworth Press.
This book includes descriptions of family systems theory interventions for a variety of presenting problems. Each chapter is authored by a different practitioner who helps the reader get a sense of the creative approaches that can be used in family intervention.

References

Avnir, Y., & Shor, R. (1998). A systematic qualitative evaluation of levels of differentiation in families with children at risk. *Families in Society, 79*(5), 504–514.

Bartle-Haring, S. (1997). The relationships among parent–child–adolescent differentiation, sex role orientation and identity development in late adolescence and early adulthood. *Journal of Adolescence, 20*(5), 553–565.

Bell, L. G., Bell, D. C., & Nakata, Y. (2001). Triangulation and adolescent development in the U.S. and Japan. *Family Process, 40*(2), 173–186.

Bowen, M. (1959). The family as the unit and study of treatment: I. Family psychotherapy. *American Journal of Orthopsychiatry, 31,* 40–60.

Bowen, M. (1978). *Family therapy in clinical practice.* New York: Jason Aronson.

Bowen, M. (1991). Family reaction to death. In F. Walsh & M. McGoldrick (Eds.), *Living beyond loss: Death in the family* (pp. 79–92). New York: Norton.

Carter, B., & McGoldrick, M. (Eds.). (1989). *The changing life cycle: A framework for family therapy* (2nd ed.). New York: Gardner Press.

Coco, E. L., & Courtney, L. J. (1998). A family systems approach for preventing adolescent runaway behavior. *Adolescence, 33*(130), 485–497.

Dodge, T. D. (2001). An investigation of the relationship between the family of origin and selected career development outcomes. *Dissertation Abstracts International, 62*(2-B), 1140.

Dysinger, R. H., & Bowen, M. (1959). Problems for medical practice presented by families with a schizophrenic member. *American Journal of Psychiatry, 116,* 514–517.

Entin, A. D. (2001). Pets in the family. *Issues in Interdisciplinary Care, 3*(3), 219–222.

Faber, A. J. (2004). Examining remarried couples through a Bowenian family systems lens. *Journal of Divorce and Remarriage, 40*(3,4), 121–133.

Frank, J. D., & Frank, J. B. (1993). *Persuasion and healing: A comparative study of psychotherapy* (3rd ed.). Baltimore, MD: Johns Hopkins University Press.

Georgetown Family Center. (2004). www.georgetownfamilycenter.org/index.html

Gilligan, C. (1982). *In a different voice.* Cambridge, MA: Harvard University Press.

Goldstein, E. G. (1995). *Ego psychology and social work practice* (2nd ed.). New York: Free Press.

Gottlieb, D. C. (2001). The application of Bowen family systems theory to the high school principalship. *Dissertation Abstracts International, 62*(1-B), 599.

Guerin, P. J., Fogarty, T. F., Fay, L. F., & Kautto, J. G. (1996). *Working with relationship triangles: The one-two-three of psychotherapy.* New York: Guilford.

Hertlein, K. M., & Killmer, J. M. (2004). Toward differential decision-making: Family systems theory with the homeless clinical population. *American Journal of Family Therapy, 32*(3), 255–270.

Hines, P. M., Garcia-Preto, N., McGoldrick, R. A., & Weltman, S. (1992). Intergenerational relationships across cultures. *Families in Society,* 323–327.

Howe, L. T. (1998). Self-differentiation in Christian perspective. *Pastoral Psychology, 46*(5), 347–362.

Howells, J. G., & Guirguis, W. R. (1985). *The family and schizophrenia.* New York: International Universities Press.

Kerr, K. B. (1984). Issues in aging from a family theory perspective. In K. B. Kerr (Ed.), *The Best of the Family 1978–1983* (pp. 243–247). New Rochelle, NY: Center for Family Learning.

Kerr, M. E., & Bowen, M. (1988). *Family evaluation: An approach based on Bowen theory.* New York: Norton.

Kim-Appel, D. (2003). The relationship between Bowen's concept of differentiation of self and psychological symptom status in individuals age 62 years and older. *Dissertation Abstracts International, 63*(7-A), 2467.

Knudson-Martin, C. (1994). The female voice: Applications to Bowen's family system's theory. *Journal of Marital and Family Therapy, 20*(1), 35–46.

Knudson-Martin, C. (2002). Expanding Bowen's legacy to family therapy: A response to Horne and Hicks. *Journal of Marital and Family Therapy, 28*(1), 115–118.

Larson, J. H., Benson, M. J., Wilson, S. M., & Medora, N. (1998). Family of origin influences on marital attitudes and readiness for marriage in late adolescents. *Journal of Family Issues, 19*(6), 750–769.

Larson, J. H., & Wilson, S. M. (1998). Family of origin influences on young adult career decision problems: A test of Bowenian theory. *American Journal of Family Therapy, 26*(1), 39–53.

Lastoria, M. D. (1990). A family systems approach to adolescent depression. *Journal of Psychology and Christianity, 9*(4), 44–54.

Levant, R. F., & Silverstein, L. B. (2001). Integrating gender and family systems theories: The "both/and" approach to treating a postmodern couple. In S. H. McDaniel & D. D. Lusterman (Eds.), *Casebook for integrating family therapy: An ecosystem approach* (pp. 245–252). Washington, DC: American Psychological Association.

Maloney-Schara, A. (1990). Biofeedback and family systems psychotherapy in the treatment of HIV infection. *Biofeedback and Self-Regulation, 15*(1), 70–71.

Margles, D. (1995). The application of family systems theory to geriatric hospital social work. *Journal of Gerontological Social Work, 24,* 45–54.

Marks, I. M. (1987). *Fears, phobias, and rituals: Panic, anxiety, and their disorders.* New York: Oxford University Press.

McGoldrick, M. (1996). *The legacy of unresolved loss: A family systems approach.* New York: Newbridge Communications.

McGoldrick, M., & Carter, B. (2001). Advances in coaching: Family therapy with one person. *Journal of Marital & Family Therapy, 27*(3), 281–300.

McGoldrick, M., Gerson, R., & Shellenberger, S. (1999). *Genograms: Assessment and intervention* (2nd ed.). New York: Norton.

Moore, S. T. (1990). Family systems theory and family care: An examination of the implications of Bowen theory. *Community Alternatives: International Journal of Family Care, 22*(2), 75–86.

Nims, D. R. (1998). Searching for self: A theoretical model for applying family systems to adolescent group work. *Journal for Specialists in Group Work, 23*(2), 133–144.

Prest, L. A., Benson, M. J., & Protinsky, H. O. (1998). Family of origin and current relationship influences on codependency. *Family Process, 37*(4), 513–528.

Roberts, N. H. D. (2003). Bowen family systems theory and its place in counseling psychology. *Dissertation Abstracts International, 63*(12-B), 6105.

Sawin, K. J., & Harrigan, M. P. (1995). *Measures of family functioning for research and practice.* New York: Springer.

Scaturo, D. J., Hayes, T., Sagula, D., & Walter, T. (2000). The concept of codependency and its context within family systems theory. *Family Therapy, 27*(2), 63–70.

Steelman, L. C., Powell, B., Werum, R., & Carter, S. (2002). Reconsidering the effects of sibling configuration: Recent advances and challenges. *Annual Review of Sociology, 28,* 243–269.

Stith, S. M., McCollum, E. E., Rosen, K. H., & Locke, L. D. (2003). Multicouple group therapy for domestic violence. In F. W. Kaslow (Ed.), *Comprehensive handbook of psychiatry: Vol. 4. Integrative/eclectic* (pp. 499–520). New York: Wiley.

Timmer, S. G., & Veroff, J. (2000). Family ties and the discontinuity of divorce in Black and White newlywed couples. *Journal of Marriage and the Family, 62*(2), 349–361.

Titelman, P. (Ed.). (1987). *The therapist's own family: Toward the differentiation of self.* Northvale, NJ: Jason Aronson.

Titelman, P. (Ed.). (1998). *Clinical applications of Bowen family systems theory.* New York: Haworth Press.

Walsh, J. (2003). *Endings in clinical practice: Ensuring closure across service settings.* Chicago: Lyceum.

Walsh, J., & Harrigan, M. P. (2003). The termination stage in Bowen's family systems theory. *Clinical Social Work Journal, 31*(4), 383–394.

Woods, M. E., & Hollis, F. H. (2000). *Casework: A psychosocial therapy* (5th ed.). Boston: McGraw-Hill.

Part V

Fourth Level of Family Need: Family and Personal Growth

Families on Level IV of family need have their basic needs met. There is adequate parenting, and structural boundaries and limits are relatively clear. Generally there exist generational boundaries and parent–child differentiation, and personal and family growth are the primary issues. Presenting needs often focus on the wish for greater intimacy and commitment, more adult autonomy, interpersonal competence, self-actualization, more constructive resolution of conflict, or changing destructive patterns. Based on the accomplishment of lower-level needs, this higher level of need is represented by a focus on inner richness and quality of life in the house that the family is building.

The two chapters in this section offer ways to work with families who have needs at Level IV and are experiencing growth issues at that level. The first is narrative family interventions, discussed in Chapter 11 by Williams, whose emphasis is on the meanings families make of their experiences, instead of the cause of the problem, making use of a collaborative, co-learning therapeutic relationship.

A second approach is presented in Chapter 12 by Kilpatrick and Trawick. Object relations family intervention is a bridge between working with individuals and working with families and is essentially interactional in its intervention processes.

11

Narrative Family Interventions

Nancy R. Williams, Ph.D.

Rhonda, 20, and Jamie*, 23, sat slumped on the couch in the therapist's office while the therapist gathered the details of their lives as she had been carefully trained to do: alcoholism, teen pregnancy, poverty, family violence—a legacy of pain that permeated generations of this couple's family history. The therapist, like the couple, felt a familiar despair. Where should she begin now that she knew their "real" story?

Human beings share their stories to communicate, remember, and make meaning of their life events and have done so across cultures and millenniums. It is the way that memories are harnessed to capture the complexity of experience as they serve to shape belief systems about culture, self, and others. Helping professionals are trained to listen to the stories that they are told by the families that they serve as they simultaneously interpret, assess, and make sense of the information that they are gathering. Often, however, they forget that there is more, much more, to the story, or that there are multiple stories or that stories can change through changed perceptions. Throughout this chapter, we will revisit Rhonda and Jamie to get a glimpse of their life journey through the lens of narrative therapy.

Needs

The storytelling process has been described as a way of transmitting "cultural and family beliefs that guide personal expectations and actions" (Walsh, 1998, p. 48).

*Names and details have been changed to protect anonymity. The author would like to acknowledge Dr. David Kurtz for his creative assistance in this chapter and Lindsay Lewis, research assistant.

194

Reciprocally, as people's stories have shaped culture, so, too, have people been shaped by the stories, or narratives, that the prevailing culture has adopted about them. Narrative therapy is an approach to working with individuals, couples, and families that utilizes these stories/narratives as the point of intervention to bring about change. This theoretical model, referred to as the third wave in family therapy theory (behind psychodynamic and family systems) has been gaining momentum in the family therapy field since the 1980s and continues to broaden its appeal and to influence practice in the human service arena. In fact, according to Nichols & Schwartz (2004), it is the "leading" approach to family therapy.

Proponents of narrative therapy regard this approach as much more than a set of techniques. They see it as a revolutionary paradigm shift that challenges the tenets adhered to in family systems theories and traditional clinical approaches to mental health treatment. Some narrative theorists refer to narrative therapy as "narrative-informed" therapy as it draws from the theories and research from a diverse range of disciplines, such as philosophy, anthropology, sociology, and linguistics, as well as family therapy and psychology (Angus & McCleod, 2004). Narrative theorists hold the view that people seek out therapy when the narratives that dominate their lives become oversaturated with problems—their life story is filled with pain and suffering (White & Epston, 1990). The re-storying process within the narrative approach challenges the status quo viewpoint and creates possibilities for alternative meanings and, correspondingly, alternative ways of acting.

Goals

Michael White (1993), one of the primary architects of the narrative therapy movement, claims that the meaning that people make of their stories influences their actions and behaviors. Narrative therapists take the position that the narratives that people adopt act as filters that determine which features of their experience will be chosen to be focused on, and what meaning will be given to the experience. However, while narratives offer strategies for adapting to the inevitable adversities in life, this process can also become the vehicle for cultural oppression. It is through the construction of narratives that the dominant culture is translated and becomes embedded into our personal frame of reference as accepted truths. These adopted truths can serve to shape self-destructive and constricting thoughts and behaviors even while providing a template for survival. Thus, a narrative approach to family intervention addresses and challenges stories that disempower and pathologize individuals and families.

Empowerment is also reflected in the collaborative relationship between client and therapist. An essential aspect of this approach is that the family members are viewed as the experts on their own lives through the validation of the meaning their problem stories are given. It is through this respectful collaboration with families that clients are enabled and empowered to bring forth their "alternative" stories. Instead of the more conventional view that problems are inherent either within the individual or the family, narrative therapy promotes the view that problems exist as a perception. Nichols & Schwartz (2004) contrast the difference between family systems approaches and a narrative approach by claiming that instead of focusing on "self-defeating patterns of behavior, the narrative metaphor focuses on self-defeating cognitions."

The Role of Culture

The narrative approach has a particular "fit" with social work values, since it directly addresses social issues of power, oppression, and social justice, often overlooked in more traditional, intrafamilial, and intrapsychic models of practice. In this approach, the impact of the cultural experience on the members of those diverse groups who remain outside the dominant cultural narrative is considered central (Gremillion, 2004; Goddard, Lehr & Lapadat, 2000; Laird, 2000; Nylund & Nylund, 2003; O'Dell, 2000; Semmler & Williams, 2000; Waldgrave, 1998; White, 1991). Blanton and Vandergriff-Avery (2001) focus on the notion of relational and positional power in marital work, exploring the negative effects of the labeling of gender within cultures. They suggest that therapists "challenge cultural injustices that oppress or marginalize individuals so preferred ways of relating can be seen as valid choices" (p. 300) through exploring gender expectations. Laird suggests that cultural narratives have such a strong impact that they are, in fact, the pivotal metaphors that clinical practitioners should focus on in work with individuals, couples, and families. She adds her voice to White and Epston (1990) and Madigan (1991) in cautioning professionals to be aware that because the therapeutic situation lies within the domains of power and knowledge, the therapeutic process always includes the possibility of social control and is never value-free, apolitical, or context-free.

Knowledge of the self is described as being largely defined by the cultural practices that clients and therapists alike engage in (Semmler & Williams, 2000). As such, narrative therapists view identity to be formed within a relational context. Freedman and Combs (1996) observe:

> A central tenet of the postmodern worldview in which we base our approach to therapy is that beliefs, laws, social customs, habits of dress and diet—all the things that make up the psychological fabric of "reality"—arise through social interaction over time. In other words, people together construct their realities as they see them. (p. 23)

Additionally, therapists approach the therapeutic situation with their own narrative that may limit or shape what they think is relevant or important in a client's story (Hart, 1995). As a result, therapists and family members alike are subject to the constraints of race, gender, culture, and theoretical position (Fish, 1993; Laird, 2000; Waldgrave, 1998; White, 1989b). Emphasis is placed on therapists being aware of their own personal and cultural narratives and the necessity of helping professionals vigorously attend to a process of "depriviteging" their own stories to be able to hear the narratives of others. Hart (1995) also warned therapists to be aware of their own narrative, which may limit or shape what is chosen for re-authoring in a therapeutic situation.

Theoretical Foundations and Basic Tenets

Michael White, an Australian social worker, is credited with the initial conceptualization of the narrative therapy model in the early 1980s. His ideas evolved in collaboration with David Epston, a clinician from New Zealand who injected the notion of community empowerment, and Cheryl White, who introduced him to the feminist perspective. The model that evolved from their collaboration is rooted in a postmodern framework while drawing from existential philosophy. The narrative approach recognizes social and political influences and constraints and embraces the belief that reality is a social construct. The narrative tradition claims to stand theoretically distinct and independent from other traditional theories and frameworks of human behavior that view pathology as the root of problems. Depending on the framework, narrative theorists suggest that pathology or blame have been passed between the individual or the family system in traditional practice theories like a hot potato. Epston (1984) argues that these approaches seek to rank individuals according to notions of pathology and "correct" behavior that is predetermined. The implication is that "truth" is possessed by the therapist (messengers of society) and will somehow be forced upon the "dysfunctional" and probably "resistant" client. Conversely, the narrative model assumes a more objective and, hence, nonjudgmental attitude toward human variation that avoids pathologizing and places particular value on personal responsibility and empowerment (Anoretic & Anoretic, 1991). Freedman and Combs (1996), prominent proponents of narrative therapy work with couples, comment:

> Narrative therapists are interested in working with people to bring forth and thicken stories that do not support or sustain problems. As people begin to inhabit and live out the alternative stories, the results are beyond solving problems. Within the new stories, people live out new self images, new possibilities for relationships, and new futures. (p. 16)

Although sharing similar theoretical, postmodern roots, narrative therapy and the solution-focused therapy defined by Steve de Shazer also have distinct differences (Chang & Phillips, 1993). Specifically, these authors note differences in therapeutic intent and the stance toward the problem. Despite important differences, narrative and solution-focused therapies both focus on strengths and solutions, placing these methods at the cutting edge of the social-constructionist, postmodern perspective. Some of the major theoretical and philosophical influences that profoundly affected White and Epston (1990) include the writings of Michel Foucault, Gregory Bateson, and Jerome Bruner. Their contributions are reflected in the following three categories of assumptions that underscore the narrative model: Foucault's theory of power and oppression, Bateson's theory of problems, and Bruner's theory of change.

Theory of Power and Oppression

Michel Foucault (1965, 1979, 1980) a French philosopher, focused his work on the distribution of power within society that objectified, marginalized, and dehumanized some social groups while upholding the social status of others. He asserted that power is maintained through standards set by the standard bearers of a society (i.e., doctors, teachers, politicians, therapists, and celebrities), who promote oppression of deviant groups through "expert" judgments that serve to categorize and stereotype these groups. Society adopts the position of its model experts through the internalization of a shared narrative (i.e., social construct) that perpetuates oppressive attitudes and beliefs. Thus the culture shapes behavior and trains individuals to conform and, in turn, to judge those who refuse or are unable to follow the prescribed norms. Those who conform to the dominant or expert knowledge are accepted, but nonconformists come under the "gaze" of others and are viewed in a pejorative way.

Psychotherapists are trained to identify deviations in behavior and label individuals with clinical diagnoses such as are found in the DSM-IV (American Psychiatric Association, 1994). Labels such as obsessive-compulsive, alcoholic, codependent, and even borderline have found their way into everyday language. Family therapists also have their own language for categorizing or labeling families by using terminology such as *enmeshed, dysfunctional,* or *emotionally disengaged,* which serves to place blame and pathologize the family. The language of the broader society is also filled with words and phrases that label behavior that is considered less than acceptable or abnormal, such as "gay/alternative lifestyles," or even "single parents" (Besa, 1994). Drewery, Winslade, and Monk (2000) emphasize the importance of recognizing the power and influence of the use of words in creating frameworks for tangible consequences that impact people's lives and become predictors of expected future behavior.

Drawing extensively on Foucault's ideas, Michael White espoused forming a therapeutic coalition with individuals and families to protest oppressive social and cultural forces that become incorporated into problematic beliefs. One of the cornerstones of his approach is the claim that the person/family/system is not the problem, "the problem is the problem." Creative exchanges called "externalizing conversations" (Tomm, 1993) are not merely designed to remove the stigma from the person with the problem but a political process of empowering individuals and families to objectify the problem and to unite with the therapist to protest its oppression. For example, Western women have labored under the cultural construct that to be thin is to be beautiful, and they seek to attain physical perfection (control) through their weight. Many of these women have come to see themselves as under the influence of anorexia (rather than being anorectic) and have begun to take a stand against anorectic ways for themselves and others. In fact, "Anti-anorexia/Anti-bulimia leagues," the brainchild of David Epston, have sprung up in Australia, New Zealand, and Canada. The purpose of these leagues is to mobilize individuals and families who are being tyrannized by those disorders to unite their energies (Nichols & Schwartz, 2001). Vodde & Gallant (2002) suggest that this sort of political activism demonstrates a unique bridge between micro and macro practice in the field of social work, provided by the practices in narrative therapy.

Theory of Change

According to Edward Bruner (1986) and Jerome Bruner (1990), stories provide the primary means for individuals to structure or organize their lived experiences. As life stories are told with their inevitable gaps and inconsistencies, lives are changed through the process of interpreting situations and filling the gaps with both experiences and imagination. As these narratives or stories are enacted or performed, they affect lives. In fact, White (1988) asserted that life is a process of reauthoring lives and relationships.

The narrative therapist who is presented with a problem-filled story such as the case of Rhonda and Jamie challenges it by focusing predominantly on previously disregarded exceptions (or unique outcomes) to the story that is presented. The narrative therapist attempts, with the family, to cocreate around the exceptions of new ideas, new information, and new perceptions that will challenge former presuppositions and create a context for change (Anoretic & Anoretic, 1991). Problem-saturated beliefs are challenged, and possibilities for alternative ways of behaving are enhanced. These alternative ways compose the new story that can gradually replace the steadily less influential old. In the case of children, it is often effective to tune into their fantasies and imaginations as well as their behaviors. These can be rich sources for identifying exceptions and authoring solution focused stories. According to Carlson and Kjos (2002), it is in this reauthoring process that the seeds of hope can be found.

If the therapist who was mentioned in the opening passage of this chapter had been trained in the narrative approach, she would have realized that exploring the couple's family history out of context of what the couple saw to be their problem led to a missed opportunity to learn about the couple and the way they viewed themselves and each other, as well as their problem. She also would have known that it would have set the stage for the negative labeling that could contribute to the oppression and sense of hopelessness of this young family. White argues that the search for a cause is itself a problem, leading to vicious cycles of blame and guilt. Since the focus in the narrative model is on the meanings that are attributed to problems, rather than on their causes, it would have assisted the couple in exploring their problem story from their vantage point. A narrative therapist would have believed that it was important to hear and amplify how any new actions might be different than the old, problem-saturated version in which the couple saw themselves as being trapped, betrayed, and victimized. Her first step though would have been to validate the feelings the couple had in relation to their problem, to hear their story, and to acknowledge its power and influence on them, thus conveying an atmosphere of respect, trust, and empathy for both Rhonda and Jamie.

Theory of Problems

Drawing on the works of Bateson (1972, 1979), narrative therapists subscribe to the notion that problems are *not* inherent in individuals or families. Problems are viewed as arising when people assign narrow and self-defeating interpretations about themselves to events that occur. These self-defeating cognitions are often culturally imposed, and narrative therapists refer to these cognitions as the client's "dominant" or "problem-saturated" story—the primary or dominant story that the client believes. Thus, these restricted views may prevent people from noticing information about their own strengths and abilities that could help them deal with the problems in their lives. This is the point at which families and individuals often seek therapy (White & Epston, 1990). Too often, well-meaning therapists, such as the therapist who focused on Rhonda and Jamie's family story, reinforce this restricted view, the one often most of interest to professional helpers. This is not the only option, however. The problem and its oppression of individuals can be deliberately "placed" by the therapist outside the individual or family. In this method, the cause is not sought, and the focus is instead on developing a deeper understanding of how the individuals themselves understand the problem.

Since the underlying assumption is that reality is invented, narrative therapists believe that the concept of the self as a monolithic entity does not exist, since the self is essentially determined by situation and by the people with whom the self is interacting. Bruner (2002) argues that "in effect, there is no such thing as an intuitively obvious and essential self to know, one that just sits there ready to be portrayed in words" (p. 4). He suggests that the self is fluid and evolves during interaction with others and situations. Drawing from the work of Markus and Nurius (1986) and Parry and Doan (1994), McQuaide (2000) describes this process as a "confederacy of selves." For example, the self we are with our friends is different than the self we are with our family, which is different from the self we are at work. Even within those groups, we are different with the various group members and are different depending on our mood and circumstance. Who we are is constantly in flux and always in the process of being reinvented. White refers to this notion as "the constituted self" in describing how meanings are cocreated between individuals and others as they communicate. McQuaide (2000) postulates that each of these selves has its own narrative and, "The different ways a person can story (his or) her life (. . . self-narratives) can be sources of strength and resilience or sources of weakness and vulnerability" (p. 72). Thus we all have parts that are resilient and other parts that are less so depending on the circumstance, and it is the job of the therapist to enhance and empower the already existing, if dormant, resilient selves.

Assessment

Assessment from the narrative perspective is not concerned with diagnoses or classification into pathologizing categories, but rather is as an intervention itself, concerned with the bringing forth of stories from a stance of respectful curiosity. Assessment occurs through enactment of a person's stories rather than through the uncovering of facts. When stories and their meanings are revealed, strengths emerge at every step of the therapeutic process. Alternative stories can deconstruct and challenge the old story and are being cultivated throughout the process. Thus, assessment and treatment are not considered separate processes, but become intertwined and interdependent.

The concept of a symptom's function is foreign to the narrative approach (Chang & Phillips, 1993), and the labeling of such serves merely to distract from the problem and its effects on the individual or family. In the narrative model, symptom functionality is replaced by the view that problems are inevitable and that restraints have prevented the discovery of effective solutions. As these negative explanations are employed, the pertinent question is not, Why are things this way? but, What has stopped things from being different? (Anoretic & Anoretic, 1991). In the following case example, Rhonda and Jamie, a young couple dealing with the effects of an affair, sought counseling to salvage their marriage.

Unrealized Potential: The Story of Rhonda and Jamie

Rhonda and Jamie, the parents of four-year-old Dawn, came to the family counseling center at the recommendation of their pastor. The referral came as a result of discovering Jamie's brief affair with Rhonda's cousin, who had been living with them temporarily. Devastated, Rhonda insisted that he move out, and the couple had tumultuously been dealing with the problem ever since it happened. Because the couple live in a rural county, seeking out marital counseling required that they drive 100 miles round trip and each take time off from work in order to make their appointments. Rhonda and Jamie had been high school sweethearts and married when Rhonda became pregnant as a junior in high school. They each had grown up and continue to live in a rural county among a large extended family. Jamie works as a maintenance man at an apartment complex, a job he describes as hating. They have been married for four years and have one child, a daughter, that Rhonda self-describes as being overly attached to. The child is cared for during the week by Jamie's mother. Rhonda acknowledges that she is "paranoid" when it comes to leaving her daughter and has taken to worrying more and more about leaving her. The first few sessions were spent focusing on the presenting problem: the affair and how it had taken hold of their lives.

While the dominant culture might be inclined to view this couple as dysfunctional, their cultural norms are such that marrying young, dropping out of high school, teen pregnancy, and extended family involvement are the norm. The news of a difference was not that they were facing marital problems; the real news was that they were seeking help in a way that was new and different for them. Since narrative therapists are not problem solvers, they are more interested in partnering with people to enhance their awareness of the way in which cultural forces have lulled them into accepting problem-saturated ways of living. Narrative therapists are less concerned with formulating therapeutic goals than they are with coauthoring with clients new, preferable stories about themselves. The focus is on enabling people to separate themselves from the problem by convincing them that the problem is the problem itself and not the person. Once free from the old problem, people have room to rewrite new scripts for their lives.

Intervention Approaches

The Therapeutic Process

According to White (1991) a central component of the narrative approach is a "deconstruction," which involves "procedures that subvert taken-for-granted realities and practices" (p. 121). The dominant story of a troubled family is usually fraught with a sense of helplessness and blame-filled descriptions of each member and the relationships among the members. Using a narrative approach to treatment, the therapist facilitates the bringing forth of what is called the "problem-saturated story"—typically, the presenting problem. Each selected memory carries meaning or personal significance that allows people to make sense of and find continuity in their experiences. The meanings that humans attach to situations and events influence their behavior around those events. Without planning or intending to, individuals support and maintain problems by cooperating with the problem until it seems to develop its own lifestyle or "career" (White & Epston, 1990). Through the use of empathic listening and carefully constructed questions, the narrative therapist "maps" the influence of the problem (Monk, Winslade, Crocket, & Epston, 1997), thus acknowledging its influence on the family.

In the case of Rhonda and Jamie, the therapist began by searching for meaning around the affair. She asked them a series of "curious" questions, such as, "What did the affair mean to you as a couple and as individuals?" "How did the affair affect you?" "What's different about today when you talk about the affair than when you first found out about it?" "What did it mean for the affair to be with your cousin?" "How has the affair affected your family relationships?" One of the outcomes of the affair is that it enabled the couple to seek out professional counseling and put some distance between themselves and their families. Since the couple lived over an hour's drive from the counseling office, it also "forced" them to have some time alone with each other while driving to and fro. The therapist saw that as an opportunity to further ask the couple, "What is it about the two of you that you have been able to use this affair as an opportunity for the two of you to fight for the relationship and the possibility of a different life together?" and, "What does it say about your relationship that you are willing to travel so far and make such a huge commitment to work on your relationship?"

Therapeutic Strategies and Intervention Approaches

Narrative interventions include an eclectic collection of treatment methods, any or all of which may include the use of "curious" questions to enable family members to explore other aspects of their lived experiences. Through this process, they are able to recall alternative stories that often draw on previous successes. Several of the more commonly used techniques are described in the following paragraphs. The order in which they are listed is intended to reflect a somewhat logical sequence, although some of these methods can be repeated many times or possibly even eliminated. The process should be seen as rather more like loops and curves than steps. It becomes the therapist's job, through a process of therapeutic conversations, to assist in drawing out and identifying experiences from the past that are exceptions to the individual's problem-saturated, old story. The exceptions or unique outcomes are evidence that, on occasion, the person has successfully challenged the problem and has mustered the strength to overpower it. As the significance and impact of the exceptions are explored and elaborated, the individual's sense of personal efficacy intensifies. Exceptions, with their new, reauthored meanings, become part of the new story's history. The therapist, and eventually the client, can then decline to accept the validity of the old story (Hewson, 1991; White & Epston, 1990).

1. Normalizing the Problem. The success of the narrative model is dependent on the collaborative bond that is established between the therapist and the client. One of the impacts of shared stories is the cultivation of empathy in the listener, which McLeod (1999) described as a co-construction of a relational process that is central to developing strong helping relationships.

Rhonda and Jamie's therapist, in seeking to understand them and their problem, began by asking many questions, phrasing them in a way that helped the couple think about their situation in a sightly different way. This questioning process helped them to feel validated and safe with the therapist and allowed the therapist, in the process, to begin to view their story more objectively. It also enabled the therapist to shift the focus from shame and blame between the couple to uniting them against a problem that they shared in common: the disrupting effects of the affair. After hearing Rhonda's detailed description of her story of betrayal and rejection, the therapist normalized their experience by observing that, while both Rhonda and Jamie appeared to be under the influence of a great deal of sadness, anger, and loneliness because of the affair, it was completely understandable, given that their marriage had suffered such a blow. The therapist believed that it was her role to hear and amplify any new versions of their story that were different from the old, problem-saturated version. She began by commenting on the couple's commitment in joining together to fight for their marriage. In doing so, the therapist marveled at the distance, time, and trouble the couple were investing by coming to therapy.

2. Externalization of the Problem: The Problem Is the Problem. Frequently, individuals and families have had previous experience with therapists who have labored with them to "work through" or "come to terms" with particular "pathologies" or "dysfunctions." As a result, clients are often restrained by the belief that blame needs to be assigned to somebody who has intentionally maintained

or caused a problem or that the problem reflects a character defect or personality weakness. Externalizing the problem challenges these notions.

Rhonda was filled with anger toward Jamie, expressing her sense of betrayal, pain, and anger in a litany of accusations and repetitive tirades that left them both feeling helpless and hopeless. Her ruminations prevented her from being able to receive the support that she wanted from her family, friends, and especially from Jamie. The therapist began by asking a series of questions aimed at deconstructing the experience, such as, "How has this affair affected you as individuals and as a couple?" and, "What has the affair meant to you as individuals and as a couple?"

The sometimes-humorous technique of naming the problem—such as referring to alcohol as "Al"—enables clients to focus their energies on combating the problem itself. This externalization process allows people to visualize the solution in terms of the collaborative process of forming a team to combat the problem. Externalization is more than a reframing and depersonalizing of the problem. It is a way for families to gain control over the problem. Therapist and family members work together to define the problem situation or pattern as something outside of and distinct from the "identified patient." As the problem is shaped through metaphor into an "entity" that can be named, the individual or family can distance themselves from the problem, challenge it, and defeat it (Neimeyer, 1993a; Winslade & Smith, 1997).

3. Mapping the Problem. As part of the early, assessment/intervention phase, therapist and client(s) explore reciprocal patterns that become apparent and that are shown to have been supporting the problem. The problem and its impact on the individual's and family's life and relationships are scrutinized at length. The narrative therapist asks each family member to give a detailed, no-holds-barred account of the distressing effects of the problem and the extent to which each individual has been supervised (dominated, pushed around, controlled) by it. Gold, Morris, and Gretchen (2003) advocate combining intergenerational aspects of the client's narrative as a way to conceptualize and intervene with the family's history. Part of the mapping process is exploring the influence (effect) of the person on the problem. White (1986) has referred to these combined questions as the mapping of the relative influence of the problem in the life of the person, and the person in the life of the problem.

Rhonda and Jamie's therapist began by assessing the influence that the problem was having on each of them as well as on the marriage. Together they discovered that the problem was bigger than the affair, that Jamie had been very unhappy in his job and that had spilled over into their marriage. Jamie also felt quite negatively about himself and was extremely self-critical. Once Rhonda's anger was explored and diminished, his story, one of desperate futility around his work situation that had little to do with Rhonda, was deconstructed. She was able to hear how "unmanly" he felt in his limited job, and a new narrative began to emerge regarding the young man who shyly shared that he taught himself to become computer savvy, had quietly rebuilt a computer, and had dreams of studying computer science. Rhonda was able to express her pride in his knowledge.

4. News of a Difference. "News of a difference" is news that makes a difference. It provides a twist that allows the individual and family to see and experience the old story in a new way. The changed meaning provides a new story line for daily living. The individuals are encouraged to acknowledge their progress through amplifying and recognizing the significance of small changes and shifts of behaviors away from the problem. In being helped to recognize the incremental improvements that they are implementing in their lives—how they are "going against" their dominant story line—the family members are empowered to change the story that dominates their view of themselves. People tend to cling to the story that they are used to, long after it serves them or is even an accurate depiction of their current reality. News of a difference empowers the family to recognize and acknowledge that changes are occurring, and they are responsible for the change. This is accomplished through a collaborative process of cocreating and witnessing the new or alternative stories that emphasizes optimism and empowerment. The therapist becomes a cheerleader who painstakingly amplifies successes.

Since the affair had such power in the marriage, the therapist felt that Rhonda's rumination represented her need to be listened to. The therapist set a structured dialogue that allowed one partner at a time to speak and then experience the other partner simply repeating back what was said, with guidance from the therapist to stay on track. Rhonda went first, and at the end of the exercise the therapist helped Jamie validate her feelings. Through this exercise, Rhonda's anger shifted significantly so that at the end, she was actually able to inject a note of empathy and hope for the future of their marriage. In this experience, Rhonda was able to viscerally experience "news of a difference"—that is, experience being heard. Most of the rest of the session was spent exploring the couple's extraordinary triumph in being able to talk about such a loaded, painful topic.

The structured dialogue enabled Rhonda to dive beyond the current story to richer, unexplored territory, and while doing so, she felt her husband genuinely struggling to understand her deeper experience. As the dialogue progressed, she moved from her rage and sense of betrayal and a familiar sense of hopelessness to see change, allowing her to explore a sense of possibility—her needs, hopes, and expectations for the future. As the dialogue ended, she began to experience her husband as a partner who was capable of working with her to comprehend her larger vision for their future.

At the next session, there was a visceral demonstration of difference. Simply watching the couple's entrance into the therapy room in the first few minutes, it was obvious to the therapist that a palpable change had occurred. A sense of harmony was evident in the couple's eye contact, body language, level of laughter, and ease of relating. Rhonda and Jamie reported having spent the previous weekend on an unprecedented outing together away from their town, family, and child. They were literally bubbling over with new energy, and there was a sense of connection and trust. In this session, Jamie began to construct a new story of possibility around his work as he experienced and celebrated the couple's triumphant rewriting of their story.

   5. Therapeutic Questions. The narrative therapist asks many gentle, curious, respectful questions in the process of interventive interviewing. It is assumed that questions will elicit experiences of exceptions, which is the stuff of re-storying (Tomm, 1987; White & Epston, 1990). "Curious" questions, by and large, are the means by which restraining patterns are revealed and challenged and new opportunities are discovered for positive, affirmative, more flexible action around the problem. As part of this search, any information that represents positive moves toward change is noticed, seized on, and highlighted. Language and metaphors are used creatively to highlight the relative influence of the problem. The following are illustrations of types of questions the therapist used with Rhonda and Jamie in laying the groundwork for the re-storying of their narrative:

   a. Opening space for possibilities:
   • To Jamie:
      How have you been able to begin to see the possibility of another way of supporting your family?
   • To Rhonda:
      How have you been able to move beyond your anger?
   • To both:
      How have you been able to see the importance of seeking counseling?
      How have you been able, despite all the obstacles, to have hope for your marriage?
      How have you been able to open yourself up to hear what your partner is really saying?
   b. Effect (of change) questions to amplify news of a difference:
   • So what has it been like for you to spend a day together fighting for your family?
   • So what has it been like for you to feel heard by Jamie?
   • How have the changes that you have experienced affected your daughter and the rest of your family?
   • What is it about the two of you that makes you able to use this affair as an opportunity to fight for the relationship?
   c. Preference questions:
   • Do you prefer these differences or the old way?
   • What has it been like for you to come to counseling today versus the first time?
   d. Story development questions/news of a difference question:
   • If you were to run a video in your head, what scenes might be there now that would not been there before?
   • If I were a fly on the wall, what would I hear you saying now in tone or words that might be different now from then?
   • Creating a song, poem, or a letter they write together or the therapist writes to them.

    e. Meaning questions:
- What does it say about you as a couple that you were able to fight so hard for your marriage?
- What does it say about you that you made the time to travel so far?

    f. Future:
- As you continue on this same path, what do you imagine your relationship will look like in the future?
- How do you see yourselves continuing to communicate effectively?

6. Exceptions Questions. These questions focus on situations of successful, exceptional outcomes that do not square with the dominant, problem-filled story. These are the overlooked times when the problem did not get the upper hand but are not recognized yet as victories worth acknowledging by the client.

Rhonda and Jamie's therapist also inquired about how the couple's ability to communicate was different from previous occasions in their married life when they had been less able. The therapist helped bring forth the emergence of a different narrative, one in which Rhonda and Jamie were capable of discussing difficult things and becoming closer as a result. This experience helped the couple to begin to frame how they wanted their relationship to be in the future.

7. History of Exceptions Questions. Sometimes called unique account questions, they help uncover past clues to accounts of current competence. Michael White (1991) urged therapists to treat these discoveries as significant and as intriguing mysteries "that persons can only unravel as they respond to the therapist's curiosity about them. As persons take up the task of unraveling such mysteries, they immediately engage in storytelling and meaning-making" (p. 30).

Rhonda and Jamie were encouraged to remember and describe situations in which they had felt comfortable and content in their relationship. They came to see that the affair was not the norm and that they had, in fact, had many more good times than bad. Other examples of questions from Rhonda and Jamie's sessions:

- How have you been able to see the importance of coming to counseling?
- How have you, despite all the obstacles, managed to hang on to hope in your marriage?
- How have you been able to open yourself up to hear what your partner is trying to say?

8. Significance Questions. These questions search for and reveal the meanings, significance, and importance of the exceptions. Questions of significance help draw attention to the importance of the exception and the possibility of new meanings. For example, Rhonda and Jamie were asked:

- What do you think these discoveries reveal to you/me/your family about your motives and what is important to you and your life?
- In more fully appreciating your achievement, what conclusions might you reach about what your marriage stands for?

9. Spectator Questions. These are sometimes called experience-of-experience questions; they invite individuals to imagine how other people that they have known might experience them. For example, Rhonda and Jamie's therapist asked them:

- If I had been able to look in on your earlier life, what might I have seen you doing that would reveal to me how you have been able to take this step?
- Of all who have known you, who would be the least surprised that your marriage has been able to meet this challenge and what would they have seen that would enable them to predict it?

10. Collapsing Time and Raising Dilemmas. This technique highlights the relative influence of the problem. It also allows individuals to peer into the past and future to consider how the problem might have developed, how it is likely to evolve, and how to make a decision around the resulting dilemma: Is it worth the effort to fight for the marriage? Some questions that the couple's therapist introduced to them are as follows:

- Is your marriage more of a problem for you now than, say, six months ago?
- If you were to continue to allow this affair to get the best of you, in what other ways would you invite your friends and people with whom you will have relationships in the future to treat you as fragile and protect you from their opinions?

11. Enhancing Changes. Reinforcing changes can be accomplished through the respectful challenge of a client's dominant story. This serves to motivate individuals to reexamine their narratives, leading to an amplification of changes already under way. The goal here is to demolish the problem-saturated version and to begin to reauthor a more adaptive story. Children and adolescents seem particularly open to this method and respond with energy and devotion to proving the problem-saturated story to be wrong. Motivational questions or comments may include the following:

- To a teen: "But wait a minute, you told me that you were always sad, and now you're telling me that you were happy on Saturday! Are you telling me that you were able to keep sadness out of your life on Saturday?"
- To a parent: "You said you noticed that Billy kept fear from pushing him around and you were able to go to the mall. I don't get it! I thought you said fear controlled him all the time! Something is different here. What happened?"

12. Predicting Setbacks. This can be done before the dilemma is even settled. Because the problem-saturated story still dominates, setbacks are virtually inevitable and, thus, they must be anticipated and their distress expected and planned for. However, this needs to occur in a manner that highlights and encourages self-efficacy. In the following questions, the couple's therapist cautioned them:

- If you are really determined to make a radical change in your marriage, do you think you'll be able to handle a setback? Or will you be tricked and seduced into using something like an affair again?

13. Letters and Audiotapes. This is a powerful tool for continuing and reinforcing the dialogue between therapist and family members. Therapist-authored letters and tapes can be rich sources for summarizing sessions, writing up case notes and sharing them with the client, highlighting emerging new stories, and rendering lived experience into a narrative or story. The therapist can ask "curious" questions (such as those already indicated) that may cause individuals to further reflect on their circumstances and that may unearth new meanings, affirm exceptions and unique outcomes, and pose new ideas or possibilities. Following a session in which the couple struggled with the powerful aftermath of the affair, Rhonda and Jamie's therapist sent them a letter:

> Dear Rhonda and Jamie,
>
> I have been thinking about our meeting today and thought it would be useful for all of us if I put into writing some of the things we talked about. Please let me know next time we meet if there are things that I missed or need to understand more fully.
>
> When we first met, you explained that you both were fighting a particularly painful battle for your marriage. Rhonda, I am very curious about how you have managed to overcome your anger and to trust the relationship again, just as I am curious, Jamie, about how you have managed to find the courage to fight so hard for your family in spite of your fear. I understand that this has been far from easy. In fact, I can't help wondering how the two of you have used the strength of your marriage to combat the effect of the affair, and I wonder if your marriage is perhaps stronger as a result.
>
> Rhonda, you also talked about how preoccupation with the affair was leading you "by the nose," and I couldn't help wondering how you managed to stand up to preoccupation a few weeks back in spite of the formidable power it has. I was thinking how, even in our meeting, preoccupation attempted to convince all of us that your withdrawal was the only remedy. From your experience, do you think it's true that withdrawal is a remedy? Do you think withdrawal and preoccupation have teamed up against both of you to strengthen each other's place in your life, or have they assisted you as you strive to develop your full potential?
>
> Jamie, you have mentioned how, despite all obstacles, you have decided to continue to fight for your marriage. How have you been able to do that? Also, how have you begun to see another way to support your family, like working with computers? When did it occur to you that you had possibilities and options?
>
> I have many more questions but am hoping I haven't already overwhelmed you. If any of these thoughts or questions are interesting to you, we can discuss them more fully when we meet or, if you feel inclined to write or draw a response, that would be great. (adapted from Winslade & Smith, 1997)

14. Reflecting Team. This is a method introduced by Tom Andersen (1991) as a way to explore available but unasked questions during family therapy conversations. A team of observers (from one to several), functioning as an audience, silently listens to the therapist and family. At a designated time, the therapist invites the team to share its observations with one another about what they have just observed. The family and therapist silently listen to the team, which reflects on the story of the family with positive and curious comments and questions. Questions often begin with "I seemed to notice . . ." or "I couldn't help but wonder what would happen if . . ." The team attempts to be sensitive, imaginative, and respectful and to avoid any negative connotations, advice, or criticism. They introduce new ideas, bring out unnoticed exceptions, and expand the family's new story. This process usually lasts about five minutes, after which the family and therapist can jointly reflect on the reflecting team's conversation.

15. Certificates and Celebrations. These acknowledgments can serve as a tangible affirmation of a defeat of the problem or a new description of an individual. Certificates mark celebrations of victories, and actual celebrations—complete with balloons, cake, and punch—signify that problems have been successfully challenged and defeated. These personal affirmations contribute to an individual's new story. To illustrate, Michael White (White & Epston, 1990) has a professionally printed certificate, complete with photo and logo, that reads, in part:

MONSTER-TAMER & FEAR-CATCHER CERTIFICATE

This is to certify that _____ has undergone a Complete Training Programme in Monster-Taming and Fear-Catching, is now a fully qualified Monster-Tamer and Fear-Catcher, and is available to offer help to other children who are bugged liars. (p. 193)

Another certificate, suitable for an adult, reads:

ESCAPE FROM GUILT CERTIFICATE

_____ is over guilt. Now that guilt doesn't have such a priority in her life, she is able to give herself a priority in her own ~ This certificate will serve to remind _____ and others, that she has resigned from the position of super-responsibility in the lives of others, and that she is no longer vulnerable to invitations from others to live their life for them and to put her life to one side. (p. 199)

Evaluation

Despite the impressive treatment effects noted in many case studies by Michael White and others, there continues to be a dearth of empirical research that examines the effectiveness of narrative methodology. This is mostly likely due to the narrativist conclusion that traditional quantitative investigatory methods with an emphasis on measurement and positivist thinking are at odds with the values espoused by the narrative and postmodern school. At the core of this dialogue is the issue of epistemology. With a different view on the nature of reality itself, reality and accompanying "normalcy" become moving targets, shifting with each family's narrative. Thus, narrative therapists have mostly used the case study method to testify to the method's effectiveness and have been slow to experiment with ways of using quantitative methods to measure success. (See "Applications of Narrative Approach to Other Levels of Need" section for illustrations of problems for which case studies have been published.) However, as qualitative methodological approaches that are perhaps more compatible with capturing the process of change in this approach—such as phenomenology (Moustakas, 1994), grounded theory (Glaser & Strauss, 1967; Strauss & Corbin, 1990), and the case study method (Merriam, 1988)—continue to achieve higher credibility, the literature will reflect more research.

A recent ethnographic study focusing on therapists' experiences in the use of narrative therapy (O'Connor, Meakes, Pickering, & Schuman, 2004) reveals that they perceive the narrative approach to be successful with clients in reducing presenting problems. They also report that the therapists have noted more enthusiastic successes, observing marked improvement in their clients and greater satisfaction in the development of a personal agency with them. Thus, the therapists viewed the narrative approach as highly respectful. Among the limitations of this approach were the requirement for specialized training to facilitate this approach, the challenges to effectively addressing family violence, the relatively dense time commitments and staff requirements (for use of reflecting teams), and the use of consulting/reflecting teams, which, while rich and helpful for the clients, can be overwhelming and threatening for the therapists.

Applications to Families at Other Levels of Need

Examples of applications of the narrative approach to a wide variety of individual and family problems:

- Couple/relationship therapy (Blanton & Vandergriff-Avery, 2001; Brimball, Gardner, & Henline, 2003; Butler & Gardner, 2003; Butler & Bird, 2000; Freedman & Combs, 2000; Neal, Zimmerman, & Dickerson, 1999; Snyder, 2000)
- Working with children (Epston & Ronny, 2004; Goddard, Lehr, & Lapadat, 2000)
- Substance abuse (Anoretic & Anoretic, 1991; Lyness, 2002; Man-kwong, 2004; Winslade & Smith, 1997).
- Dissociative disorder (Gallant, Brownlee, & Vodde, 1995)
- AIDS (Dean, 1995; Rothschild, Brownlee, & Gallant, 2000; White & Epston, 1991).
- Domestic violence (Augusta-Scott & Dankwort, 2002; Drauker, 2003; Jenkins, 1990; Tomm, 2002; Wright, 2003).
- Gay/lesbian issues (Behan, 1999; O'Dell, 2000)
- Anorexia/bulimia (Dallos, 2004; Epston, 1993a; Epston, Morris, & Maisel, 1995)
- Grief (McQuaide, 1995; White, 1989a)
- Trauma (Bhuvaneswar & Shafer, 2004; Hardy, 2002; Lapsley, 2002; Shalev, 2000)

- Spirituality (Abels, 2000; Carlson & Erickston, 2000; Faiver, Ingersol, O'Brien, et al., 2001; Ramsey & Bleiszner, 2000; Feinstein, 1997)
- Support groups (Jones, 2004)
- Multiple sclerosis (Eeltink & Puffy, 2004)
- Women's issues/sexual abuse (Cowley, Farley, & Beamis, 2002; Gremillion, 2004; Verko, 2002).

Ethical Challenges

There are several ethical challenges for narrative family interventions, among them:

1. Seeing any interpretation as being as good as any other.
2. Inattention to power differences in family and community regarding interpretations.
3. Assuming that the narrative approach can reach the best solutions for anyone.

These challenges deserve discussion and consideration.

Summary

Narrative therapy is a postmodern approach to individual and family therapy that is rooted in social constructionism and uses the storytelling process as a primary therapeutic metaphor. This approach, credited to Michael White, an Australian social worker, and referred to as the third wave of family therapy, can be viewed as a reaction against the effects of the imposition of the dominant narratives of human behavior on culture. This shaping process has been reflected in older models that are viewed as blaming the individual (psychodynamic) or blaming the family (family systems). This model places great emphasis on a collaborative therapeutic alliance between the therapist and the client in which they team together to challenge old stories and cocreate new realities. Problems are investigated based on the meanings that a client assigns rather than on their causes. Assessment/ intervention occurs as the problem-saturated story is carefully deconstructed and through therapeutic strategies such as "news of a difference," as strengths are focused on and exceptions emerge that actively challenge the client's belief in the old story. These strategies involve carefully worded questions that are aimed at making the problem, not the person, the problem a process called externalization of the problem. Through this process, the relative influence and power of the problem on the person is assessed, and the resources the individual used to combat the problem are validated and celebrated. At this point, the influence of the person on the problem takes center stage through the uncovering of exceptions to problematic situations. "Curious," gentle, respectful questions can be raised about each exception, such as its history, its significance, and its spectators/audience. Setbacks can be anticipated and plans made to deal with them and, if possible, a reflecting team can provide new descriptions and previously unnoticed exceptions. Letters, certificates, and celebrations are used to amplify the content of the sessions and provide continuity to what has been accomplished between and after sessions.

Discussion Questions

1. What is meant by the notion that there is not one self but a multiplicity of selves?

2. Explain the idea that one's self can only be defined in relationship with others.

3. Why does narrative therapy emphasize the meaning of problems rather than their causes?

4. What is meant by the phrase "problem-saturated story"?

5. What is the role of assessment in narrative therapy?

6. What is meant by the phrase "the problem is the problem"?

7. What are some of the key ideas that narrative therapists rely on to increase the likelihood that therapy is a process of cocreation rather than therapist directed?

8. What roles do oppression and power play in the life of a person's presenting problem?

9. What role can externalization of the problem play in de-escalating the oppressive story of the problem?

10. What role can exceptions play in helping to reauthor a person's story?

11. What value do letters, celebrations, and reflecting teams have in narrative therapy?

12. How can the narrative approach be used with families that are perceived to be functioning at each of the four levels?

13. If you were to use the narrative perspective, how would the way in which you see yourself working with families be different from the way it is now?

Internet Resources

www.narrativeapproaches.com/
www.california.com/~rathbone/pmth.htm
www.acs.ucalgary.ca/~strongt/
www.narrativespyche.com
www.massey.ae.nz/~alock/virtual/narrativ.htm

Suggested Readings

Andersen, T. (Ed.). (1991). *The reflecting team: Dialogues and dialogues about the dialogues.* New York: Norton.
The development of a new strategy in therapy is presented, in which professionals and clients trade places, exchange conversations, and open up new possibilities for change.

Dialogues are exchanged in collaborative discussions among family, therapist, and reflecting team and result in the dissolving of traditional therapeutic boundaries.

Angus, L. E., & McLeod, J. (Eds.). (2004). *The handbook of narrative and psychotherapy: Practice theory and research.* Thousand Oaks, CA: Sage.

This volume presents narrative theory and appled research and practice from a number of different disciplines. The editors have attempted to incorporate the varying voices and traditions that have contributed to the current narrative-informed field of therapy.

Anoretic, M., & Epston, D. (1989). The taming of temper. *Dulwich Centre Newsletter* (Special ed.), 3–26.

This issue includes articles by Anoretic (Temper taming: An approach to children's temper problems—Revisited) and Epston (Temper tantrum parties: Saving face, losing face, or going off your face!). Anoretic's article discusses temper and behavior problems from a narrative viewpoint, as well as the development of his ideas in dealing with these issues. Epston's article presents a method for dealing with out-of-control temper in children or adults. The approach is simple, economical, and amusing for all concerned as it teaches individuals to substitute self-control for the control of others.

Anoretic, M., & Kowalski, K. (1990). Overcoming the effects of sexual abuse: Developing a self-perception of competence. In M. Anoretic & C. White (Eds.), *Ideas for therapy with sexual abuse.* Adelaide, S. Australia: Dulwich Centre.

Drawing from both the narrative approach and the model of brief solution-focused therapy, the authors approach the issue of sexual abuse qualitatively, not unlike other issues in therapy. They propose a framework for enhancing the perception of self as competent rather than as victim.

Freedman, J., & Combs, G. (1996). *Narrative therapies: The special construction of preferred realties.* New York: Norton.

Drawing from the narrative approach, the authors present practical information to the clinician intent. Issues of practice power, sociocultural context, and ethics are addressed in this acclaimed book.

Gilligan, S., & Price, R. (Eds.). (1993). *Therapeutic conversations.* New York: Norton.

Emerging from a conference held in Tulsa in June 1992, the book's contributors are well known within the traditions and spheres of narrative family therapy tradition, solution-focused tradition, and conversational therapies. Chapter authors respond to each other's positions and perspectives. Contributors include John Weakland, David Epston, Michael White, Steve de Shazer, Karl Tomm, and Michele Weiner-Davis.

Lieblich, A., McAdams, D. P., & Josselson, R. (Eds.). (2002). *Healing Plots: The Narrative Basis of Psychotherapy.* Washington, DC: American Psychological Association.

This book is the third volume in a series entitled *The Narrative Study of Lives.* This volume explores the relationship between therapy and narrative and how stories impact the therapeutic process. The selection of chapters describe therapeutic process from a variety of perspectives and settings.

Metcalf, L. (1991). Therapy with parent-adolescent conflict: Creating a climate in which clients can figure what to do differently. *Family Therapy Case Studies, 6*(2), 25–34.

Responsibility and protection are contrasted with freedom and independence as being the conflicting needs of parents and adolescents. As conflicts increase, guilt and blame often result. The examples given demonstrate a climate in which families can decide on alternative behaviors and resolve their conflicts. Ideas are used from both the brief solution-focused model and from the narrative approach.

Monk, G., Winslade, J., Crockett, K., & Epston, D. (Eds.). (1997). *Narrative therapy in practice: The archaeology of hope.* San Francisco: Jossey-Bass.

This instructive book reflects a collaboration of practitioners who have appled narrative therapy to diverse populations. It is filled with instructive, illustrative examples that describe the application of this approach in creative and hope-filled ways.

Tomm, K. (1988). Interventive interviewing: Intending to ask lineal, circular, strategic, or reflexive questions? *Family Process, 27,* 1–15.

> This article and the two preceding it (Interventive interviewing I and II, *Family Process, 26,* 3–13, 167–183) discuss questions based on circular rather than lineal assumptions. A framework is offered that distinguishes four major groups of questions with guidelines for their use. Lineal assumptions lead to lineal and strategic questions; circular assumptions lead to circular and reflexive questions. The categories of questions are discussed regarding their effects on families and on therapists.

White, M. (1991). Deconstruction and therapy. *Dulwich Centre Newsletter, 3,* 21–40.

> White presents theory and case studies illustrating externalization of the problem and relative influence questioning. He explains deconstruction and the place of meaning in narrative. The article includes discussion of issues of power and of the influence of Michel Foucault. It relates discussion of power back to examples. White challenges therapists to question the notion of "expert power" in therapeutic situations.

White, M., & Epston, D. (1990). *Narrative means to therapeutic ends.* New York: Norton.

> Letters, documents, and certificates become a respectful and often playful means to encourage the restorying of experience. The narrative approach is explained. Many examples are offered, suitable for children, adolescents, and adults. In addition, the restraints of power and the political implications inherent in therapy are discussed.

References

Abels, S. L. (2000). *Spirituality in social work practice: Narratives for professional helping.* Denver: Love Publishing.

American Psychiatric Association. (1994). *Diagnostic and Statistical Manual for the Human Sciences, IV.* Washington, DC: American Psychiatric Association.

Andersen, T. (Ed.). (1991). *The reflecting team: Dialogues and dialogues about the dialogues.* New York: Norton.

Anoretic, M., & Anoretic, D. (1991). Michael White's cybernetic approach. In T. Todd & M. Selekman (Eds.), *Family therapy approaches with adolescent substance abusers.* Boston: Allyn & Bacon.

Anoretic, M., & Epston, D. (1989). Temper taming: An approach to children's temper problems revisited. *Dulwich Centre Newsletter,* 3–11.

Angus, L. E., & McLeod, J. (Eds.). (2004). *The handbook of narrative and psychotherapy: Practice theory and research.* Thousand Oaks, CA: Sage.

Augusta-Scott, T., & Dankwort, J. (2002). Partner abuse group intervention: Lessons from education and narrative approaches. *Journal of Interpersonal Violence, 17*(7), 783–805.

Bateson, G. (1972). *Steps to an ecology of the mind.* New York: Ballantine.

Bateson, G. (1979). *Mind and nature: A necessary unity.* London: Wildwood House.

Behan, C. (1999). Linking lives around shared themes: Narrative group therapy with gay men. *Gecko: A Journal of Deconstruction and Narrative Ideas in Therapeutic Practice, 2.* Retrieved September 1, 2004, from www.dulwichcentre.com.au.

Besa, D. (1994). Narrative family therapy: A multiple baseline outcome study including collateral effects of verbal behavior. *Research on Social Work Practice, 4*(3), 309–325.

Bhuvaneswar, C., & Shafer, A. (2004). Survivor of *that* time, *that* place: Clinical uses of violence survivors' narratives. *Journal of Medical Humanities, 25*(2), 109–127.

Blanton, P., & Vandergriff-Avery, M. (2001). Marital therapy and marital power: Constructing narratives of sharing relational and positional power. *Contemporary Family Therapy, 23*(3), 295–308.

Brimball, A. S., Gardner, B. C., & Henline, B. H. (2003). Enhancing narrative couple therapy process with an enactment scaffolding. *Contemporary Family Therapy: An International Journal, 25*(4), 391–415.

Bruner, E. (1986). Experience and its expression. In V. Turner & E. Bruner (Eds.), *The anthropology of experience*. Chicago: University of Illinois Press.

Bruner, J. (1990). *Acts of meaning*. Cambridge, MA: Harvard University Press.

Bruner, J. (2002). The narrative creation of self. In L. E. Angus & J. McLeod (Eds.), *The handbook of narrative and psychotherapy* (pp. 3–14). Thousand Oaks, CA: Sage.

Butler, M. H., & Bird, M. H. (2000). Narrative and interactional process for preventing harmful struggle in therapy: An integrative model. *Journal of Marital and Family Therapy, 26*, 123–142.

Butler, M. H., & Gardner, B. C. (2003). Dynamically adapting enactments to couple reactivity: Five developmental stages of enactments over the course of therapy. *Journal of Marital and Family Therapy, 29*, 311–327.

Carlson, J., & Kjos, D. (2002). *Theories and strategies of family therapy*. Boston: Allyn & Bacon.

Carlson, T. D., & Erickson, M. J. (2000). Re-authoring spiritual narratives: God in person's relational identity stories. *Journal of Systemic Therapies, 19*(2), 65–83.

Chang, J., & Phillips, M. (1993). Michael White and Steve de Shazer: New directions in family therapy. In S. Gilligan & R. Price (Eds.), *Therapeutic conversations*. New York: Norton.

Cowley, C. B., Farley, T., & Beamis, K. (2002). "Well, maybe I'll try the pill for just a few months . . ." Brief motivational and narrative-based interventions to encourage contraceptive use among adolescents at high risk for early childbearing. *Families, Systems & Health: The Journal of Collaborative Family HealthCare, 20*(2), 183–105.

Dallos, R. (2004). Narrative therapy: Integrating ideas from narrative and attachment theory in systemic therapy with eating disorders. *Journal of Family Therapy, 26*(1), 40–66.

Dean, R. G. (1995). Stories of AIDS: The use of the narrative as an approach to understanding in an AIDS support group. *Clinical Social Work Journal, 23*(3), 287–304.

Drauker, C. (2003). Unique outcomes of women and men who were abused. *Perspectives in Psychiatric Care, 3*(1), 7–17.

Drewery, W., Winslade, J., & Monk, G. (2000). Resisting the dominating story: Towards a deeper understanding of narrative therapy. In R. A Neimeyer & J. D. Raskin (Eds.), *Constructions of disorder: Meaning-making frameworks for psychotherapy*. Washington, DC: American Psychological Association.

Eeltink, C., & Puffy, M. (2004). Restorying the illness experience in multiple sclerosis. *Family Journal, 12*(3), 282–287.

Epston, D. (1984). Guest address: Fourth Australian family therapy conference, Brisbane, September 24th, 1983. *Australian Journal of Family Therapy, 5*, 11–16.

Epston, D. (1992). "I am a bear": Discovering discoveries. In D. Epston and M. White (Eds.), *Experience contradiction narrative and imagination* (pp. 173–188). Adelaide, S. Australia: Dulwich Centre Publications.

Epston, D. (1993a). Workshop on anorexia. Charter-Peachford Hospital, Atlanta, GA.

Epston, D. (1993b). *The approach of the Anti-Anorexia (Bulimia) League*. Auckland, New Zealand: Family Therapy Centre.

Epston, D., Morris, F., & Maisel, R. (1995). A narrative approach to so-called anorexia/bulimia. *Journal of Feminist Family Therapy, 7*(1,2), 69–96.

Epston, D., & Ronny. (2004, March). *Narrative therapy with children and their families: Taming the terrier*. Retrieved from www.narrativeapproaches.com.

Faiver, C., Ingersoll, R. E., O'Brien, E., & McNally, C. (2001). *Explorations in counseling and spirituality: Philosophical, practical and personal reflections*. Australia: Brooks/Cole.

Feinstein, D. (1997). Personal mythology and psychotherapy: Myth-making in psychological and spiritual development. *American Journal of Orthopsychiatry, 67*(4), 508–521.

Fish, V. (1993). Poststructuralism in family therapy: Interrogating the narrative/conversational mode. *Journal of Marital and Family Therapy, 19*(3), 221–232.

Foucault, M. (1965). *Madness and civilization: A history of insanity in the age of reason*. New York: Random House.

Foucault, M. (1979). *Discipline and punish: The birth of the prison*. London: Peregrine.

Foucault, M. (1980). *Power/knowledge: Selected interviews and other writings*. New York: Pantheon.

Freedman, J. H., & Combs, G. (1996). *Narrative therapies: The special construction of preferred realities.* New York: Norton.

Freedman, J. H., & Combs, G. (2000). Narrative therapy with couples. In F. M. Dattilio & L. J. Bevilacqua (Eds.), *Comparative treatments for relationship dysfunction.* New York: Springer Publishing, 342–361.

Gallant, J. P., Brownlee, K., & Vodde, R. (1995). "Not with me you don't!" A story of narrative practice and dissociative identity disorder. *Journal of Contemporary Family Therapy* [Special Issue on the Story and Storytelling], *17*(1), 143–157.

Glaser, B., & Strauss, A. (1967). *The discovery of grounded theory.* Chicago: Aldine de Gruyter.

Goddard, J. A., Lehr, R., & Lapadat, J. C. (2000). Parents of children with disabilities: Telling a different story. *Canadian Journal of Counselling, 34*(4), 273–289.

Gold, J., & Morris, G. (2003). Family resistance to counseling: The initial agenda for intergenerational and narrative approaches. *Family Journal, 11*(4), 374–380.

Gremillion, H. (2004). Unpacking essentialisms in therapy: Lessons for feminist approaches from narrative work. *Journal of Constructivist Psychology, 17*(3), 173–201.

Hardy, K. (2002). Coming to terms with the events of September 11th (interview). *The International Journal of Narrative Therapy and Community Work, 1.*

Hart, B. (1995). Re-authoring the stories we work by: Situating the narrative approach in the presence of the family of therapists. *Australian and New Zealand Journal of Family Therapy, 16*(4), 181–189.

Hewson, D. (1991). From laboratory to therapy room: Prediction questions for reconstructing the "new-old" story. *Dulwich Centre Newsletter 3,* 5–12.

Jenkins, A. (1990). *Invitations to responsibility: The therapeutic engagement of men who are violent and abusive.* Adelaide, South Australia: Dulwich Centre Publications.

Jones, A. C. (2004). Transforming the story: Narrative applications to a stepmother support group. *Families in Society, 85*(1), 129–139.

Laird, J. (2000). Culture and narrative as metaphors for clinical practice with families. In D. H. Demo, K. R. Allen, & M. A. Fine (Eds.), *Handbook of family diversity* (pp. 338–358). New York: Oxford University Press.

Lapsley, M. (2002). The healing of memories (interview). *International Journal of Narrative Therapy and Community Work, 2.*

Lyness, Kevin P. (2002). Alcohol problems in Alaska natives: Risk, resiliency, and native treatment approaches. *Journal of Ethnicity in Substance Abuse, 1*(3), 39–56.

Madigan, S. (1991). Discursive restraints in therapist practice: Situating therapist questions in the presence of the family. *Dulwich Centre Newsletter, 3,* 13–20.

Man-kwong, H. (2004). Overcoming craving: The use of narrative practices in breaking drug habits. *International Journal of Narrative Therapy, 1.*

Markus, H., & Nurius, P. (1986). Possible selves. *American Psychologist, 41,* 954–969.

McLeod, J. (1999). A narrative social constructionist approach to therapeutic empathy. *Counseling and Psychology Quarterly, 12*(4), 377–394.

McQuaide, S. (1995). Storying the suicide of one's child. *Clinical Social Work Journal, 23*(4), 417–428.

McQuaide, S. (2000). Women's resilience at midlife: What is it? How do you mobilize it? In E. Norman (Ed.), *Resiliency enhancement: Putting the strengths perspective into social work practice* (pp. 70–82). New York: Columbia University Press.

Merriam, S. (1988). *Case study research in education: A qualitative approach.* San Francisco: Jossey-Bass.

Monk, G., Winslade, J., Crockett, K., & Epston, D. (Eds.). (1997). *Narrative therapy in practice: The archaeology of hope.* San Francisco: Jossey-Bass Publishers.

Moustakas, C. (1994). *Phenomenological research methods.* Thousand Oaks, CA: Sage.

Neal, J. H., Zimmerman, J. L., & Dickerson, V. C. (1999). Couples, culture, and discourse. In J. M. Dovovan (Ed.), *Short-term couple therapy.* New York: Guilford Press.

Neimeyer, R. A. (1993a). An appraisal of constructivist psychotherapies. *Journal of Consulting and Clinical Psychology, 61*(2), 221–234.

Neimeyer, R. A. (1993b). Constructivist psychotherapy. In K. T. Kuehlwein & H. Rosen (Eds.), *Cognitive therapies in action: Evolving innovative practice.* San Francisco: Jossey-Bass.

Nichols, M. P., & Schwartz, R. C. (2001). *Family therapy: Concepts and methods* (5th ed.). Boston: Allyn & Bacon.

Nichols, M. P., & Schwartz, R. C. (2004). *Family therapy: Concepts and methods* (6th ed.). Boston: Allyn & Bacon.

Nylund, D., & Nylund, D. A. (2003). Narrative therapy as a counter-hegemonic practice. *Men & Masculinities, 5*(4), 386–395.

O'Connor, T., Davis, A., Meakes, E., Pickering, R., & Schuman, M. (2004). Narrative therapy using a reflecting team: An ethnographic study of therapists' experiences. *Contemporary Family Therapy, 26*(1), 23–39.

O'Dell, S. (2000). Psychotherapy with gay and lesbian families: Opportunities for cultural inclusion and clinical challenge. *Clinical Social Work Journal, 28*(2), 171–182.

Parry, A., & Doan, R. E. (1994). *Story re-visions: Narrative therapy in the post-modern world.* New York: Guilford Press.

Ramsey, J. L., & Blieszner, R. (2000). Transcending a lifetime of losses: The importance of spirituality in old age. In J. H. Harvey & E. D. Miller (Eds.), *Loss and trauma: General and close relationship perspectives.* Philadelphia: Brunner-Routledge.

Rothschild, P., Brownlee, K., & Gallant, J. P. (2000). Narrative interventions for working with persons with AIDS: A case study. *Journal of Family Psychotherapy,* 1–13.

Semmler, P., & Williams, C. B. (2000). Narrative therapy: A storied context for multicultural counseling. *Journal of Multicultural Counseling and Development, 28*(1), 51–62.

Shalav, A. (2000). Treating survivors in the acute aftermath of traumatic events. Retrieved September 1, 2004 from www.ncptsd.org.

Shalav, A. (2000). Psychosocial resources in the aftermath of natural and human-caused disasters: A review of the empirical literature, with implication for intervention. Retrieved September 1, 2004 from www.ncptsd.org.

Shuler, P., Gelberg, L., & Brown, M. (1994). The effects of spiritual/religious practices on psychological well being among inner city homeless women. *Nurse Practitioner Forum, 5*(2), 106–113.

Snyder, M. (2000). The loss and recovery of erotic intimacy in primary relationships: Narrative therapy and relationship enhancement therapy. *Family Journal-Counseling and Therapy for Couples and Families, 8*(1), 37–46.

Strauss, A., & Corbin, J. (1990). *Basics of qualitative research: Grounded theory procedures and techniques.* Newbury Park, CA: Sage.

Tomm, K. (1987). Interventive interviewing: Part I. Strategizing as a fourth guideline for the therapist. *Family Process, 26,* 3–13.

Tomm, K. (1993). The courage to protest: A commentary on Michael White's work. In S. Gilligan & R. Price (Eds.), *Therapeutic conversations.* New York: Norton.

Tomm, K. (2002). Enabling forgiveness and reconciliation in family therapy. *The International Journal of Narrative Therapy and Community Work, 1,* 65–69.

Verko, J. (2002). Women's outrage and the pressure to forgive: Working with survivors of childhood sexual abuse. *The International Journal of Narrative Therapy and Community Work, 1,* 23–27.

Vodde, R., & Gallant, J. P. (2002). Bridging the gap between micro and macro practice: Large scale change and the work of Michael White and David Epston. *Journal of Social Work Education, 38*(3), 439–459.

Walsh, F. (1998). *Strengthening family resilience.* New York: Guilford Press.

Waldgrave, C. (1998). The challenge of culture to psychology and postmodern thinking. In M. McGoldrick (Ed.), *Re-visioning family therapy: Race, culture and gender in clinical practice.* (pp. 404–413). New York: Guilford Press.

White, M. (1986). Family escape from trouble. *Family Therapy Case Studies, 1,* 29–33.

White, M. (1988/1989, Summer). The externalizing of the problem and the re-authoring of lives and relationships. *Dulwich Centre Newsletter,* 3–21.

White, M. (1989a, Spring). Saying hullo again: The reincorporation of the lost relationship in the resolution of grief. *Dulwich Centre Newsletter*, 7–11.

White, M. (1989b, Summer). Family therapy training and supervision in a world of experience and narrative. *Dulwich Centre Newsletter*, 27–38.

White, M. (1991). Deconstruction and therapy. *Dulwich Centre Newsletter, 3,* 21–40.

White, M. (1993). Deconstruction and therapy. In S. Gilligan & R. Price (Eds.), *Therapeutic conversations* (pp. 22–61). New York: Norton.

White, M., & Epston, D. (1990). *Narrative means to therapeutic ends.* New York: Norton.

White, M., & Epston, D. (1991). A conversation about AIDS and dying. *Dulwich Centre Newsletter, 2,* 5–16.

Winslade, J., & Smith, L. (1997). Countering alcoholic narratives. In G. Monk, J. Winslade, K. Crocket, & D. Epston (Eds.). *Narrative therapy in practice: The archaeology of hope.* San Francisco: Jossey-Bass.

Wright, J. (2003). Considering issues of domestic violence and abuse in palliative care and bereavement situations. *The International Journal of Narrative Therapy and Community Work, 3,* 72–74.

12

Object Relations Family Interventions

Allie C. Kilpatrick, Ph.D.,
and Elizabeth O. Trawick, M.D.

Object relations family therapy is a relatively new model of family treatment. Its origins are in two separate schools of thought whose streams have merged into a dynamic body that is having a major impact on family therapy today. Not unlike the mighty, milky-white Amazon where it merges with the black waters of the Negro River, but remains separate before finally mingling, psychoanalysis and family therapy have run together and commingled before finally merging to form object relations family therapy.

Object relations theory is considered to be the bridge between psychoanalysis—the study of individuals—and family theory—the study of social relationships. It may be defined as

> the psychoanalytic study of the origin and nature of interpersonal relationships, and of the intrapsychic structures which grew out of past relationships and remain to influence present interpersonal relations. The emphasis is on those mental structures that preserve early interpersonal experiences in the form of *self and object-images*. (Nichols, 1984, p. 183)

Object relations theory is an existing general framework in psychoanalysis and psychiatry that provides the means for understanding the earliest developmental phases of childhood. Using this orientation, which gives primacy to the need for a human relationship even at birth, clinicians and researchers have studied the development of individuals in relation to the people around them from earliest infancy. In recognizing that the newborn baby has an ego, a part of the

220

personality that copes with internal and external reality, object relations theorists have been able to understand early modes of mental functioning based on fantasies of splitting, projection, and introjection that occur in the processes of attaching to and differentiating from the family. These processes allow for the building up of an internal structure, the personality, which consists of condensations of the individual's own unique biopsychosomatic innate givens (the id) blended with experiences of others (resulting in an enriched ego and a superego). It is now recognized that this internal structure building, though most intense in the young, continues throughout life in response to ongoing relatedness. When positive, these early processes lead to a person's having a sense of his or her self as a valuable individual dependent on and working within an indispensable matrix. When negative, the person experiences little sense of self as differentiated from the matrix on which life is felt to absolutely depend and relies on projective identification as a primitive defense mechanism to relieve emotional pain.

These processes, first described by psychoanalysts, have now been recognized in families and larger social groups. The lack of differentiation of family members has become one of the cornerstones of Murray Bowen's work (1978) in understanding families, as well as Helm Stierlin's work (1976) in studying larger social group functioning (Slipp, 1984). When personality structure does not develop, enmeshment within the family group interferes with recognition of individual needs, which then cannot receive attention. This leads to impoverishment of individuals and thus of the group.

Family Needs

Object relations concepts developed as a way to understand psychotic, borderline, and narcissistic conditions. They continue to provide the most useful tools for treatment of these conditions, in which mental functioning remains at an immature level, with massive use of defenses such as splitting and projective identification. With recognition that groups such as families may function in ways similar to immature individuals by joining to utilize early and immature defense mechanisms, the path was paved to develop interventions that interpret these processes within the family setting. Thus object relations family interventions (ORFI) are indicated whenever family patterns of resolving problems and relieving emotional pain rely on defensive functioning rather than on evaluation of reality with containment of emotional states followed by appropriate action. ORFI may be possible primarily in families functioning at Levels III or IV, where basic needs are met and family structure is stable enough for the family to meet regularly together. But ORFI may also be helpful in Level I and II families, when painful emotional states such as terror or depression are overwhelming the family's ability to maintain structural cohesiveness. Thus, ORFI is also useful for all family levels following severe trauma, when resulting emotional states overwhelm the family's usual patterns of processing emotion. At such times, the therapist's ability to know and modulate emotional states for the family may diminish actions that are damaging and may lead to deeper change in the family system.

Within the family system, the modes of mental functioning discovered by psychoanalysts may promote or disrupt attachment, bonding, love, caring, development, and intimacy, depending on whether they are used as a means of communication with self and others or as a barrier against communication. To explain, projective identification was first described in 1946 by Melanie Klein, an English psychoanalyst, as a way of ridding the self of unwanted painful or terrifying experiences, which were projected into the object, who then came to be experienced as identical to the unwanted part. This was thought to be essential in early infancy, allowing for nurture of the growing ego by taking in good experiences while there was freedom from the bad. Overreliance on projective identification in infancy or its persistence after infancy was thought to be a sign of impaired ego development. As described by Grinberg, Sor, and Bianchedi (1977), Wilfred Bion, a student of Melanie Klein's, recognized that for the infant, projective identification is also the means of communicating with the mother. Neuroscience researchers such as Schore (1994, 2000) have begun to describe the neural pathways through which the nonverbal infant seems to "give" to the mother emotional states representing needs for physical care and love. Through internal, neural processes of her own, the mother unconsciously and consciously considers the communication and responds. According to Bion, the infant introjects and internalizes the mother's response and attitude to the projection, thus learning early in life the meaning of its inner world and internalizing a listening attitude toward its self. When this process works "good enough," a term used by Donald Winnicott (1965), another English psychoanalyst, to describe adequate mothering, the stage is set for a lifelong process of intimate communication both verbally and nonverbally with projective processes. When the process does not work between the mother and the infant, the stage is set for a lifelong unconscious process of using projective processes to rid oneself of unwanted inner experiences. Because barriers are built against the unwanted parts that are felt to be in others, communication is interrupted. Carried to an extreme, reality may be so altered that an individual becomes psychotic. To a lesser extent, misperception of certain aspects of another person commonly occurs.

Within family units, systems of projective identifications develop and may persist throughout life. As with individuals, these projections may function as communications with both conscious and unconscious responsiveness to needs of individual members. Or the projections may function as a means of getting rid of the unwanted. In this case, the family develops collusive systems of projections, in which one member may carry a projection for another member in exchange for a need being met or a projection being accepted by the other. Carried to the extreme, families using a projective system become poorly functioning, as reality testing is altered and action may be taken to protect against contact with the unwanted.

In a paper presented at the 2004 International Psychoanalytic Congress, Isidoro Berenstein of Buenos Aires, Argentina, described the family as a multi-personal, intersubjective organization with an unconscious structure, which he called the Unconscious Family Structure. In this organization, the members are mutually linked in ways that are largely unconscious. In family therapy, the object relationships that are talked about in individual therapy are present and enacted. The presence of linked "others" allows the unconscious family structure to be reached in a way that is not possible in individual therapy as mental processes come to be lived out in the session. Discommunicative projective systems, which are extremely common and cause a multitude of difficulties, can then be addressed.

The three most common marital complaints—lack of communication, constant arguments, and unmet emotional needs—are understandable in this context. The remarkable and common experience of hearing several people describe one event with a totally different memory and emotional reaction can be comprehended with the recognition that each may be experiencing the other as an unwanted part of the self, thus altering reality of the interaction. Intimacy, emotional and sexual, is blocked by these processes. To make matters worse, because the family has become a system with an unconscious structure in which members depend on each other to carry projections, pursuit of individual goals is in conflict with relational goals and so are undermined (Finkelstein, 1987). Enmeshment with unclear emotional boundaries results. To varying degrees, the family is experienced as a needed but hostile and controlling web.

As a result of these shared, unconscious, internalized object relations, children often develop symptoms and become the "identified patient" who is jealous, hyperactive, angry, or even ill. When children have illnesses or learning difficulties, families may respond inappropriately and with rejection, as the child may represent an unacceptable aspect of the parents or other siblings. At other times, parents may find ambivalent pleasure in allowing gratification of unacceptable desires by their children and then will be unable to limit behavior that is also disturbing. Thus children are confused by their parents' "double messages" and are truly in a bind as they sense their parents' pleased excitement with the unwanted behavior. Siblings may join parents in choosing one child as the recipient of projections. The child is then in the distressing position of accepting the role demanded by the projections in exchange for vital provisions. Not uncommonly, this child is unable to develop a sense of self and becomes depressed. ORFI in situations like this is necessary so that each family member can come to carry and be responsible for his or her own being, freeing each to develop.

Object relations family interventions deal with shared, unconscious, internalized object relations. Focusing on the interaction and interdependence of individual dynamics and family system functioning is crucial in the application of an integrated understanding to family interventions. The family is perceived not as a set of individuals but as a system comprising sets of relationships that function in ways unique to that specific family, the unconscious family structure. The immediate goal is not symptom resolution, but a progression through the current developmental phase of family life with an improved ability to work as a group and to differentiate among and meet the individual members' needs. Thus this model is especially relevant for Level IV families.

In regard to whether or not ORFI is indicated for a specific family, we must remember that psychological maturity is not necessarily related to socioeconomic status. Applegate (1990) explored aspects of object relations theory within the socio-cultural context of family constellations, child-rearing practices, race, and ethnicity. The interrelationship of the internal world of object relations and the external world of multiculturalism is offered as a clinically useful way of examining issues arising from ethnic differences. Slipp (1988) observes that ethnicity alone has not been found to be an issue in ORFI's relevance. Although there are differences between ethnic and racial groups, basic mental functioning of splitting with projection and introjection is common to all people. If the clinician is skilled and able to experience intense emotional states, these processes will be recognized and content specific to various ethnic and cultural groups will be identified and interpreted. In regard to sexual orientation, therapists generally use the same treatment methods with traditional and same-sex couples (Parker, 1996). One must remember, however, that lack of societal supports and resources, as well as societal sanctions imposed by the dominant culture, must be addressed within the therapeutic dialogue. Families that are functioning at Level IV may come to the clinician with problems described as internal or interpersonal conflicts, anger, blaming, lack of communication, desire for growth and greater intimacy, loss of confidence in self or spouse, depression, loneliness, or isolation. These families generally want an understanding of these situations and are reflective. The next section presents a case in which ORFI is an effective explanatory and interventive method.

Family Case Assessment

Assessment of families for ORFI does not necessarily follow the common pattern of history taking, because, as with psychoanalysis, the way and order in which information is presented is essential to understanding the interactional difficulties. In other words, the mode of presentation is data to aid in diagnosis. Furthermore, as it is essential that the therapist be available to enter into the process as a recipient of projections of emotions, the therapist must remain nondirective and available from the beginning to hear the family. Though history is taken nondirectively, by the third to fourth interview the family's ability to use ORFI can be determined based on their cooperativeness in providing linked information and their response to a holding environment and interpretive interventions.

In this context, an important source of information in assessment is the so-called countertransference reaction of the practitioner. The concept of countertransference has evolved in psychoanalysis. Originally, it implied an unacceptable emotional reaction on the part of the therapist that interfered with understanding. With a deeper appreciation of the power and necessity of projective processes to communicate noncognitive and unverbalized thoughts and emotional states, the emotional reaction of the therapist has come to be viewed as essential to understanding. Without the therapist's having an actual experience, the individual or family in therapy will often feel they have not been heard, even when the interpretation is intellectually correct. Recognition of the importance of countertransference has placed a responsibility on the therapist, who must work to allow emotional reactions to be alive while maintaining the capacity to reflect and think of the reactions without responding reflexively with action. Indeed, the therapist must discern reactions that are in fact due to his own emotional blocks, a task that requires self-knowledge. The following case, as told by the practitioner, demonstrates this process.

At age 68, Al, a prosperous retired executive, called to seek treatment for his 61-year-old wife, who was in the midst of her fourth severe depression. He and his married children wished to bring her in, as she could not come herself. Indeed, when seen, Mary seemed barely functional: She spoke only in a whisper if at all, moved slowly, and had an extremely downcast, deadened expression. She said she saw no reason to live but had no suicidal plans. Al spoke for his wife, explaining that she had become depressed several weeks before during a trip to Europe with their son and daughter-in-law. He had a wonderful time, though it was somewhat difficult driving in strange countries, and he had depended on his competent son, of whom he was proud. His wife, however, had become more and more depressed as the trip went on, eventually withdrawing to hotel rooms and causing great discomfort in the group. All agreed that perhaps it was the rainy weather. As his wife sat motionless, the family explained that she had always been moody, especially so in the last seven to eight years, when she had begun to have severe episodes of depression. Al never felt depressed and could not understand depression. He had always worked and gotten along with people. He was a peacemaker, and it made his wife mad. He simply did not get angry. Since Al's retirement seven years before, Mary had become more depressed, wanting to be with him almost all the time. He, however, wanted time to golf with the boys and was troubled that she "punished" him by withdrawing to the back of the house after he spent a day away. On the trip, he had wanted to be with other people; she had wanted to be in the room with him at night and complained that her feet hurt and she would like to put them up on his lap and relax. As Al spoke, Mary sat motionless, and the children silently looked away, I became aware of a deep feeling of hurt, angry longing that seemed to be present, drawing them together and pushing them apart at the same time. And I was aware of my internal response, a wish to make peace as a mother might between two of her children, accompanied by an urge to tell them to knock it off, behave, and stop whining. On the surface, the consultation was about Mary's pain, but Al spoke for Mary, seeming to author the story of her depression as if he knew of it. The children seemed to agree that Al had the story right and wished their mother to be "corrected." I made a statement recognizing the longing each experienced without assigning it to any one person and was careful to avoid labeling Mary as the "ill patient." All wished to continue, and Mary seemed to move a little more freely. Al took her arm to help her as she left the room.

In assessing this original session, I thought that Mary was "holding" depression for all the family members and was overwhelmed. I was struck by the focus of the family on correcting the situation, not simply denying it. Mary seemed to accept the family's projections of emotional pain, and I wondered what the family accepted for her in return, why she was willing to engage in this painful collusion. I was aware that I had a mixed reaction of wishing to be helpful but feeling annoyed and critical at the same time. I was struck by the family's level of functioning, wish to work together, and positive response to my containing the emotional pain. Thus, despite Mary's deep depression, I elected to continue this approach.

In subsequent sessions, attended by Al and Mary and sometimes the grown children, Al focused on his frustration that their life was not happier since his retirement. He had thought there would be time to play golf with his friends and to travel. He wanted more time with his son and daughter and perhaps to go on a trip alone, something he had never done. Instead, he found that his children seemed more distant and he was tied to Mary. Mary, a housewife who had many artistic interests and volunteer activities, quietly whispered that she thought that they would finally be together. It emerged that, since their marriage 42 years before, Al had worked long hours, often getting home in time to read to the children and go to bed himself, only to be up at the crack of dawn and off to work. Weekends were devoted to church and children's activities when Al was not working at home. Mary had always felt lonely but had tolerated the situation because she felt it was for the family, and the children were doing well. And she thought that some day "Al will retire and it will be my turn." Al had not noticed her loneliness or any emotional unhappiness in the family or himself. He had enjoyed the children, and Mary agreed that he was a wonderful father. The grand picture, recreated in interactions within the first few sessions and in their perceptions of their life together, was of Mary as frighteningly sensitive, demanding, and depressive; Al as happy, content, hardworking, engaged, and devoid of unpleasant emotion other than criticism of Mary. The children had grown into competent adults, but with difficulties in tolerating feelings, seeming to agree with their father that their mother felt and demanded too much. In their own choice of partners, they had responded to dynamics within the family. Their daughter, always closest to her father, married a man who had not attended college but ran a blue-collar business and would always be home for dinner and weekends. Their son, perceived as sensitive and artistic like his mother, was highly successful at a business that he ran from his home while his wife worked long hours away from home. They had chosen to have no children.

Dialogue of retirement and the trip was associated with a feeling of depression, which Mary silently expressed by slumping more in the chair and which Al denied by turning the focus to curing Mary's depression, perhaps with medication. Rather than labeling Mary as the ill patient, interventions focused on depression as related to Al's retirement and aging. When these subjects were present, I experienced feelings of sadness and fear, but family members turned to Mary and focused on her as depressed. As I interpreted the feelings of loss and fear for the future that arose in relationship to Al and Mary's aging, the family was able to shift the focus from Mary and began the human process of accepting losses. The process of projective identification was operative within the family, but when painful effects were contained in the therapeutic setting and identified by interpretation, the family responded, indicating that they were good candidates for ORFI.

As we explored the onset of Mary's depression, a similar process became apparent: Al had avoided feeling humiliated when he depended on his competent son to drive him around by focusing on his pride in his son; his son had focused on his joy at being with his kind father rather than on worry about his father; Mary felt more and more incapacitated by depression, showing the way in which she carried the painful effect. In return, Al complained but remained extremely dependent on her, never leaving her side. So Mary had a constant companion, which fulfilled strong lifelong needs of dependency, reinforcing the pattern. Furthermore, in the third session, Mary began to evoke criticism from the family by not accepting sympathy instead of correction, indicating that she had a need to be criticized. She began to seem angry at me, as if I were taking something from her.

In this continuing assessment, I noted that the dynamics of the family were active and that I had become an observing participant. The family's ability to include me indicated the ego strength to relate and to form transferences with me. Even when unpleasant, the family members were able to consider my comments. I thus knew that the ability to tolerate good and bad was present, meaning that the family could consider their emotional states.

The collusive pattern that had been present throughout the couple's long and stable marriage had limited intimacy. Only over the course of several years of therapy were the underpinnings of this pattern understood as emotional states that could be identified and located in the rightful partner. Each partner fulfilled a function of containing or fulfilling longings for the other and of representing past objects. Both had grown up in large families during the Great Depression. Al was the fourth son, followed by a sister, brother, and another sister. Mary was the fifth child, preceded by four brothers, and followed by one younger sister. Al presented stories of an idealized view of childhood, such as of admiring his wonderful older brothers whom he watched run and play, and then criticized Mary's neediness. Exploration revealed that, for Al, Mary represented the younger baby sister whom he, as a toddler, stayed home with while he watched his big brothers run off. Most significantly, he had to watch his sister be the baby, carried and held by his mother, in a way that he had still wanted. Originally, his neediness had been projected onto the baby sister, who was internalized by him as a resented representation of need. This internal representation had been reprojected (transferred) onto Mary throughout their relationship and had become more intense as he became more needy with aging. When his son became more competent than he, able to drive around easily in a strange country, his experience of his early life was strongly activated, as he again became the weak child left with baby sister and mother, who had no time for him. Mary became depressed, and he became annoyed with her, as he had felt toward his mother when she had no time to be with him.

As this picture of Al emerged, more of Mary's life experience became apparent. Her father was distant, often at work in the same blue-collar profession as their disappointing son-in-law. Mother, remembered as a well-respected, hardworking, self-reliant housewife, was dominant. She felt that her mother was not to be crossed and seemed to do little to oppose her, though she had often longed to go off with her brothers, who always left her. She also experienced her mother, a fantastic housekeeper, as focused on tasks and critical of any interferences. Even though she was the first girl, she did not feel she had been enjoyed by her parents. After high school, she had left home for a larger city and found employment as a secretary, where she met Al, already employed as a professional in the same company. From the beginning, his position paralleled that of admired older brothers, all of whom had left her. This experience primed Mary to accept the role of "wife at home waiting," but with the leftover pains of feeling that she was an unliked, bothersome baby, which were transferred into the marriage. A part of her internalized object world was a mother who did not deem feelings to be important but insisted on getting on with the tasks of maintaining a home and raising a family. For Mary, her mother had been internalized as so critical that she would have difficulty bearing the burden of it. Inducing her family to criticize her had thus allowed her to engage in a projective identification in which others carried the criticism. Resistance in therapy occurred when the family became less criticizing and more understanding. Then Mary had to accept responsibility for her internal sense of always feeling criticized and to work through her relationship with her mother.

A significant tension arose even in the beginning sessions—that of each of us waiting for another to speak or respond. Mary had said that she was always waiting for Al, and this was recreated in the therapeutic setting. As I contained the painful tension and followed its lead, information arose that contributed to our understanding that this was a shared internal experience of both Mary and Al, as both had felt themselves to be always waiting for mother's attention. This common experience was dealt with in their habitual way of Al's taking actions that caused Mary to experience the feeling and then Al rejecting her if she expressed it. It could be seen that each of the children had internalized parts of this pattern, which continued into the next generation. As we worked to follow the emotional states as they became alive, the patterns were altered in all family members. As pointed out by Thomas Ogden (1997), internal object relationships are not fixed, but are fluid sets of thoughts, feelings, and sensations that are continually in movement and always susceptible in newly experienced context. Thus even unconscious patterns can change as the intersubjective experience of the family is altered.

Treatment Goals

Safety of each family member is always a concern. In this case, the potential of suicide by Mary required evaluation. As the treatment progressed, the possibility that awareness of intense feelings that had been avoided throughout life could overwhelm Al, causing him to become suicidal, required ongoing assessment.

Once safety is established, in ORFI the goal is always to enable the family to engage so that the fundamental drive for relatedness will be met in the unique manner of each family. Interventions aim to support the family as a work group, so that impediments to relatedness can be identified and resolved. Impediments include family-of-origin issues, such as multigenerational transmission of conflicts and maladaptive roles, resistance to accepting and tolerating painful emotions, and attempts to control rather than to empower other members.

Goals directed toward specific symptom removal or achievement of desired behaviors are incompatible with ORFI, as they usually reflect attempts to manipulate or control the group and impede the family's being with the therapist in a way that reveals interactive projection–collusion processes. As the therapist identifies the collusive processes, a potentially destructive process is broken, allowing a more constructive relativeness in which individual and group development is supported.

Intervention Approach: Theory Base and Tenets

Object relations family intervention comes from the application of object relations theory to family systems. Object relations theory and its therapeutic approach regard the individual's inner world and external family as components of an open system. It can be used to develop typologies of family interaction and treatment that take into consideration the intrapsychic influences on family patterns, which in turn affect the client's personality. Thus psychoanalysis and family treatment complement each other to enhance the theoretical understanding in both fields and to foster an intervention approach that is dependent not on the theoretical orientation of the clinician but on the needs of the client family.

Historically, Freud is recognized as the father of psychoanalysis and contributed theories that are the foundation of object relations. As described by Hamilton (1989), in Freud's early biological theories infants were conceptualized as having drives directed toward an object (*Instincts and Their Vicissitudes*, 1915), so that the infant sought gratification from an object, usually the mother. Psychological growth occurs when drives are frustrated and the organism seeks increasingly effective means of energy discharge. The goal is maintenance of the organism, the infant, without recognition of or focus on the object. Freud's later theories were the beginning of object relations theory. In *Mourning and Melancholia* (1917) he described introjection following the loss of a loved person as a means of maintaining a sense of continuing to be with the person receiving fantasied gratification. In his last work, *Splitting of the Ego in the Mechanism of Defense* (1940b), he described splitting as a defense mechanism of the ego, which resulted in a lifelong coexistence of two contradictory dispositions that do not influence each other. Splitting, projection, and introjection form the core concepts of all object relations theories in psychoanalysis and ORFI.

As described by Gomez (1997), object relations theory was a British development of psychoanalysis that arose in the mid-twentieth century with the recognition that relatedness is the core of all human interaction from the beginning of life. The need for others is not only biological, it is also the *need to be experienced by the other* in order to develop a sense of one's own existence. The term *object* shifts from a biological concept of functions that satisfy urges to an existential experience essential for development of mind and personality, in which a person lives a dual reality, internal and external. Working about the same time and commingling concepts, Melanie Klein (1935, 1936, 1937, 1940) and Ronald Fairbairn (1952) refined theories of splitting into good and bad objects and recognized the importance of introjection and projection for the buildup of personality structure, particularly the ego and superego. Continuing these theories, Winnicott (1965) developed the concept of the holding environment as an essential aspect of mother–infant relationship paralleled later in that of therapist–patient. Baliant (1952, 1968), Guntrip (1968), and Bowlby (1953, 1969, 1973, 1980) extended these ideas to concepts of attachment theory. Wilfred Bion (1962a, 1962b, 1963), working in the late mid-twentieth century, extended knowledge of projective identification to recognize its importance as a normal means of communication operative in all groups. Object relations theory originally referred to internal objects but has been extended primarily by American analysts to include relations with external objects.

Although the basic tenets of ORFI are based on psychoanalysis, they continue to be modified. Specific historical tenets and concepts are now presented as they are currently used in assessment and interventions.

Freud (1940a) originally mentioned **splitting** as a defense mechanism of the ego and defined it as a lifelong coexistence of two contradictory dispositions that do not influence each other, as mentioned earlier. Kernberg (1972), in tracing the process of splitting through developmental stages, states that splitting of the "all good" (organized around pleasurable mother–child interactions) and "all bad" (derived from painful and frustrating interactions) self-images, object images, and their affective links occurs from 2 to 8 months. The separation of the self from object representations occurs from 8 to 36 months. Splitting into good and bad persists, and this is seen as the fixation point for borderline patients. Following the splitting is the integration of the good and bad emotional images so that the separate self and object representations are each both good and bad. It is at this point that the ego, superego, and id become firmly established as intrapsychic structures and that the defenses of splitting are replaced by repression. Slipp (1984) sees this stage as the fixation point for neurotic pathology. In the last stage, internalized object representations are reshaped through actual current experiences with real people. A goal of ORFI is to assist in the development of this integration and reshaping.

Introjection is a crude, global form of taking in, as if those fragments of self–other interactions are swallowed whole. It is the earliest, most primitive form of the internalization of object relations, starting on a relatively crude level and becoming more sophisticated as the child grows (Nichols, 1984). The child reproduces and fixates its interactions with significant others by organizing memory traces that include images of the object, the self interacting with the object, and the associated affect. Good and bad internal objects are included, each with images of the object and the self. However, the resulting internal image does not completely parallel the actual external experience, which has been altered by projection of an already existent internal state. For example, a frustrated, enraged infant is likely to perceive mother as angry even when she is not and to store the image of her as an angry mother fused with itself as bad. To prevent this internalization, the mother must be able to provide a holding function, contain the anger, and respond in a way that alters the state of the infant and thus the perception of mother/self which is introjected.

Projective identification is a defense mechanism that operates unconsciously. Unwanted aspects of the self are attributed to another person, and that person is induced to behave in accordance with these projected attitudes and feelings (Nichols, 1984). For instance, in the case example, Al is unable to accept his sadness, anxiety, and longings to be held and supported, and projects them onto Mary. Mary, unable to tolerate the internal criticism of an introjected critical mother, projects this aspect of herself onto Al and her children. The concepts of transference (Freud, 1905), scapegoating (Vogel & Bell, 1960), symbiosis (Mahler, 1952), trading of dissociations (Wynne, 1965), merging (Boszormenyi-Nagy, 1967), irrational role assignments (Framo, 1970), and family projective process (Bowen, 1965) are all variants of Klein's (1946) concept of projective identification. The phenomenon of projective identification as a life and clinical experience is most thoroughly described by Grotstein (1981) and Ogden (1982).

Collusion is an integral part of projective identification. The recipient of the split-off part of the partner does not disown the projection but acts on the conscious or unconscious message (Stewart, Peters, Marsh, & Peters, 1975). For example, the need for a "weak" woman requires that both partners agree to the assigned roles. Each spouse's ego identity (which includes both good and bad objects) is preserved by having one or more bad objects split off onto the partner. Thus each partner disowns his or her bad-object introjects and needs the other to accept the projection of these introjects in a collusive manner (Piercy et al., 1986). Dicks (1963) believes that this collusive process continues because both spouses hope for integration of lost introjects by finding them in each other. Clinicians using object relations theory attempt in various ways to help couples own their introjects and begin seeing their spouses for the people they really are, not projected parts of themselves.

Winnicott (1958) builds on his notion of good enough mothering with the idea of a holding environment. If the good enough mother (or primary nurturing person) provides a holding environment that is safe, secure, responsive, nurturing, nonretaliating, and supportive of separation–individuation, the child can achieve a firm sense of identity and a lifelong capacity for developing nonsymbiotic object relations.

Scharff and Scharff (1987) develop this concept further by defining the role of the father (or secondary nurturing person) as supporting the holding of the mother physically, financially, and emotionally; the father holds the mother as she holds the baby. This contextual holding provides an environmental extension of the mother's presence that later extends outward to grandparents and family, neighbors, and others. Feminist-informed object relations theory additionally considers the influence of gender on the holding environment. Sex role differentiation and shifting sex role mores are considered to affect the holding environment that is created within the couple, marital, and family settings (Juni & Grimm, 1994). Traditional concepts of masculine and feminine roles are challenged with the emergence of new realities that defy gender specification. A holding environment that typifies excessive power imbalances between partners may be understood within the context of early object relations (Silverstein, 1994). The need for dominance and power, particularly in the area of sexual arousal and pleasure, has been suggested to evolve from excessive control or coercion by a powerful parental object during early psychosexual development.

These concepts of the holding environment also apply to working with families. The clinician needs to provide a holding environment for the family by providing safety, competence, and concern for the whole family and by engaging with the central issues of the family, being caring, interactive, and understanding. The concept of containment introduces a specifically mental ability of the therapist to allow unknown feelings, sensations, and thoughts of the family members to live within the boundaries of the therapist's being and so to be known, identified, and returned to the family in tolerable form and doses. Within this "therapeutic envelope," Al and Mary could tolerate their own experience and then accept the other as different, even if disagreeably so.

As to the current status of ORFI, there is no overall integrated theory. Various theorists have developed their own perspectives over the years, and others have made attempts at integration. One is Framo (1972), who calls his approach a "transactional" one. It leans heavily on the notion of projective identification as applied to a family system and offers a new way of presenting transference. He builds on Fairbairn's notion of the fundamental need for a satisfying object relationship. When a child interprets the parents' behavior as rejection or desertion and cannot give up the parent, it internalizes the loved but hated parent in the inner world of self as an introject (as if swallowed whole) or a psychological representation. In the course of time, as the person begins to force close relationships into fitting this internal role model, these split-off or divided introjects become important. Framo sees the introject of the parent as a critical issue in family therapy, and one that is much neglected. Framo tries to put together a basically intrapsychic concept, introjects, with a system concept. In doing so, he draws out the implications in Bowen's (1978) formulation of family theory for object relations theory.

Boszormenyi-Nagy and Spark (1973) are also concerned about introjects and object relations. They see family pathology as a specialized multiperson organization of shared fantasies and complementary need gratification patterns that are maintained for the purpose of handling past object loss experience.

Monumental groundbreaking work has been done by D. Scharff (1982), J. Scharff (1989), Scharff and Scharff (1987), and Slipp (1984, 1988). For Scharff and Scharff (1987), ORFI derives from the psychoanalytic principles of listening, responding to unconscious material, interpreting, developing insight, and working in the transference and countertransference toward understanding and growth. The immediate goal is not symptom resolution but progression through the current developmental phase of family life with improved ability to work as a group and to differentiate among and meet the individual members' needs. Slipp (1984, 1988) studied diverse patient populations and their families to explore the interaction and interdependence of individual dynamics and family system functioning. His ultimate goal is to apply an integrated understanding to family treatment.

ORFI's basic tenet is that treatment of the individual and treatment of the family are theoretically and therapeutically consistent with each other, and both are parts of an open system. The two levels of the intrapersonal and the interpersonal are in a constantly dynamic relationship with each other. An assumption is that resolving problems in the relationships in the client's current family necessitates intrapsychic exploration and resolution of those unconscious object relationships that were internalized from early parent–child relationships. Another assumption is that these early influences affect and explain the nature of present interpersonal problems (Blazina, 2001).

Application to Families on Level IV

Families who have needs on Level IV are generally introspective and reflective, and yearn to be more self-actualizing. There may be problems of inner conflict or difficulties with intimacy. Although we may still be treating symptomatic people, our goals have to do with the development of an inner "richness": insight, more sensitive awareness of the relational world, and an understanding of legacies and heritage. In all cases we would hope to deepen awareness of the inner world and to improve understanding of history, style, and unmet yearnings.

A very important aspect is the spiritual therapies that help families discover the transcendent aspects of their beings. ORFI is a useful adjunct to all spiritual therapies because interventions that allow for a fuller experience of self, free of internal images or projections of others, support an engagement with transcendence and assumption of responsibility for mature spiritual experience as described by Young-Eisendrath and Miller (2000).

Spirituality is enhanced by ORFI particularly when families share unconscious experiences of guilt. It is common for parents to feel that they have harmed their children by inadequate parenting, hostile emotions, or a failure to protect them from adverse experiences in life. Experiences of guilt lead to self-criticism and thus to a shutdown of experience of self. The pathway to spirituality is blocked. Verbalization of thoughts and feelings that have been condemned by guilt leads to a realistic mourning and sadness and to an assumption of responsibility rather than intolerable guilt. Mentalization of the reality of having less than the ideal parents than we wanted and of being less than the ideal that we wished to be can occur. Thus, acceptance of our place in the world of our family can be enhanced. With acceptance, pain and anger diminish, leaving openness to spiritual experience.

In ORFI, the therapeutic environment is established by the therapist's encouragement of open dialogue in a safe, mutually helpful atmosphere. The family practitioner generally maintains a neutral stance that respects each member's autonomy. The practitioner avoids assuming a directive approach but attends to other material produced in the session as described by Slipp (1988). The past is linked to the present through interpretation of the transference, particularly the ways it is acted out interpersonally in the ongoing family relationships. In order to facilitate the acceptance of these interpretations, the therapist needs to join the family empathetically and to create a safe and secure holding environment where space for understanding is provided. In the research of Sampson and Weiss (1977), creating such a holding environment has been found to be the most crucial element for change and growth. The practitioner's stance with the family is one that reflects an awareness that he or she affects and is affected by the family (Slipp, 1988). ORFI fosters the kind of meaningful shared intimacy with respect for one another's individuality that the philosopher Martin Buber (1958) so aptly described as the "I–thou relationship."

Family practitioners who have not experienced Level IV work may be unprepared to deal with clients for whom meaning, awareness, and spiritual growth are issues. Some practitioners would not acknowledge the importance, or even the existence, of an inner world. If such practitioners encounter families who have Level IV needs, referral to a more existentially oriented practitioner would seem appropriate.

Interventions and Techniques

In ORFI, a vital part of the practitioner's role and function is assessment. Scharff and Scharff (1987, p. 155) cite six major tasks to achieve in the assessment phase to determine if ORFI would be effective.

1. The provision of therapeutic space, which includes trust and openness.
2. Assessment of developmental phase and level to determine tasks to be accomplished.
3. Demonstration of defensive functioning to determine ego strength.
4. Exploration of unconscious assumptions and underlying anxiety to determine intervention needs.
5. Testing of the response to interpretation and assessment format to see if they are ready for understanding and insight.
6. Making an assessment formulation, recommendation, and treatment plan.

These major tasks may be accomplished in a more structured assessment phase. Slipp (1984, pp. 204–205) reviews the steps in such an assessment process (Table 12.1).

TABLE 12.1   Assessment Process in Object Relations Family Therapy

- **Explore the presenting problem** of patient and its background.
  1. Does it seem related to overall family functioning and/or to stress from a family life cycle stage?
  2. What has been done so far to remedy the problem?

- **Establish an individual diagnosis** for each family member including a judgment concerning the level of differentiation and the use of primitive or mature defenses.
  1. Gather data on the client and family development.
  2. Note any ethnic differences or conflicts.

- **Evaluate family constancy** to determine if parents can maintain their own narcissistic equilibrium, or if patient is needed to sustain their self-esteem and survival.
  1. Does a rigid homeostasis or defensive equilibrium exist that binds and prevents the patient from individuating and separating?
  2. Is there pressure for personality compliance within the family, or social achievement outside the family?
  3. What affiliative, oppositional, and alienated attitudes exist?

- **Explore precipitating stress** and its relation to a loss or other traumatic event (negative or positive) or a transitional point in the family life cycle that has disrupted homeostasis.

- **Define individual boundaries** for members. These may be rigidly too open (a symbiotically close relationship) or too closed (an emotionally divorced and distant relationship).
  1. Are generational boundaries intact, or are there parent–child coalitions?
  2. Are the parental coalition, the subsystems, and authority hierarchy intact?

- **Define the family boundary** to see if it is too open (symbiotic relations persist with family of origin) or too closed (family is isolated from community without social support system).

- **Determine the ability to negotiate differences and problem solve** through verbal dialogue involving respect for one's own and others' views, opinions, and motivations versus an egocentric controlling viewpoint resulting in coercion and manipulation.

- **Observe communication patterns** for evidence of spontaneous versus rigid stereotyping, distancing, or obfuscating; level of initiative versus passivity; rigidity of family rules; and the power-role structure.

- **Evaluate the loving and caring feelings** amongst members that allow for separateness (rather than acceptance only by conformity) and provide warmth, support, and comfort.

- **Define the treatment goals** in terms of difficulties that have been uncovered, and present the frame or boundaries of the treatment process.

Source: Slipp, 1984, pp. 204–205.

Superceding all other areas of the assessment process is the importance of each clinician's assessment of their own countertransference reaction. Is one present and usable? Is the countertransference tolerable? Are there indications that the family may present situations that parallel the clinician's own unresolved emotional distresses? Because countertransference is deeply personal, consultation may be necessary to fully assess the potential impact of a family on the clinician's emotional life and the ability of the clinician to tolerate and interpret the family's distresses.

In addition to the ethnic differences or conflicts mentioned earlier, attention must also be given to other sociocultural–environmental factors that influence the family. Impacts of the entire ecosystem must be considered in the assessment process.

There are some specific techniques that ORFI uses in the beginning, middle, and last phases of treatment, which Slipp (1988, pp. 199–200) has outlined as a guide for clinicians (Table 12.2).

TABLE 12.2   Phases of Treatment in Object Relations Family Therapy

- During the beginning phase of treatment the techniques are to
  1. Develop a safe holding environment through empathy, evenhandedness, and containment; an environment that facilitates trust, lowers defensiveness, and allows aggression to be worked with constructively.
  2. Interpret the circular positive or negative systemic interaction in a sequential non-blaming manner by
     a. Defining its origin.
     b. Defining what was hoped to be gained.
     c. Describing its effects.

- During the middle phase of treatment, the techniques are to
  1. Interpret projective identification by
     a. Reframing its purpose to give it a positive aim.
     b. Linking it with a genetic reconstruction.
     c. Clarifying why an aspect of the self needs to be disowned and projected. This process diminishes defensiveness, enhances the therapeutic alliance, and facilitates continued work with the reowned projective identification.
  2. Use the objective countertransference as a tool to understand the transferences and to provide material for interpreting projective identification.

- During the last phase of treatment, the techniques are to
  1. Work through individual conflicts and developmental arrests in the intrapsychic sphere. This process is gradual and may continue in individual therapy after the family treatment terminates.
  2. Terminate treatment.

Source: Slipp, 1988, pp. 199–200.

Evaluation of Effectiveness

Because symptom reduction is not the goal of this model, it cannot serve as the measure of effectiveness. The presence or absence of unconscious conflict, because it is not apparent to family members or outside observers, is difficult to measure. Therefore, assessment of effectiveness depends on the subjective clinical judgment of the therapist and on the family's reactions. With the current emphasis on scientific evidence and cost effectiveness, would these measures be considered sufficient? Clinicians would answer yes, as they consider the clinician's observations to be entirely valid as a means of evaluating theory and treatment. Blanck and Blanck (1972, 1987), discussing Mahler's methods and model, state that clinicians who employ Mahler's theories technically do not question the methodology or the findings, for they can confirm them clinically. This is a form of validation that meets as closely as possible the experimentalist's insistence on replication as a criterion of the scientific method. Along these same lines, Langs (1982) posits that the ultimate test of a therapist's formulation is in the use of these impressions as a basis for intervention. He states further that the patient's reactions, conscious and unconscious, constitute the ultimate litmus test of these interventions, and that true validation involves both cognitive and interpersonal responses from the patient.

The views held by current, eminent object relations family therapists are similar. Slipp (1988) holds that meeting the goals of treatment is the criterion that both the family and therapist use to consider ending treatment. These general goals do not lend themselves to empirical measurement but to subjective assessments by therapists and families. Scharff and Scharff (1987) state that, at termination, the family can provide the holding environment for the members that is so necessary for attachment and growth. The family is able to return to or reach an appropriate developmental level so that they fit with the individuals' developmental needs for intimacy and autonomy. Slipp (1988) describes the end result as the restructuring of the internal world of object relations with resultant modification of the family's interpersonal relations. Each individual self is experienced as separate and less dependent on external objects to sustain self-esteem and identity. The family will be able to function as a group in a more intimate and adaptive fashion that meets each member's needs.

Although outcome studies have been, primarily, uncontrolled case studies, Dicks (1967) reported on a survey of the outcome of couples therapy at the Tavistock Clinic. He rated 73 percent of a random sample of cases as having been successfully treated. Others have investigated specific tenets of the ORFI theory and provided further empirical evidence of their existence (Slipp, 1984).

Application to Families Functioning at Other Levels

As discussed previously, object relations theory is very useful in understanding a vast array of needs behaviors, problem areas, and symptomatology. This understanding can be applied to families who have needs on any level. Although object relations theory has been utilized extensively to study and treat borderline and narcissistic personality disorders, it is now being used to understand and treat diverse populations and families.

As Slipp (1988) has stated, although ORFI is appropriate for families who desire and can tolerate intensity and closeness, it is certainly not restricted to only those families. As families develop trust and become closer in the intervention process, the treatment itself can serve as a model for more open and intimate relationships among family members. Thus the growth produced could enable the family to move to a higher level of relating.

A significant, though not the only, variable in selecting the most suitable type of family therapy for a specific family's level of need is the family's socioeconomic level. Clients who have Level I needs with overriding poverty and social problems want help that is more immediate and less abstract. Slipp's (1988) study showed that the ORFI approach is particularly fitting for and effective with middle-class families, as well as with a blue-collar population. These families would typically have Level II, III, and IV needs. On the basis of his study findings, ORFI with lower socioeconomic–level families is least effective and not recommended.

Scharff and Scharff (1987), however, caution clinicians that it should not be assumed that the poor or the culturally or intellectually disadvantaged cannot benefit from ORFI. Some families will fit cultural stereotypes of concrete thinking and dependency on directives and gratification, but others will take to a more reflective approach. Although this type of intervention is not for all families, it is for those that demonstrate an interest in understanding, not just in symptom relief.

More recently, ORFI has proved useful in treating families of all levels who have experienced traumatic events. During and after experiences of trauma, intense, distressful emotions are stimulated. These emotions resonate with past experiences, remembered in the unconscious of the family, so that established patterns of splitting and projection are activated or intensified. Many families do not have well-established, useful psychological processes for dealing with these experiences. Therefore, after traumas, family members may become more distant and alienated. Interventions that provide a holding of the emotions followed by accurate verbalizations that allow each member to become more aware of their individual experience are effective in preventing the fracturing of families following traumas. This allows for the development of a space within the mind where the experience is felt and represented, or in analytic terms, held. This process, described by Fonagy and Target in several publications (1996, 2000, in press; also, Fonagy, Gergely, Jurist, & Target, 2002), promotes emotional experiences that would otherwise be projected or put into action, rather than becoming processed thought.

Ethical Challenges

There are some ethical challenges that need to be considered when object relations family interventions are used. A primary concernn is that of maintaining a central position with the family. This means that the therapist would be allied equally with all members of the family and not become invested in, or identified with, the perspective of one member. This is especially challenging when the practitioner allows his or her own feelings to be active in the process. Monitoring counter-transferences is essential to prevent "favoritism."

Along the same lines, confidentiality may become an issue. A family member may call the practitioner, outside the boundaries of the family session time, re-questing information or help. Maintaining the boundaries of the family is essential. Having confidential information from one or more members compromises the practitioner's central position within the family. All information belongs to the family.

Summary

Object relations family treatment can be effective with families who have their basic physical and nurturant needs met, are capable of abstract thinking and in-sight, and are interested in understanding and changing destructive patterns of behavior, achieving greater intimacy and commitment, reworking meanings, and rewriting their life stories. These patterns may involve poor communication, con-flict, lack of differentiation, weak personal and intergenerational boundaries, in-consistent family structure, and rules. Therefore, ORFI is ideally suited for many Level IV families and can be very effective with Level II and III families. It is gen-erally not recommended for Level I families.

Discussion Questions

1. What are ORFI's basic tenets, and how do they apply to the case example given?

2. What are the similarities and differences of introjection, projective identification, and collusion?

3. Do ethnicity and gender issues impact the use of ORFI?

4. How are family object relations interventions different from those of individual object relations interventions?

5. From your own practice, identify an individual or family that demonstrates "split-ting." Briefly explain why the defense mechanism is evidenced in the person's be-havior. Can you find projective identification and collusion as well?

6. What is the "holding environment," and how can it be developed and utilized in applying the techniques of ORFI?

7. How is the pain of Level IV families different from that of Level I, II, and III fami-lies in view of object relations theory?

Internet Resources _____

http://object-relations.com/metprog.html
This is a good source for information and resources about object relations theory and practice. This site has links to reading lists, training programs, and papers from the Met Center's programs.
www.objectrelations.com
This site has resources on object relations theory and practice.
www.sonoma.edu/users/d/daniels/objectrelations.html
Reviews object relations theory as seen by its nine leading proponents.

Suggested Readings _____

Applegate, J. S. (1990). Theory, culture and behavior: Object relations in context. *Child and Adolescent Social Work Journal, 7*(2), 85–100.
Aspects of object relations theory are explored within the sociocultural context of family constellations, child-rearing practices, race, and ethnicity.

Fairbairn, W. R. D. (1954). *An object-relations theory of the personality.* New York: Basic Books.
A seminal work in object relations theory that has had a significant influence on the later work of Dicks, Bowen, Framo, and others. Required reading for those interested in the role of object relations in psychopathology.

Finkelstein, L. (1987). Toward an object relations approach in psychoanalytic marital therapy. *Journal of Marital and Family Therapy, 13*(3), 287–298.
Describes the features that distinguish psychoanalytic marital therapy from other forms of marital therapy, describes how object relations theories can be applied to psychoanalytic marital therapy, and indicates certain directions for further study.

Scharff, D. E., & Scharff, J. S. (1987). *Object relations family therapy.* Northvale, NJ: Jason Aronson.
Represents the Scharffs' efforts to develop a psychoanalytic object relations approach to families and family therapy. The Scharffs demonstrate that object relations theory provides the theoretical framework for understanding and the language for working with the dynamics of both the individual and the family system.

Silverstein, J. L. (1994). Power and sexuality: Influence of early object relations. *Psychoanalytic Psychology, 11,* 33-46.
This article challenges traditional concepts of masculine and feminine roles with the emergence of new realities that defy gender specification.

Slipp, S. (1988). *The technique and practice of object relations family therapy.* Northvale, NJ: Jason Aronson.
This book extends the clinical application of object relations family therapy that Slipp began in an earlier book. He further develops the application of his family typology to the treatment process with specific attention to techniques and process.

References _____

Applegate, J. S. (1990). Theory, culture and behavior: Object relations in context. *Child and Adolescent Social Work Journal, 7*(2), 85–100.
Baliant, M. (1952). *Primary love and psychoanalytic technique.* London: Hogarth.
Baliant, M. (1968). *The basic fault: Therapeutic aspects of regression.* London: Tavistock.

Berenstein, I. (2004). *Psychoanalysis of families.* Paper presented at the International Psychoanalytic Congress, New Orleans, LA.

Bion, W. (1962a). *Learning from experience.* London: Heinemann.

Bion, W. (1962b). A theory of thinking. *International Journal of Psycho-analysis, 43,* 110–119.

Bion, W. (1963). *Elements of Psycho-analysis.* New York: Basic Books.

Blanck, G., & Blanck, R. (1972). Toward a psychoanalytic developmental psychology. *Journal of the American Psychoanalytic Association, 20,* 668–710.

Blanck, G., & Blanck, R. (1987). Developmental object relations theory. *Clinical Social Work Journal, 15,* 318–327.

Blazina, C. (2001). Part objects, infantile fantasies, and intrapsychic boundaries: An object relations perspective on male difficulties with intimacy. *The Journal of Men's Studies, 10.*

Boszormenyi-Nagy, I. (1967). Relational modes and meaning. In G. H. Zuk & I. Boszormenyi-Nagy (Eds.), *Family therapy and disturbed families.* Palo Alto, CA: Science and Behavior Books.

Boszormenyi-Nagy, I., & Spark, G. (1973). *Invisible loyalties.* New York: Harper & Row.

Bowen, M. (1965). Family psychotherapy with schizophrenia in the hospital and in private practice. *Comprehensive Psychiatry, 7,* 345–374.

Bowen, M. (1978). *Family theory in clinical practice.* New York: Jason Aronson.

Bowlby, J. (1953). *Child care and the growth of love.* Harmondsworth: Penguin.

Bowlby, J. (1969). *Attachment and loss. Vol. I: Attachment.* London: Hogarth.

Bowlby, J. (1973). *Attachment and loss. Vol. II: Separation: anxiety and anger.* London: Hogarth.

Bowlby, J. (1980). *Attachment and loss. Vol. III: Loss: Sadness and depression.* London: Hogarth.

Buber, M. (1958). *I and thou.* New York: Scribner.

Dicks, H. V. (1963). Object relations theory and marital studies. *British Journal of Medical Psychology, 36,* 125–129.

Dicks, H. V. (1967). *Marital tensions.* New York: Basic Books.

Fairbairn, R. (1952). *Psycho-analytic studies of the personality.* London: Routledge and Kegan Paul.

Finkelstein, L. (1987). Toward an object-relations approach in psychoanalytic marital therapy. *Journal of Marital and Family Therapy, 13*(3), 287–298.

Fonagy, P., Gergely, G., Jurist, E., & Target, M. (2002). *Affect regulation, mentalization and the development of the self.* New York: Other Press.

Fonagy, P., & Target M. (1996). Playing with reality I: Theory of mind and the normal development of psychic reality. *International Journal of Psychoanalysis, 77,* 217–233.

Fonagy, P., & Target M. (1996). Playing with reality III: The persistence of dual psychic reality in borerline patients. *International Journal of Psychoanalysis, 81*(5), 853–874.

Fonagy, P., & Target M. (in press). Playing with reality IV: A psychioanalytic theory of external reality. *International Journal of Psychoanalysis.*

Framo, J. L. (1970). Symptoms from a family transactional viewpoint. In N. W. Ackerman (Ed.), *Family therapy in transition.* Boston: Little, Brown.

Framo, J. L. (1972). Symptoms from a family transactional viewpoint. In N. W. Ackerman, N. Lielg, & J. Pearce (Eds.), *Family therapy in transition.* New York: Springer.

Freud, S. (1905). *Fragment of an analysis of a case of hysteria: Collected papers.* New York: Basic Books.

Freud, S. (1915). *Instincts and their vicissitudes. Collected Works: Vol. 7.*

Freud, S. (1917). *Mourning and melancholia. Collected Works: Vol. 14.*

Freud, S. (1940a). An outline of psychoanalysis. *Standard Edition, 23,* 139–171.

Freud, S. (1940b). *Splitting of the ego in the mechanism of defense. Collected Works: Vol. 23.*

Gomez, L. (1997). *An introduction to object relations.* New York: New York University Press.

Grinberg, L., Sor, D., & Tabak de Bianchedi, E. (1977). *Introduction to the work of Bion.* New York: Jason Aronson.

Grotstein, J. S. (1981). *Splitting and projective identification.* New York: Jason Aronson.

Guntrip, H. (1968). *Schizoid phenomena, object relations and the self.* London: Hogarth.

Hamilton, G. N. (1989). A critical review of object relations theory. *American Journal of Psychiatry, 146*(12), 1552–1560.

Juni, S., & Grimm, D. W. (1994). Sex roles as factors in defense mechanisms and object relations. *Journal of Genetic Psychology, 155,* 99–106.

Kernberg, O. F. (1972). Early ego integration and object relations. *Annals of the New York Academy of Science, 193,* 233–247.

Klein, M. (1935). A contribution to the psychogenesis of manic-depressive states. In *Love, guilt and reparation.* London: Hogarth.

Klein, M. (1936). Weaning. In *Love, guilt and reparation.* London: Hogarth.

Klein, M. (1937). Love, guilt and reparation. In *Love, guilt and reparation.* London: Hogarth.

Klein, M. (1940). Mourning and its relations to manic-depressive states. In *Love, guilt and reparation.* London: Hogarth.

Klein, M. (1946). Notes on some schizoid mechanisms. *International Journal of Psycho-Analysis, 27,* 99–110.

Langs, R. (1982). *Psychotherapy: A basic text.* New York: Jason Aronson.

Mahler, M. S. (1952). *Psychoanalytic Study of the Child: Vol. 7. On child psychosis and schizophrenia: Autistic and symbiotic infantile psychoses.*

Nichols, M. (1984). *Family therapy: Concepts and methods.* New York: Gardner Press.

Ogden, T. H. (1982). *Projective identification and psychotherapeutic technique.* London: H. Karnac.

Ogden, T. H. (1997). *Reverie and interpretation, sensing something human.* Northvale, NJ: Jason Aronson.

Parker, G. (1996). Personal communication with A. Kilpatrick.

Piercy, F. P., Sprenkle, D. H., et al. (1986). *Family therapy sourcebook.* New York: Guilford Press.

Sampson, H., & Weiss, J. (1977, March). Research on the psychoanalytic process: An overview. *The Psychotherapy Research Group,* Bulletin No. 2, Department of Psychiatry, Mt. Zion Hospital and Medical Center.

Scharff, D. E. (1982). *The sexual relationship: An object relations view of sex and the family.* London: Routledge & Kegan Paul.

Scharff, D. E., & Scharff, J. S. (1987). *Object relations family therapy.* Northvale, NJ: Jason Aronson.

Scharff, J. S. (Ed.). (1989). *Foundations of object relations family therapy.* Northvale, NJ: Jason Aronson.

Schore, A. N. (1994). *Affect regulation and the origin of the self: The neurobiology of emotional development.* Mahwah, NJ: Erlbaum.

Schore, A. N. (2000). Attachment and the regulation of the right brain. *Attachment and Human Development, 2,* 23–47.

Silverstein, J. L. (1994). Power and sexuality: Influence of early object relations. *Psychoanalytic Psychology, 11,* 33–46.

Slipp, S. (1984). *Object relations: A dynamic bridge between individual and family treatment.* New York: Jason Aronson.

Slipp, S. (1988). *The technique and practice of object relations family therapy.* Northvale, NJ: Jason Aronson.

Stewart, R. H., Peters, T. C., Marsh, S., & Peters, M. J. (1975). An object-relations approach to psychotherapy with marital couples, families and children. *Family Process, 14*(2), 161–178.

Stierlin, H. (1976). The dynamics of owning and disowning: Psychoanalytic and family perspectives. *Family Process, 15*(3), 277–288.

Vogel, E. F., & Bell, N. W. (1960). The emotionally disturbed as the family scapegoat. In N. W. Bell & E. F. Vogel (Eds.), *The family.* Glencoe, IL: Free Press.

Winnicott, D. W. (1958). *Collected papers: Through pediatrics to psycho-analysis.* London: Hogarth.

Winnicott, D. (1965). *The maturational processes and the facilitating environment.* London: Hogarth.

Wynne, L. C. (1965). Some indications and contraindications for exploratory family therapy. In I. Boszormenyi-Nagy & J. L. Franco (Eds.), *Intensive family therapy.* New York: Hoeber.

Young-Eisendrath, P., & Miller, M. (Eds.). (2000). *The psychology of mature spirituality, integrity, wisdom, transcendence.* London: Routledge.

Part VI

The Family in the Community: Ecosystem Implications

Throughout this book we have been working within the overall metatheories of ecological systems and social constructionism as the philosophical and theoretical base for working with families on four levels of family need. Each type of family intervention for each level of need includes ecological and system implications. As discussed in Chapter 2, the ecological system includes the microsystem, mesosystem, exosystem, and macrosystem. Many of these levels of ecosystems are included in the interventions in the various chapters. However, this concluding section serves to bring these all together with a focus on the community and the total sociocultural environment within which the family functions and has their needs met—or not met. This concluding section integrates the theoretical and philosophical underpinning from Part I and the microsystem level interventions from Parts II through V with the ecosystem implications of working with families at the macrosystem level. It helps the practitioner to see the larger contextual issues when working with individual families.

In Chapter 13 Kilpatrick, Turner, and MacNair emphasize the community as "replete with opportunities for self-empowerment and enrichment" and, at the same time, "fraught with dangers with impediments to self-fulfillment." They examine the community as the broader context in which families can thrive, survive, or break down. A primary goal is to eliminate the barriers and impediments that prevent family practitioners from becoming involved with larger community issues that have an impact on family functioning at all levels. Two models that address family needs on a community level are presented.

13

The Family in the Community

Allie C. Kilpatrick, Ph.D., John B. Turner, D.S.W., and Ray H. MacNair, Ph.D.

This chapter examines the community as the broader context in which families survive, thrive, or break down. The ecosystems perspective on the community touches on many aspects that affect families in crucial ways. Communities vary in the extent to which they meet the needs of their members. There needs to be a dual focus in family work—on the family system and its social environment. Emphasis is directed to a holistic and integrative analysis of patterns of human service networking which are intended to overcome the fragmentation found in many community service systems. Finally, two models of addressing family needs on a community level are presented.

For many people, the term *community* connotes a place characterized by social warmth, common values, and economic and personal security. Perhaps most families would welcome such a haven in which to raise a family. Too often for some, the community is a place with social and physical risks that threaten the well-being of families. For many, especially the poor living in urban and rural neighborhoods, their social environment is not a healthy place for families. The movie *Boys in the Hood* dramatically illustrates the tension that can exist between families and neighborhoods. Either the family lacks the skills and resources needed for survival or it lacks the skills to negotiate with the community. Good or bad, the neighborhood community is where families live, and its impact on families must be considered (Ewalt, Freeman, & Poole, 1998).

The family practitioner and agency may find that, in addition to interventions directed toward helping family members become more competent in performance of family functions, interventions in the neighborhood, community, and the larger society directed toward making them more supportive of families need to occur.

The Case of Mrs. Y.

Mrs. Y. wrote a letter to the local newspaper claiming that her rights and those of her family as citizens were being denied by her neighbors who wished to "run her off of the street." She claimed that her neighbors, and Mrs. X. in particular, actively discouraged other children from playing with her four children. The Y. family consisted of her husband, the four children, and her sister-in-law and brother-in-law. The sister-in-law was chronically ill. They lived in a four-room house. Mrs. Y. said that this house was a real improvement over the two-room house in which they had previously lived for 18 months. She told her family worker that where they had lived before there had been no outside space where the children could play. She stated that her husband sometimes held two jobs in order to make ends meet. The worker observed that the children were undisciplined. Managing the family seemed to be a bit too much for Mrs. Y., yet she clearly did not want to search for new housing.

The family worker learned that Mrs. X. was a black woman who was thought by Mrs. Y. to be 65 years old or older. She learned that Mrs. X. was a college graduate and that her father had founded a prominent church in the city. Mrs. Y. said that Mrs. X. thought of herself as belonging to the "elite." She had no children.

Later the worker spoke with Mrs. X., who readily admitted to applying pressures to force the Y. family to move. Mrs. X. indicated that several white and black families wanted the Y. family off the street and refused to allow their children to play with the Y. family's children. They especially did not like the conduct of Mrs. Y.'s older boys. Conversation with a neighborhood club leader verified that strong social pressure was being directed against Mrs. Y. by some of her neighbors to isolate the family and pressure them to move from the street. It was also acknowledged that Mrs. X. was the leader in this effort.

What are the options for intervention in this situation? What objectives can the family worker seek with the Y. family? Should interventions be attempted with the neighborhood? If so, how might that be accomplished?

Dual Focus

The Y. family illustration highlights the dual focus needed in family work—the family system and its social environment of neighborhood, community and larger society. The need for the agency and family worker to pursue such a dual focus is critical in high-risk neighborhoods and communities. This is especially required in the case of poor families. In such areas, even though some solid citizens reside in them, families are more likely to be confronted with violence, crime, poor quality housing, negative peer pressure on youth and adults, low school performance, social, political, and physical isolation, poor air quality, racial, cultural and class differences. (See Chapter 3, "Contexts of Helping: Commonalities and Human Diversities."

Ideally, families could be encouraged and assisted in finding housing outside of high-risk living areas. In many cases this is not realistically possible. Intervention

in community situations that threaten families must be considered when reloca-
tion is not the answer.

To exercise the community intervention options, it is essential that the
agency understand and agree that community intervention is agency policy. Such
interventions, where indicated, are necessary for success in efforts to help families.
This means (1) training and supervision of the practice of community interventions and (2) acceptance of community action as a legitimate function by the
agency staff, administration, and board.

Definition of Community

The family is located in the center of a nest of surrounding geopolitical systems:
(1) the neighborhood, (2) city and local community, (3) state and county, (4) regional, and (5) national. Within the boundary of each is the potential for providing support or harm to families (Figure 13.1). Likewise, the agency and other

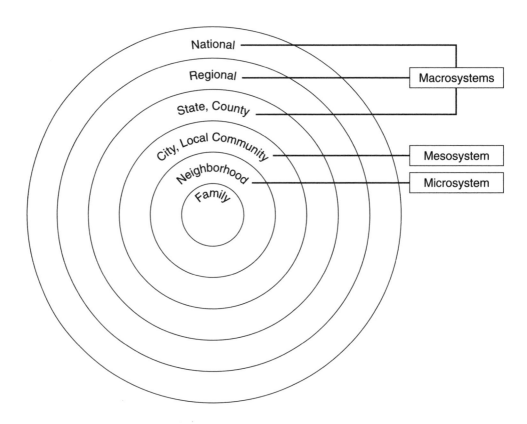

FIGURE 13.1 *Levels of Community Systems*

institutions, both private and public, are located in one or more of the concentric circles. Each may want and may possess some capacity to influence policy and actions regarding family policy.

Each community (geopolitical system) will possess to some extent the following general characteristics (Turner, personal communication, 2005):

1. A constellation of social relationships and roles maintained over time.
2. An identifiable functional interdependence.
3. A specified locality.
4. A common value system.
5. Social stratification (distribution of power).
6. Communication channels.
7. Social control/normative behavior.
8. Production of goods and/or services.
9. Intercultural tolerance.

It is obvious that communities vary in the extent to which they meet each of these characteristics. In some cases, the variation is to such an extent that the community can be described as dysfunctional or disorganized. Also, families may be members of more than one community and, as members, are expected to conform to the requirements of more than one community that may be at odds with each other. This is frequently the case with youth gangs in urban neighborhoods and is often a source of problems for the family.

Family Practitioner and Agency Helping Function in Community

1. Helping Family Members Use Community Resources

It is not unusual to discover that family members are not using community resources that are available to them. Studies have shown that low-income families are reluctant to approach formal-looking institutions like schools, libraries, health centers, policy makers, city housing, inspection departments, and the like. Also, these services may be located outside of the immediate neighborhood. Transportation may be a deterrent in terms of both cost and convenience. The family worker needs to have a familiarity with such resources, including knowledge of key staff members in community institutions. In some instances, it will help to accompany family members to the resource on their first visit. It is also possible to have a volunteer accompany them on first visits in selected cases. In some neighborhoods, it may be unsafe for children and women to travel without someone accompanying them. It is also not unusual to find that parents are reluctant to attend or join groups such as street clubs, PTAs, and civic groups, because they lack confidence in speaking at such groups or they are ashamed of their dress.

2. Documentation of Family Problems Related to Community Conditions

Negative or troublesome conditions faced by family clientele should be documented for prompt consideration by the agency for referral or some other course of action. It is important that such documentation and a means of determining how and when to act should be agency policy. Feedback to the practitioner is essential. Referrals to another human service agency, to city housing, to police, to the local school, or to legal aid are among the courses of action. The agency may also call for an interagency conference group on an ad hoc or continuing basis to plan a course of action.

3. Promoting a Community Development Program: Long-Range Planning

Finding adequate housing in a good neighborhood is a huge challenge to family programs. Of course, if housing could be found in quality neighborhoods, the effort involving documentation could be significantly downsized. Family programs need to urge city and county officials to a greater effort to maintain and improve neighborhoods.

In many communities, public and private groups are taking steps to redevelop neighborhoods and communities. These are multidiscipline and multiagency efforts designed to improve housing, streets, playgrounds, and police protection. They involve a large amount of citizen participation. Efforts like this could be called for by the boards of family programs.

Instead of thinking in terms of a multiplicity of so-called social problems, each demanding special attention and a different remedy, we can view them all as different symptoms of the same disease (Frank, 1948, pp. 1–2).

Two Models That Address Family Needs on a Community Level

The next section proposes two models that address family needs on a community level. These are (1) a goal-directed community human services system and (2) comprehensive community initiatives.

A Goal-Directed Community Human Services System

This goal-directed model is based on the assumption that there are at least three types of human services: those directed at survival (Level I families), those focused on self-empowerment (Level II and III families), and those geared for self-realization and prevention (Level III and IV families). Examples of survival-oriented services are unemployment compensation, food stamps, Temporary Assistance to Needy Families (TANF, formerly AFDC), homeless shelters, psychiatric hospitals, youth detention centers, runaway shelters, and detoxification facilities. Corresponding self-empowerment services are training and job placement services, public housing in which rent is paid, outpatient mental health, youth home placement or family preservation service, and addiction treatment and support groups.

Self-realization and prevention services are career development programs, housing subsidies through Section 8 of the U.S. Housing Act, individual or family therapy, education for child rearing, and preventive action systems. The term *preventive actions systems* refers to inventive self-help organizing and empowerment activities that pull together at-risk populations prior to the outbreak of problems, such as teen pregnancy or teen drug addiction. For example, teen councils have been known to organize preventive actions systems of volunteers to mentor younger people, clean up neighborhoods, or offer community services.

For too long American society has been content to offer minimal survival services, or less, to Level I families. Self-empowerment has often been an espoused objective, but often the optimism and sense of professional efficacy required for success have been lacking. Limited resources and clearly documented effectiveness have been barriers to the development and maintenance of self-empowerment and self-realization/prevention services.

Nevertheless, an array of programs at all three levels is available in most urban communities. It is the goal-directed interconnection that is often missing. If survival, self-empowerment, and self-realization/prevention programs were clearly linked, a sense of effectiveness would be more likely. Each program should be designed to demonstrate achievement at one level, readiness to go to the next level, and preparation to receive families from previous levels. Practitioners should be prepared to guide families at Levels I and II from one set of goals to the other when their progress warrants the connection. A goal-directed human services networking system will demonstrate its eagerness to prepare families for and receive them at the next level. Progress should be documented so the public can be made aware of programs' achievements. A model of the three types of goals and their interconnections can be offered visually, as in Figure 13.2.

The model suggests that communitywide policies be established that encourage agencies to link with each other through information systems and goal setting with clients. Resources would be expected to follow clients through their connections within the networking system. Connections between programs are thus established that link TANF with child care, education, job training programs, and employment services. Finally, family practitioners will be primed for a networking practice through community workshops that focus on an awareness of the availability of program connections and the policies that guide those connections. A sense of optimism can thus be generated among families that the service system is set up to work for them.

The challenge for community human service networks is threefold: (1) to promote a culture among providers, middle managers, and top managers that

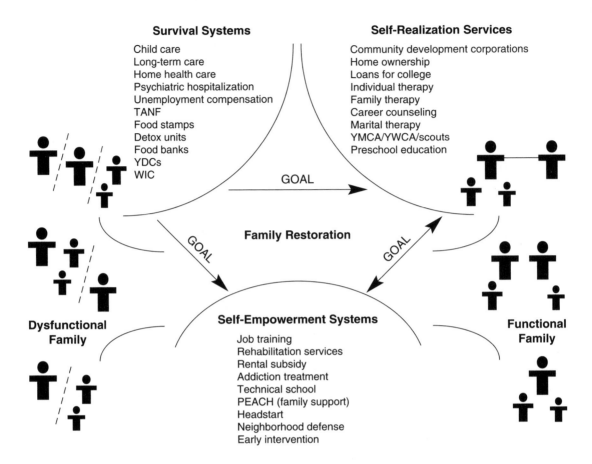

FIGURE 13.2   *Community Human Service Networking Systems, Linking Policies, Programs, and Practices*
MacNair, 1995.

they are part of a broader system of accountability; (2) to focus on the perception of client family members of their own readiness for different kinds of services; and (3) to structure a networking system that honors the specialized problems of individual family members and at the same time integrates the service plan together with the family as a whole. Family practitioners could participate in such a system with a greater sense of confidence that their efforts will receive recognition as they move families forward.

Comprehensive Community Initiatives

A second model is known as Comprehensive Community Initiatives (CCI). These have emerged again over the last 20 years and serve as a development strategy for the disadvantaged communities in the United States. Followers of this strategy believe it to be the best approach to address the "compounding and interrelatedness of social problems" (Ewalt, 1997, p. 413).

CCI uses coalitions of public and private agencies, religious organizations, neighborhood groups, community leaders, and individuals in the community who work together on neighborhood councils, task forces, planning committees, and advisory boards to identify family needs in the community and to develop and implement a comprehensive plan for multisystem change (Kurzman, 1985). CCI includes macrolevel, mesolevel, and microlevel strategies as discussed previously in this chapter.

CCI has been described primarily as an urban strategy. However, recent literature has demonstrated that CCI is just as applicable to rural settings (Messinger, 2004). Messinger states that CCI can be broken down into seven components, and most components found in urban literature can also be found in rural areas. These seven components include level of approach, the intervention target, organizational involvement, citizen participation, consensus approach, strengths-based philosophy, and an incremental approach.

The literature on urban CCIs presents five challenges that are inherent in the CCIs. Messinger (2004) states that the rural initiative encountered most of those challenges, but with some differences in the effects of these problems. The five challenges consist of the following:

1. *Lengthy Process:* The long time necessary for planning, implementation, and evaluation.
2. *Citizen Participation:* The formidable task of including low-income citizens in a meaningful way.
3. *Professional Roles.* Conflicts among professionals involved in planning.
4. *Politics.* The uncontrollable effect of local and external economics and politics on these initiatives.
5. *Complexity of Evaluation.* The complexities of evaluating a CCI.

An explanation of the fifth challenge is given by Kubisch, Weiss, Schorr, and Connell (1995). They assert, in writing for the Aspen Institute Roundtable on CCIs for Families and Children, that the attributes of CCIs are difficult to evaluate because they include operating to make change across systems (horizontal complexity), operating to make change on different levels (vertical complexity), the importance of context, the flexible and evolving nature of the interventions, the breadth of the range of outcomes being pursued, and the absence of appropriate control groups for comparison purposes.

In concluding her analogy of CCIs in meeting family needs in both urban and rural areas, Messinger asserts that "the careful maintenance of interpersonal relationships so important in a rural community might be constructive to urban initiatives that operate in a more geographically targeted area" (2004, p. 546).

Summary

The two models of community family practice that are suggested here are ones that emphasize the community as replete with opportunities for self-empowerment and enrichment. At the same time, the community is fraught with dangers and with impediments to self-fulfillment. The models recognize the differences between communities in the level of positive and optimistic organizing that takes place among disadvantaged (Level I and II) families and on behalf of such families.

In addition to recognizing the variations in community attitudes and behavior, it is suggested that family practitioners participate in community development and prevention activities that have the potential for expanding opportunities and reducing self-defeating forms of pessimistic behavior. Individual family practice must be distinguished from group, neighborhood, or community-level activities. The social constructivist practitioner can, however, encourage individual participation when an assessment shows a readiness for it. This approach is consistent with the Family Empowerment and Social Justice model proposed by Haynes and Singh (1993).

The practitioner may also wish to refer to Gaudin's (1984) concept of "social work roles"; Kruzich's (1988) chapter in Chilman, Cox, and Nunnaly, "Helping Families with Income Problems"; and finally, Parsons, Hernandez, and Jorgensen's (1988) generalized practice model, "Integrated Practice: A Framework for Problem Solving." These models merge an individualistic model of family practice with models that focus on the collective activities of education groups, neighborhood organization, self-help, community planning, and legislative action. Clearly, these models reduce or eliminate the division and cleavage that are felt between clinical practitioners and macrolevel practitioners. This is the major thrust of the multilevel view of families and family practice.

Discussion Questions

1. Explain why a dual focus is needed in family practice.

2. Discuss what the agency must be prepared to do in order to support practitioner efforts to ensure support from communities for families.

3. How does the cultural mix of a community affect the level of trust required in community building?

4. In performing an assessment of community human services networks, what features of network structure and function would you look for? What kinds of networks work best in the long run?

5. If you could design a community human services networking system for families, what would it look like?

6. In what ways could the two models of community family practice complement each other?

Internet Resources _____

www.communityiniatives.com
> Offers much training on the model, workshops, programs, and coaching on the comprehensive community initiative strategy.

www.ncrel.org/sdrs/areas/pa0cont.htm
> More on communities and families.

Suggested Readings _____

Buell, B. (1952). *Community planning for human services.* New York: Columbia University Press.
> This research report is based on a tracking study of over 100 families with multiple problems and a sense of being lost in the community network of agencies. It is the first to document the fragmentation of services and establish the need for integrative practices among agencies. It is a landmark study.

Chilman, C., Cox, F., & Nunnaly, E. (Eds.). (1988). *Families in trouble: Vol. I. Employment and economic problems.* Beverly Hills, CA: Sage.
> The editors present a compilation of articles on the issues families face with the threat of unemployment and loss of income, subjects that family practitioners must address if they are to deal with social justice issues on the individual and family levels. The articles are seminal.

Fraser, M., and Galinsky, M. (1997). Towards a resilience-based model of practice. In M. Fraser (Ed.), *Risk and resilience in childhood* (pp. 265–273). Washington, DC: NASW Press.
> The authors discuss the person in an environment and the interplay of individual characteristics and contextual influences as determinants of human behavior.

Gaudin, J., Wodarski, J., Arkinson, N., & Avery, L. (1990–1991). Remedying child neglect: Effectiveness of social work interventions. *Journal of Applied Social Sciences, 15*(1), 97–123.
> The authors describe a networking intervention study with neglectful families. The intervention consisted of personal networking, volunteer linking, employing neighborhood helpers, and social-skills training. A variety of measures were used to assess the results of the intervention.

Guitterez, L., Alvarez, A., Nemon, H., & Lewis, E. (1996). Multicultural organizing: A strategy for change. *Social Work, 41*(5), 501–508.
> Concepts of community organizing are developed that take into account issues of cultural competence, social justice, family, and neighborhood empowerment. The role of the social worker is differentiated by virtue of how they identify with the ethnicities of the family and neighborhood.

Lassen, M. (1995). *Community-based family support in public housing.* Cambridge, MA: Harvard Family Research Project.
> The author describes efforts in eight public housing communities to work with neighborhood and community resources in helping families to help themselves.

MacNair, R. (1981). *Case coordination: Designing interagency teamwork.* Athens: Institute of Community and Area Development, University of Georgia.

Nelson, G. M. (2000). *Self governance in communities and families.* San Francisco: Berrett-Koeler.
> The author explains why partnerships between people and social institutions are essential to the well-being of both. The book describes how to work to achieve these partnerships.

Schorr, L. B. (1997). *Common purpose: Strengthening families and neighborhoods to rebuild America.* New York: Anchor Books.
> Inspiring tales and hard evidence of our social programs' success in helping disadvantaged children and families toward better lives, on a scale that is large enough to matter.

References

Ewalt, P. L. (Ed. in Chief). (1997). The revitalization of impoverished communities (Special issue). *Social Work, 47*(5).

Ewalt, P. L., Freeman, E. M., & Poole, D. L. (Eds.). (1998). *Community building: Renewal, well-being, and shared responsibility.* Washington, DC: NASW Press.

Frank, L. K. (1948). *Society as the patient.* New Brunswick, NJ: Rutgers University Press.

Gaudin, J. (1984, May). Social work roles and tasks with incarcerated mothers. *Social Casework,* 279–286.

Haynes, A. W., & Singh, R. N. (1993). Helping families in developing countries: A model based on family empowerment and social justice. *Social Development Issues, 15*(1), 27–37.

Kruzich, J. (1988). Helping families with income problems. In C. Chilman, F. Cox, & E. Nunnaly (Eds.), *Families in trouble series: Vol. 1. Employment and economic problems.* Newbury Park, CA: Sage.

Kubisch, A. C., Weiss, C. H., Schorr, L. B., & Connell, J. P. (1995). Introduction. In A. C. Kubisch, J. P. Connell, L. B. Schorr, & C. H. Weiss (Eds.), *New approaches to evaluating community initiatives: Concepts, methods, and contexts* (pp. 1–21). Washington, DC: Aspen Institute.

Kurzman, P. A. (1985). Program development and service coordination as components of community practice. In S. Taylor & R. W. Roberts (Eds.), *Theory and practice of community social work* (pp. 95–124. New York: Columbia University Press.

MacNair, R. (1995). The family in the community. In A. C. Kilpatrick & T. P. Holland, *Working with families: An integrative model by level of need* (pp. 218–229). Boston: Allyn & Bacon.

Messinger, L. (2004). Comprehensive community initiatives: A rural perspective. *Social Work, 49*(4).

Parsons, R., Hernandez, S., & Jorgensen, J. (1988, September/October). Integrated practice: A framework for problem solving. *Social Work,* 417–421.

Appendix

Ethics Cases and Commentaries

The ethics cases and commentaries in this appendix are taken from NASW, (1998). *Current Controversies in Social Work Ethics: Case Examples* (1998). Each example first lists the primary relevant citation of a standard of the NASW Code of Ethics (1996). Other applicable standards are listed in chronological order and are not ranked.

Case 1

An undocumented Mexican woman lives in southern California with her husband and two school-age children. Her husband is frequently physically and verbally abusive to her. She cannot drive and has little facility with English. She is completely dependent on her husband for transportation and assistance with English. She loves her husband and wishes he would not abuse her but fears he may abuse the children if she is not at home. Because she feels she has few options, she rarely seeks medical help. A friend insisted she seek help from the local shelter for battered women, and when she went there, she met with a social worker, who is feeling caught between the shelter's philosophy of encouraging women to leave abusive homes and her client's desire to return home. The social worker understands that through occasional stays at the shelter, her client may become more self-determining and assertive and eventually find safe alternatives for herself and her children. The shelter's board of directors is considering a policy that women must leave abusive situations to receive ongoing services.

NASW Code of Ethics: 1.01; 1.02; 1.05; 1.15; 2.06a; 3.09b

Commentary

Surely the social worker's understanding of cultural factors in this situation is essential to inform her work with and understand the behavior of this client. It is her responsibility to help the client identify and clarify her goals and perhaps develop their priority. The social worker may need to develop a long-range strategy that ensures some continuity of service, despite the interruptions. If the shelter can offer counseling services to clients who are not residing in the shelter, she could work with the client toward strengthening her resolve to change factors in her life and toward obtaining help for the husband. The social worker should initiate a legitimate study of clients' real needs in the context of agency resources and guide the policy and program development of the agency accordingly. If there is not a resolution of the conflicting factors, the social worker should explore other community resources that could better serve the client on an ongoing basis.

Case 2

A child protective services worker must present recommendations to the court regarding placement for the 10- and 12-year-old daughters of a recently deceased lesbian mother. Since their separation five years ago, the mother's former lesbian partner has paid monthly child support and all medical and dental costs for the girls. She has also maintained positive relationships with the girls and their mother, visiting regularly and taking the children on vacations. She and the mother had an unwritten understanding that the former partner would become the guardian for the children should something happen to the mother. The biological father maintains only occasional contact with the girls and has arranged for a few visits to his mother and sisters. The father and mother were never married. The social worker favors placing the girls with their father because of her religious convictions in which homosexuality is considered immoral.

NASW Code of Ethics: 1.02; 1.01; 1.03c; 1.05b,c; 1.14; 4.02; 4.06a; 5.01b; 6.01

Commentary

Although the children are not of an age to make a final decision regarding with whom they will reside, their preferences still must be sought and weighed. Limitations in their self-determination should not relate to a social worker's preferences for heterosexual environments, a value she may hold as a private individual but which should be distinguished from her professional position. The girls have grown up with lesbian parental figures, and the social worker's competence should encompass an understanding of such. Social justice issues are inherent in the development of a plan for these youngsters and an optimal environment for them. The social worker's recommendation to the judge is likely to be a significant factor in the outcome for the young clients.

Case 3

A first-year MSW student has a field placement at a city psychiatric hospital. Her first unsupervised intake interview is with the wife of a well-known physician, who has published many articles. During the intake, the student learns that the client has been treated over many years at various mental health facilities. Believing that all other possible forms of treatment have been exhausted without lasting success, the client's husband has recommended hospitalization, and the client has agreed. During the intake interview, the client reveals that her husband has been involved in romantic affairs with other women. The social work student completes the interview, makes a provisional diagnosis, and decides against recording specific assertions made by the woman.

NASW Code of Ethics: 1.07a; 2.05a,c; 3.04a,c

Commentary

This is the MSW student's first unsupervised intake interview, which may mean it is the first interview the student has conducted alone. She has access to a field instructor, however, and the case should be discussed carefully with the instructor. Is there anything to argue that because the client's information has not been verified and the information conveyed relates to a prominent person that extra care should be taken to protect the physician's privacy? The competence of the student to make a decision regarding what should be included in the record and to make a provisional diagnosis is questionable. The field instructor and the agency-based supervisor of the student bear ultimate responsibility for case decisions and should be involved in determining the significance of information.

The *Code of Ethics* states that social workers should not solicit private information from clients unless it is essential to the provision of service. Furthermore, information included in the record should be directly relevant to the care and treatment of the client. At the same time, social workers should keep accurate records and include sufficient information to facilitate delivery of services and ensure continuity of services. Is the wife's perception of her husband's behavior based on fact? Is her perception significant to her condition? The student should discuss the case carefully with the field instructor and consult with the agency supervisor to determine the recording procedure that is required and the usual information that is recorded. Every effort should be made to protect the rights of the client, the privacy of her husband, and the policies of the hospital.

Case 4

A clinical social worker meets weekly for therapy with a 15-year-old female client. During a session, the client reports that she is dealing drugs and has begun seeing a boyfriend who just completed a six-month jail sentence for selling drugs. The client's parents have forbidden contact between their daughter and her boyfriend and have asked the social worker to inform them if their daughter reported that she is seeing the boy again. The social worker believes that her client trusted her not to pass on this information to anyone else and that disclosure might permanently impair the trust in their relationship. However, the social worker told her client when they first began their sessions that she could not promise to keep confidential any statements that indicate a threat to harm self or others. The social worker is concerned for her client's safety with the boyfriend but also is far more concerned about her illegal involvement in the sale of drugs and the dangers she may face from the drug trade.

NASW Code of Ethics: 1.07a,c,d; 1.01; 1.02; 1.03a

Commentary

The social worker must struggle among obligations to her primary client, a minor; to her parents, who are inevitably part of the client system; and to society, whose laws are intended to protect. She can seek to work with the client toward the goal of achieving consent to bring the parents into active work as a family unit. The social worker would endeavor to support the client and work toward accomplishing consent to reveal the relationship but with the goal of establishing a growing alliance with her parents. Or she can weigh the dangers to the client of the renewed relationship with her boyfriend plus the betrayal of the collateral clients' (the parents) expectations for the protection of their daughter and decide that revealing the information to them constitutes a compelling exception to confidentiality. If she decides on the latter course of action, the primary client (the daughter) must be informed in advance of the disclosure.

Case 5

Social workers regularly discuss client progress and receive supervision at a community mental health center's weekly case review. In the case review, a social worker reports that her client has recently discovered that he is HIV positive, and she requests help in considering changes in his treatment plan in light of this information. Another social worker, who is treating the wife of the recently diagnosed HIV positive client, learns of her client's husband's HIV status because she attends the same case review. She knows that the couple is having unprotected sex and that the wife is unaware of her husband's HIV status.

NASW Code of Ethics: 1.07c,d,q; 2.05a

Commentary

The value of confidentiality is frequently challenged in providing services to clients. Although social workers should protect the confidentiality of a client, there are limitations, and the possibility of an exception should be addressed with the male client. The social workers participating in the case review are obligated to keep confidential all cases discussed, yet there may exist sufficient compelling reason to breach a client's confidence. The exception that requires a disclosure to prevent serious, foreseeable, and imminent harm to the client's wife must be considered as a basis of the social worker's decision making. The client's wife is at high risk of becoming HIV positive, thus providing a compelling reason to breach confidentiality. In working with the husband, the social worker needs to provide information, incentive, and details about her obligation to breach his confidentiality if the client takes no steps to inform and protect his wife.

Case 6

A social worker who specializes in marriage and family counseling sometimes works with couples who decide to divorce. In one such case, the social worker receives a subpoena to provide testimony regarding his sessions with the divorcing couple. The husband's lawyer has recommended that the social worker be asked to give a deposition, and the wife and her attorney have agreed; both have provided signed consents for release of information. In his sessions with the husband, the social worker learned that the husband had had an affair that his attorney is unaware of. Although the social worker does not believe it is in the husband's interest that he testify, he considers that he is being ordered "by a court of law or other legally authorized body" to disclose "confidential or privileged information."

NASW Code of Ethics: 1.07d,e,f,g,j; 1.06d

Commentary

It is not unusual for social workers to be subpoenaed to testify about their contact with clients. As in this case, social workers may be subpoenaed in conjunction with divorce proceedings. As a general rule, social workers should not disclose confidential information without their clients' consent or unless they have been ordered to do so by a court of law. If a court of law or other legally authorized body orders social workers to disclose confidential or privileged information without a client's consent and such disclosure could cause harm to the client, social workers should request that the court withdraw or limit the order.

In this particular case, the social worker should have discussed with the husband the possibility that the social worker's knowledge of the husband's affair, if disclosed during the deposition, could be harmful to the husband's legal interests. The social worker should have given the husband an opportunity to consider this possible consequence when the social worker obtained the husband's informed consent for the social worker to testify. The requirement to inform clients of the limitations of confidentiality applies whether social workers disclose confidential information on the basis of a legal requirement or with client consent. In addition, social workers who provide services to two or more people who have a relationship with each other, such as couples, should clarify with all parties which individuals will be considered clients and the possibility of conflicts of interest among them.

Case 7

A social worker employed in a well-respected sectarian mental health agency met with his supervisor to discuss treatment of an HIV-positive adolescent client's disclosure that he has anonymous sex with men. The following week the social worker's supervisor, espousing agency policy—whether formal or informal—advised him that his client's case must be closed because he poses a safety risk to the other adolescents in the program and because the agency's reputation could be tarnished for serving gay boys with AIDS.

NASW Code of Ethics: 1.16b; 3.07d; 3.09c,d; 4.02; 6.04b

Commentary

The central conflict is the client's right to treatment regardless of sexual orientation and the social worker's obligation to the agency. A sectarian agency has a legal right to develop policies according to its religious beliefs. However, the social worker has a professional obligation not to discriminate against a client based on sexual orientation. In terms of the mission of a mental health agency that employs social workers and other mental health professionals, how the agency could morally justify discrimination by refusing services to this client should be questioned. The manner in which it is doing so amounts to a requirement that the social worker abandon the client. This has both ethical and legal implications. The sectarian organization, by the nature of its mission grounded both in social work values and religious values, should be helped to recognize its moral responsibility to this client. The *Code of Ethics* requires that social workers, as a part of their commitment to employers, inform them of their ethical obligation as prescribed by the *Code*. Moreover, the social worker has the responsibility to help administrators create a work environment that helps their employees carry out their ethical responsibilities.

In situations such as these, the social worker may have to consider whether he or she can continue employment with an agency where there is a conflict between one's professional values and an agency's prerogatives. Religious agencies should make their policies based on religious values and how these are expected to be carried out in practice clear at the time of contracting with an employee. All of the relevant facts are needed to determine one's ethical action; the situation suggests the need for consultation.

Glossary

Note: These definitions are based on how the terms are used in this book.

accommodation The process of adjustment of family members to each other in order to coordinate their functioning, or a therapeutic tactic used by practitioners, especially in structural family interventions, to adapt to the family style in order to create a therapeutic alliance.

alignment Who is with or against the other in the transaction generating the problem.

amplification Used by a solution-focused therapist when a client mentions positive changes. The therapist asks numerous questions to help the client expound on these changes.

attachment theory Concepts about the stages that children go through in developing social relationships and the influence of this development on relationships in later life.

behavior rehearsal A technique used in social learning family interventions, in which the practitioner suggests desired behavior and then encourages the person or family to behave similarly through demonstrations, role plays, or descriptions.

boundary What defines who is in or out of a family relationship vis-à-vis the focal issue, as well as what their roles are in this interaction.

brief family therapy Short-term interventions that are usually goal oriented, active, and focused. They emphasize resolving the presenting problem rather than seeing it as a symptom of underlying dysfunction.

brokerage A function of case managers to identify, locate, and obtain needed community resources for individuals and families.

case management A procedure for planning, securing, and monitoring services on behalf of a person or family from a variety of relevant agencies and resources.

circular causality The recursive nature of interactions of the family and other systems where the behavior of one component affects the behavior of all others.

circular question Used by a solution-focused therapist to assist family members in understanding the motivation for their behaviors; namely, "What do you think she thinks?"

coaching In Bowen's family theory, the practitioner's role is to be both a role model for individual family members in the differentiation of self-process and a facilitator or coach as they explore their families of origin.

cognitive restructuring Procedures that attempt to modify or restructure disruptive or maladaptive thought patterns that may result in maladaptive behaviors by changing feelings and actions.

collusion An integral part of projective identification in object relations theory, where the recipient of the split-off part of the partner does not disown the projection but acts on the conscious or unconscious message.

confidentiality A principle of ethics where the family practitioner or other professional may not disclose any information about the individual or family without that person's or family's consent. This includes identity, content of verbalizations, or opinions.

consulting break A break taken by a solution-focused therapist to consult with or without a team regarding recommendations to make to a client following a session.

coping question Used by a solution-focused therapist to switch the client from problem-talk to solution-talk; namely, "Given all of these problems, how do you cope?"

cultural pluralism The coexistence and mutual respect for differences and strengths of cultures and groups other than one's own.

customer The person in solution-focused therapy who is the most motivated to effect change.

detriangulate In Bowen's family theory, this intervention consists of pointing out the triangulation process in order to withdraw a person from the buffer or go-between role, usually with parents so as not to be drawn into alliances with one against the other. This is many times more helpful than dealing with the presenting issues.

developmental transitions The movement of persons or families from one life stage to another. This is a time of greater stresses, problems, and conflicts, as tasks from the previous stage are consolidated and progress toward the tasks of the next stage is begun.

differentiation In family systems theory, this is the psychological separation of intellect and emotion in the differentiation of self, and also the ability of family members to separate their identities, emotions, and thoughts from other family members' in terms of autonomy and independence. This is the opposite of fusion or enmeshment.

eclecticism The use of many theories together or in sequence, or selected parts of them used in combination. Caution is urged in the selection of theories to use together.

ecological systems perspective A metatheory that shows the systemic relatedness of family variables and the environment, and allows for multiple intervention methods and practitioner roles.

ecology A science that studies the relationships that exist between organisms and their environment. In human ecology, it relates to how humans adapt or achieve goodness of fit with the environment.

ecomap A diagram used to show reciprocal influences between a family and their environment. It would include extended family members, relevant social institutions, and environmental influences.

ecosystem A concept pertaining to the physical, biological, and social environments of family members and the interaction between every relevant component contained therein.

effectiveness Producing a definite or desired result. Research into the effectiveness of different theories can help us determine their validity; however, because many theories are not prescriptions for actions but are about ideas and

interpretations, the research findings do not give us all the answers about usefulness.

empowerment The process of helping a person or family increase their influence and strength over their own lives and circumstances.

enactment Where a family lives out its focal struggle in a therapy session that approximates its experience at home.

encopresis The inability to control one's bowel functions; an elimination disorder.

enmeshment In structural family theory, this is where boundaries are blurred between family members, so that there is little autonomy or independent functioning.

environment The conditions, circumstances, and influences of ecological or situational forces that affect the development and behavior of individuals or groups in a particular setting.

equifinality The premise that the same result may be reached from different beginning points.

Eriksonian theory Erik Erikson's conceptualization of human psychosocial development through eight stages of life. Each stage has a task to be accomplished before the next stage can be reached. There are conflicts or danger at each stage that could interfere with development.

ethnic competence The ability to behave in a manner that is congruent with expectations of various ethnic groups, thus demonstrating respect for the family's cultural integrity.

ethnocentrism The belief that one's own culture or ethnic group is superior to others.

ethnographic interviewing Learning about specific cultures or groups by going into their natural settings, as is done when family preservation workers go into a family's home and community to provide services.

exceptions to the rule Instances where a problem behavior did not exist or was successfully overcome; used in solution-focused therapy.

exosystem This system represents the social structures, both formal and informal, that influence, limit, or constrain what happens there. Exosystem practice would focus on community-level factors that have an impact on the way people function.

externalizing problems A technique in the narrative approach of getting families to view problems as external to them, thus motivating them to strengthen exceptions to the problems and control them.

family preservation Intensive services based on family strengths which are provided to families whose children are at imminent risk of out-of-home placement.

family structure The pattern of organization underlying family interactions.

first-order change In systems theory, this is a temporary and superficial change in the family system and the way it functions which leaves the basic structure and functioning of the system unchanged.

formula tasks Very general tasks that are scripted by the solution-focused therapist for use with any client regardless of the presenting problem.

fusion Fusion occurs when blurred intellectual and emotional functioning within an individual parallels the degree to which that person loses autonomy and differentiation with other family members.

generic Relating to more basic universal characteristics or patterns like those commonly found in all families, such as boundaries and authority.

genogram A graphic presentation of a multigenerational relationship system where recurring behavior patterns within the family system can be traced.

grounded theory A concept from qualitative research methods that refers to developing a theory inductively through identifying common themes across a number of qualitative case studies or the results of such efforts (as contrasted with more deductive reasoning from grand theory to explanations for more specific circumstances).

habitat The place where a person or family lives, including the physical and social setting within cultural contexts.

hedging words Words used by a solution-focused therapist to suggest to a client movement or change in a positive direction (*might, seems, could*).

holistic An individual or family is seen as more than the sum of all its parts, and problems are more than specific symptoms. Physical, social, psychological, spiritual, and cultural influences are integrated.

homeostasis A dynamic balance or equilibrium in a family or other system where one or more variables are very stable.

hypnotic situations Nontrance-induced situations developed by the solution-focused therapist that result in the client becoming more susceptible to a therapeutic suggestion.

idiographic research The study of an individual, couple, or family where baselines are established and repeated measures are used to determine results of interventions. The results may be replicated with other individuals, couples, or groups.

idiosyncratic Characteristics that are unique to a particular family with their own expectations, meanings, interactions, and behaviors that would not be representative of other families.

indigenous workers Members of a community who work with helping professionals in providing services such as those used in family preservation.

introjection In object relations theory, a primitive form of identification involving a process where an individual takes in the characteristics of other people, which then become part of the individual's own self-image.

joining A process whereby the practitioner enters the family system and relates to all members individually and to subsystems, thus developing a therapeutic alliance so that treatment goals may be reached.

levels of need Used specifically in this book to refer to families' specific needs, where lower-level needs must be met before higher-level needs are addressed.

life stage theory The idea that every period of life, including that of an individual, couple, or family, has certain goals and dangers inherent in it that serve to modify behavior and order priorities. Each higher stage builds on the accomplishments of the previous stage or may be hampered by unfinished tasks.

macrosystem The larger system that includes the overall broader context and culture. Macrosystem practice would work toward improvements in the general society through such means as political action or community organization.

maintenance An accommodation technique that is supportive of a family's structure as it is. The practitioner may relate to other family members through this structure, as, for example, a parent as the central figure.

Mental Research Institute (MRI) The original developer of "brief therapy," this institute is in

Palo Alto, California, and the model is based on the work of Gregory Bateson. MRI involves a cybernetic systems approach to working with families which focuses on observable behavioral interactions and the interventions that alter the system.

mesosystem   The system that incorporates the interactions of individuals, families, and groups within the person's microsystem. Mesosystem practice would focus on interpersonal relationships within these systems.

metaphor   A figure of speech containing an implied comparison, where a word or phrase ordinarily used for one thing is applied to another to express feelings, imagination, or objective reality.

metatheory   A comprehensive system of thought that covers a wide area of practice and that would accept the inclusion of other perspectives and methods.

microsystem   This system represents the individual in family and group settings that incorporate the day-to-day environment. Microsystem practice would focus on interventions on a case-by-case basis to deal with the problems faced by individuals and families.

mimesis   A therapeutic tactic used especially by structural family practitioners as an accommodation technique, where the practitioner imitates or mirrors a family's style and communication and behavioral patterns in order to gain acceptance and accomplish goals.

miracle question   A future reality coconstructed between the solution-focused therapist and client, in which the present problems do not exist; namely, "If a miracle happened and your problems no longer existed, what would you be doing differently?"

modeling   Used in social learning theory to encourage the imitation and acquisition of behaviors observed in others that have led to more desirable outcomes.

multiculturalism   Understanding, appreciating, and valuing cultures other than one's own with their own uniquenesses and strengths.

narrative   A story created by a person or family where objective and subjective experiences are selectively arranged, which serve to organize and give meaning to the person or family.

niche   The particular role or status of an individual or family in its community and environment resulting from accommodation to this environment.

normalizing   A therapeutic technique that depathologizes problems in a way that changes perceptions of the situation, gives relief to the family, and deemphasizes the problem.

object relations theory   An interactional systems theory that views the basic human motivation as the search for satisfying interpersonal relationships. It is based on early parent–child interpersonal relationships, which the child internalizes and which become the model for later interpersonal relations in the family of origin, mate selection, family of procreation, and other intimate relationships.

oppression   When a group, institution, or government places severe restrictions on or withholds power from other groups or institutions.

power   The relative or comparative influence of the participants upon one another in the interactions that create the problem.

Premack principle   A social learning principle that requires the completion of a desired activity or low-probability behavior before doing a preferred activity or high-probability behavior; also known as "Grandma's law."

prescription   Recommendations made to a family by a solution-focused therapist following a consulting break with or without a team. Generally consists of compliments, reframes, and a task.

presuppositional questioning   In solution-focused interventions, a family is led to believe that a solution will be achieved by implying the occurrence of a specific event or selecting a specific verb tense. For example, saying, "What good things happened since last session?" instead of "Did anything good happen since last session?"

projective identification   An unconscious defense mechanism and interactional style of families where unwanted aspects of the self are attributed to another person, thus inducing that person to act according to these projected feelings and attitudes in an act of collusion.

relabeling   A therapeutic intervention that involves reframing a problem in more positive terms so that it is perceived differently and so that the person or family can respond to it differently and in a healthier way.

resilience The ability to withstand and rebound from crises and adversities.

restructuring The process of producing change in a family system through changing its structure; for example, strengthening the boundaries around the spousal subsystem.

scaling question Used by the solution-focused therapist to gauge the severity of a problem; namely, "On a scale from 1 to 10, with 1 being terrible and 10 being good, how would you rate your problem?"

second-order change In systems theory, this is a basic and lasting change in the structure and functioning of a family.

self-help organizations These are formally structured groups, such as Parents Without Partners or Alcoholics Anonymous, that provide mutual assistance for group participants who have a common problem with which some of the members have coped successfully.

service networks The linking of formal or informal persons, agencies, or organizations on behalf of a person or family in order to make the services available, accessible, and need-satisfying.

shaping A procedure used especially in behavioral therapy where an area of competence or desired behavior is acknowledged and reinforced.

social constructionism A metatheory where behaviors and relationships are seen in terms of organized efforts to create meaning out of personal experiences. Reality is seen as constructed by the person or family, family functioning is based on shared meanings, and the family practitioner becomes a coauthor of a living story with them.

social learning theory This theory focuses on reciprocal relationships and uses principles from social and developmental psychology and learning theory for understanding and treating behavior.

solution-focused intervention A style of intervention that emphasizes solutions or exceptions that families have already developed for their problems rather than the problems themselves.

spirituality The dimension of life that contains the meaning people give to their lives, their standards of morality, and their definition of the social context within which they practice their beliefs.

splitting In object relations theory, a primitive defense process where a person separates the good from the bad in an external object and then internalizes this split perception. These splits can then be projected upon other people.

strategic family interventions A therapeutic approach where the practitioner designs interventions to resolve specific problems that will, at the same time, require the family system to modify other interactions. The focus is on second-order change and breaking the recursive sequence that seems to be maintaining the problem.

structural family therapy A model of therapy that works through immediate experience to solve present-day key issues by altering the underlying structure of people's relationships.

symbiosis An intense emotional attachment where the boundaries between individuals become indistinct, and they react as one as in an undifferentiated ego mass.

Tarasoff decision A 1976 ruling by the Supreme Court of California in the case of *Tarasoff* v. *Regents of the University of California*, stating that, under certain circumstances, psychotherapists whose clients tell them that they intend to harm someone are obliged to warn the intended victim.

therapeutic alliance The capacity of the practitioner and family systems to mutually invest in and work together toward their goals.

therapeutic contract The agreement that the family and the practitioner have worked out together concerning what the problem is and how they will work on it. Goals, methods, mutual obligations, and timetables may be a part of the formal or informal agreement.

triangle In family systems theory, this is a three-person system that results when a dyad under stress pulls in a third person to dilute the stress and maintain the system. The triangle is considered to be the smallest stable emotional system.

triangulation In family systems theory, it can refer to any triangle where the conflict of two persons pulls in a third person and immobilizes this third person in a loyalty conflict. Most commonly it involves two parents and a child.

underorganization Family structures that have not achieved the constancy, differentiation, and flexibility they need to meet the demands of family functioning.

yes-set A hypnotic situation developed by the solution-focused therapist, in which the therapist manages to elicit affirmative responses from the client generally during the delivery of the prescription. This yes-set is meant to make the client more susceptible to a therapeutic suggestion.

Name Index

Note: Page numbers followed by *f* indicate figures; those followed by *t* indicate tables.

McColdrick, M., 179
McCollum, E. E., 168
McCroskey, J., 82, 88
McDonald, L., 142
McGehee, E., 62
McGoldrick, M., 95, 173, 176, 177, 187–188, 190
McGoldrick, R. A., 187
McGovern, M. P., 85
McLeod, J., 195, 203, 213
McNally, C., 212
McNamee, S., 25
McQuaide, S., 200, 211
Meador, R. G., 96
Meakes, E., 211
Medora, N., 185
Meezan, W., 82, 88
Merriam, S., 211
Messinger, L., 251
Metcalf, L., 214
Meyer, C. H., 16, 30
Miller, G., 165
Miller, J. B., 50
Miller, M., 233
Minahan, A., 102
Minuchin, S., 7, 14, 37, 85, 95, 116–118, 120–123, 126, 149
Mitrani, V., 123
Molnar, A., 146, 150
Monk, G., 198, 202, 214
Montalvo, B., 14, 116, 122
Moore, K., 162
Moore, S. T., 102, 173
Morris, F., 211
Morris, G., 204
Morris, P. W., 136
Morris, R., 40, 47
Morris, S. B., 133, 139
Morrison, D. H., 85
Moses, B. S., 88
Mott, S., 162–163
Mount, B., 97–98
Moustakas, C., 211
Moyers, B., 62, 63
Myers, L., 100

Nakata, Y., 170
Naleppa, M., 105, 110
Nash, M., 43
Neal, J. H., 211
Neimeyer, R. A., 204
Nelson, G. M., 102, 253
Nelson, K. E., 77, 78, 80–83
Nelson, T. S., 162–163

Nemon, H., 253
Nichols, M. P., 18, 19, 26, 123, 195, 196, 199, 220, 230, 231
Nims, D. R., 184
Noguiera, J., 123
Northey, S., 123
Norton, D., 40, 41f
Nunnally, E., 146, 253
Nurius, P., 200
Nylund, A., 196
Nylund, C., 196

O'Brien, E., 212
O'Connor, G., 110
O'Connor, T., 211
O'Dell, S., 196, 211
Ogden, T. H., 228, 231
O'Hanlon, W. H., 24, 30, 146, 149
Onnis, L., 123

Paquin, G. W., 7
Parker, G., 224
Parks, L., 72
Parry, A., 200
Parsons, R., 252
Passmore, J. L., 133, 136, 139
Patterson, C. J., 48
Payne, M., 15, 27
Peck, J. S., 123
Peck, M. S., 68
Pecora, P. J., 82
Pellar, J. E., 149, 165
Perez-Vidal, A., 123
Peters, M. J., 231
Peters, T. C., 231
Phelps, A., 66
Phillips, M., 197, 201
Pianta, R., 78–79
Pickering, R., 211
Piercy, F. P., 231
Pincus, A., 102
Pinderhughes, E., 42, 45, 46, 50
Pine, B. A., 83
Pinsof, W. F., 10f, 37, 38, 50
Pippin, J. A., 8
Polak, F., 149–150
Polansky, N. A., 3, 77, 79
Polkinghorne, D. E., 24, 32
Pomeroy, E. C., 162
Poole, D. L., 244
Powell, B., 172–173
Prest, L. A., 63
Price, R., 214
Prigoff, A., 40

Puffy, M., 212

Ramsey, J. L., 212
Rapp, C., 100
Reed, H., 62
Reed-Ashcraft, K., 88
Rehr, H., 102
Reid, W. J., 105, 110
Renae, C., 90
Rhodes, S. L., 95
Rice, S., 62
Richmond, M., 36, 101
Ricoeur, P., 24
Riley, J., 95–96
Rivard, J., 77, 81–83
Robbins, J. M., 62
Roberts, N. H. D., 185
Roberts-DeGenaro, M., 101
Robin, A., 137
Robinson, M., 98, 100, 110
Rogers, C., 36
Ronny, 216
Rose, S., 100
Rosen, H., 30
Rosen, K. H., 168
Rosenthal, J. A., 95
Rosman, B. L., 14, 116, 117, 122, 123
Rothman, J., 98
Rothschild, P., 211
Rubin, A., 101
Rush, A. J., 85
Russell, B., 151

Saayman, G., 123
Salcido, R., 86
Saleebey, D., 100
Salley, M. P., 82
Salus, M., 78
Sampson, H., 234
Sandau-Beckler, P., 86
Santisteban, D., 123
Sarbin, T. R., 23
Sarup, M., 32
Satir, V., 149
Saunders, E. J., 78, 82–83
Sawin, K. J., 173
Sayger, T. V., xxv, 115, 133, 136, 139, 142
Scamardo, M., 162
Scharff, D. E., 231, 232, 234, 237, 238, 240
Scharff, J. S., 231, 232, 234, 237, 238, 240
Schlesinger, E. G., 39

Subject Index

Note: Page numbers followed by *f* indicate figures; those followed by *t* indicate tables.

Celebrations, in narrative family
  interventions, 210
Certificates, in narrative family
  interventions, 210
Change
  and narrative family
    interventions, 199, 208
  and solution-focused
    interventions, 147, 151, 152
  theory of, 199
Charity Organization Societies
  (COS), 101
Chemical Use, Abuse, and
  Dependency Scale, 85
Child abuse, defined, 78
Child neglect
  defined, 78
  parental factors in, 79
  poverty and, 79–80
Children
  ethical practice concerning, 54
  family structures and, 47–48
  narrative family interventions
    and, 211
  poverty and, 46–47
  solution-focused interventions
    and, 162
  structural family interventions
    and, 123
Child Well Being Scales, 88
Chores, assigning extra, 137–138
Circular causality, in family
  systems view, 19
Circular question, in solution-
  focused interventions, 158
Client diversity, 38–48
  cultural democracy, 39–42
  ethnic sensitive practice, 39–42
  family structures, 47–48
  gender justice, 42–44, 54
  multiculturalism, 39–42, 224
  poverty, 46–47
  power and powerlessness, 44–46
Coaching, in family systems
  interventions, 183
Codes of ethics
  American Association for
    Marriage and Family Therapy
    (AAMFT), 55, 61
  National Association of Social
    Workers (NASW), 58–61
Cognition, in spiritually sensitive
  practice, 65
Cognitive behavioral interventions

in family preservation, 86–87
in social learning family
  interventions, 134
Collaboration, in narrative family
  interventions, 205–206
Collapsing time, in narrative family
  interventions, 208
Collusion, in object relations family
  interventions, 222, 226, 227, 231
Common Human Needs (Towle), 2
Communication skills training, 138
Communion, in spiritually sensitive
  practice, 65
Community, family in, 243, 244–252
  agency and, 247–248
  case study, 245
  community human service
    networking systems, 250*f*
  comprehensive community
    initiatives, 250–251
  definition of community, 246–247
  dual focus and, 245–246
  family case management, 100
  family practitioner and, 247–248
  goal-directed community human
    services system, 248–250
  nature of, 244
Community development
  programs, 248
Compassion, for clients, 67
Comprehensive Community
  Initiatives (CCI), 250–251
Concentration-camp survivors, 150
Confederacy of selves, 200
Confidentiality, 36
  ethical practice concerning, 54–55
  with object relations family
    interventions, 239
Conflict
  in ecosystems perspective, 22
  in family systems interventions,
    170, 171
Conners' Parent Rating Scale, 162
Conscience, in spiritually sensitive
  practice, 65
Constructionism. *See* Social
  constructionist perspective
Consulting break, in solution-
  focused interventions, 148–149,
  152, 155
Contexts of helping, 35–49
  client diversity and, 38–48, 54, 224
  helping relationship in, 36, 37*t*
  therapeutic alliance in, 36–38

Coping, in ecological view, 17
Coping question, in solution-
  focused interventions, 158–159
Coping skills training, in social
  learning family interventions,
  134
Council on Social Work Education,
  62
Countertransference, in object
  relations family interventions,
  224–225, 232–233, 236, 239
Couple/relationship therapy
  narrative family interventions
    and, 194, 201–210, 211
  solution-focused interventions
    and, 162
Criminals with high recidivism,
  solution-focused interventions
  and, 162
Crisis intervention theory, 81, 83–84
Cultural Assessment Grid, 40, 42*f*
Cultural democracy, 39–42
Culture
  goal-directed community human
    service system and, 249–250
  in narrative family interventions,
    196–197
  structural family interventions
    and, 123
Cup-is-half-full approach, 150
Curious questions, in narrative
  family interventions, 202, 206,
  209

Deception, ethical practice
  concerning, 55
Decision making, 56–58
  cycle of reflection in, 60*f*
  ethical, 56–58, 59*f*, 60*f*
  interpersonal orientation in, 56
  of practitioner, 56
  source of authority in, 56
Dependency, in object relations
  family interventions, 227
Depression, in object relations
  family interventions, 223,
  225–228, 231
Deprivileging, in narrative family
  interventions, 196–197
Detriangulation, in family systems
  interventions, 175–176, 181, 182
Developmental-ecological model
  (Belsky), family preservation
  and, 77–80, 85

and ethnic sensitive practice, 39–42
gender and, 42–44
in narrative family interventions, 196, 198–199
social class and, 40–42
theory of, 198–199
theory of problems and, 200
Orthopedic patients, solution-focused interventions and, 162

Parental projection, in family systems interventions, 171
Parenting groups, solution-focused interventions and, 161
Parenting Stress Index, 85
Participation, ethical practice concerning client, 55
Patriarchy, challenges to, 43
Personality development, in family systems interventions, 172–173
Postmodern feminism, 42–44
Postmodern worldview, 196, 197, 212
Poverty, 46–47
American children and, 79*t*
child neglect and, 79–80
Power
defined, 45
differences in, 26, 44–46
in narrative family interventions, 196, 198–199
nature of, 117
needs of practitioner and, 46
powerlessness and, 44–46
theory of, 198–199
as useful construct, 45
Power to Care, The (Wilson), 46
Practitioner. *See also* Assessment; Intervention
clinical relationship in family systems interventions, 174–175
compassion for clients, 67
decision making by, 56
ethical challenges, 69–70, 89, 108–109, 123–124, 140, 163–164, 186–187, 212, 238–239
family in community and, 247–248
personal narrative in narrative family interventions, 196–197
power needs of, 46
roles in family case management, 104
therapeutic alliance and, 36–38

Predicting setbacks, in narrative family interventions, 208
Preference questions, in narrative family interventions, 206
Premack Principle, 137
Prescription, in solution-focused interventions, 155, 160
Preventive actions systems, 249
Privileges, loss of, 138
Problems, theory of, 200
Problem-saturated ways of living, 201–203
Problem-solving skills
in social learning family interventions, 134, 138–139
in solution-focused interventions, 147
Projection
defined, 171
in family systems interventions, 171
in object relations family interventions, 222, 223, 224–228, 230, 236, 238
Psychoanalysis
defined, 220
object relations family interventions and, 220
Psychodynamic theory, in family systems interventions, 176
Psychosomatic illness, family structure and, 123

Questions
assessment, 173–174
coping, 158–159
curious, 202, 206, 209
effect (of change), 206
exceptions, 207
history of exceptions, 207
meaning, 207
news of a difference, 205–206
preference, 206
significance, 207
spectator, 208
story development, 206
therapeutic, 202, 206–208
unique account, 207

Reality testing, in object relations family interventions, 222
Reauthoring process, 199
Redirecting, in family systems interventions, 180
Reflecting team, in narrative family interventions, 209–210

Reframing
in family systems interventions, 178–179
in social learning family interventions, 136–137
Relatedness, in ecological view, 17
Relativism, 26
Relaxation training, 136
Repression, in object relations family interventions, 230
Respect, 36
Role assignments, in object relations family interventions, 231, 232
Rules of conduct, 53

San Antonio Model (SAM), 40
Scaling question, in solution-focused interventions, 154, 159
Scapegoating, in object relations family interventions, 231
Second level of family need. *See* Level II families
Self-control strategies, 137
Self-determination, in decision making, 56
Self-efficacy, and family systems interventions, 185
Self-empowerment, 249
Self-knowledge, in narrative family interventions, 196
Self-management skills training, 136–138
Self-realization services, 249
Sexual abuse, narrative family interventions and, 212
Significance questions, in narrative family interventions, 207
Single-parent households
family structures and, 47–48
poverty and, 46
Social class
community resources and, 247–248
object relations family interventions and, 237–238
oppression and, 40–42
Social constructionist perspective, 23–27
applications of, 25
assumptions of, 24–25
caveats in using, 26–27
described, 23–25
ecosystems perspective versus, 27–30, 29*t*
principles of, 27*t*